CAPTAIN SWING

THE HOME OF THE RICK-BURNER.

Acknowledgment to "PUNCH"

CAPTAIN SWING

By

E. J. HOBSBAWM
and
GEORGE RUDÉ

W · W · NORTON & COMPANY
New York · London

W. W. Norton & Company, Inc., 500 Fifth Avenue. New York. N.Y. 10110
W. W. Norton & Company Ltd., 37 Great Russell Street, London WC1B 3NU

First published in the Norton Library 1975
by arrangement with Pantheon Books

Published simultaneously in Canada by
Penguin Books Canada Ltd,
2801 John Street, Markham, Ontario L3R 1B4.

Books That Live
The Norton imprint on a book means that in the publisher's estimation it is a book not for a single season but for the years.
W. W. Norton & Company, Inc.

Library of Congress Cataloging in Publication Data
Hobsbawm, Eric J
Captain Swing.
(The Norton library)
Reprint of the ed. published by Pantheon Books, New York.
Bibliography: p.
Includes indexes.
1. Agricultural laborers—Great Britain. 2. Agriculture—Economic aspects—England. 3. England—Rural conditions. I. Rudé, George F. E., joint author.
II. Title.
HD1534.H58 1975   338.1'0941   75-23442

ISBN 0-393-00793-6

Printed in the United States of America
4 5 6 7 8 9

CONTENTS

LIST OF ILLUSTRATIONS

MAPS

PREFACE

The writing of this book has been divided between us: E.J.H. has been mainly responsible for the Introduction, Chapters 1–4, 9, 15 and Appendix IV; and G.R. for Chapters 5–8, 10–14 and Appendices I–III. But we have collaborated closely throughout in both planning and writing the book. It is strictly a joint enterprise and not merely the stringing together of two sets of chapters written by two independently operating authors.

We wish to express our thanks to the secretaries and directors of The London Assurance and the Norwich Union Fire Insurance Society and to the librarians and archivists in London, Aylesbury, Bedford, Cambridge, Carlisle, Chelmsford, Dorchester, Gloucester, Hereford, Hobart, Huntingdon, Ipswich, Leicester, Northampton, Norwich, Oxford, Reading, Sydney, Taunton, Trowbridge and Worcester, who have placed their records so freely at our disposal. Our special thanks are due to the late Peter Eldershaw, archives officer of Hobart, Tasmania, who gave us so unstintingly of his skill and energy and whose tragic and untimely death last year has robbed Australia of one of its most gifted and devoted public servants.

We are also indebted to Miss Carol Coombe and Miss Ruth Meyerowitz who, as research assistants, have helped in the preparation of the book; and to Professor Norman Gash, Miss A.M. Colson and Dr. Monju Dutt for permitting us to draw on their unpublished theses, concerned respectively with the labourers' movement in Berkshire, Hampshire and the south-eastern counties; the extent of our debt to them will become evident in Chapters 5, 6, 7 and 10. Mr. Rex Russell has made available to us his expert knowledge of the farm labourers of Lincolnshire and his notes on the local press and local sources. It is not possible to measure the benefit we have derived from the discussions arising from papers we have read to various groups of colleagues and students during the time we have been working on this subject, but it is considerable. Mrs. Diana Wood in London and Mrs. Eileen Pennycote in Adelaide have been largely responsible for typing the manuscript. The index was compiled by Mrs. Betty Lloyd.

Finally, we express our gratitude to Cambridge University Press for permission to reproduce Caird's Map of England in 1850 from Clapham, *Economic History of Modern Britain*, Vol. 1.

We have confined our bibliography to a list of contemporary

sources, both manuscript and in print, and to works dealing specifically with the agitations of farm-labourers in our period. Other works we have used are listed in the reference notes.

E. J. H.

February 1968 G. R.

INTRODUCTION

"Hodge"; "the secret people", "brother to the ox". Their own inarticulateness, our own ignorance, are symbolised by the very titles of the few books which have attempted to recreate the world of the English farm-labourer of the 19th century. Who were they? Nobody except themselves and the rulers of their villages knew or cared, nobody except the clergyman or (much more rarely) dissenting minister entered the few basic facts of their obscure lives in the parish register: birth, marriage and death. The directories of their county, which recorded the details of their parishes, their landlords, their inn-keepers, village artisans, shopkeepers and carriers in extraordinary detail, said nothing about them. If they could write—and in 1830 most could not—they would have little occasion to, except perhaps, laboriously, to some daughter or sister "in service" in a town too remote to be visited, some brother or son in the army. Except for their gravestones and their children, they left nothing identifiable behind them, for the marvellous surface of the British landscape, the work of their ploughs, spades and shears and the beasts they looked after, bears no signature or mark such as the masons left on cathedrals.

We know little about them, because they are remote from us in time. Their articulate contemporaries knew little more, partly because as townsmen they were ignorant about the country or cared nothing for it, partly because as rulers they were not allowed to enter the self-contained world of the subaltern orders, or because as rural middle class they despised it. It is a salutary exercise for the modern historian to read—in most cases vainly—through the opulent volumes of that monument to the gentleman's view of the countryside, the older volumes of the Victoria County History, in search of *any* information about the rising of 1830, a movement which, after all, affected upwards of 20 counties. Or, for that matter, of any but the most jejune information about the labourers. It is equally instructive to glance through the reports of those well-meaning explorers, the 19th century collectors of folklore or "popular customs", and to observe the triumph with which they brought back from their forays into their neighbouring lanes, elementary information which every cottage child learned at its mother's breast. The vicars of Victorian England found medieval documents a less recalcitrant source than their parishioners. As for the townsmen, their ignorance was quite startling. The Liberal politicians of the 1840s, always anxious to comment on the abuses of squire and parson in the interests of Free Trade and in order to palliate the horrors of their own towns, often display an insouciance about the facts of the labourer's life which reflects both a fundamental lack of interest and a virtually total lack of knowledge. The publishers of broadsheets and ballads for the urban mass market could not fail to notice so dramatic and newsworthy an event as the riots of 1830, but the few London pamphlets and broadsheets on the subject might have been written about Sweden rather than Kent. "Captain Swing", for instance, may be treated as an honest but wronged yeoman farmer rather than a labourer.* Indeed, the very term "Captain Swing" and its association above all with rural incendiarism reflect the journalistic creation of the city and not the reality of the countryside, for as we shall see, incendiarism was only a marginal aspect of the rising—it became the characteristic form of rural unrest only *after* 1830—and there is no evidence that any labourers except perhaps in some small parts of Kent ever believed themselves to be following any "Captain Swing".

The task of this book is therefore the difficult one, which nowadays —and rightly—tempts many social historians, of reconstructing the mental world of an anonymous and undocumented body of people in order to understand their movements, themselves only sketchily documented. It is technically fascinating to an extent which the layman can scarcely grasp, and we cannot be sure that we have avoided the consequent temptation to put our pleasure above the reader's. For there is a real difference between the attitude of the researcher, whose reward is the sheer rock-climber's entertainment of ascending what has hitherto been regarded as impassable, and the attitude of both historian and reader which is to ask: where have we got? From their point of view several days' or even weeks' intensive work on some particularly tricky problem—let us say, the question of how many threshing-machines were destroyed, or the relation between the pattern of landownership and riotousness—may be worth no more than a line or two, especially if, as is so often the case, these questions cannot be satisfactorily answered. The researcher will inevitably be tempted to record his exploration and not only its results.

We may well have done so. That is why it may be useful at the outset to explain what we have tried to achieve in this book and what is new in it.

* Cf. The genuine Life of *Mr.* Francis Swing (1831)—our emph.

The historiography of the labourers' rising of 1830 is not large, that of the rest of agrarian agitations and riots in the first half of the 19th century negligible. Nevertheless, in addition to a few unpublished dissertations of uneven merit* and a valuable monograph on the East Anglian riots of 1816,† it contains one classic of modern social history, J. L. and Barbara Hammond's *The Village Labourer* (London 1911), one of the most distinguished products of the only era of British history until the present which took a really serious interest in the farm-workers. Virtually all subsequent references to the rising in general historical works are based on the Hammonds, and what little is known of it by the general public is what is known of their book. The Hammonds brought two major assets to their task: a profound sympathy for the predicament of the British labouring poor in the transition to industrial capitalism, and a fairly systematic use of the then neglected Home Office Papers in the Public Record Office, which remain to this day the major source for our knowledge of early 19th century social agitations. On the other hand—and we do not say this in order to diminish the merits of our admirable predecessors—they also suffered from several avoidable and unavoidable weaknesses. In a sense they simplified both their picture of social change in general, and of the events of 1830 in particular, in order to dramatise them more effectively. To take merely three examples. In their account of the degradation and pauperisation of the village labourers they laid far too exclusive an emphasis on the process of "enclosure", which was one, but by no means the only or in many instances the most important element in rural proletarianisation. In their description of the situation in the early 19th century, they greatly oversimplified both the nature and the prevalence of the "Speenhamland System" of poor relief, at least in its extreme form. And in their narrative of the events of the "last labourers'" rising, they not only neglected the fact that it was not in fact quite the last act of rural rebellion, but also relied too exclusively on the activities of the Special Commissions of repression, which were active in only parts of the country. This led them to underestimate the extent of the movement; e.g. to pay unduly little attention to such areas as East Anglia where it was dealt with by other methods. The degree of their underestimate is quite substantial. A fuller investigation of court proceedings—in Assizes, Quarter and even Petty Sessions of different but relevant dates—shows that they did so by about one-third.

* See Bibliography.

† A. J. Peacock, *Bread or Blood* (London 1965).

In addition to such avoidable weaknesses, their book suffers from the inevitable obsolescence of any work written almost sixty years ago. Our knowledge of both the agrarian economy and agrarian society in the 18th and early 19th century has progressed considerably. What is more to the point, we are today more keenly aware of certain kinds of problems—of economic development, of social structure, of collective behaviour, of the interaction between the social-economic base and the ideology of various social strata, than Liberal Radical historians of Edwardian England could be. It is not so much that the material for the study of the 1830 rising has increased all that much. Substantially, our narrative of events is based on sources, most of which were known in 1911, in the Public Records, in the newspapers, and in various records and publications, and most of which were probably already accessible. (The main exception, and the major body of new manuscript material utilised, are the Australian convict records which both supplement the Hammonds' study of the repression of the rising and throw valuable light on its social composition.)* It is true that the establishment of County Record Offices and a half-century of research and bibliography have made the task of today's historian of the rising much simpler, though also more nomadic. But the main reason for writing another book about Captain Swing is not that we can add substantially to what was already known, or knowable, about the *events* of 1830—though it is obviously important to show that these were even more widespread and serious than even the Hammonds thought—but that we are now able to ask new *questions* about them: about their causes and motives, about their mode of social and political behaviour, the social composition of those who took part in them, their significance and their consequences.

This book therefore supersedes the Hammonds', in every respect except one: they will probably continue to be read with pleasure when we are only consulted to provide footnotes. Nevertheless, they are now superseded. This does not mean that our work is exhaustive, though it is unlikely that on the actual events of 1830 we have failed to consult any substantial body of source-materials or monographs. Much of our work, such as the discussion of the economic and social development of the labourers in the generations which preceded the rising, the nature of village society and social agitation, the causes of the riots and the variations in their pattern, and their social and econ-

* There are also a few memoirs and private papers which were not accessible or known in 1911, but they do not add anything of major significance to our knowledge.

omic consequences, concerns questions which cannot be answered exhaustively on the basis of an identifiable and limited body of sources, and some of which can hardly be answered at all in the present state of research. Some of them can barely be answered at all by means of the methods of old-fashioned individual artisan research to which we have had to limit ourselves. Ours is not by any means the last word on the social movements of British farm-labourers in the first part of the 19th century, in so far as such a phrase has any sense in history. In terms of modern social history, it is one of the first. We can only hope that by treating Captain Swing at such length, we do not discourage subsequent workers. There remains plenty for them to do.

What, then, have we done? We have tried to describe and analyse the most impressive episode in the English farm-labourers' long and doomed struggle against poverty and degradation. Their history between the industrial revolution and the middle of the 19th century is a tragic one; perhaps of all classes of English society the most tragic, though surpassed in horror and bitterness by the fate of the Irish and Scots Highland peasantry. They were already in existence as a class in the 18th century. What happened between say 1750 and 1850 was not the destruction of a peasantry in the normal sense of the word, and the substitution of an agricultural proletariat, for the basic tripartite division of the English land—a small number of very large landowners, a medium number of tenant-farmers employing hired labour, and a large number of wage-workers—was already substantially in existence, in all but a few untypical regions and localities. What happened was rather that a rural society which was in some senses traditional, hierarchical, paternalist, and in many respects resistant to the full logic of the market, was transformed under the impetus of the extraordinary agricultural boom (and the subsequent, though temporary recessions) into one in which the cash-nexus prevailed, at least between farmer and labourer. The worker was simultaneously proletarianised—by the loss of land, by the transformation of his contract and in other ways—and deprived of those modest customary rights as a man (though a subordinate one) to which he felt himself to have a claim. This happened at a time when his economic situation deteriorated sharply. He became not merely a full proletarian, but an underemployed, pauperised one, and indeed by the time of the 1830 rising he retained little of his former status except the right to parish relief, though even this was to be withdrawn from him within a few years. Yet he was a proletarian only in the most general economic sense. In practice the nature of his labour, and of the rural society in which he lived and starved, deprived him even of the relative freedom of the urban and industrial poor, and certainly made it difficult for him to develop or to apply those ideas and methods of collective self-defence which the townsman was able to discover.

Eventually he did so, though the combined force of village radicalism in politics and agricultural trade unionism was feeble enough, even when supplemented by the power of a growing rural labour shortage. But in the half-century from the mid-1790s to the mid-1840s he was left to improvise his resistance as best he might. He could hardly *not* resist. His situation was such as to make some sort of rebellion inevitable. And indeed from time to time it broke out in various ways: perhaps here and there in the hard years of the mid-1790s, certainly in the Eastern counties in 1816, and again in East Anglia in 1822, all over the East and South of England in the autumn and winter of 1830, and again, more scattered in 1834–35, and (mainly in the Eastern counties) in 1843–44. The subject of our book is the greatest of these rebellions, but it was not the only one of its kind.

The object of these movements was not revolutionary. Their immediate purpose was economic, though the predicament of the proletarian did not clearly dominate them until 1830, when the almost universal demand was for higher wages, for better employment and/or for improvements in the system of social security (i.e. the Poor Law). The old-fashioned hostility to those believed to be responsible for high prices—shopkeepers and middlemen—which was still very important in 1816, had by then ceased to be of any significance. Nobody demanded the land—but then nobody had even before 1830. Land reform was then as later a nostalgic dream of townsmen, but not a serious concern of rural proletarians. But, at least until 1830, and perhaps until 1834–35, behind these immediate and virtually (though not formally) trade unionist demands, there was a wider objective: the defence of the customary rights of the rural poor as freeborn Englishmen, and the restoration of the stable social order which had—at least it seemed so in retrospect—guaranteed them. This was an objective which the labourers shared with other strata of rural society, and it gave to the rising of 1830 in some counties something of the air of a general manifesto of county against town, of past against future, carried by the labourers but signed also by farmers and even gentry. The most extraordinary aspect of this solidarity between the labourers and their employers and rulers was the surprising support these gave to the Luddism of the poor. The rising of 1830 was the greatest machine-breaking episode in English history—and by far the most successful—because the rioters did not need to break threshing-machines by force. For reasons which we shall analyse below, their Luddism was not only tolerated, but in many instances actually welcomed.

Nevertheless, the solidarity of rural society was an illusion. The insignificance of mere sympathy as a political or economic force has rarely been better illustrated than in 1830, when the bulk of the counties' rulers agreed that the labourers' demands were just, indeed modest, and ought to be conceded, though the government in London, full of ideology and the fear of revolution, took a different view.* Sympathy gained the labourers little except, in those counties in which the repression of the riots was left to the local administration, a lesser degree of barbarism in their punishment. Neither gentry nor farmers were prepared to make the slightest economic or social sacrifice for the sake of a justice they admitted, though they were prepared to make concessions to force. The New Poor Law of 1834 knocked the last nails into the coffin of their ancient belief that social inequality could be combined with the recognition of human rights. After 1830, and especially after 1834, the labourers knew that they had to fight alone (or at all events without rural allies) or not at all. For another twenty years or so they waged a silent, embittered, vengeful campaign of poaching, burning and rural terror—now sometimes actually directed against the gentry itself—which erupted into epidemics of incendiarism and cattle-maiming at moments of acute distress, notably in 1843–44. But these were rearguard actions of a minority. The majority remained inert and passive until the rise of the agricultural workers' trade unions in the 1870s.

The weapons with which the labourers fought were archaic, though their use was sometimes new. In the Eastern Counties machine-breaking and incendiarism, for instance, appear first on any scale in 1815, though the first reached its climax in 1830, the second after the defeat of Swing. But neither needed much in the way of social in-

* Sheer ignorance played a large part in this, as usual. Even so sympathetic an urban observer as T. L. Peacock presented the 1830 rioters in *Crotchet Castle* as the "Jacquerie" and made them clamour for arms. In fact, as we shall see, there can rarely have been a movement of the despairing poor so large and so widespread which used, or even threatened, so little violence.

ventiveness, and this was also true of the more ambitious forms of organised protest and demand. Essentially these modified the traditional collective practices of the village, which had once served only to organise the annual feasts, the processions and waits, the rural ritual (sometimes by this period barely concealed under the utilitarian hood of the "village friendly society"), for purposes of social agitation. The village or parish remained the political universe; the band of mobile activists or the snowballing mass march through the neighbouring parishes, was the only conscious method of spreading agitation from one settlement through a wider area. Nor are there many signs of a new political or social ideology. On the contrary, there is evidence that the labourers still accepted the ancient symbols of ancient ideals of stable hierarchy. Their demands were just: they must be lawful. The King himself must have authorised them.

However, the English village of the early 19th century was plainly not a dark backwater totally insulated from knowledge and contact with the more dynamic sectors of society. Village radicals (as often as not the shoemakers, whose literacy and intellectualism were proverbial), radical craftsmen and shopkeepers in small market-towns, provided a link with the wider world and formulated ideas and programmes which the labourers sometimes made their own, if only because rural craftsmen and others of the kind so often acted as their spokesmen and organisers. Indeed, as we shall see, the rising of 1830 is incomprehensible without such contacts. There were plenty of reasons for rebellion, but it is doubtful whether it would have occurred on so vast a scale when it did, without the double stimulus of the French and Belgian revolutions abroad, and the revival of intensive political agitation in England. And we may add, it is doubtful if it would have been suppressed with such ferocity had it not coincided with a moment of acute political crisis in national affairs. But these were stimuli from outside. Were there any signs of the development of a new consciousness among the labourers themselves? Possibly in a few places we can discern such signs in the early spread of certain non-conformist sects, such as the Primitive Methodists and Bible Christians, which were later to be closely associated with rural trade unionism. At all events in at least two centres of the 1830 riots (North Walsham in Norfolk and Elham in Kent) such sects had already begun to establish themselves.

What we have tried to do therefore is to describe and analyse an entire epoch of the English farm-labourers' history, that of the rise and fall of their improvised, archaic, spontaneous movements of resistance to the full triumph of rural capitalism, in the light of the greatest movement of this kind. It was as near to a national movement as so spontaneous and unorganised an upsurge could be. For the limits of its spread were not those of organisation or ideology, but of economic structure. Agricultural England in the first half of the 19th century could be divided into a roughly corngrowing South and East, a primarily pastoral West; and also into a low-wage South and a not quite so abysmally paid or treated North. The line dividing corn from pasture ran approximately from Scarborough on the Yorkshire coast to Weymouth in Dorset; that dividing North from South, also approximately, from Chester to the Wash (see map 1). The rising of 1830 occurred essentially in the low-wage South and East, i.e. in the area comprising the counties of Norfolk, Suffolk, Essex, most of Cambridge, Bedford, Huntingdon, Hertford, Middlesex, Kent, Surrey, Sussex, Berkshire, Wiltshire, Hampshire and parts of the counties of Northampton, Buckingham, Oxford, Gloucester, Somerset and Dorset. It was not the whole of England—but in so far as England remained an *agricultural* country, it contained the core of those of its areas in which, in the first half of the 19th century, the rural and farming population continued to predominate, and where modern industry and (with the exception of London) the big city were still marginal phenomena. "Swing" was a rural movement. Perhaps its great tragedy was that it never succeeded in linking up with the rebellion of mine, mill and city. But it is not the historian's task to speculate on what might have been. His duty is to show what happened and why. We have tried to do so.

PART 1

BEFORE SWING

I

AGRICULTURAL ENGLAND

Agricultural England in the 19th century presented a unique and amazing spectacle to the enquiring foreigner: it had no peasants. In practically all the countries from which visitors were at all likely to come to the United Kingdom, the bulk of the people who earned their living by tilling the soil consisted of families owning or occupying their own small plot of land, cultivating it substantially with the labour of their members, and indeed very often—perhaps mostly—still practising subsistence agriculture, even when they sold some of their produce in the market, supposing they had a surplus. (That peasant serfs in feudal societies were obliged to work also on their lord's farms does not mean that on their own holdings they were not peasant farmers in the sense just described.) Such peasants still form the bulk of the population of the soil in some parts of the world and the bulk of the cultivators of the soil in many regions, including most of Europe. At the time of the first industrial revolution they were even more common. In 19th century Britain they were not entirely absent. They predominated in Ireland, and the thinly populated regions of Wales and the Scottish Highlands, perhaps in parts of Northern England such as the Pennine dales, and local concentrations could be found here and there in other parts. Yet in England these were already unimportant minorities. When 19th century politicians and pamphleteers spoke of the English "peasantry" they did not mean direct family cultivators, but agricultural wage-labourers.

In fact, the English agricultural population divided into three unequal segments. At the top stood a small number of landlords, who between them owned most of the land. The first attempt to discover how the land of Britain was owned (in 1871–73) revealed that about 1,200 persons owned a quarter of the United Kingdom and about 7,200 owned half, though it certainly underestimated the concentration of landed property. It could be argued that in England and Wales not more than 4,000 proprietors owned four-sevenths of the land, and that most of the rest of "landowners" probably consisted of small freeholders in towns and suburbs rather than of yeomen or small country gentlemen.[1] This comparative handful of giant landlords rarely cultivated their estates themselves, except for the odd home farm or model holding. Essentially they rented them out to tenant-farmers who actually exploited them. In 1851, when the first nationally reliable figures were collected,[2] there were about 225,000 farms in Britain, about half of them between 100 and 300 acres in size, and all of them averaging just over 110 acres. In other words, what passed for a small farm in England would certainly have counted as a giant farm beside the smallholdings of typical peasant economies.* Just over 300,000 people described themselves as "farmers and graziers". These cultivated their farms essentially by employing the 1·5 million men and women who described themselves as agricultural labourers, shepherds, farm-servants, etc.

In other words, the typical English agriculturalist was a hired man, a rural proletarian. There is no doubt that beside him all manner of smallholders survived (but as often as not they might be small rural tradesmen, craftsmen, carters, etc., with a hay-field or market-garden, who did not regard themselves as farmers), and even some people who could be classified as peasants. However, socially speaking the marginal members of a rural lower-middle class were assimilated to the rest of the "lower orders", and distinguished from the farmers.[3] Of course, rural society consisted not only of those actually engaged in landownership or farming, but also of the numerous craftsmen, shopkeepers, carters, innkeepers, etc., who provided the services necessary to agriculture and village life, not to mention the less numerous professional men who provided those necessary to farmers and gentry; and of course the Church, which went with the Squire. Parishes in which more than three-quarters of the families were engaged in agriculture were not too common, even when there was no particular local industry or manufacture.† Nor ought we to forget the various rural industries, either domestic and cottage manufactures (such as the straw-plaiting of Bedfordshire) or the small (mainly textile) nuclei still fairly widely spread through even the most agricultural counties, with some notable exceptions.‡

* Thus in France (1882) out of 5·7 million "exploitations" 4·9 millions were less than 26 acres, 700,000 (described as "medium-sized") were between 26 and about 100 acres, and only 140,000 ("large" and "very large") were over 100 acres. In Germany (1882) only just over 6 per cent of holdings were over about 50 acres.

† Thus in the purely agricultural Hundred of Hartismere (Suffolk) only about one-third of the parishes had more than 75 per cent of their families engaged in agriculture; rather under a quarter had half or less of their families in agriculture (1831 Census).

‡ By 1851, according to the map attached to the census, there was a large area south of the North Downs, and covering also most of East Kent, Hampshire and Berkshire, as

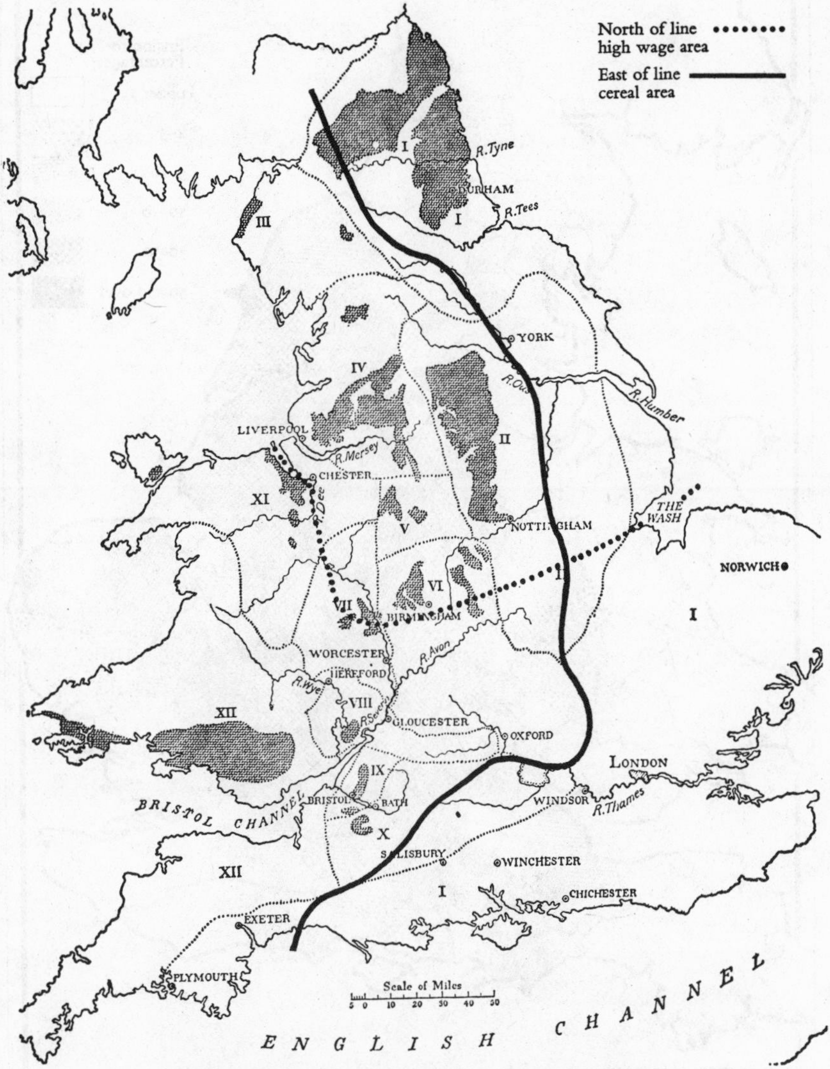

ENGLAND: AGRICULTURAL STRUCTURE

After Caird (reprinted in J. H. Clapham, *Economic History of Modern Britain*, I, *The Early Railway Age*, p. 147)

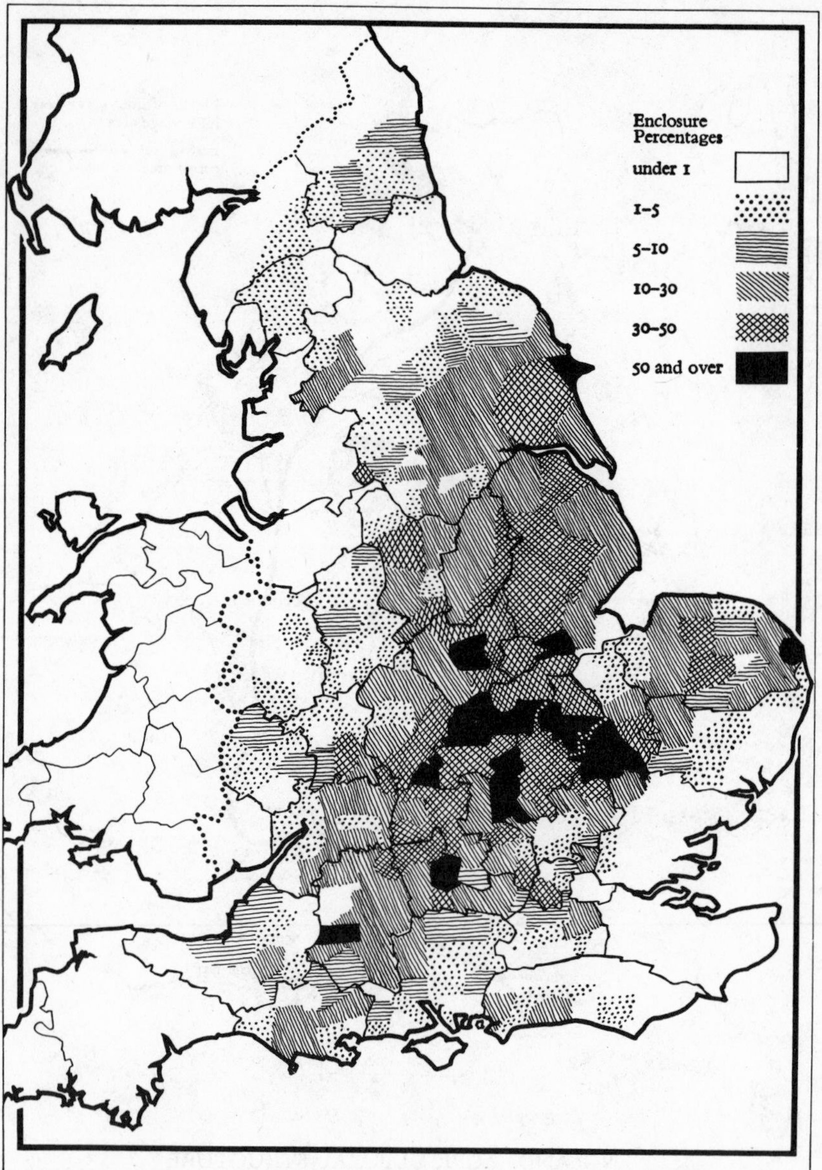

ENCLOSURE OF COMMON FIELD BY ACT
18TH–19TH CENTURIES

After E. C. K. Gonner, *Common Land and Inclosure*

Just when the English peasantry disappeared, and English farming came to be dominated by the triple division into landlords, tenant-farmers and hired labourers, has been a matter of argument for a long time. The most common opinion today is that this structure had come into existence in broad outline by the middle of the 18th century at the latest, i.e., before the start of the Industrial Revolution.[4] The agrarian changes which accompanied the passage to industrialism (say, 1760 to 1850), did not turn a feudal countryside into a capitalist one, nor did they simply transform family subsistence cultivators or small market peasants into proletarians. Several centuries of English history had already done most of that. Nevertheless, it is evident that in the period of the Industrial Revolution profound changes were taking place in the British countryside. Every schoolchild is familiar with the parliamentary "Enclosures" which, between 1750 and 1850 turned well over 6 million acres, or something like *one-quarter* of the cultivated acreage from open field, common land, meadow or waste into private fields, thus incidentally creating the characteristic hedge-patterned landscape of much of the English countryside. Three-quarters of the 4,000 private Acts of Parliament which thus revolutionised English farming and landscape (especially in a great inverted triangle of country with its apex at Portland Bill and its corners in North Yorkshire and East Norfolk)[5] were concentrated in the 1760s and 1770s, and again during the revolutionary and Napoleonic Wars (1793–1815). Between 1750 and 1840 the population of England and Wales multiplied by rather more than two. Yet it was estimated that in the 1830s home production of grain covered 98 per cent of British consumption, that is to say, that British cereal farming had not much less than doubled its output*—a very dramatic rise for so traditional a form of production as farming. It is inconceivable that such vast changes should not have had equally profound repercussions in rural society.

Before we try to assess these, let us see what industrialisation actually meant to the British agricultural producer. It meant in the first place, and mainly, a permanent boom in the demand for food for the growing towns, the rising numbers of the non-agricultural workers, and indeed the expanding population in general. (For reasons which do not concern us here, there was no real possibility of massive and regular

well as another zone covering much of Lincolnshire, almost all of Cambridgeshire, West Norfolk and a good deal of Suffolk, which lacked any kind of non-agricultural industries or manufactures.

* In the 18th century the country still had a persistent export surplus of grain.

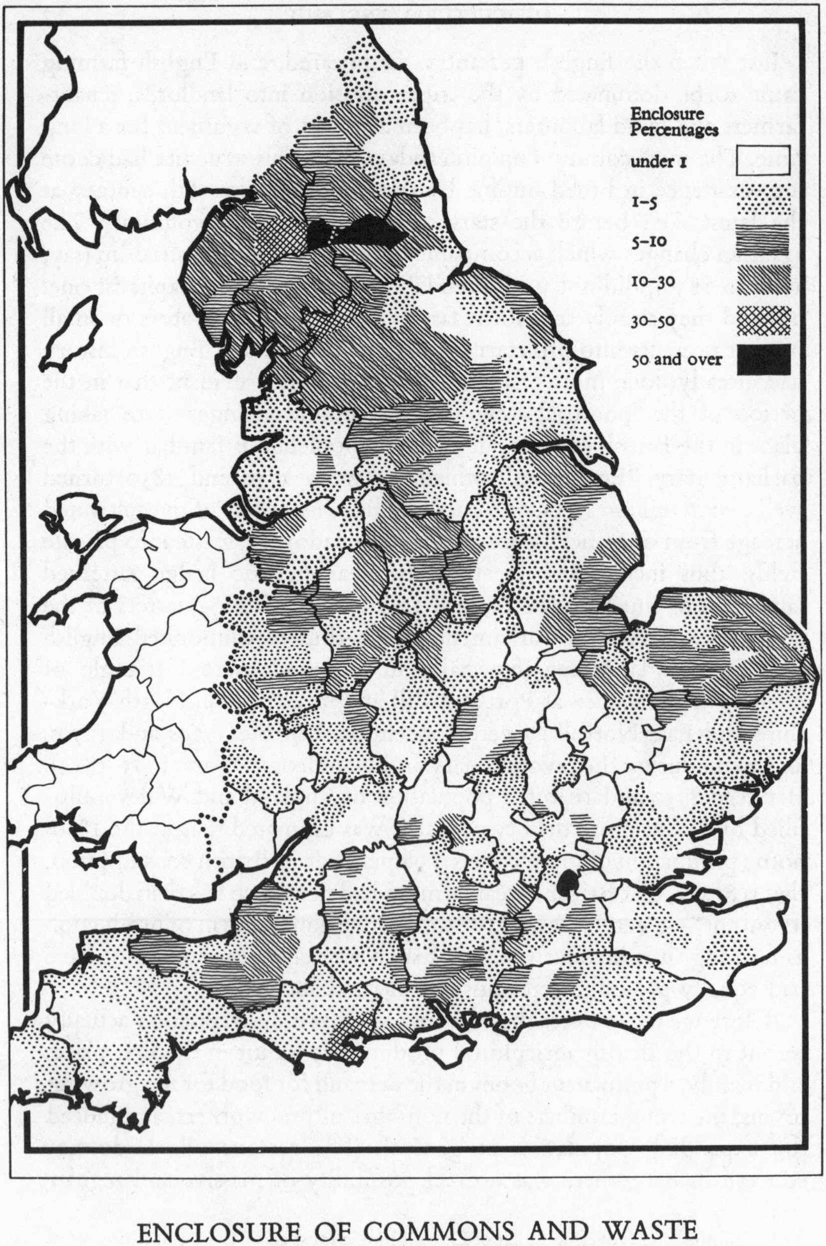

ENCLOSURE OF COMMONS AND WASTE
BY ACT 18TH–19TH CENTURIES

After E. C. K. Gonner, *Common Land and Inclosure*

imports of basic foods from outside the United Kingdom until past the middle of the 19th century.) The expansion of English farming in this period was essentially one of food production (including, of course, drink), and not significantly of the production of raw materials for industry. In the areas which lent themselves to tillage (as many hilly regions of the North and West, or heavy lands as yet incapable of effective drainage, did not), it was essentially the expansion of the production of bread of some or other cereal, which was still the staple food, the "staff of life".* The great waves of enclosure were primarily for grain production (especially during the wars of 1793–1815 when the cereal fields crept farther up the hillsides and onto the moorlands than at any time between the late 13th century and the production drives of the Second World War). However, geography, the nearness of large towns with their miscellaneous demand for food, and even the crop-rotations recommended by the experts, ensured a good deal of mixed farming; and so did the defects of transport, which made it impossible to transport perishable products very far before the railway boom of the 1840s, and obliged the producers of meat to drive their livestock for long distances and then to fatten it up near the final market (e.g. in the Home Counties and parts of East Anglia).

Broadly speaking, demand kept pace with, or ran ahead of, supply for the whole of the period from the middle of the 18th century until the arrival of massive cheap overseas food imports in the third quarter of the 19th century. Yet the prices of farm produce, and with them the prosperity of agriculture, fluctuated very considerably. Leaving aside short-term fluctuations, such as those which drove prices sharply upwards in years of poor harvests, the most striking movement, as the following table of annual average wheat prices for England and Wales shows, was the very large rise during the revolutionary and Napoleonic wars, and the very substantial fall in the years which followed them. (See table overleaf.)

This table shows that wheat prices after the Napoleonic Wars were consistently higher in each five-year period than they had been before the wars; and indeed, except for four such periods,† the *lowest* prices

* "In this period bread was undoubtedly the staple of life for the 80 or 90 per cent of the population that made up the working classes. Often enough it was practically the total diet, supplemented by tiny quantities of butter, cheese, bacon and tea; fresh meat was a luxury rarely seen at the tables of the poorest labourers." J. Burnett in Barker, McKenzie and Yudkin, *Our Changing Fare* (London 1966), p. 70.

† Characteristically these were the periods which saw the Parliamentary enquiries into the state of agriculture of 1821, 1833 and 1836, and the split in the agrarian-based Tory party.

Annual average wheat prices in England and Wales, 1771–1850

Period	Average for period	Highest price	Lowest price
1771–75	51·5 s	54/3	48/7
1776–80	40·2	46/11	34/8
1781–85	48·6	54/3	43/1
1786–90	47·2	54/9	40/0
1791–95	53·6	75/2	43/0
1796–1800	73·7	113/10	51/10
1801–05	80·0	119/6	62/3
1806–10	88·0	106/5	75/4
1811–15	97·2	126/6	65/7
1816–20	80·8	96/11	67/10
1821–25	57·3	68/6	44/7
1826–30	61·6	66/3	58/6
1831–35	52·6	66/4	39/4
1836–40	61·2	70/8	48/6
1841–45	54.8	64/4	50/1
1846–50	51·9	69/9	40/3

never fell below 50 shillings, which would have been considered extremely high prices before 1795. Yet landowners and farmers after 1815 measured their prosperity not against the remote pre-war years, but against the abnormal boom profits of 1795–1815, when the golden sovereigns had rolled in, when credit had been easy, when marginal land had been leased at inflationary rents, money borrowed in the confidence that prices would stay up, and luxury articles accumulated in the parlours of farmers who saw themselves as potential gentlemen, and on the backs of their wives and daughters who saw themselves even more passionately as ladies. After the dramatic fall of prices there is no evidence that British farming was going to rack and ruin. Taking the good years with the bad, prices remained pretty well stable until the very substantial improvements in agricultural methods from the 1830s on pushed up productivity. But there can be no question that in the years from 1815 to 1850 the British farming community saw itself under extreme pressure. The various Corn Laws (1815–46) were attempts to maintain prices by exploiting the political strength of a "landed interest" grossly over-represented in Parliament. It was equally natural that the farmers should seek to cut their costs by all means in their power—at the expense of their labourers.

Contrary to the traditional textbooks, British farming did not achieve its great increase of output during this period by an "Agricultural Revolution" similar or analogous to the contemporary Industrial Revolution. Before the 1840s there was little mechanisation, except, in most of the region which concerns us in this study, the threshing-machine,[6] though this spread during the wartime years of labour shortage. There was virtually no application of steam-power, and very little application of such modern sciences as chemistry (fertilisers) and the biological disciplines. With the exception of the new means of transport—canals, improved roads and coastal shipping, and in the 1840s, but hardly before, railways—farming made no great use of the Industrial Revolution; even the new earthenware pipes for the drainage of exceptionally heavy clay lands did not come into wide use until the middle of the 19th century. Essentially, agriculture achieved its remarkable increase in production partly by bringing new land (i.e. former waste or rough pastureland) under cultivation, partly by applying the best of traditional farming methods more widely, adopting certain common-sense innovations which had long been practised here and there* and, perhaps as important as anything, by applying systematic business calculation to farming. "The peasant", it has been observed, "does not operate an enterprise in the economic sense; he runs a household, not a business concern." The farmer, on the other hand, runs "primarily a business enterprise, combining factors of production purchased in a market to obtain a profit by selling advantageously in a products market".[7] But even among farmers, especially among those that have emerged gradually and slowly out of a pre-capitalist society, there are degrees of economic rationality. The impetus of the growing market for food turned British landowners and farmers with increasing rapidity into business calculators.

So far as the landlord was concerned, economic rationality consisted in linking his land as closely as he could to the market (e.g. by encouraging improvements in communications) and in getting the maximum rent from the most business-like tenant-farmers, i.e. of arranging his tenancies on such terms as to encourage the most profitable production by farmers. How far landlords actually did this is not so clear. The richest of them had such vast rent-rolls in any case that a little extra hardly counted much, unless they went in for particularly opulent luxury living; and their habit of not actually exploiting much of their land directly kept them somewhat out of touch with the realities of the farming business. (Of course, the aristocracy and gentry

* The crop-rotations and breeding methods associated with such names as Robert Bakewell and "Turnip" Townshend and popularised by the agricultural propagandists of the late 18th century, were not new. It is now accepted that, in so far as they were not taken over from the Low Countries, they were developed in England well before the middle of the 18th century.

did spend their rents freely: between 1760 and 1830 country-houses were built and rebuilt at a rate hardly ever paralleled before and never since, and those notably expensive pastimes, hunting and shooting, developed as never before.) There was probably much less rationalisation of leases than the agricultural "improvers" advocated and hoped for. Even in the mid-19th century, when the subject for the first time—characteristically—came under the scrutiny of Parliament,[8] tenancy right was a jumble of local custom and innovation, which on balance probably gave the tenant rather better than market terms. The mere fact that the term "rack-renting", which means merely charging a pure market rent, developed the connotation of inhuman hardness, is significant.

In fact, for various reasons the tenant almost certainly had rather the better of the bargain with the landlord. He was, much more obviously and necessarily, in the business of making profit, for he had fewer other resources, and certainly he had much less incentive to buy or hold on to estates for non-economic reasons, such as the status of gentleman and potential member of Parliament which only landowning conferred,* or the tradition of paternalism, of exercising "influence" in the county, of being, in short, at the top of a traditional rural—and national—hierarchy. He paid his rent, but at the same time was in one way or another subsidised by the landlord, whose productive expenditure, tenancy and credit terms, etc., diminished his own capital investment. Lastly, if times really got intolerably bad, the farmer had the advantage of being indispensable. Just because England was *not* a peasant country, efficient tenant farmers were not so easy to find. There was not (as we shall see) a queue of land-hungry peasants or smallholders waiting to occupy every vacant plot. And in so far as there was, they would not necessarily make the business-minded, large-scale market farmers who produced the maximum rents for an estate. Landlords, who would not have hesitated to turn their bankrupt or expired smallholders off the land neck and crop (as they habitually did in Ireland or the Scottish Highlands), might find it to their advantage to give the efficient big English tenant long credit, to cut or excuse his rent temporarily, since the alternative was to have the land uncultivated and degenerating.

* But, of course, the city businessmen and other newly-rich who bought themselves into the gentry by the purchase of estates in suitable (and correspondingly expensive) areas of the country, such as the Home Counties, might have more sense of book-keeping than more ancient families of the nobility and gentry.

There is, in fact, a good deal of evidence that throughout this period the large farm increased at the expense of the smaller, the big tenant at the expense of the lesser tenant or declining smallholder and family cultivator.[9] Hence it is misleading to speak of "farmers" as though they formed a homogeneous social group. The smaller men held their own during the wars, when sky-high prices and easy credit enabled even the marginal operator to make money. The postwar depression and the credit-squeeze which came with the return to the gold standard plunged them into trouble again, and when they complained they had cause to. They were probably being eliminated faster than at any time within living memory. This process of concentration in farming, it is generally agreed, continued well into the latter part of the 19th century.

The large tenant-farmer, on the other hand, could look after himself at most times. Economically and socially he played a disproportionately large part in farming, and he was the man the visiting foreign experts had in mind when they talked about the novelty and progress of English farming. From the labourers' point of view he was a remote —an increasingly remote—boss. For, as overseas observers noted with amazement, used as they were to European peasants and American working farmers, *he did not work*. "They rarely do any personal labour whatsoever," said that knowledgeable reporter of comparative agriculture, Henry Colman.[10] They supervised and gave the proverbial pig the proverbial prod while leaning over the proverbial gate. Economically their importance was capital. Thus in Suffolk out of some 5,000 farms rather over one-third employed six or more labourers each, and a little less than one-fifth employed ten or more, which was by no means unimpressive even by contemporary non-agricultural standards.*

The farmer might complain about his rent in bad years, but he would complain even more passionately about two payments which were far less flexible and were not offset by any incidental advantages: tithes and taxes. Of these *tithes* were a particular burden, and as we shall see, drove farmers in some regions into common cause with their labourers while making the clergy easily the most unpopular sector

* J. Glyde, *Suffolk in the 19th Century* (London, 1856), p. 336, gives the following figures:

686 farms had 1 labourer.
1,931 farms had 2–5 labourers.
793 farms had 6–9 labourers.
933 farms had 10 or more labourers.

of the landowning classes. The tithes consisted of the compulsory payment of one-tenth of the yearly produce of land and stock, either in kind or, by the early 19th century, increasingly in money, fixed in endless and ill-tempered wrangles of negotiation between agriculturalists and clergymen.[11] This flat 10 per cent impost on farming incomes and improvements was probably not as much of a brake on agricultural progress as the propagandists argued. Very often, indeed, it may have been borne largely (in the form of lower rents than might otherwise have been charged) by the landlord, who therefore—unless he was himself the "lay impropriator" of tithes—tended to share his tenants' dislike of them.[12] But, since it only incompletely reflected changes in prices, the tithe fell with particular weight on the farmer in bad times, and the demand for their commutation, reduction or abolition grew at such times. In fact, a few years after the labourers' rising they were commuted into "a corn rent, fluctuating in value according to the septennial average of wheat, barley and oats".[13]

Tithes opposed the farmers to the clergy. Taxes, or rather the most important of them, the local rates—and especially the most burdensome of these, the Poor Rate—opposed them to one another, but even more obviously, to the labourers. We shall consider the situation of the labourers and the problems of the Poor Law further on. Here we need merely note that the Poor Law had become, especially since 1795, a supplement to wages (most generally in the form of a childrens' allowance for large families), and one which increasingly allowed the employers to pay far less than a living wage in the certainty that the rates would bring it up to at least (i.e. in practice at most) a bare subsistence minimum. But as we have seen, the employment of labour was very uneven, whereas the Poor Rate fell equally on all ratepayers, whether they employed labour or not. In other words, those who did not employ labour subsidised those who did, those who employed little subsidised those who employed much, while the non-agricultural ratepayers, and especially the small shopkeepers, artisans etc., subsidised the farmers.

Still, there was constant pressure on the farmer to rationalise his enterprise. How did this affect his relations with the labourer?

Unfortunately we know very little about the poorest strata of the English rural population, of which the agricultural labourers formed the largest part. The early statisticians (basing their estimates mostly on intelligent guesswork) did not always distinguish between what Gregory King called "labouring people and out-servants" and "cottagers and paupers" or within those categories or between agricultural and non-agricultural labourers. Joseph Massie in 1760 thought the farming community was composed of about 150,000 families of farmers, 200,000 of "husbandmen" and 200,000 of "country" labourers as distinct from London ones (which does not necessarily mean only farm-workers).[14] This means very little except that in general the proportion of labourers to farmers seems to have been rather lower than it became later,* and that the categories of proletarians and marginal smallholders or cottagers were not very easy to distinguish.

The first major consequence of the agrarian changes during the Industrial Revolution was almost certainly that the problem disappeared, because the characteristic member of the rural poor was now a landless proletarian, relying almost exclusively on wage-labour or on the Poor Law for his or her living. "Enclosure", said the Hammonds, "was fatal to three classes: the small farmer, the cottager and the squatter." There is probably not much force in the argument that enclosures proletarianised the small farmer, though argument on this question continues. Yet even recent students who take a positive view of enclosures find that "there is indeed a great deal of truth" in the Hammonds' view so far as the cottagers are concerned.[15] "Before enclosure the cottager was a labourer with land, after enclosure he was a labourer without land", as the Hammonds put it. Those who had built a cottage on some patch of common or waste, or who relied on common or waste lands keeping a pig or two, a cow and maybe some geese, and to collect firewood or whatnot from them, could not but be disastrously hit by their division into pieces of exclusive and fenced-off private property in which they no longer had a share. More often than not this might mean that they could no longer manage to maintain an economic independence, however miserable and tenuous, and had to become labourers, or, if they had been part-time labourers before, to work full-time. Enclosure dissipated the haze which surrounded rural poverty and left it nakedly visible as propertyless labour. That it might lead to more and more regular local employment—at least for a time—did not compensate for the poor man's loss of independence. The social history of the 19th century village in much of England is the story of poor men's attempts

* But, of course, to compare the number of labourers with that of *all* farmers can be highly misleading, since many of them employed only or mainly family labour. The correct comparison, which we cannot make until the census of 1831, is between "farmers employing labour" and "labourers".

to escape from the economic and social dependence on those who gave them employment and relief. And anyway, as the whole of this book bears witness, employment in the village diminished and grew more uncertain.

Nevertheless, we should not exaggerate the effect of enclosures by themselves. They were a special case of a more general situation: the growing inability of tiny marginal cultivators to hold out in a system of industrialised manufactures and capitalist agriculture. For (and here the excessive stress on enclosure misleads) the proletarianisation of the rural poor proceeded everywhere in southern, midland and eastern England, and the worst pauperisation was found in areas which were quite unaffected by the parliamentary enclosures of 1760–1830, often because they had never been "open", as much as in those which were more recently enclosed.* The marginal cultivator is always immensely vulnerable, because he can rarely be genuinely self-sufficient. If he tries to be, the failure of the harvest may throw him temporarily onto the market as a purchaser of food at famine prices. If he relies partly on the sale of a little specialised produce, a good year (i.e. low prices) or the competition of others like himself may wipe out his little profit, while he still needs to buy goods and supplies. His domestic production of some manufactured articles during the slack winter season may be—and with the growth of industrialisation is likely to be—knocked out by the competition of factories, of more specialised "manufacturing villages" or of others like himself, anxious to work for ever-diminishing prices to make at least *some* extra cash. He has in fact no alternative except to rely increasingly on such wage-labour as is available locally—and in agricultural areas that meant, substantially, farm-labour—or on emigration. We need not pursue the various ways in which he could gradually sink below the threshold of even partial independence.[16] The only thing that could conceivably have held him above it, though in a community of impoverished and backward ignorance, was the traditional system of mutual aid and collectivity, such as we can still observe in 20th century Ireland.[17] But England was no longer that kind of society. It was moving rapidly away from what it had maintained of such a society from the past. Instead of the village community (as symbolised by open field and common) there was now enclosure. Instead of mutual aid and

* But as we shall see (pp. 179–80 below) Chambers and Mingay, *op. cit.*, p. 104, are quite wrong to say that "there was obviously no connection between the revolt (of 1830) and enclosure".

social obligation, there was now the Poor Law, administered exclusively by the rulers of the countryside.* Instead of family, patronage or custom, there was now the straightforward nexus of wages, which bound the landless to the landed.

Notes to Chapter 1

1. J. H. Clapham, *An Economic History of Modern Britain*, II, p. 253.
2. The 1831 Census contains some, which have been used in this book, but mainly for the study of individual parishes and hundreds.
3. Cf. Select Committee on Agriculture (Parliamentary Papers V of 1833, Q 9443).
4. This was, incidentally, the view expressed by Karl Marx, cf. *Werke* XXIII, p. 750.
5. For the basic maps of national enclosure distribution, see E. C. K. Gonner, *Common Land and Inclosure* (London 1912). See also W. E. Tate, *The English Village Community and the Enclosure Movements* (London 1967).
6. See Appendix IV.
7. Eric R. Wolf, *Peasants* (Foundations of Modern Anthropology Series, Prentice-Hall, 1966), p. 2.
8. Cf. the *Select Committee on Agricultural Customs* (Parl. Papers VII of 1847–48).
9. G. E. Mingay, "The size of farms in the 18th century" (*Econ. Hist. Rev.*, XIV, 1961–62).
10. *European Agriculture and Rural Economy from Personal Observation* (Boston 1846), vol. I, p. 38.
11. Lawyers distinguished between predial, mixed and personal tithes, farmers mainly between the "great" or rectorial tithes (corn, beans, peas, hay and wood) and the "small" or vicarial tithes (the remainder). For this immensely complicated problem, see W. E. Tate, *The Parish Chest* (Cambridge, 1946), p. 134 ff.
12. Cf. J. H. Clapham, *op. cit.*, p. 258.
13. Ernle, *British Farming Past and Present*, p. 344.
14. P. Mathias, "The Social Structure in the 18th century" (*Econ. Hist. Rev.*, X, 1957–58), pp. 30–45.
15. Chambers and Mingay, *The Agricultural Revolution* 1750–1880 (London, 1966), p. 97, and more generally Chapter IV.
16. Cf. B. Kerr, "The Dorsetshire Agricultural Labourer" (*Proc. Dorset Arch. Soc.*, vol. 84, 1963).
17. Cf. C. Arensberg and S. Kimball, *Family and Community in Ireland* (Cambridge, U.S.A., 1940), cap. 4.

* We are not of course implying that the communal institutions and customs of the countryside were egalitarian.

2

THE RURAL POOR

The most significant, but also the most obscure, aspect of this change is the transformation of the relations between the rural rich and the rural poor, the farmers and their labour force, into a purely market relationship between employer and proletarian. The best way to illustrate this is by analysing three crucial aspects of it: the separation of employer from labourer, the labour contract, and the methods of wage-payment.

Agriculturalists distinguished very clearly between two types of hired hands: "labourers" and "servants", the former hired and paid by the week or day, or by results—it hardly mattered in normal times*—the latter by the year; the former coming in to work, the latter mostly living and boarding in the farm-house. (It therefore followed that the servant was generally unmarried, young, and remained a servant only for part of his life until he or she married and settled down independently as a labourer or cottager, perhaps around the age of 25–30 years.)[1] The "servant" was essentially part of the employer's household, and hence servants got their wages largely in kind while being under the employer's discipline and at his or her disposal for their entire waking time; or rather for such tasks and times as people in their position were by custom expected to work. In return, of course, they had security all the year round. It is easy to sentimentalise or misinterpret such arrangements. England was not a country in which family structure (even that of the extended family which included servants, clients and other dependants) prevailed over or replaced class structure.[2] Even the small farmer who worked beside his servant in the field, yard or barn was perfectly aware of the difference between his son and his milkmaid, his daughter and his horseman. Yet the relation between master and servant was equally clearly not quite that between mere employer and mere worker. Their lives were intertwined, for better or worse—and many a youngster at the constant beck and call of the farmer would reckon it was for worse. They worked and ate together, at the same table. The young men and women did not expect to stay for ever. Such a relation-

* "The regulating medium for all task-work is the value of the day's labour", wrote John Boys in the *General View of the Agriculture of Kent* (1796), p. 161.

ship was not necessarily confined to house-servants. In many places the harvesters also, hired for the longest and most labour-intensive task of the year, were boarded and lodged on the farm, cooked for and served by the farmer's wife, daughters and maids, working together with the farmer and his sons, and joining with the family in the "harvest home" celebration which was the emotional culmination of the agricultural year, and the symbol of human and class co-operation in labour.

The servant was normally hired by the year, at the Hiring Fairs or Mops where the young men flocked from various parts of the county to display and enjoy themselves, the carter with a bit of whip-cord in his hat, the dairymaid with a strand of cow-hair in her bosom, the cowman with one on his hat. An entire body of custom and folklore accumulated around the process of annual hiring and leaving, such as the Pack Rag Day (often combined with May Day) when servants hired by the year packed up their clothes before spending a week at home or joining a new master.[3] After harvest, Michaelmas, or (as Marshall observed) in the North more logically Martinmas, in November when there was less to do,[4] in other instances May, were the most usual times for these occasions, which as usual attracted the displeasure of the economists and the puritans:

> "Let me now", wrote Mr. Austin in 1843, "call your attention to one of the most destructive sources of evil to which the character of the young female is exposed in the agricultural districts. In many counties it is the custom to hire lads and girls for farm-work at what are called 'Statute Fairs', known among the poor as 'Staties', 'Mops' and 'Wakes'. Some second-rate country town is in general the scene of these assemblages: a few shows, a few stalls for the sale of toys, etc.; a good many itinerant singers and sellers of ballads, many of which are of the most obscene character; a certain number of public houses and beershops, comprise the chief attraction of the fair. The business part of it consists in the exhibition of a large number of young lads and girls, dressed in all the finery they can muster, that they may be seen, as they think, to the best advantage to be hired on the spot by those masters or mistresses who come to such places to seek servants. . . . Those only who have witnessed them can form any idea of the scenes of vice which these fairs become late in the day. I know of no language of reproach too strong to apply to them . . ."[5]

Harvesters—also often hired for a longer period (i.e. in principle the "harvest month")—would also sometimes be hired at similar local fairs,[6] sometimes with the formal pledge of a shilling or a drink to commit the bargainers. Statute hiring provided some legal security. Shorter hires—most usually by the week, sometimes by the day, more often by the task, were naturally more easily terminable, and could amount to little more than casual labour. Payment was complex, but three broad categories can be distinguished:[7] The "servants" were paid by the year, plus their keep and extra allowances in kind (e.g. small beer and ale) and where necessary some incentive supplements, and worked for as long as required. Weekly labourers were paid by time and in cash, again with varying allowances in kind and possible incentive payments. Task-work was performed by the piece. Special tasks such as harvesting would be paid in various ways, ranging from a straight wage for the whole harvest (normally plus food, drink, a "harvest home" supper and some gleaning and free carting of wood or the like) to a straight piece-contract, sometimes negotiated by teams of men who pitted their wits in judging the nature of the harvest, the weather, etc., against the farmer's.

Essentially the annual work consisted of those jobs which went on all the year round, such as most obviously the care and handling of animals, supervisory jobs, regular work in yard or barn, kitchen work, but also, very often, such long-term winter tasks as threshing.[8] (The servant thresher was supposed to thresh a customary or fixed stint per day and received extra payment for more.) The bailiff and housekeeper, if there was one, the carter, ploughman (or anyone else who had to look after the horses), the cowman and shepherd, the dairy and kitchen maids, the regular "first man" or "second man", the thresher and any lads and girls about the house, tended to be hired by the year, lodged and boarded. In practice this might well mean, as in Hertfordshire, that "a great part of the labour of farmers is performed by annual domestic servants",[9] and this was certainly the case in Scotland and the North, and we may suppose also in the mainly pastoral regions. Apart from the special problem arising out of the haymaking and harvest, which required far more labour than any farm could rationally employ all the year round, the main jobs which could not be done by the servants plus the family would be such things as hedging and ditching, timber-felling, hoeing and draining, manuring, shearing, roadwork, specialised repairs and maintenance and the like, which would be done by labourers paid by time or piece, or by specialised craftsmen hired for the task. Naturally, it is impossible to generalise or, in the absence of any but fragmentary information, to make a realistic estimate how much of the labour force in any of the southern and eastern counties in the mid-18th century consisted of each category of labour. The agricultural writers were at best interested in total labour costs per unit of size or output, and since in most cases the conventional standard of a good day's work provided the real guide to pay (whether by time or piece), it did not much matter who performed it. At best a hard-headed calculator like Marshall would express his view, which was almost certainly correct, that an in-servant probably cost the farmer more than a poor labourer in maintenance, especially if kept "in the luxurious style in which farm servants in *this* country expect to be kept".[10]

This type of relationship reflected not only the technical nature of farming (with its combination of steady annual and extremely fluctuating seasonal work), but also a social pattern and an economic conjuncture. Socially, it fitted in best with a society in which distinctions of wealth and status among cultivators were not very great. (As we shall see, the growing "luxury" of the farmers and their growing social differentiation from the poor was later blamed for the decline of the common meal at the common table, which symbolised the old system.) A few large farmers; a good many medium farmers with an in-servant or two, recruited from among the sons and daughters of peasants or smallholders without enough land or tillage fully to employ their large brood, and making ends meet by seasonal wage-work for others; some more or less permanent labourers, craftsmen and other specialists: such would be the rural structure most suited to the traditional pattern of employment. (Indeed, the *General View of the Agriculture of Berkshire* in 1813 lamented "that good servants are every year more scarce and difficult to be found. The best domestics used to be among the sons and daughters of little farmers . . . but since that valuable order of men has been so generally reduced in every county, and almost annihilated in some, servants are of necessity taken from a lower description of persons.")[11] Mixed agriculture would lend itself better to it than monoculture, for the labour demands of, say, livestock and dairy farming were less than those of corn-growing and their busy seasons were different. The one could supplement the peak requirements of the other. Traditional and relatively unchanging agriculture lent itself better to it than rapidly changing farming practice, for when the nature of all rural tasks was familiar to one and all, and the standard of a good day's work established by the long practice of generations, there were only marginal problems of incentives and efficiency.* In terms of costs, payments in kind (e.g. the board and lodging of in-servants) made more sense when prices for farm products were low, stable or declining than if they were high or rising; lodging servants when the cost of building cottages was relatively high. That is, supposing the employer was responsible for it. In terms of labour supply, one might argue that a preference for long hires fitted in best with a fairly permanent shortage of hands at all but the traditional peak seasons, so that it paid each employer to keep a small pool of labour available at all times, because he might not be able to get hands at short notice, and/or a fairly modest level of normal employment, so that it paid the worker to prefer steady employment at a low income to the occasional possibility of higher wages. Paradoxical though it sounds, both these situations can co-exist quite happily in traditional semi-peasant agriculture. However, it is a mistake to read too much economic calculation into the pattern of employment. Much of it was traditional, and—as the agricultural improvers were never tired of pointing out—the old-fashioned farmer, however greedy for money, was a poor hand at rationalising his activities.

Inevitably the great changes in farming, combined with the succession of a long inflation of farm-prices, a wild boom in the war-years, and a drastic deflation afterwards, undermined traditional labour relations. In the long run they were also wrecked by the appearance of something which had hardly ever been reckoned with before, a *permanent* surplus of labour in the countryside. This was due in the first instance to the growth of population from the middle of the 18th century, but especially in the new century. Between 1701 and 1751 it is estimated that the purely agricultural counties of England—all but one were in the area at least marginally affected by the "Swing" rising[12]—remained virtually stable at 1·5 million inhabitants; between 1751 and 1801 they rose to about 2 millions, by 1831 to the remarkable figure of 2·9 million (i.e. by 50 per cent in 30 years). What affected the labour market was not of course mere numerical increase, but the failure of agricultural employment to rise correspondingly, the failure of non-agricultural employment to develop sufficiently in the farming

* As is shown by the practice of employing harvesters and threshers on a straight time-basis, which assumed that they would *at least* produce the expected or necessary daily stint.

counties, and perhaps most obviously, the failure of the surplus population to migrate. Of course emigrants left these counties. At all times the majority of them lost men and women by migration, and between 1781 and 1801 all without exception had net losses.* Yet the safety valve of emigration—mostly, from the south-eastern and eastern counties, to London—began to close.

Migration from Agricultural Counties 1700–1801 (to nearest 000)

Period	Population	Estimated Natural Increase	Estimated Emigration	% of natural increase migrating
1701	1,563			
1751	1,540	125	147	100
1801	2,046	654	261	40
1831	2,876	1,280	371	29

* *Source:* Deane and Cole. Counties: Beds., Berks., Bucks., Cambs., Essex, Herts., Hereford, Hunts., Lincs., Norfolk, Oxon., Rutland, Suffolk, Sussex, Wilts.

A diminishing proportion of the natural increase left. It was not human biology but human society which created the surplus labour in the countryside.

Fortunately, though we have little statistical material, there is overwhelming evidence that the old systems of employment declined.[13] We are sometimes able to date the decline even more precisely. The October "Jack and Joan" fair at Canterbury (Kent) had already become vestigial by 1799, when complaints about the scarcity of yearly servants along the Kentish coast, and about their lack of humility, were already familiar.[14] By 1833, though there was still long hiring at Michaelmas and Lady Day, it was no longer, they said, at hiring fairs: the labourers simply made the rounds of local farmers. Living-in was said to have disappeared in the Weald "since the early part of the War when Wages rose and the Demand for Labour in the County of Kent was very great". In Norfolk, "forty or fifty years ago", an expert claimed in the early 1840s, most servants lodged in. It was so no longer. "The system of weekly wages was the first blow towards weakening the ties which had hitherto bound the farm-servant, under all circumstances, to his employer." Another witness recalled in 1830:[15]

> "When I was a boy I used to visit a large Farmhouse, where the Farmer sat in a room with a Door opening to the Servants' Hall,

* Of the rest of the "Swing" counties all had net losses by migration between 1801 and 1831, but Hampshire gained a little between 1781 and 1801. (Surrey, being dominated by its London sector, is omitted from this list.)

and everything was carried from one Table to the other. Now they will rarely permit a Man to live in their Houses; and it is in consequence a total Bargain and Sale for Money, and all Idea of Affection is destroyed."

The shortening of the period of hire is particularly striking, for by the mid-19th century even weekly contracts, widespread in the south, were in fact daily or even casual, since farmers paid nothing for periods when work was impossible (e.g. when it rained).[16] The man or woman who was lucky enough to work with beasts still had some security of employment since "it might put employers to great inconvenience if their shepherds or stockmen left them on a week's notice",[17] but even here the contract might be reduced from a year to a month, and there was a distinct tendency in counties with a labour surplus to hire even horsemen, stockmen and shepherds by the week, the day, or even—in Suffolk—by the hour.[18] In a word, the farmhand became essentially a casual labourer, hired and dismissed at will, and lacking even the guarantee, as he set out in a misty dawn, that he would return home that night with any earnings at all. The decline of payments in kind reduced him, except at harvest when every hand was needed, to nothing but a precarious cash-wage, which might or might not cover his modest subsistence costs. The many local variations do not disturb this sombre generalisation.

The reasons for this relentless proletarianisation of the farm-labourer can be analysed a little more closely than we have done so far. They were economic, social and institutional, in that order of importance. The very nature of the expansion of agriculture, i.e. as we have seen largely the expansion of cereal crops, intensified the transformation of the servant into the casual labourer, for cereal culture minimises the regular all-the-year-round work and maximises the seasonal fluctuations of labour demand.* But economically the two most powerful impetuses for the transformation of in-servants into labourers, income in kind into cash payment, and long into shorter hires were the rise in the price of farm-produce and the increasing reserve army of labour. With rising prices it would obviously pay a farmer to sell as much of his produce on the market as he could, paying his labourers cash and

* "The difficulty of finding constant employment for a large staff of farm hands all the year round exists chiefly in the great corn-growing districts in the winter months, after the autumn ploughing and sowing has taken place and the roots have been taken up." Wilson Fox, *Wages and Earnings of Agricultural Labourers in the United Kingdom* (Cd 346 HMSO 1900), p. 10.

letting them buy their own food; or in other words throwing the burden of inflation on them. (Anyway, as Marshall observed, they always ate too much of the master's food; it would do them good to live more frugally on their own.) The famine years of the 1790s and the boom prices of the wars brought the point home to the dullest and most traditional of farmers. "The great advance in the price of provisions", as was observed of Bedfordshire (1813), "has apparently contributed to diminish the number of domestic servants of every description."[19] Or, as William Cobbett put it with his usual bluntness:

> "Why do not farmers now feed and lodge their workpeople, as they did formerly? Because they cannot keep them upon so little as they give them in wages. This is the real cause of the change."[20]

During the war years the labourers might be willing to accept the change in return for higher cash wages. As soon as the war was over, and with it the temporary labour shortage, or the willingness of farmers to pay good cash, it became only too obvious that employers could get as much cheap labour as they wished. "If a servant in agriculture leaves his place", observed the Rector of Whatfield (Suffolk) to the Poor Law Commission, "it is seldom indeed he can get another except as an occasional day labourer. Labourers now seldom live under their employers' roofs for these reasons: the number of unemployed labourers is such, that a Farmer is always sure of hands when he wants them. It is cheaper to hire day labourers . . . than to maintain Servants in the House, especially as they are always sent home on a rainy day."[21] There was no longer any point, as there had been still in the war years, in offering the worker better terms in the hope of keeping a sufficient labour force available for the peak demand. Conversely, during the Depression there was a greater incentive to pay out good money only for such days or hours when a man actually did work.

At the same time there were social reasons for the change. Time and again observers note that "since farmers lived in parlours, labourers are no more found in kitchens" or attribute the change "to the alteration of manners which a greater wealth and a larger occupation of land have introduced among the Farmers".[22] As the social and financial gulf between them widened, the farmer was no longer content to work by the side of his man and to eat the same food, let alone at the same table.* But the reluctance was not only on one side. In a

* Batchelor, *op. cit.*, p. 585, noting a tendency in Bedfordshire to abandon even the traditional boarding of harvesters, rightly feared "that this practice has a tendency to

rapidly changing society, the labourers themselves were often no longer so ready to accept the traditional discipline of the domestic servant. The young men disliked in-service.[23] The high cash wages of the early war years might encourage them to seek independence:

> "The Wages that a Servant received in a Farmer's Family bore no Proportion to those he got out of it; he became dissatisfied with his situation; and the Farmer, in consequence of the Alteration of Circumstances, and the high Prices which prevailed during the War, got above his Situation, and was ready to part with all his Men, whom he considered rather Incumbrances and Annoyances to him; and thus, by mutual Consent, the Masters and the Labourers parted."[24]

Not to the labourer's advantage.

Finally, there were institutional reasons for the change: the fear of giving labourers a "settlement" in the parish by employing them for a year, thus making them chargeable to the local poor-rate. However, though this was much mentioned in the discussions on the subject before the Poor Law Commission, it was almost certainly only of marginal importance. This difficulty could have been and was often got round by some small legal trick, such as employing a man for only fifty weeks in the year. The fear of giving "settlements" to outsiders cannot explain the transition to weekly, and indeed daily, hire.

One by one, with the inevitability of tragic drama, the defences of the village labourer against the traditional troubles of the poor, were thus stripped away. He found himself naked in what had, without many people noticing, become a much harsher social and economic climate than he had been used to. One final twist of historical irony completed his degradation. It arose out of the fundamental question in the minds of every employer: "How much shall I pay my worker?" It was price-inflation which stimulated the growth of farming from the middle of the 18th century to the end of the Napoleonic Wars, and, at least in some of the early decades, labour was by no means abundant. The fear in the minds of farmers was not so much of paying high or rising cash wages, when they could afford them, as of committing themselves *permanently* to high wage-rates, which they might be unable to afford in less prosperous times. As the agricultural improvers

dissolve the bond of union which ought at that time to subsist between a farmer and his labourers: their mode of living as well as every other attendant circumstance, tends to repress their spirit and activity"; i.e. snobbery could actually diminish productivity.

collected their reports, time and again they took down such phrases as "the rise of labour has been from 1s. to 1s. 4d. in ten years", "the price of labour in twenty years risen half".

As we have seen, farmers adopted the most obvious way of avoiding or at least minimising flat increases in guaranteed wages, namely the transfer of as much work as possible to payment by results or to casual employment for short periods.* The real difficulty was that the labourers' income was by custom, convention and justice a *living* wage, though a very modest one. What happened when the price of provisions kept rising, apparently without limit, for generations, and occasional dearth sent it rocketing? This situation arose with particular acuteness in the hard years of the middle 1790s.[25] It was at this moment that the rulers of the countryside, following the example of the magistrates of Berkshire in conference at Speenhamland, chose what turned out to be a disastrous alternative to the simple increase in basic wage-rates. They decided to subsidise low wages out of the local rates, in cases where the labourers' family income fell below the subsistence level, either because the price of bread was too high or the number of children too large. The "bread and children" scale, though never law, was almost universally adopted.

For the next forty years the "Speenhamland system" in one form or another, hung like a millstone round the necks of all rural classes in southern England. The "Poor Law" was no longer something to fall back on in times when a man could not earn his living, it became the general framework of the labourer's life. The distinction between worker and pauper vanished. We must conclude this chapter with a discussion of its nature.[26]

A fundamental contradiction lay at the heart of English agrarian society in the period of the Industrial Revolution. Its rulers wanted it to be both capitalist and stable, traditionalist and hierarchical. In other words they wanted it to be governed by the universal free market of the liberal economist (which was inevitably a market for land and men as well as for goods), but only to the extent that suited nobles, squires and farmers; they advocated an economy which implied mutually antagonistic classes, but did not want it to disrupt a society of ordered ranks.

"In the prosperity of agriculture", observed N. Kent[27] in 1796,

* They had traditional experience of this problem in the harvest when labour shortage could double the basic wage—admittedly for a limited period—quite apart from extra earnings by piecework and payments in kind.

"there are three persons who have a natural tye upon each other: the gentleman of landed interest—the farmer—and the labourer. Their degrees of interest are different, but their connexion must be permanent, as they cannot subsist without the aid of each other. Protection is due from the first—humanity from the second—and obedience from the third." The language would have been comprehensible to a medieval ideologist. The irony of this statement is that it envisages a society of employers and labourers, that it is applied to the country of the greatest capitalist development in agriculture, and that it pretends to guarantee, of all things, the "prosperity" of an agriculture which rested on diametrically opposite assumptions. We may note in passing that such views as these—and Kent was merely expressing the commonplaces of country gentlemen's after-dinner talk—took no notice of either the State or that part of the economy which lay beyond the local market town.

Thanks to the preponderant political power of the "landed interest" the universal market of capitalism stopped short of land. This was not freely bought or sold, except at the margin of the great and legally buttressed monopoly of the nobility and gentry. The prices of landed produce were also to some extent exempt from market-forces. The politically decisive "landed interest" attempted after the French Wars to stop them from falling; nobody objected to their rise. Success was indifferent, since the factors determining farm-prices were not fully under the control of county members of Parliament or "Corn Laws". Both these limitations of the capitalist market can be explained as mere self-interest. However the Speenhamland version of the Poor Law, which was in essence an attempt to limit the third type of capitalist market, that for *men*, cannot be entirely so explained, though it was among other things a useful alternative to the granting of higher wage-scales. It was at bottom an attempt to maintain the ancient ideal of a stable though unequal society, while combining it with the aspects of agrarian capitalism advantageous to landlords and farmers. Hence, as has been rightly, if ironically observed:

> "No measure was ever more universally popular. Parents were free of the care of their children, and children were no more dependent on their parents; employers could reduce wages at will and labourers were safe from hunger whether they were busy or slack; humanitarians applauded the measure as an act of mercy even though not of justice and the selfish gladly consoled themselves with the thought

> that though it was merciful at least it was not liberal; and even the ratepayers were slow to realise what would happen to the rates under a system which proclaimed the 'right to live' whether a man earned a living wage or not."[28]

It flowed naturally out of the traditions of that unique set of institutions, the English Poor Law, which was itself part of a larger social code, mostly formulated under the Tudors, though substantially modified after the Restoration. The Tudor code, in its essentials, believed that men should labour (and must be forced to do so if they did not want to) at just wages fixed annually and locally by the Magistrates. If for one reason or another they could not labour or earn their living, then they must be maintained, educated, medically cared for and buried by their community, i.e. the parish. I.e. the social code provided, in modern terms, both a productivity policy (forced labour), an incomes and prices policy, and a system of social security, but except for the first—labour enforcement was the job of the Poor Law authorities—they did not overlap. The Poor Law dealt with those people who did not fall under the other great instrument of law, the Statute of Artificers. The major addition to this code was the Act of Settlement of 1662, which confined relief strictly to the natives of the parish, or those who had established a "settlement" there, thus at one and the same time saving ratepayers from an influx of paupers or potential paupers, and guaranteeing the employers of the parish a local pool of labour. The system was essentially *local*, though under Elizabeth and the early Stuarts attempts were made to establish national control and co-ordination, and again in the 18th century there was a tendency to enlarge the unit of administration by combining parishes in "unions", and to make it more flexible in other ways, as by permitting occasional relief outside the village poorhouse or union workhouse. It was, of course, economically quite anachronistic, and made tolerable only by the gradual obsolescence of many of its provisions. On the other hand, socially it worked, at least in the countryside—so long as the number of the poor who could not maintain themselves remained manageable. In the 18th century the rural Poor Law ceased to be an instrument of labour compulsion. "Still, by and large the nearly 16,000 Poor Law authorities of the country managed to keep the social fabric of village life unbroken and undamaged."[29]

It was this system that the Berkshire magistrates tried to transform into something quite different: a last barrier against the advance of that part of rural capitalism which they did not like. The "Old Poor Law" has recently been defended by post-liberal economists as a rational device for maintaining, at slight social cost, a large number of rural surplus labourers who could not, at that period, have yet been employed in industry or the towns, and who could certainly not have all been employed at a living wage in agriculture.[30] On paper this makes sense. Its cost was not high—at the peak of expenditure (between 1815 and 1820) England and Wales paid out rather more than 3 per cent of its income, comparable to the percentage of the national income which went on unemployment relief in the 1930s.[31] The most universal principle of supplementing wages was the entirely acceptable one of a family allowance for large families.[32] It is quite legitimate to point out that the architects of the New Poor Law of 1834 were attacking, not only the abuses of the "Old Poor Law", but *all* welfare payments to families whose breadwinner is at work, i.e. the very principle on which modern Britain is conducted. However, it is a mistake to apply abstract economic reasoning, however humanitarian, to a situation which cannot be understood except in its context.

Speenhamland was not intended to achieve the results which Keynesian or socialist economists have in mind. It was no doubt an emergency measure, introduced at a time of famine, designed to hold off mass unrest, but which had the advantage of doing so without raising the market rate of wages. It was an instinctive escape of country gentlemen into the world they knew best—the self-contained parish dominated by squire and parson, and indeed it reinforced that supremacy, by making the village totally dependent on the decisions of its rulers, and wrecked the modest attempts to make the Poor Law slightly less parochial, by riveting it firmly to its local area and nowhere else. Henceforth it would be madness for a labourer, sure of at least his crust at home, to venture anywhere else. But its tragedy lay above all in the desire to combine agrarian capitalism (the determination of the wage by supply and demand) and the traditional "right to live" of even the poorest man, while at the same time setting its face against the only thing which could have at least provided some defence against the fall in wages, the combination of the workers.

Consequently it achieved the worst of both worlds. The traditional social order degenerated into a universal pauperism of demoralised men who could not fall below the relief scale whatever they did, who could not rise above it, who had not even the nominal guarantee of a living income since the "scale" could be—and with the increasing expense of rates was—reduced to as little as the village rich thought fit for a labourer. Agrarian capitalism degenerated into a general lunacy, in which farmers were encouraged to pay as little as they could (since wages would be supplemented by the parish) and used the mass of pauper labour as an excuse for not raising their productivity; while their most rational calculations would be, how to get the maximum subsidy for their wage-bill from the rest of the ratepayers. Labourers, conversely, were encouraged to do as little work as they possibly could, since nothing would get them more than the official minimum of subsistence. If they worked at all, it was only because their fathers had done so before them, and because a man's self-respect required him to.

Nobody can measure the dehumanisation or, in economic terms, the fall in productivity which resulted. (It was probably this last, rather than the actual cost of the Old Poor Law which made the criticisms of it increasingly shrill and desperate. In 1832–33 twelve English counties reported declining productivity of labour in between 50 and 76 per cent of their parishes,* *all of them wholly or partly in the "Swing" area*, and only six counties reported that it had declined in 15 per cent or less of theirs,† none of them in the "Swing" area.) Faced with the combination of rising poor rates and falling productivity, the "Old Poor Law" reacted by giving the vicious spiral another twist. The poor were starved even further. Between 1815–20 and 1830–35 the English poor law expenditure per head of the population diminished by almost a third, and as a percentage of the national income almost by half.‡ What this meant is that the subsistence minimum of the 1790s, itself hardly on the generous side, was progressively whittled away. In 1795 the Berkshire magistrates recommended an allowance of 3½ gallon loaves for a man, and 1½ for every other member of his family; in 1816–21 in Northamptonshire, Cambridge and Essex they thought he could live on 2 gallon loaves or a little more, plus 1½ for his wife; in Hindon (Wilts.), 1817, on 1⅗, with 1$\frac{1}{10}$ for a woman; in Dorset (1826) 1½ and 1$\frac{1}{16}$, in Hampshire (1822) on 1 gallon loaf.[33]

* Sussex, Bucks., Beds., Wilts., Berks., Norfolk, Cambs., Dorset, Hants., Surrey, Middlesex, Gloucester.

† Westmorland, Rutland, Durham, Stafford, Northumberland, Cumberland. M. Blaug, "The Poor Law Report Re-examined" (*Jnl. Econ. Hist.* XXIV, 1964, pp. 236–7).

‡ Mulhall's estimate:

Period	pence per inhabitant	per cent of national income
1815–20	152	3·23
1830–35	114	1·75

The Poor Law was not only made cheaper, but more deterrent. As we shall see, attempts to cut the relief scales still further helped to precipitate the rising in 1830 in several places.

It is difficult to find words for the degradation which the coming of industrial society brought to the English country labourer; the men who had been "a bold peasantry, a country's pride", the sturdy and energetic "peasantry" whom 18th century writers had so readily contrasted with the starveling Frenchmen, were to be described by a visiting American in the 1840s as "servile, broken-spirited and severely straitened in their means of living"[34] (unlike the "civil, cleanly, industrious, frugal and better-dressed" French). Everything conspired to impoverish and to demoralise them. They lost what little traditional right and security they had, and gained instead not even the theoretical hope which capitalism held out to the urban labourer, the legal equality of rights in the liberal society, the possibility of ceasing to be a proletarian. Instead, another, less human, more unequal hierarchy closed in upon them—the farmer who talked to them like a squire, the squire who drove them out for partridge and hares, the collective conspiracy of the village rich who took their commons, and gave them instead their charity in return for their servility, and on whose whim depended their livelihood. They did not even sell their birth-right for a mess of pottage. They simply lost it. They and they alone paid for the failure of British rural society to combine tradition and capitalism, for they got the benefits and hopes of neither. Stretched on the rack between the pauperisation of a caricatured market economy and the social oppression of those who grew rich from it, they lacked even the only real resource of the British labouring poor, the capacity to constitute themselves a class and to fight collectively as such. This book is in a sense the story of their attempt to do so, and—at least in the first half of the 19th century—its failure.

It would be easy to draw a horrifying picture of the poverty and degradation into which the English farm-labourer fell as a result of the economic and social developments in the countryside of which he, and he almost alone, bore the burden. From that day to this those who observed him, or who studied his fate, have searched for words eloquent enough to do justice to his oppression. We do not wish to compete with those of our predecessors who have already found them, from William Cobbett's cry of rage about the men found dead behind hedges with nothing but sour sorrel in their famished bellies[35] to the noble pity of the Hammonds' *Village Labourer*. It would be possible to accumulate the statistics of misery, the figures of the incomes on which grown men were expected to maintain a family (it was rarely possible for even the fully employed to do much more than pay for the bare necessities of food, except from the one substantial lump sum they got in the year, the harvest-earnings), the even more grotesque pittance on which single paupers were supposed to live, family budgets, the bleak dietaries of cottage life. Fortunately the subject is moderately well documented, and readers may be referred to a fairly copious literature.

Let us instead be modest, and conclude this chapter with the impression collected by a visiting foreign expert, a man with wide experience of agriculture in various countries, and one who was plainly reluctant to abandon the politeness due from a guest to those who had shown him much kindness in his tours. The English farm-labourer, thought Henry Colman in the 1840s, was in general comfortably clad, but poorly fed. With many exceptions they were "wretchedly lodged". "They seem to me to grow old quite early." "In a very low condition, ignorant and servile", slow and loyal, they went about their tasks. "I cannot help thinking", said this visiting American, "that the condition is a hard one in which incessant and faithful labour for so many years, will not enable the frugal and industrious to make some small provision for the period of helplessness and decay, in a country where the accumulations of wealth in some hands, growing out of this same labour, are enormous."[36] And nor can the historian.

Notes to Chapter 2

1. For servants staying till the age of 25–30, Poor Law Comm. Rural Questions 38 (Starston, Norfolk).
2. For an exaggerated version of the "family" interpretation of English society, Peter Laslett, *The World We Have Lost* (London, 1965).
3. *British Calendar Customs: England* I (London, Folklore Society 1936), pp. 243–4.
4. W. Marshall, *Minutes . . . on Agriculture in the Southern Counties* (1799 edn.), I, pp. 185 ff.
5. *Reports of the Special Assistant Poor Law Commissioners on the Employment of Women and Children in Agriculture* (London 1843), p. 75. From the report on Wilts., Dorset, Devon and Somerset, where annual hiring maintained itself better than elsewhere.
6. T. Batchelor, *Gen. V. Agric. Bedfordshire* (1808), p. 582. Wilson Fox, *Report on Wages of Agric. Labour* (1900).
7. Rev. A. Young, *Gen. V. Agric. Sussex* (1808), p. 404.

8. Cf. Batchelor *op. cit.* 581 for Bedfordshire, C. Vancouver, *Gen. V. Agric. Hampshire* (1813), p. 382, A. Young, *Gen. V. Agric. Hertfordshire* (1813), p. 217, for annual hire of threshers.
9. A. Young, *op. cit.*, p. 217. Cf. also *V. C. H. Berkshire*, II, p. 222.
10. Marshall, *Minutes* I, pp. 302–4.
11. W. Mavor, *Gen. V. Agric. Berks.* (1813), p. 416.
12. Beds., Berks., Cambs., Essex, Hereford, Herts., Hunts., Lincs., Norfolk, Oxon., Rutland, Suffolk, Sussex, Wilts. The source of these demographic estimates is P. Deane and W. A. Cole, *British Economic Growth* 1688–1959 (Cambridge 1962).
13. The most systematic exposition of agricultural contracts and wage systems in the later 19th century is the *Report on the Wages and Earnings of Agricultural Labourers in the United Kingdom* by Wilson Fox (Cd. 346, London, HMSO, 1900), which should be consulted for comparison, but also for the occasional anomalies such as the maintenance of some payment in kind in Hampshire, Wiltshire and the South-west.
14. *British Calendar Customs, loc. cit.*, p. 97; J. Boys, *Gen. V. Agric. Kent* (1796), p. 165; *S.C. on Agric.* V of 1833, Q 5194–9.
15. *Lords Ctee on Poor Law* (Parl. P. VIII of 1830–31, pp. 26–7, 186; R. N. Bacon, *History of the Agric. of Norfolk* (London 1844), pp. 142–3. For similar evidence regarding Norfolk, *S.C. on Poor Law Amendment Act* 1837, Q 1143, *R.C. on Poor Law* 1834, Rural Questions 38 Costessey, Starston), for Bedford, *Poor Law Ctee* 1837 11442–53; Somerset, Wilts., 1833, *S.C. on Agric.* 9437, 1244–7, Suffolk, Rural Q. 38 (Chediston).
16. Cf. W. Hasbach, *A History of the English Agricultural Labourer* (London 1908), pp. 406, 411; Wilson Fox, *loc. cit.*, pp. 10–12, for the recognition that this was in fact casual or daily hire.
17. Wilson Fox, *ibid.*
18. *Suffolk Farming in the 19th Century*, ed. J. Thirsk and J. Imray (Suffolk Record Soc., vol. I, 1958), p. 32. For examples of such short hires from Kent, Somerset, Surrey, Herts., Hunts., Norfolk, Suffolk, Sussex, at the end of the century, A. J. Spencer's Report in *R.C. on Labour* (Parl. P. XXXV of 1893).
19. T. Batchelor, *Gen. V. Agric. Beds.* (1813), p. 580.
20. *Polit. Reg.*, 20 October 1825.
21. *R.C. Poor Law* 1834, Rural Questions 38, Suffolk. Cf. also answers for Chediston, Burghclere (Hants.), etc.
22. *Loc. cit.*, Rougham (Suffolk), Chilmark (Wilts).
23. *R.C. Poor Law*, Rural Questions 38, Rougham, Whatfield (Suffolk), Downton (Wilts.).
24. T. L. Hodges, M.P., speaking about the Weald of Kent, *S.C. on Poor Laws*, 1830–31, pp. 26–7.
25. For these, see W. M. Stern, "The Bread Crisis in Britain 1795–96" (*Economica*, vol. 31, 1964), pp. 168–87.
26. By far the best discussion we know is in K. Polanyi, *Origins of Our Time* (London 1945), caps VII–IX. This is a brilliant and unduly neglected book. A modern discussion by an economist, M. Blaug, "The Myth of the Old Poor Law and the Making of the New" (*Jnl. Econ. Hist.*, XXIII, 1963, pp. 151–84).

27. *Gen. V. Agric.* Norfolk, p. 192.
28. Polanyi, *op. cit.*, p. 85.
29. Polyani, *op. cit.*, p. 92.
30. Blaug, *loc. cit.*
31. Mulhall, *Dict. of Statistics*, art. Paupers. However, since the rates were raised locally and pauperism was much heavier in the Southern counties, the actual burden on some regions was of course heavier.
32. The propaganda of the New Poor Law reformers of 1834, whose disingenuousness was very great (cf. M. Blaug, "The Poor Law Report Re-examined", *Jnl. Econ. Hist.* XXIV, 1964, pp. 229–45), exaggerated the prevalence, after the Wars, of direct subsidies to wages.
33. Hammonds, *op. cit.*, I, pp. 181–2.
34. H. Colman, *The Agricultural and Rural Economy of France, Belgium, Holland and Switzerland* (London 1848), pp. 25–6.
35. *Polit. Register*, 6 November 1830, p. 711.
36. H. Colman, *European Agricultural and Rural Economy from personal observation* (Boston–London 1846), pp. 40–2, 64.

3

THE VILLAGE WORLD

There were, as we have seen, plenty of causes for the labourers' unrest, and it is indeed difficult to see how they could *not* have revolted. Nevertheless, causes are not the same as acts. Human beings do not react to the goad of hunger and oppression by some automatic and standard response of revolt. What they do, or fail to do, depends on their situation among other human beings, on their environment, culture, tradition, and experience. We must therefore look next at the social and mental world of the southern labourer, and especially on what he knew about collective organisation and protest.

Rural Englishmen, with few exceptions, lived in *parishes*, that is to say in territorial units whose administrative centre was the Anglican church (where their births, baptisms, deaths, and marriages were solemnised and registered, where they attended divine worship and which provided the official channel for communications to them from higher authority). All lived in parishes governed formally by the local committees of the rate-paying wealthier parishioners (vestries, overseers of the poor), who organised the social administration of the parish and such other collective functions as they had to, e.g. the appointment of the parish constable, or maintenance of roads.[1]

The parish was a very real unit in the lives of labourers, and the development of the Poor Law made it, as we have seen, their inescapable cage. Inside the parish they had their "settlement" and therefore their social security; outside it they were at best tolerated foreigners, at worst deportable paupers. For the purposes of their lives the parish boundary was more important than the county line, much more important than the frontiers and shores of England. What went on outside of it was none of their direct business. Thus in 1822 the men of Shimpling (Norfolk) stopped a threshing-machine which a farmer of Burston had sent for and dragged it back to their parish. As soon as it had crossed the parish boundary, *but not before*, they smashed it to pieces.[2]

Yet the parish was evidently not the only unit of their lives. It was in some senses too small, in others too large. Many farmers employed labour from other parishes, and many labourers relied on such employment, especially where the regional surplus was concentrated in a few pauperised "open" rural slum-villages whence people tramped, or were taken by labour contractors in gangs, to their places of work. Nor was the parish the basic unit of the nobility and gentry who thought mainly in terms of "the county", ruling it and its subdivisions at the Petty and Quarter Sessions, but in times of trouble increasingly also through special conferences (such as the meeting of the Berkshire magistrates at Speenhamland which changed the Poor Law in 1795), at county protest meetings, and through the informal network of understanding between magnates and gentlemen. All parishes had a symbolic representative of the hierarchy of rule in the parson, himself more often than not a landowner and magistrate, and by his style of life and habits a member of the gentry. Some—a varying proportion, greater near London than outside the Home Counties—had a "seat" or "seats", i.e. a resident squire or nobleman; or in a few areas a sizeable concentration of gentlemen-residents (e.g. around Amesbury in Wiltshire, in the Alton–Alresford area of Hampshire, around Hawkhurst in Kent). Only where a village was "close", i.e. where all or most of it belonged to a single owner, especially a resident one, was the circle of the parish world entirely closed: provided most employment was also in the parish. This situation was most likely to arise in relatively small villages.

Nor was the parish the unit of communications. The *market* (weekly, or bi-weekly) linked it to the nearest town, the *fair* to the centre of administration or to some county-wide or even regional centre of movements and transactions. Thus when there were hiring fairs in Gloucestershire, they existed at only a few places: Cheltenham, Cirencester, Gloucester, Newent, Tetbury and Tewkesbury, and perhaps elsewhere. In the Suffolk Hundred of Hartismere, with over thirty parishes, they coincided with the Petty Sessions, which were held at Stoke and Botesdale.[3] Berkshire had 17 places with regular fairs, Hampshire 42, of which at least three were still used for hiring in the early 19th century; and so on.[4] Moreover, for most people the neighbouring parishes, even if inhabited by traditional enemies and rivals, were part of the normal universe and range of social action. We shall see the labourers in 1830 habitually move outside their parishes into the rest of their small universes (see chapter 10 below). Still, if the labourer's horizon was bounded by the "small universe" rather than the parish, and thus included the market-town, the fair, and perhaps areas as far as 15 or 20 miles distant, it is likely that after 1815 increasing dependence on the Poor Law riveted him more tightly to his home territory, and consequently made him more dependent than before on those whose movements and horizons were less circumscribed: artisans, shopkeepers, carters, hawkers, and those coming or returning from the great outside world.

In another sense, however, the parish was too large or indiscriminate a unit of life. In practice it did not necessarily coincide with the real unit of *settlement*, which was (speaking broadly) either the *village* or the scattering of small hamlets and farms or cottages, or a combination of the two. In Sussex, for instance, the coastal plain was an area of villages, the Downs were empty but with large villages distributed at their foot, the Weald (as in Kent) a region of small farms and scattered dwellings, with the occasional small township as a regional centre. The village had its own communal shape, structure and institutions, though it might also—so far as the inhabitants were concerned—be a complex of neighbourhoods which the urban foreigner overlooked. It would have the church, perhaps a village green (but many large villages straggled along a road), probably at least two public houses (the one a man went to and the one he didn't), resident craftsmen and perhaps members of the middle class and gentry. The great region of nucleated villages was the area formerly under common fields, i.e. a large inverted triangle with its apex in West Wiltshire and its base a line stretching from Great Yarmouth to the northern borders of Yorkshire, and its centre in the East Midlands.[5] The scattered settlement, much more common in the west, the east and south-east, and parts of the south, where common and common field had never existed or long died out, had no such obvious cohesion, and perhaps implied much more coming and going of people, and a less sharp consciousness of the village boundary. The church and its surrounding houses, shop, green, etc., were like the modern suburban shopping centre, the point of regular contact for the settlement, and not its very existence. Of course the poor men's cottages and cabins, which grew up throughout the area of even a nucleated parish, were never in such close contact with the village. They might, for instance, be some miles from the village pub, and the modest beerhouses which sprang up (especially after the Act of 1830)[6] in all kinds of back lanes, to the horror of farmer, parson and squire, acted as their centres.[7] Can we generalise that in the scattered settlement the social control of the ruling classes was less direct? If so, we must always remember that the stimulus for action was more likely to work where men habitually and daily met in large numbers.

Moreover, there was at least one type of village where social structure and control were proverbially loose: the very large so-called "open" villages which often lived in a sort of symbiosis with the surrounding smaller or "close" parishes, providing them with labour. The large village was, sometimes by its very tradition and structure and like the small provincial town, much less of a landed monopoly of the nobility and gentry, especially when it had a fair or was a decayed town. In Wiltshire, for instance, Pewsey and Ramsbury, though in a zone of very large (mainly absentee) owners, contained a lot of plots owned by shopkeepers, artisans, and the like, who tended to run up cottages for rent to labourers, thus attracting the otherwise homeless and creating those straggling rural slums which so preoccupied the reformers of rural life. In "close" villages the planning was under the effective control of the local squire or gentry, and as often as not the size of the settlement and the building of cottages were kept down in order not to interfere with the amenities and "picturesque view" of country house and park.* Several such villages became proverbial "problem settlements": Castle Acre in Norfolk, where neighbouring farmers recruited the "gangs" of women and children for their field-labour,[8] Ixworth in Suffolk, and others. Certainly if criminality is any index of the tightness or looseness of social control, the large or open village had more of it. In the Thingoe Hundred of Suffolk, three out of the five villages with abnormally high criminality were "open". (There were altogether 27 "close", 11 "open" and nine unclassifiable parishes.)[9] In the Hartismere Hundred of the same county three of the five criminal villages had above 750 inhabitants in 1831 (there were altogether six parishes of this size out of over 30), and none of them were obviously "close". In Cosford Hundred the four largest parishes were also among the six most criminal. Large or small, concentrated or scattered, the settlement was a place which provided meeting-points. The little "village parliaments" of neighbours talking over the business and gossip of the day or season were the least formal;[10] the church the most formal. In 1830 we find examples of labourers' movements starting on Sundays in the church (as at Ringmer in Sussex), and in 1834 protests against the new Poor

* It is impossible to generalise about the validity of the frequent complaints that squires and large farmers actually pulled down cottages, though this certainly happened, and when it happened, left bitter and long memories. In Tisbury (Wilts.), a large village near numerous parks and countryhouses, an act of this kind by Benett of Pyt House, one of the county MPs, in 1817, was still remembered in 1965. For the Pyt House affair see below, pp. 125-6.

Law which took the form of church boycotts, the people demonstratively leaving the church and "smoking pipes in the cemetery" (at Wroughton in Wiltshire), or walking out "every poor man, woman and child . . . to the number of 150".[11] It was natural to arrange for more formal negotiating meetings with the local farmers and gentry in church or churchyard, as in Horsham (Sussex) and Thatcham (Berks.).[12] Similarly other formally or informally localised institutions —the Hundred Pound in Brede (Sussex), the space in front of the vestry rooms (Pulborough, Sussex), the village green or a field near the church (Kentish Weald) could provide places of assembly and discussion. However, the general impression is that such movements began more often with informal groups and propagated themselves by the silent consensus of the poor, until they reached the point of open demonstration in front of the house of farmer, rector or squire.

It was natural that the inn, a natural centre of meeting and discussion, saw the start of many such movements, though the innkeeper might not always be happy about this: he depended on the goodwill of the notables who licensed him. Still, in the pre-temperance era the inn was the automatic locus of secular organisation, from the village club even to the Petty Sessions, and the less formal and official beerhouses were constantly accused of being centres of subversion, i.e. of discussion. The inn, where not the only secular meeting-place, was often one of two,[13] so it could not help but become a vehicle of politics. It is not an accident that in East Kent, where the machine-breaking began, Saturday and Sunday night, when the men left the pubs, saw the start of action. Just so in 1816 the Littleport riots (Isle of Ely) began when men of that village left the *Globe* inn after a meeting of the local Benefit Club.[14] The fact that in many smaller villages the publican or beerhouse keeper was himself also a small craftsman or trader, brought him closer to the labourers.*

Nevertheless, these units of administration or settlement were not communities if that word implies that the ties of locality prevailed over those of class. Or rather, they were communities only within the limits of the village poor. When a "threatening paper" signed simply "North Curry" and "Stoke St. Gregory" was distributed round that area in 1834, it was evident that the men who signed it with the name of their villages did not regard the "jentelmen" and farmers whose

* In the Erpingham Hundred of Norfolk we find publicans who were also wheelwrights, carpenters, butchers, joiners, coopers, brickmakers, shoemakers, bakers and blacksmiths.

ricks they offered to burn, as part of the collective.[15] Of course even the traditional common institutions of the village recognised, or even insisted on, its internal economic inequality. Waits, mummers or any of the other ritual processions of village life would not have been complete if the performers had not also collected money from the wealthier villagers "for good cheer", but also *as of right*. These were indeed the ritual occasions when the customary order of social relations was briefly stood on its head, a built-in safety valve for the tensions which exist in all stratified societies. Thus on Plough Monday (the first Monday after 12th Day) the labourers in Cambridgeshire used to go round the parish cracking whips as though calling the plough team (but also as though exercising coercion in general) "till the householder contributes to the fund for good cheer".[16] We shall see later how practices of this kind took on a different colouring in the context of the labourers' rising of 1830. Nevertheless, in the traditional village a balance between tension and co-operation between different groups had been maintained. The horrors of the period from 1760 to 1830 destroyed it. Eighteenth-century writing on English agrarian society does not insist on the sullen hatred of the poor for the rich. Nineteenth-century records increasingly do, especially in certain counties. "All friendly relation between the Farmers and the poor ceases" it was reported from Burghclere (Hants.) to the Poor Law Commission. "Revenge", it was said in Bramshaw, "want of good feeling" between the classes in Minstead, both in the same county.[17]

The upper classes probably did not realise, until riot and incendiarism taught them differently, quite how much they had been excluded from the village community by the poor. The squire still saw himself in his ideal role as the paternal protector, the farmer as strict but humane, and both saw the labourer as obedient, grateful and fundamentally at one with the traditional hierarchy of rank. They were not quite wrong. As we shall see, there is evidence that in 1830 the labourers and their sympathisers did not normally want a disruption of the old society, but a restoration of their rights within it, modest, subaltern, but *rights*. Moreover, as we shall see, the labourers had some reason to believe that their demand was acceptable. The gentry almost certainly, a proportion of the farmers probably, resented and resisted the disintegration of the old order and would have liked to maintain it. They were not, like the industrialist middle class, conscious of creating a new capitalist order, and proud of it. What they failed to see was that their very actions as landowners and farmers, the very fact of their growing wealth and changing styles of life, turned their attachment to the traditional order into empty phrase. What they did was to create an order in which the poor were pauperised and rightless, and rank and wealth became caste superiority, and the labourers' silence and humility in the face of their "betters" hid sentiments similar to those of Mississippi Negroes in the face of the whites. Each village increasingly hid two villages: the official parish, whose citizens the new County Directories recorded—the landowners, resident gentry, farmers, publicans, etc.—and the dark village, whose members they did not.

Yet the official and the dark village overlapped to some extent. The "poor" included not only the labourers and their like, but all other little men who maintained some sort of economic or social independence of parson, squire and farmer—e.g. the craftsmen and perhaps some small traders—and such larger traders as depended mainly on the custom of the poor, and therefore maintained contact and perhaps sympathy with them. "I do not think a respectable character ever enters them", said the Rev. Robert Wright of Itchen Abbas (Hants.) about the beerhouses; but an occasional tradesman and "sometimes shoemakers and people of that description" did, at least in Tilehurst (Berks.). They were kept by labourers, but also by cottagers, by carpenters and blacksmiths (Essex), by carpenters and shoemakers (Berks.), by blacksmiths and carpenters (Sussex), or more generally by "a little kind of petty tradesman who will rather get their bread any other way than by hard labour"—i.e. by those who sought economic independence from their "betters".[18] Indeed at Ingatestone (Essex) there had been "a meeting of all the parish" at one of these dens of unrespectability in 1830 "determined not to serve as special constables".[19] The line between the village and its rulers did not run between those who laboured for wages and those who did not, but between "the people" as a whole and the rich. As we shall see, this fact was to provide the labourers' movement with plenty of leaders, organisers, spokesmen and activists from outside their ranks.

Among the labourers themselves, certain groups were, by their situation or their choice, more likely to welcome acts of protest. In the first instance, there were the young unmarried men, who suffered most from pauperisation, since they received least from the parish, and were most likely to be forced into the most degrading and useless kinds of parish labour, e.g. on the road-gangs which provided only too justified centres of disaffection. The most active were also the most discontented. It is a safe bet also that those whose work isolated them most from discipline and social control were likely to be potential dissidents, such as the shepherds, a proverbially wild group in most rural societies.* Men who maintained a certain economic independence of squire and farmer, however miserably, were in a better position to rebel. And indeed, it is likely that men who resented humble dependence often chose such independent occupations. For the labourers there were few, except the increasingly important activity of commercial poaching and, in some coastal regions, smuggling or the occasional resource (as in the hinterland of Poole harbour, Dorset) to the sea.[20] Poachers and smugglers—in the nature of things mostly young or strong men with no prejudice against violence—and those who organised their work, were notoriously involved in the risings of 1816 and 1830. On the other hand, such "natural rebels" among the agricultural workers were likely to be the least educated and "ideological" of their kind.

The genuine and public rebel was probably much rarer; a figure whose humble heroism is difficult to conceive nowadays. Such a one was Thomas Davis of Swallowfield, "one of the most active young men and best labourers" but, alas (as his betters recorded), a bad character, in spite of the seven children who made him as a pauper totally dependent on the good will of his betters. He acted, on occasion, as spokesman for his comrades. During the 1830 riots he was the *only* man in the village who resisted the pressure of squire and farmer and refused to be sworn in as a special constable. He was alone: the rest were too frightened to act. This may have been a mercy for him, for he would otherwise have been commemorated in some Tasmanian convict register rather than in the pages of the Royal Commission on the Poor Law.[21] Let us in passing pay him the tribute due to a very brave man, and through him to the many others of his kind, whose names nobody now remembers.

Among the non-labourers certain occupations lent themselves perhaps even more readily to political dissidence. The shoemakers were, as always, the typical artisan intellectuals: often we find them doubling as parish clerks, because of their superior education.[22] The

* The religious convention which makes shepherds a symbol of gentleness rests on (*a*) their relation to sheep not men and (*b*) the fact that, being marginal men in agricultural society, they belong to those ritually and magically powerful, though formally often despised classes which play so great a part in religious life. Mountains are the frequent locations of visions, shepherds have them (as Prof. A. Dupront has reminded us).

builders were also active, and if other craftsmen such as tailors appear more rarely, it is only because there were few of them in the villages. (The artisans from neighbouring towns are another matter.) Of the more respectable tradesmen, perhaps the publicans who depended heavily on the patronage of labourers were the most sympathetic, and those whose sympathy was most useful in the preparation of protest movements.

The non-labourers among the poor also provided one, perhaps the only, certainly the chief link of the labourers with the world of the written word, of wider national ideology and politics. For their universe was largely illiterate, their own resources of struggle and aspiration tradition and oral communication. In 1840 only 395 letters and 54 newspapers a week were posted or delivered in Faringdon (Berks.), 320 in Wantage, 241 and 51 in Wokingham (compared to 2,820 and 1,213 in the town of Reading, 2,906 and 714 in the upper-class centre of Windsor).[23] The actual global rates of illiteracy around 1840 (when the first official figures become available) ranged from 60 per cent in Bedfordshire to a surprising minimum of 30 in Dorset, a median of 48 per cent, as the following Table shows:

Illiteracy in the "Swing" Counties, 1838–39 (per cent)

County	Men	Women	Both	County	Men	Women	Both
Norfolk	44	49	46	Kent (pt)	29	40	34
Suffolk	46	53	49	Surrey (pt)	33	36	34
Essex	46	54	50	Sussex	31	43	37
Cambs.	45	54	49	Hants.	32	36	34
Beds.	55	66	60	Wilts.	44	56	50
Herts.	52	57	55	Dorset	20	40	30
Bucks.	42	55	48	Somerset	36	47	42
Hunts.	46	56	51	Berks.	44	45	44
Lincs.	28	47	38	Oxon.	35	43	49
Northants.	37	51	44	Gloucs.	32	44	38

But these were, of course, gross underestimates, since they were based on the numbers signing the marriage registers with a mark, and the ability to scrawl one's own name is no effective test of literacy. In practice, and especially among farm-labourers, ignorance was much greater. A report from Bucks. suggested that of adult labourers and their wives one in six could read, one in ten write. A Kentish area investigated because of a local movement of revolt (see below, p. 291) showed that even among children over 14 in 1839 only about a quarter could read and write, a little under half could do neither. In Norfolk (1841–42) it was believed that among the labourers "very few of the adults of either Sex, from Twenty to Fifty", could read or write.[24] Of the labourers tried in Suffolk for incendiarism in 1843–44 nine could read and write, in one fashion or another, 17 were quite illiterate and 13 partly illiterate.[25] And if they could read, the chances were that they had access overwhelmingly to devotional literature, as in Norfolk.[26]

What were these resources? Ideologically they consisted of the usual luggage of the pre-political poor, the belief in the rights of poor men by custom, natural justice and indeed law which must not be infringed by the rich. Egalitarianism, democracy or other more revolutionary slogans seem to have entered the village rather from the Radical nuclei of the neighbouring small towns, or through the literate and conscious craftsmen and small traders within it; perhaps also through religious sectarianism, where there was a tradition of rural dissent. (There is no great evidence that the expanding new sects, like Primitive Methodism, were at this stage very politically-minded in the village: their eyes were fixed on another world.)* Among the political statements emanating from the 1830 rising we can normally distinguish fairly clearly between those of evidently Radical phraseology, which say relatively little about the labourers' social plight, and those semi-literate ill-scrawled missives which are clearly from labourers themselves, and conversely rarely say anything about Placemen, Taxes and the Funding system, except perhaps to observe its irrelevance. "You have often-times blinded us", said the pseudonymous signatories of the letter to "the Gentlemen of Ashill", "saying that the fault was all in the Place-men of Parliament: but now you have opened our eyes, we know they have great power but they have nothing to do with the regulation of this parish."[27]

Labourers' movements were therefore likely to be localised, and they were always reluctant to believe—like most peasant movements of the past—that the King's government and Parliament were against them. For how could the fount of justice be against justice? The men of Otmoor misinterpreted a legal declaration that their entire Enclosure Act was null and void, and immediately rioted.[28] The men of Weston in the 1830 rising even thought that in some curious way they had the authorities on their side. We shall find other similar

* There are very few signs of religious terminology in the statements of protest from labourers, except for such vague phrases as "Gentlemen, these few lines are to inform you that God Almighty have brought our blood to a proper circulation, that have been in a very bad state a long time, and now . . . we mean to circulate your blood with the leave of God." A. J. Peacock, *op. cit.*, pp. 65–6.

examples later, such as the men of Crowhurst who refused to withhold taxes because "it was the King's money and it wouldn't do". There is no evidence that, in spite of a constant animus against the clergy and a growing one against the farmers and gentry (at least in some parts) the movements up to 1830 sought any subversion of the social order. They sought its regulation. No doubt the general moderation of their atmosphere was partly, and paradoxically, due to the fact that they were movements of an agricultural proletariat and not a peasantry. Peasants, however unrevolutionary, want land, and lack of land is against natural justice. The remarkable characteristic of the proletarianised labourer was that he no longer wanted land, but higher wages and good employment. As we shall see, there were virtually no examples of anyone connected with these movements demanding land.

Organisationally, the labourers had occasion to observe the fairly elaborate political and administrative activities which went on around them: the vestries with their elected officers and other assemblies and committees of local government, the periodic parliamentary election campaigns and public meetings, the parish, hundred, or county meetings and protest campaigns of their betters, particularly in the depressed years of 1815–22 when the organised pressure on Parliament for the relief of agriculture was both militant and widespread. Such activities may have given men the idea that action was possible or imminent, but they belonged by definition to property-owners and rate-payers, and few labourers were either. They could provide as little guide to labourers' organisation as shareholders' meetings do to trade unions.

On the other hand even the poorest had experience of two or perhaps three types of organised collective activity: for labour, for ritual purposes, and perhaps for certain customary functions of the entire village such as beating the bounds. Co-operative labour was generally organised hierarchically (as in the farmer's harvest) or quite informally, but we also know of egalitarian work-organisation by independent gangs, bargaining through elected, or at all events democratically accepted foremen or "captains", most usually in connection with harvest labour. Interestingly enough, poaching gangs also seem to have been organised in a similar way, the proceeds being equally divided among the members. Unfortunately such organisations, though demonstrably common in many agrarian societies, are very poorly documented, at least in Britain.[29] However, it is likely that the activist gangs in 1830 were inspired by such experiences.

The second, and perhaps more important experience of organisation was ritual. It included such occasions as the preparation of the annual village feast—generally around Whitsun in the south—and of the ritual processions (mummers, waits, etc.) of certain sections of the village, such as the young men and women, the ploughmen, milk-maids and the like. Two characteristics of these rituals are particularly to the point. They generally included or culminated in a procession round the parish or neighbourhood, and they normally involved the collection of money or gifts. Both these characteristics are found in the protest movements of the labourers, which frequently had an atmosphere of festiveness, ritual and formality about them, such as the wearing of best clothes, of ribands, the blowing of horns, etc. (See chapter 10 for examples.) More specifically, a "purser" or "treasurer" was often appointed "to take charge of the contributions" as in the Plough Monday processions in the Isle of Ely. It is significant that the one formal officer we find most frequently among the riotous mobs was such a "treasurer", as in the Isle of Ely in 1816, in Berkshire in 1830, and elsewhere. It was the hypocrisy of frightened lawyers which was to turn the familiar procedure of collecting money from the upper ranks, which was widely adopted in 1830, into the crime of "robbery" or "extortion" for which, unlike the breaking of threshing machines, the death penalty could be given.

How far did the voluntary organisations existing in the village serve as a school or nucleus of social movement? By far the two most important were the Friendly Societies or Benefit Clubs (much encouraged by the humanitarian gentry in the late 18th century) and the dissenting sects. Neither were comprehensive organisations; both included, in fact or even by definition, only a minority.* Neither seem to have played a major part as such, though in 1816 the Littleport riot grew out of a Benefit Club meeting.† This is not to say that the presence or absence of a Friendly Society or group of religious dissenters was irrelevant to the strength or militancy of a local movement. As we shall see (see below, chapter 9) it was not. But neither of these bodies acted as important centres or models of organisation, as for instance the Primitive Methodists were later to do in the Agricultural Labourers' Unions, and the complaints of the upper classes rarely

* Thus the Netheravon Friendly Society limited its membership to a maximum of 150 (Wilts.).

† Mr. Peacock's valuable book on the subject may exaggerate their value as "a meeting-place at which freemason-like secrecy was observed" (*op. cit.*, p. 56). Labourers never had much difficulty in keeping their thoughts and discussions secret from their betters.

mentioned dissenters and even more rarely Benefit Clubs among the causes of the 1830 rising, whereas—for instance—they habitually mentioned beer-houses.[30] Friendly Societies, were of course purely village organisations, and indeed often formally confined to one village and exercising communal ceremonial functions: the preparation of the annual feast in which members took part in their special colours ("each member is required to bring his bunch of ribbons, blue and red, and to follow the band, and to walk in regular order, that the Society may pay their respects to their different friends in the neighbourhood").* The branches of the national Affiliated Orders had hardly penetrated the southern counties by 1830, and if they had, were confined to non-agricultural workers. The sects were virtually the only voluntary bodies with national affiliations to possess groups in the villages, for secular political bodies hardly reached beyond the provincial towns. The occasional talk by hysterical parsons and others about the delegates of Political Unions who "constantly attend those (beerhouses) and there they enrol members",[31] was, like most similar statements, devoid of serious content. On the other hand there is no doubt that small-town Radicals, especially in Kent and East Sussex, systematically tried to extend their agitation into the countryside, and that, as we shall see, much of the 1830 rising bears the marks of this influence. But the evidence for any radical or other permanent organisation or combination by labourers in the villages is thin.†

What experience of actual social protest by the poor did the villagers of the early 19th century have? Certainly between 1760 and 1830 they often experienced enclosure, whether of open fields or (in the Swing area more often) commons, which led to protest actions. As we shall see, the memory of enclosure contributed to the outbreaks of 1830, and it is highly likely that places with a tradition of protest against them, learned something from past actions.[32] In the neighbourhood of small country-surrounded parliamentary boroughs, labourers must have witnessed, and perhaps on market or fair days been involved in, the meetings and riots of what was then a notably turbulent activity.

* Rules of the Netheravon Friendly Society (1840). The Bromham Society, also in Wilts., wore "purple first to the hat, next blue Pink in the middle—that is to be made up in a Cockade and not tied loose round the hat". The Seend Society (Wilts. 1800) wore "purple, pink and white, not less than a yard and a half of each sort", Potterne (1793) "blue and red ribbons in the hat, one yard each, and a rod in hand".

† But in Barton Stacey (Hants.) fires were started in December 1831 and 1832 by labourers victimised for joining a Political Union. (Poor Law Commission XXVIII of 1834, p. 303.)

There were the occasional conflicts of parish politics. But above all, there were the familiar kinds of recurrent social unrest in times of dearth or high prices—the riots against millers, shopkeepers and other dealers. It is possible that the hard times of the middle 1790s produced the first of that series of rural waves of discontent which, as we shall see, continued until the 1850s. As we have seen, the Speenhamland system was in its origins largely a device to allay such rural unrest at this time. Doubtless most of the 1795 riots were still essentially directed against dealers. Yet already the characteristic demand for higher wages as well as lower prices occurred. In Thatcham (Berks.) some 300 collected in 1800 to demand either the one or the other. In West Dean (Sussex) a round robin had already been circulated. No doubt further research will discover other examples of such concerted action, most probably in East Anglia.

The war-years diminished such movements, but their memory lived on. What is more, after 1795 the labourers had a constant occasion for collective protest in the Poor Law—the last and perhaps the only "right" which they retained and, as the evidence of their shocked superiors shows, cherished and defended. "That relief which formerly was and still ought to be petitioned as a favour", wrote Arthur Young of Suffolk in 1797, "is now frequently demanded as a right." To a certain W. Peter it all proved "the general degradation which has taken place in the moral habits and feelings of the lower orders of society. To accept parochial charity was formerly a disgrace, it is now demanded as a privilege."[33] We dare say that the labourers would have preferred to have other rights to demand. Yet the men who pressed, and indeed sometimes terrorised, the village notables in defence of their constantly threatened pittance, were demonstrating not moral degradation but its opposite, collective self-respect. And though there is some evidence that the parishes in which the informal action in defence of poor relief was most successful were those in which more formal movements had less appeal in 1830,[34] the defence of their rights to relief was probably the best schooling available to the potential village militant in many parts of South and East England.

Notes to Chapter 3

1. The classical discussion is S. and B. Webb, *History of English Local Government* I, "The Parish and the County" (London, 1906).
2. *The Times*, 11 March 1822.

3. *British Calendar Customs, loc. cit.*, III, p. 87; J. Glyde Jr., *The Suffolk Garland* (Ipswich 1866).
4. *The Journey-Book of England: Berkshire* (London, C. Knight & Co., 1840), p. 32; G. A. Cooke, *Topographical and Statistical Description of the County of Hants.* (London 1819); *Robson's Commercial Directory*, 1835.
5. Cf. Map D in E. C. K. Gonner, *Common Land and Inclosure* (1912).
6. See below, p. 88.
7. The *S.C. on the Sale of Beer* (Parl. P. XV of 1833) complains that labourers prefer to frequent the beerhouse in the next parish, presumably to be less under the eye of their immediate rulers (Q. 34).
8. *Report on the Employment of Women and Children* 1843, pp. 221 ff.
9. For criminal villages, J. Glyde, *Suffolk in the 19th Century* (London 1856), p. 138; for close and open ones in Thingoe, A. Wilson Fox in *Parl. P. XXXV* of 1893–94, pp. 52–3 (Cambridge 1961).
10. Cf. M. K. Ashby, *The Life of Joseph Ashby of Tysoe*, pp. 140 ff., for a good description.
11. *Brighton Herald*, 20 November 1830; *Devizes and Wiltshire Gazette*, 27 March 1834.
12. Hammonds II, pp. 59 ff.; A. L. Humphreys, *Bucklebury* (Reading 1932), pp. 378 ff.
13. In two Norfolk Hundreds 25 parishes had one inn, 16 two and only seven (including the small towns) three and more; in a Suffolk Hundred 13 parishes had one inn, eight 2 and three 3 or more. Beerhouses have been omitted, as have parishes without a recorded inn. Source: White's *History, Gazetteer and Directory* for Suffolk (1844) and Norfolk (1845).
14. A. J. Peacock, *Bread or Blood* (London, 1965), p. 95.
15. *Devizes and Wiltshire Gazette*, 30 October 1834.
16. *British Calendar Customs*, II, p. 95.
17. See chapter 15 for further discussion on this point.
18. S.C. On the Sale of Beer (*Parl. P.* XV of 1833) Qs. 74 ff. 1802–3, 434, 2072, 3132.
19. *Ibid.*, Q. 498.
20. Barbara Kerr, *loc. cit.*
21. R.C. Poor Law, XXIX of 1834, p. 302.
22. E.g. in Hampshire (1859) in Abbott's Ann, Bullington, East Woodhay, Hurstbourne Tarrant, Highclere, Liss, Selborne, Sherfield and the Wallops, to take only the area of the riots. White's *History*, etc. of Hampshire (London, 1859).
23. *Journey Book of England: Berkshire* (London 1840), p. 31.
24. R. K. Webb, "Working Class Readers in Early Victorian England" (*Eng. Hist. Rev.*, LXV, 1950, pp. 335–6.
25. H. o. Lords Papers 258 of 1844: *Ages and Descriptions of persons committed for trial for Incendiary Offences in Norfolk and Suffolk.*
26. *Report on the Sanitary Condition of the Population* (London, 1842) (p. 140 for Holkham).
27. A. J. Peacock, *op. cit.*, p. 65.
28. Hammonds, I, p. 89.
29. D. F. Schloss, *Methods of Industrial Remuneration* (London 1892) has precisely

one sentence about "self-constituted cooperative gangs", though noting that they were "common".

30. In the Rural Questions of the Poor Law Commission there is one place in Berkshire which mentions "Ranters". In 1822 a Norfolk parson mentioned as an additional (but not principal) factor in the unrest "there are several of the inferior meeting-houses, the pulpits of which are filled by those illiterate preachers whose doctrines are of the most dangerous tendencies", by which he apparently meant Calvinist. R. Hindry Mason, *The History of Norfolk* (London 1884), p. 496.
31. *S.C. on Sale of Beer* (Parl. P. XV of 1833, Q 14).
32. Cf. P. Olivey, *North Curry* (Taunton 1901) for one such activist area. 1834 Poor Law Com. Rural Q 53 ascribed the 1830 riots here to "revenge of expropriated smallholders".
33. Quoted in A. J. Peacock, *op. cit.*, p. 35.
34. E.g. the Suffolk parishes in which smuggler, poachers and paupers "extorted the scale allowance from reluctant overseers by threats of violence". *2nd Ann. Rep. of Poor Law Commissioners*, 1836, p. 148.

4

FROM WATERLOO TO REVOLUTION

The history of the farm-labourers' battles against their tragic fate is wrapped in almost total obscurity. Yet it is certain that their struggle began to enter a new and acute phase in the last years of the Napoleonic Wars, and particularly after Waterloo. The end of the wars turned the potential crisis of agriculture into an actual one; an artificial war-time boom into a correspondingly acute and prolonged recession. The demobilisation of anything up to 250,000 men from the armed forces within a short period swamped the rural labour market, which was already glutted with excess labour, with even greater numbers of the unemployable. All this at a time when the labourer was peculiarly denuded of protection. The Speenhamland policy had opted for relief rather than high wage-rates and in so doing taken away the labourer's safest guarantee, a living wage, and substituted the much weaker one of a minimum family income for paupers. During the boom years of the war the labourer had at least worked, and therefore earned wages. But the fatal decision of the war years—his own as well as the farmer's—for short contracts and money wages left him defenceless when there was simply too little work to go round. The agrarian depression enclosed rural labour in a diminishing and increasingly vicious circle. The employer hired as little and as briefly as he could, relying on the parish to maintain the unemployed. The parish could do so only at increasingly astronomic expense, and in turn the rate-payer (i.e. to a large extent the employer of labour) cut down his labour requirements even further, as his expenditure on poor relief rose. The insane logic of this process reached the point of tragic absurdity when decent men "are driven, without the pretext of a complaint, from services of long standing with masters to whom they had become attached", because someone else had sacked his labourers and "if X has turned off 20 of his men; if I'm to pay their wages he'll have to pay yours".[1]

For the labourer there were only five methods of protest or self-defence. He could protest against wage-cuts or demand higher wages, but in the nature of the situation he could do so only occasionally, at moments of mass mobilisation, and with little hope of permanent success. He could take a desperate grip on the one economic asset he still possessed, the right to poor relief within his parish, thus transforming what gentry and farmers had regarded as a temporary alternative to wage-increases into a permanent and an inflexible system of social security, almost impossible to destroy by purely local power, and tending—when not reduced by deliberate harshness and brutality—to become steadily more expensive and, since it had to bear an increasing proportion of the labourers' income, steadily less efficient. He could seek a relief from poverty in crime—in the simple theft of potatoes or turnips which constituted the bulk of the offences which he would himself regard as criminal, and in poaching or smuggling, which he would not. It was, of course, not a mere source of income, but also a primitive assertion of social justice and rebellion. Fourthly, he could resort to terror, i.e. in practice to incendiarism which threatened the farmer with greater losses than he might sustain by yielding to the demands of his labourers. Last, and most ambitious, he could attack the very basis of his unemployment by destroying the machines which, in his view, intensified or even created it. He could also, in theory, use a variety of political devices—petitions, delegations to petty and quarter sessions, etc., but his lack of political rights and inexperience put these beyond his effective use in most cases.

The absence of adequate statistical sources makes it impossible to measure the progress of rural poverty and degradation with any accuracy or in any detail. We know that *unemployment* certainly increased in the post-Napoleonic period, but we have no general figures to measure its progress and fluctuations year by year. There are plenty of data about individual villages at particular times and some more general enquiries, but these can merely serve as illustrations of the sheer scale of the problem and the difficulty of generalising about it. A few of such wider enquiries may be mentioned. In 16 parishes of the Kentish Weald in 1823, 8,263 out of 21,719 inhabitants were paupers, and 682 men (supporting an unknown number of dependants) were totally unemployed all the year round. Benenden, Biddenden, Hawkhurst, Rolvenden, Staplehurst and Woodchurch each had 60 or more men totally out of work, and only two parishes had less than ten. The situation in 1826 was no better.[2] In the Blything Hundred of Suffolk there were in 1830 2,500 to 3,000 able-bodied men: 1,001 of these (with 602 wives and 2,399 children) were unemployed. In Baddington 60 out of 110 were without work in January of 1830, in Stradbroke 70 out of 110, in Fressingfield 110 out of 140, in Framlington three-quarters.[3] In Cosford Hundred (Suffolk), a pauper census in 1832—which is not, however, the same as an unemployed census—revealed that roughly 4,100 out of a population (1831 census) of 7,900 in 18 parishes were paupers.[4] Such figures are not necessarily typical. A return for 426 Norfolk parishes, presumably for the whole year of 1831, gives an unemployment percentage of only 12,[5] but a more detailed enquiry in 10 parishes wholly or partly owned by Lord Suffield, and by no means selected for their poor conditions, gives an average of 16 per cent for, presumably, 1830.[6] On the other hand a fairly comprehensive return for Cambridgeshire of some 120 parishes shows extreme local inequalities. Half the parishes reported no permanent unemployment (though this may have meant only that it was concealed by work-spreading and systematic under-employment), and heavy unemployment was clearly concentrated in certain regions and villages: Gamlingay had 70 out in winter, 50 in summer, Isleham 70 in winter, Soham 80, Histon 40–50, Willingham 62, Melbourn 40.[7]

Under-employment was constant, except perhaps at the height of the harvest, and sometimes even then. Yet it is clear that the main burden of unemployment was concentrated in the winter months, and this was the reason for the almost universal hostility to the threshing machines, which took away the standard winter labour.* Manual threshing in the old days went on throughout November, December and January at least.[8] It could amount to a quarter of the entire annual labour requirements of the farm. Threshing machines had been introduced in some quantity during the labour-shortage of the war years, yet they continued, curiously enough, to spread even in subsequent years of depression and surplus cheap labour, though many farmers were by no means enthusiastic about them.[9] For the labourers this was an unqualified tragedy, for it left them, or threatened to leave them, totally dependent on relief for the hardest part of the year. The threshing machine thus became the symbol of their misery. Even in regions where it was of no serious significance, the very existence of an individual machine, especially if recently introduced or in particularly hard winters, mocked their hunger. The demand for work inevitably became the demand for the destruction of this machine,

* Not quite universal. Able-bodied young men, who could earn good money with the machines, were not against them. In one place in Dorset there was an actual demand to restart the stopped machines in December 1830, but this was quite exceptional. Kerr, (1962), p. 175.

and other kinds of agricultural machinery do not seem to have attracted anything like this general hatred.

Unemployment figures, however significant as indications of the labourers' misery, are too patchy to throw much light on the accumulation of despair which broke out in 1830, and therefore cannot explain why it did so then and not before. We are rather better informed about the Poor Law, which gave rise to a mass of literature and miscellaneous official returns, unfortunately so miscellaneous as not to lend themselves very easily to generalisation. Two essential facts about it must be constantly borne in mind. The first is that, by the end of the Napoleonic War, thanks to Speenhamland (using the term in its most general sense) the labourer, even when in employment, was as likely as not a pauper who depended for part of his family income on the parish. Even in the early 1830s family allowances, for instance, were given (normally to those with three or more children) in 82 per cent of the reporting parishes in Sussex, 74 per cent in Hants. and Suffolk, 73 per cent in Berks., 72 per cent in Wilts. and Oxford, 71 per cent in Bucks., 67 per cent in Northants. and Devon, 66 per cent in Essex, 54 per cent in Hunts. and about 50 per cent in Norfolk, Cambridge and Kent. (It will be observed that most of these were Swing counties.)* In extreme cases it could be said with little exaggeration that the farmworker could no longer strictly be described as a wage-labourer. The remarkable percentages of pauperism mentioned in an earlier paragraph—over a third in the Weald, over half in the Cosford Hundred—are thus explained. It does not take much imagination to picture the situation of famished dependence of the 60 per cent of *all* inhabitants of Hitcham or Polstead, or of almost the entire population of Wattisham and Whatfield (all in the Cosford Hundred), or the 958 out of 1,746 inhabitants of Benenden, the half of those living in Biddenden or Goudhurst (Kent), who were paupers. In a sense, the more comprehensive the local poor law, the more the labourer was enmeshed in this web of dependence, for the more was he forced *all the time* to go cap in hand to his betters. The counties in which the system of subsidising wages was the most widespread, at all events in 1824, were East Anglia, Bedford, Cambridge and Huntingdon, Berkshire, Bucks., Oxford, Wilts. and Dorset, and—if we are to judge by the constant complaints about abuses—Sussex, or rather the Weald area of East Sussex and the adjoining part of Kent.

* Of the remaining Swing counties, the percentages were 44 for Dorset, 46 for Gloucester, and, surprisingly, only 19 in Beds.

Clapham has observed acutely that "the coincidence of the area in which wages were most systematically augmented from the rates with the area of maximum recent enclosure is striking".[10]

The second fact is that the constantly rising cost of poor relief led to increasing attempts to cut it down in the 1820s. We know that, taking England and Wales as a whole, poor law expenditure per head of population rose rapidly from the 1790s and reached a peak—at about 12s. 10d. or 3·2 per cent of the national income—between 1815 and 1820. In 1815 the global percentage of paupers stood as follows:

Paupers relieved as per cent of total population[11]

Berks.	17	Suffolk	12·25
Wilts.	15	Cambs.	11·5
Sussex, Essex	14	Kent	11·25
Dorset, Oxford	13	Herts., Norfolk, Northants.	11
Bucks.	12·75	Hereford, Leicester	10·5
Hunts.	12·5	Beds., Salop., Hants.	10

Clapham estimated that by 1830 the English farm-labourer relied on the poor law for a minimum of 15 per cent of his income, and in the Swing counties, especially those of maximum Poor Law expenditure (in 1831 Sussex, Bucks., Essex, Oxford and Bedford) for a great deal more.[12] However, 1830 was well past the peak of Poor Law generosity. In that year *per capita* expenditure on the poor in England and Wales was down to 9s. 9d., or almost a quarter below 1815–20.

How was this reduction achieved, in a decade when all the evidence concurs that rural poverty and unemployment were not diminishing and may have increased? Essentially by making the Poor Law more deterrent—or rather, harsher in administration, more humiliating, more repellent to any man with self-respect or a minimum of alternative resources. The disgusting practices reported from such areas as Sussex and the Weald in these years—virtual slave auctions, paupers harnessed to carts with bells round their necks and the like[13]—are best explained as desperate measures to drive the poor out of relief rather than by the psychopathology of individual overseers. Whatever the explanation, it is not surprising that the hatred and resentment of the poor grew, waiting only for a suitable occasion to burst into the open. The relatively good years of the early and middle 1820s probably relaxed the pressure on the rates somewhat in any case; but any sudden deterioration was likely to increase it, and to lead to panic measures of economy or deterrence. As we shall see, the winter of

1829–30 saw such a deterioration. Consequently the months preceding the rising witnessed a tightening-up of relief in various places. Allowances were reduced at Brede, the original centre of riot in Sussex (see pages 104–5); as in Eversley and the Bramhills (Hants.). In Burwash (Sussex) the riots were later ascribed in part to "the harrassing manner in which they were treated through the various plans adopted for their employment", in Eastbourne to the oppression of the unemployed, in Walsham-le-Willows (Suffolk) to the substitution of a dole in kind for money, and so on.[14] In such villages the attempt to cut down relief, or to make it even more demoralising at the very moment when it was most needed, was the straw that broke the long-suffering camel's back.

However, even the Poor Law statistics do not give us a clear picture of the movements of the labourers' conditions by which we can measure the increasing tension of their lives.

Our best available source is therefore the movement of crime, which in the agricultural areas was almost entirely economic—a defence against hunger. The following table illustrates its movements for one county:[15]

Commitments to the County Jails in Norfolk 1800–30
(Norwich, Wymondham, Aylsham, Walsingham (from 1807)*)

1800–4	250	1819	639	1826	784‡
1805–9	277	1820	811	1827	839‡
1810–14	309	1821	722	1828	745‡
1815	415	1822	943†	1829	899‡
1816	489	1823	728	1830	916‡
1817	579	1824	700		
1818	669	1825	812		

The movement of Norfolk crime shows a modest rise during the wars, a precipitous increase from 1814 to 1820, a decline until 1824 and a rise well beyond the worst levels of 1815–20 thereafter, except for a visible improvement in 1828. Between 1824 and 1830 crime rose by at least 30 per cent (allowing for the under-reporting in later years), and stood perhaps 15 per cent above the earlier peak.

Such are the figures for a single county. A simple index—so simple as to eliminate most arguments about the defects of the statistics—

* Swaffham jail, which becomes available only from 1822, has been omitted.

† "The great increase in misdemeanours this year was occasioned by the agricultural riots."

‡ Norwich Castle and Walsingham only.

can give us a more representative picture. Let us take 22 counties, which comprise virtually the whole area affected by the "Swing" movement,[16] and count the numbers in which crime increased or declined (or remained stable) in each year from 1805 to 1830. The following table is the result:

Movement of crime in 22 counties

Year	Number of cases Increase	Decrease
1806	8	14
1807	12	10
1808	8	14
1809	11	11
1810	10	12
1811	13	9
1812	18	4
1813	16	6
1814	4	18
1815	19	3
1816	18	4
1817	21	1
1818	11	11
1819	14	8
1820	6	16
1821	15	7
1822	8	14
1823	13	9
1824	14	8
1825	14	8
1826	15	7
1827	17	5
1828	4	18
1829	21	1

A number of conclusions can be drawn from this very revealing series. *First*, the relatively good situation until the last years of the war. Until 1810 the number of counties in which crime increased averaged less than half the total, between 1810 and 1829 it was below half in only four years. *Second*, there were two periods of abnormal increase in pressure: 1811–17 (interrupted by the exceptionally mild year of 1814), and 1823–29 (interrupted by the equally good year of 1828). It is obviously no accident that the outbreak of 1816 occurred as the first of these was about to reach its peak, that the rising of 1830 followed the worst year of the second—as bad a year in terms of our criminal index as any in the entire quarter-century—and that the outbreak of 1822 followed a sudden increase in economic pressure in 1821. *Third*, we note the fact that the outbreaks also followed dramatic increases in economic pressure after temporary lulls—1814, 1820, 1828 precede 1816, 1822, 1830. And *fourth*, we cannot but observe the remarkable conjunction of years which preceded 1830: 1828, as good a year as any, 1829, as bad a year as the worst in a generation that had plenty of bad years for the labourer. The study of crime therefore gives us a guide both to the long-term movements of economic pressure on the farm-labourer and to the short-term antecedents of his major outbreaks.

Can it also illuminate his growing discontent and rebelliousness? Here three kinds of offences may help us: the terrorist ones, such as rick-burning and cattle-maiming, the infringements of the game laws, and the most obviously relevant crimes, such as riot and machine-breaking. All of them were, in part at least, social crimes, for though the odd act of incendiarism might merely express some personal grudge, and poachers took game to live, larger numbers of incendiary acts clearly reflect something more than personal revenge, and everyone knows that poaching was also an act of defiance and rebellion against constituted authority, though not one which implied much political consciousness. Of all these, poaching is the most useful. Incendiarism, though it tended to increase, played a much smaller part in rural social movements before 1830 than after, though in Suffolk it had become sufficiently significant by 1815 for its victims to use the hitherto dormant act of the 1720s which allowed claims for loss through fire against the hundred.[17] In Norfolk this action was described as "unprecedented" in 1823.[18] The following curve, which represents the total commitments for arson at assizes and sessions, is interesting enough, but it represents only a relatively small number of cases; before 1829 never more than 33 (with the exception of 1822, which, as we have already seen, marked an important phase in the development of this terrorist method of struggle):[19]

Commitments for Arson, 1810–34

1810	15	1819	22	1828	14
1811	12	1820	29	1829	37
1812	31	1821	26	1830	45
1813	18	1822	47	1831	102
1814	24	1823	28	1832	111
1815	13	1824	28	1833	64
1816	33	1825	22	1834	68
1817	30	1826	17		
1818	21	1827	14		

We can deduce from it: *first* a tendency for incendiarism to flare up occasionally and to maintain itself at a fairly high level during certain periods of disturbance; *second*, a tendency for it to decline very markedly in the later 1820s; and *third*, as one might expect, for the fires to burn brightly in the times which we know to have been riotous (1816, 1822). There is clearly no simple pattern of increase. Nor should we expect one. Arson was still an exceptional and not a normal part of rural agitation.

The same is true of both cattle-maiming or -killing and machine-breaking. The former never played a significant part in England and is probably best neglected, as the number of cases is so small that the fluctuations cannot be relied on. The latter virtually occurred only during major outbreaks of unrest, and almost certainly not much before 1815. In Suffolk cases are reported as early as March 1815 (in Gosbeck, east of Needham Market), and a good many machines were broken that summer, mainly in East Suffolk; in Essex cases occurred by April 1816, though in Norfolk the first case was not reported until July.[20] It was, of course, virtually impossible to break machines except by public collective action, which by its very nature flared up only occasionally.

Offences against the game laws, on the other hand, were constant and habitual. Consequently their movement tells us a great deal more about the groundswell of village opinion, as distinct from its occasional outbursts of rage and despair. And here the trend is much clearer.[21]

Commitments for poaching: annual average

1817–20	149
1821–25	177
1826–29	281

Figures for one of the "Swing" counties most given to poaching—Wiltshire—make this even more evident.

Poaching cases before Wiltshire Assizes and Quarter Sessions[22]
annual average

1816–20	8	(18 in 1816)
1821–25	12	
1826–29	17	

Whatever the annual fluctuations, poaching increased, and rose particularly steeply in the years immediately preceding the rising of 1830. This trend was independent of the general movement of crime; thus in 1828—when, as we have seen, crime diminished in almost all Swing counties, game law offences reached their peak both nationally and in Wiltshire. If we require an index of the rising social tensions in the village, this is perhaps the best one we can get.

Pauperism, degradation, desperation and sullen discontent were thus almost universal. The Appendix to the Report of the Poor Law Commission of 1834 contains an invaluable set of answers to the "rural queries" circulated by the commissioners; among them one on the causes of the 1830 riots. Time and again the answer of the local correspondents—normally clergymen, overseers of the poor and others not notably identified with the labourers—was the same: "unemployment" (Maulden, Beds.), "distress and unemployment" (Meppershall, Beds.), "antipathy of paupers to overseers, game preservers and thrashing machines" (Sharnbrook, Beds.), "the parish system" (of poor relief) (Southill-cum-Warden, Beds.), "the game laws" (Willington, Beds.). It was due to low wages, said Coleshill (Berks.), to harsh treatment of labourers and the "desire to depress them". There was distrust between labourers and employers. And so the litany goes on, from Blunham-cum-Muggeridge in Bedfordshire to the last reporting parish of Yorkshire: "Winter unemployment, low wages, discontent" (Great Faringdon, Berks.), "Unemployment, low wages, especially for single men" (Tillington, Sussex), "distress, unemployment, low wages" (Euston, Suffolk), an unending catalogue of misery. Even that familiar figure in the mythology of the well-fed and the contented, the subversive agitator, could not explain more than a fraction of the riots; and only the correspondents from Buckenham, Norfolk (where there was indeed a good deal of instigation by farmers), Hampshire and Sussex (where the bluest of High Toryism encountered particularly militant if small nuclei of Radicals) tried to make much of him, or of the Radical press and the new beerhouses (under the Act of 1830) which were regarded as the discussion clubs of the poor. The labourer in the 1820s was desperately poor, unemployed, oppressed, helpless and hopeless. Nothing was more natural than that he should rebel, as the table overleaf demonstrates.

Yet, with the exception of one region, he showed no consistent signs of doing so before 1830. We can no doubt trace individual nuclei of militancy here and there: Thatcham in Berkshire—we shall

Causes of 1830 *Riots* (*Source: Rural Question* 53. *R.C. on the Poor Laws* 1834)

	Low Wages	Unemployment	Poor Law	Plight of single men	Contagion	Agitators, beer-shops	Indiv. Spite Revenge Hate
Beds.	2	4	6	1	0	2	1
Berks.	13	8	2	1	7	8	2
Bucks.	2	7	1	0	0	6	2
Cambs.	16	10	5	0	2	5	2
Dorset	4	2	1	0	2	4	0
Essex	8	10	0	0	0	2	0
Gloucs.	6	2	0	0	1	6	0
Hants.	18	14	3	2	3	14	1
Hereford	1	1	0	0	0	0	0
Herts.	1	2	0	0	0	2	1
Hunts.	2	3	1	0	0	0	0
Kent	15	17	4	0	1	6	0
Norfolk	15	14	5	0	1	14	2
Northants.	3	0	1	0	2	3	1
Oxford	6	1	0	0	2	3	0
Somerset	3	2	0	0	0	1	1
Suffolk	12	17	4	0	1	8	4
Sussex	21	23	5	3	5	23	3
Wilts.	9	8	2	2	2	3	0

observe its role in 1830—where there had been a dispute as far back as 1800, 300–400 labourers gathering to ask for either higher wages or cheaper food;[23] West Dean in Sussex, where there was memory of a "round robin" circulated in the hard year of 1795; or Northiam (Sussex), which had a turbulent history of parish politics and had rioted in 1822.[24] There were memories of expropriation in places like North Curry (Somerset)—we shall see this and the neighbouring settlement of Stoke St. Gregory continuing collective resistance, even after 1830, against the New Poor Law. There were of course knots of Radicals in little market-towns here and there, in small parliamentary boroughs like Horsham and Maidstone, or in the occasional centre where the small yeoman still survived, as in the Weald of Kent, but these were marginal to the universe of the labourer, though they merged with it during the 1830 rising. There was, as we have already seen, a tendency —though by no means a universal one—for silent quasi-resistance movements in the form of poaching. Sussex, Hampshire and Wiltshire were generally at or near the top of the ranking order of the "Swing" counties, while other counties became at varying times more and less devoted to poaching compared with the rest. But on the whole the observer of the southern English countryside would hardly have predicted a general outbreak of active discontent, because there was virtually nothing to announce it.

The one obvious exception was East Anglia. Here everything indicated an explosive situation, and this is not surprising; for the Eastern counties were—in parts at least—the pioneers and centres of the new commercial agriculture, the region in which the labourer's status had been most completely transformed, if only by the precipitous decline of annual hiring and living-in, and indeed by the large-scale substitution of payment by results for regular (or even daily) wages. If we can speak of mechanisation in any part of English agriculture by 1830, it is here. In 1830 there was probably only one firm in the country which described itself primarily or exclusively as "agricultural implement manufacturers", Ransomes of Ipswich (seconded by what were already well-known names beyond the region—Garretts of Leiston, Wood of Stowmarket, John Holmes of Norwich, Burrell of Thetford, Hensman of Woburn and the rest).[25] Even in 1845 the provincial machine-makers listed by an informed German student of mechanisation included nine in five eastern counties as against eight in eight southern, western and midland ones.[26] One Suffolk firm—J. Smyth Jr. of Peasenhall—claimed to have manufactured "upwards of 2,500 corn and manure-drills . . . at this establishment in the past 40 years", a high proportion of them evidently for use in the county.[27]

If poaching is an index of growing poverty and social tension, the eastern counties were in trouble: Suffolk ranked tenth or eleventh among the poaching counties of the Swing region in 1817 and 1818, fifth in 1819–20, third in the number of convictions in 1827–28 and second in 1829–30, and both Norfolk and Essex showed a similar, though less dramatic trend. If the sense of dumb hatred can be measured, it was high: in this area the reporters after 1830 mentioned "revenge on the occupiers" (Benhall, Suffolk), "revenge", "desire on the part of the labourers to retaliate upon the Farmer for the unkind treatment he has received" (Blything Hundred) more often than elsewhere. If incendiarism is any guide, the fact that rick-burning was already becoming an eastern speciality is significant. Moreover, both the major outbreaks before 1830 were virtually localised in East Anglia, that of 1816 in Norfolk, Suffolk, Essex and Cambridgeshire, that of 1822—if we except some scattered incidents elsewhere as at Stony Stratford (Bucks.)—in large parts of Suffolk and a more restricted area of Norfolk, in the main the one bounded by Diss, Wymondham, Long Stratton and New Buckenham. Since the riots of 1816—the risings in Ely, Littleport and Downham Market, and their brutal suppression—have been fully described in A. J. Peacock's *Bread and Blood* (1965), we need only refer readers to that book. The 1822 upsurge was less dramatic, except for the riots in the Diss area of Norfolk and the adjoining Hartismere and Hoxne hundreds of Suffolk which were overawed by the Suffolk Provisional Cavalry and the 9th and 16th Lancers, but more persistent and in many respects more successful.[28] At all events occupiers of Wingfield (Suffolk) abjured the use of threshing machines "on a penalty of £5", as did those of Metfield and Marlesford (Suffolk) and "a numerous meeting of Hoxne Hundred", while Sir B. Bunbury Bart. sent a circular letter recommending his tenantry to abstain from using these implements.[29] A band of labourers, six months after the end of the spring riots, still went round "most of the farmers in Norton, Haddiscoe, Aldeby, Tofts, Raveningham, Hale Green, etc." to see whether any threshing machines were in use and dismantled the only one they found in this area (between Beccles and Lowestoft), breaking nothing and dispersing with three cheers.[30] The riots appear to have started at Shimpling near Diss in February, to have built up through fires and threatening letters to a climax in early March in the same region, to have continued with scattered but widespread incendiarism and manifestations of discontent in various parts of Suffolk through April; and, as we have seen, the labourers remained mobilised until after the harvest (which was, as it happens, outstandingly good in most parts that year). As the Norfolk criminal statistics show, at least 200 men were actually jailed for their part in these disturbances in Norfolk alone. How many machines were broken, we cannot say, though there appear to have been 30 or more in the riotous area of Norfolk.[31] It was a serious enough business, and no great perspicacity was needed to predict further troubles in East Anglia in future.

Whether or not East Anglia would have rioted again in 1830 is anybody's guess. Possibly not, for its disturbances began significantly later than those in the South. At all events the eastern conditions cannot explain the general rising, starting in Kent, moving westwards, meeting local risings which began in their own local centres on the way and merging with them, until in the last ten days of November virtually all of Southern England seemed in flames, while grandees like the Duke of Buckingham wrote to Melbourne in (quite unjustified) tones of hysteria: "this part of the country is wholly in the hands of the rebels".[32]

There were, no doubt, local and specific causes for the outbreak in 1830. Here and there—in the marginally affected Midlands, possibly in the Chislehurst and Sevenoaks part of Kent—they said it was the Irish harvesters;[33] but this was clearly of no general importance, though the press made something of it. Except for St. John, Margate (in the Isle of Thanet) and Northfleet, the only Kentish parish reporting to the Poor Law Commission which so much as mentioned any Irish harvesters was West Wickham. Here and there there were local crises about poor relief—notably so in the explosive Weald area of Kent and Sussex, where the allowances had been reduced—local political excitement, and the like. In East Kent, it was the introduction of new threshing machines, or rather (in Barham) the fact that "some of the farmers, persist(ed) in using threshing machines, after a major part of the vestry meeting had agreed to and recommended their disuse".[34] If there was any evidence that the use of these machines was spreading abnormally fast in the years immediately preceding 1830, we might not have to look much farther for the precipitating cause of the rising. For the one thing which clearly united labourers everywhere was the hatred of machines which took away men's labour in the winter months when there was little else to do. Yet there is no clear evidence one way or another, and so we must continue our search.

What sort of a year was 1830? As the labourers saw it, it was first and foremost the year that followed one of the hardest periods in their appalling history. The harvest of 1827 had been good.[35] Eighteen-twenty-eight, as we have seen, was as good a year—if the term has any meaning in this context—as the labourers had known since 1814. The harvest of 1828 was poor, though the winter was mild; the harvest of 1829 was worse, and not gathered in until the snow was already on the barn in early October. Eighteen-twenty-nine was, as we know, an entirely disastrous year, as bad (if criminality is anything to go by) as 1817. The labourers must have faced the spring of 1830 with the memory of cold, hunger and unemployment, and the reflection that another winter like the last was more than flesh and blood could bear. "Fear of the winter" was the cause given (together with low wages) for the riots in Marden (Kent), and we can be quite certain that the men of Marden were not alone in their sentiments.[36] Perhaps it is worth adding that, though 1830 brought a fairly general improvement, some counties appear to have continued to deteriorate.

Crime increased in Suffolk, Herts. and—more significantly—in the contiguous counties of Hants., Wilts., Gloucester, Dorset and Devon. It was in Hants., Wilts., and Berks., as we know, that the rising reached its highest pitch of intensity. If we can put ourselves into the skins of labourers in the early autumn of 1830, as the brief and unimpressive harvest was gathered in, we can imagine the tense pessimism with which they confronted the hard part of the year.

Tenseness: but also vaguely stirred expectation. For had not a revolution broken out that summer across the Channel? Was not a general election being fought as the harvest came in, defeating the Tories after a period of rule longer than most men could remember, and bringing the Whigs to power? What did largely illiterate farm-hands know of all this? Directly, no doubt, very little, though the news certainly reached them. "Those riots and burnings came into Sussex from Kent" it was reported from Willingdon. "They were preceded by symptoms of disquietude, and an expectation of a new state of things to enrich and elevate the Poor, and impoverish and debase the Rich. Enquiries were anxiously made as to the occurrences in France and Belgium."[37] We catch the millennial note of obscure poor men's discontent here and there in other places. "Riots by reading newspapers: burning by ranting: for they all say, do what they will, it is no sin." Thus the reporter from Sutton Wick (Berkshire), where the Primitive Methodist apostles were even then preaching imminent—though doubtless not terrestrial—salvation. "Rumours came into the country, of which even the gentry could not immediately detect the falsehood, that successful and large bodies of rioters were coming down from London, and joined as they advanced by the Hampshire labourers." And the labourers of Haselbury Bryan, in their remote backwater of Dorset, summoned up the courage to ask—successfully—for an advance in wages. Perhaps, who knew, the long-delayed time for justice had at last come. "The rioters (in Weston, Somerset) were in general under the impression that their proceedings were sanctioned and encouraged by authority." For how could justice be against the King and Government? Gnarled and usually inarticulate men gossiping outside their cottages, speculating over their beer in pubs; fresh and sullen bachelors, killing the long hours of useless leisure and useless work on the pauper road gangs, argued and speculated ready to turn their dreams into hope, their hope into action.

Just so, in other countries, the news of great events which must have some relevance to the humble villager, filters down to him and is transformed into the habitual myths of peasant action: the rumour of a "new law" that is about to be passed, that has perhaps been passed already and only needs to be applied, the "manifesto in letters of gold" which a representative of the Tsar is even now carrying about the country on a white charger, promising freedom, the news that one hundred villages have already risen somewhere else, that the army of liberation is already approaching; what are the men of X waiting for? But how did the great news reach the labourers?

Almost certainly not directly from France, though there was the usual loose talk about smugglers bringing it onto Sussex beaches with the rum, and English peasants learning how to burn ricks from the example of their Norman colleagues across the Channel. The former was technically possible, though so improbable as to be not worth considering, the latter was merely another version of the habitual rationalisation of the rich. What else but foreign inspiration or agitation could produce the unexpected and unprecedented revolt of the meek and humble? Such lunatic hypotheses, the usual small-change of upper-class letters to newspapers and government departments in times of disarray and crisis, can be dismissed. The continental revolution came to the English countryside mediated through British politics, i.e. British Whig and Radical agitation.

We must remember that the French and Belgian revolutions were inscribed on the banner of the left, engaged at this very moment in victorious political battle against the forces of Toryism which had governed the country for all practical purposes since the Revolutionary Wars.* The July Revolution occurred in the midst of the election: between the start of the borough and that of the county polls (30 July, 5 August). As Halévy points out, until the end of July such subjects as the abolition of slavery and the necessity for retrenchment filled candidates' addresses, but as soon as the French king fell, *reform*, the constitution, the privileges of the aristocracy became the staple of anti-Tory electioneering. The Radicals hailed Paris and displayed tricolours; the Whigs, and the moderate middle class, were more restrained but could hardly fail to express their sympathy for Louis Philippe and their dislike of Charles X (whose coup, frustrated by the revolution, had actually been assisted, according to a current and politically

* See Halévy III cap I. However, as we have seen, Halévy is entirely wrong in denying that there were special social and economic reasons for discontent in 1830. As so often, anti-marxist prejudice has tended to mislead him on this point.

transient myth, by the Duke of Wellington, the Tory premier). No Englishman in touch, however vaguely, with the political discussion of the times, or with Radical or opposition newspapers, could fail to be aware of the French Revolution, symbol of British as well as of continental defeat for reaction. And at a time when political discussion was at its maximum, even the village labourers were drawn into it.

This evidently, was the point of the widespread accusation that the new beerhouses and the Radical newspapers which were read there lay behind the riots. The beerhouses were obvious centres for discussion, and unlike the inns, hardly frequented by the prosperous and respectable rural middle class.* (There is no evidence at all that they were, in fact, more effective centres of discussion than the village pubs.) The newspapers—from Cobbett's *Political Register* to "a paper called the *Dispatch* which has a considerable circulation amongst the

* The role of the beershops may be briefly discussed and dismissed. They opened their doors under a new Act on 10 October 1830, i.e. a few weeks before the main rising, a coincidence which ought to have suggested, if anything, that they could hardly be among its major causes, but suggested the opposite to the gentry. Their misdeeds were investigated at excessive length, and in connection with the 1830 riots, in the *S.C. on the Sale of Beer* (Parl. P. XV of 1833) by as prejudiced, bone-headed and sometimes hysterical a parcel of gentlemen and clergymen as may be found on such occasions. The main political objections to them were that they were less under the social control of the village rulers than the pubs, (*a*) because they were managed by "little petty kinds of small tradesmen who will rather get their bread by any other way than by hard labour" (Q 11), and (*b*) because they were frequented exclusively by the lower orders and therefore must be disaffected. The Rev. Robert Wright of Itchen Abbas, Hants., was unable to explain why, if this was so and the leaders of the riots had all been above the labouring status—though he admitted they did not actually include a beerhouse keeper—the beerhouses could be responsible for the trouble. (Q 205). Logical or not, he had sent the rioters to transportation or the gallows in 1830. However, among the rare collective pieces of subversion actually quoted as taking place at a beershop—at Ingatestone, Essex—was a meeting of almost the entire parish to refuse service as special constables (498). The political sins of these cottagers seem to have consisted entirely in providing meeting places for labourers beyond the supervision of their betters. As an informant of Mr. Majendie, one of the Assistant Poor Law Commissioners, put it disarmingly: "He was constable and could go into any of the public houses and perhaps escape notice and make his observations, but in the beer shops he was immediately a marked person." (Q 2649.)

The only enquiry made into the role of the beerhouses in 1830 comes from the Rape of Hastings—the Battle area of Sussex—where all parishes reported on the matter in February 1831 (p. 89 ff. Q. 1431). Of 21 whose opinions are preserved 8 had no complaints, 10 had no complaints about politics, except to note the dangers of any institution "unfrequented by any person above the rank of labourer" and which "encourages all bad characters". Brede, a riotous parish, thought they were "too private" but said the riot of 5 November had been plotted at a ginshop, because no beershop yet existed; Peasmarsh thought there must be plotting because only the poor went there, and only Battle actually reported a man who had since been sentenced for seditious talk at one of them. This was one of the most disturbed parts of the country.

worst class of newspaper readers" (Nayland, Suffolk), and "the politics they had imbibed at the beer-houses from such newspapers as the *Sunday Times*" (Great Waldingfield, Suffolk)—gave news of political agitation elsewhere and magnified the news from France. Quite certainly very few labourers actually read them.[38] But equally certainly those who did—village artisans, and their like, and the local Radicals—passed the news along by word of mouth, and by example.

For, of course, if the labourers remained initially inert, because neither the Revolution nor the revival of the Reform agitation in England had much direct relevance to their sub-political existence, the political classes were immediately moved. The perennial Radical demands, such as parliamentary reform, the fight against high taxes, tithes, placemen and sinecures and the whole system of "Old Corruption", now became slogans for action, or at least active political campaigning. Even where their agitation had no bearing on the economic issues which preoccupied the labourers, the mere fact of organised activity in the countryside or small market town could not but set an example for men who had neither the experience nor the readiness for collective self-assertion. It may well be argued that the systematic campaigns of meetings, petitions and protests of the gentry and farmers for agricultural relief were one of the factors which precipitated the outbreaks of the East Anglian poor in 1822. In 1830 they could hardly be unaffected by the spectacle of public meetings and campaigns all around them. These were not specifically addressed to them, or at any rate they hardly took part in them. When Cobbett describes his audiences in such places as Battle or Eye, he talks not of labourers, but of a public composed "almost entirely of farmers"[39] or townspeople. Yet it cannot be entirely accidental that the county in which the movement first broke out was Kent, distinguished not by any unusual poverty, but by exceptionally close communication with both London and the sea, and by a good deal of political discontent among the rural and small-town middle class.

Still, since the question of political agitators has been so often raised —Cobbett was later actually tried and acquitted for instigating the movement—we might as well look at it in greater detail. So far as Kent and Sussex are concerned the allegation is based almost entirely on the fact that at the very time of the outbreak Cobbett was on one of his south-eastern circuits. He proposed, according to the *Political Register*, to lecture at Deptford on 11 October, Gravesend on the 12th, Rochester on the 13th, Tonbridge on the 14th, Maidstone on the 15th, Battle—always a favourite stopping place—on the 16th, Lewes on the 18th, Brighton on the 19th–20th, Chichester on the 21st, and thereafter at Portsmouth, Gosport and on the Isle of Wight. Now, as we know, the first Kentish outbreaks, in what are today the south-eastern parts of London and the adjoining commuter zone (Bromley, Sevenoaks, Orpington), had begun long before—between April and early September. The second, and more expansionist outbreak in East Kent—broadly speaking in the triangle between Canterbury, Folkestone and Dover—showed itself first at the end of August and was well under way before Cobbett left the Great Wen (2–10 October). Neither area had any centre at which he or any other national Radical speakers lectured at this time. There is no reason whatever for connecting Cobbett with the Kentish rising. In Sussex, if we except the political demonstration at Battle on the actual occasion of Cobbett's visit, there was no action at all before early November, apart from one or two scattered cases of arson. However, when the movement reached that county in the first week of November—at least two weeks after Cobbett had passed—Battle and its surrounding countryside were undoubtedly the first parts affected, and, as we shall see, Radicals in the small towns and settlements of East Sussex and the Weald of Kent equally undoubtedly made common cause with, and sometimes sought to raise, the rural labourers. In other words, and once again: the political agitation of the nation and the continent reached the countryside not directly, and not even through the direct agency of national means of communication, but mediated through *local* men, local agitations and in local terms.

Among those in Kent and East Sussex the specific discontents of farmers and small shopkeepers in the Weald played an important part, and notably the question of *tithes*, which readily merged with the general anti-clericalism, anti-aristocratic and anti-corruptionist programme of the Radicals. Even they did not start the movement, for neither in the Orpington–Sevenoaks area nor in East Kent (where threshing machines were the all-important issue) did tithe agitation play any significant part. The Weald did not move until the Battle area in Sussex had given the signal, i.e. last of all parts of Kent, other than the belated Romney Marshes. In this part of Kent and Sussex also certain specific local issues dominated the agitation of the poor—the abuses of the Poor Law and in some instances the level of cottage rents which, being often paid for paupers out of the parish rates, were kept artificially high. Yet even here the activity of Radicals who took up these matters and peppered the local agitation with tricolour flags and politically conscious slogans ("Every man should live by his labour" said the document drawn up by or for the men of Rotherfield and Crowborough)[40] did not start the movement. It was the combination of small backward farmers, the fluctuating fortunes of hop production—on which, in bad times, tithes fell with particular force—the heavy unemployment, and the attempt to reverse the excessive reliance on the Speenhamland devices of the Poor Law, which made the situation in the Weald explosive. Without these the local Radicals would have been ineffective.

We can therefore sum up the causes of the outbreak of 1830 as follows. The condition of the southern labourer was such that he required only some special stimulus—admittedly it would probably have to be exceptionally powerful to overcome his demoralised passivity—to produce a very widespread movement. The economic conditions of 1828–30 produced a situation which made his already bad situation worse, and almost certainly increased both rural unemployment, the attempts to diminish in some way or another the financial burden of poor relief on the rate-payers, and the discontent of farmers and all those who depended on agriculture. The combined effect of continental revolution and British political crisis produced an atmosphere of expectation, of tension, of hope and potential action. They did not provide the actual spark. In North and East Kent it may have been Irish labourers and threshing machines, in the Weald the cut in poor relief, elsewhere in the country other local factors may have revived action here and there in those occasional villages where, for one reason or another, a tradition of resistance and action survived. The details are irrelevant. Small sparks which would have produced little except a few burned ricks or broken machines turned into a conflagration when fanned by the double wind of another winter like the last, and politics. What began at Orpington and Hardres ended in the jails of England and the convict settlements of Australia.

Notes to Chapter 4

1. *First Report of the Poor Law Commissioners*, 1835, pp. 235–6.
2. *S.C. on Emigration* (Parl. P. IV of 1826), pp. 136 ff.
3. J. Thirsk and J. Imray, ed. *Suffolk Farming in the 19th century* (Suffolk Record Soc., 1958, vol. I), pp. 134–5.
4. *R.C. Poor Law* (Parl. P. XXVIII of 1834), p. 372.
5. R. Hindry Mason, *The History of Norfolk*, 1884, p. 503.

6. *Lords Ctee on Poor Law* (Parl. P. VIII of 1831), p. 353.
7. *Ibid.*, pp. 316 ff.
8. Cf. Arthur Young, *The Farmer's Kalendar* (London, 1778).
9. The problem why they did so is not strictly relevant to the present chapter; but see Appendix IV.
10. *Economic History of Modern Britain*, I, p. 214.
11. *Lords Ctee on Poor Law*, 1831, *loc. cit.*, pp. 248–9. All other counties had less than 10 per cent, including Gloucester (9·25) and Somerset (8·5). The median and mean of all counties were 10 or just under.
12. *Op. cit.*, pp. 364–5.
13. *S.C. Poor Law* IV of 1828, pp. 18, 20, 21. *R.C. Poor Law* XXVIII of 1834, p. 177a.
14. From the answers to the Rural Questions of the 1834 Poor Law Commission. See also Eversley (Hants.).
15. R. N. Bacon, *History of the Agriculture of Norfolk*, pp. 154–5.
16. Beds., Berks., Bucks., Cambs., Devon, Dorset, Essex, Glos., Hants., Hereford, Herts., Hunts., Kent, Leics., Norfolk, Northants., Oxon, Rutland, Somerset, Suffolk, Sussex, Wilts. Surrey and Middlesex have been eliminated, as being too dominated by the a-typical movements of crime in the metropolis.
17. A. J. Peacock, *Bread and Blood* (1965). The Act was reversed in 1827.
18. The case, *Jonathan Wrench vs. the men inhabiting the Hundred of Holt*, is described as an "entirely novel" action. The plaintiff was awarded £143 15s. damages. See C. Mackie, *Norfolk Annals* (Norwich, 1901), p. 218.
19. There are various parliamentary papers giving criminal statistics before the compilation of regular returns. I have used XVI of 1818 for 1805–17; VI of 1826–27 (*S.C. on Criminal Commitments*), XIX of 1826–27, p. 235; XVIII of 1829, p. 45; XLV of 1835, p. 23.
20. A. J. Peacock, *Bread and Blood*, pp. 70–2; Mackie, *op. cit.*, p. 138.
21. Figures before 1817 are not comparable, because of the change in the law in 1816.
22. County of Wilts: *Statistics of Crime from 1801 to 1855, compiled by the governor of the county gaol* (Salisbury, 1855).
23. A. L. Humphrey, *Bucklebury* (Reading 1832), p. 377. The Volunteers who dispersed them also marched through Newbury, Highclere and Upper Hurstbourne, centres of riot in 1830 and presumably believed to be disaffected even then.
24. Poor Law Comm.: XXXIV, 1834 Rural Questions, 53.
25. Cf. Pigot & Co., National Commercial Directory (South), 1830, Robson's Commercial Directory (1839), the three volumes of the Post Office Directory (1845). In 1830 Tasker of Andover—a victim of the riots—still described himself as "Blacksmith".
26. W. Hamm, *Die landwirthschaftlichen Geräthe und Maschinen Englands* (Brunswick, 1845).
27. Advertisement of 1841 in B.M. 1891 c.2.
28. In the absence of any published historical account, we have consulted the *Annual Register*, *The Times*, HO 41/6 and 7 and HO 40/17 for 1822 in the Home Office Papers (Public Record Office), R. Hindry Mason, *The History*

of Norfolk (London 1884), pp. 495 ff., and C. Mackie, *Norfolk Annals* (Norwich, 1901), pp. 205–6.

29. *The Times*, 8 April, 6 September.
30. *Loc. cit.*, 20 September.
31. Nineteen machines went in the Wymondham area, another 9 or 10 can be discovered from press reports, though there may be some overlap. Hindry Mason, *loc. cit.*
32. *Memoirs of Viscount Melbourne*, by Wm. Torrens MP (London 1878), I, p. 348.
33. Rural Questions, *loc. cit.*
34. Rural Questions (Barham).
35. Data about weather and harvests from T. H. Baker, *Records of the Seasons, Prices of Agricultural Produce and Phenomena observed in the British Isles* (1883), and E. L. Jones, *Seasons and Prices* (1964).
36. The same sentiments are reported from East Kent in HO 52/8, 6 October, and from the men of several parishes assembled at Hurstmonceaux (*Brighton Guardian*, 30 March 1831). We owe these references to Dr. M. Dutt.
37. Rural Questions, *loc. cit.*
38. "There is very little reading of tracts and newspapers among the poor" reported a sensible clergyman from Berkshire, sensible enough also to reject the fairy-tales about agitators in gigs and on horseback. If they read any newspapers, it was because of some item of local interest, for "they take no concern in any politics beyond those of their village". *R.C. Poor Law*, XXIX of 1834, p. 300.
39. *Rural Rides* (Everyman Edition), II, p. 220. The date is March 1830. In fact, at Battle one-third of the audience were in smock-frocks.
40. P.R.O. TS/4051. Reference supplied by Dr. M. Dutt.

PART 2

THE RISING

5

THE RIOTS IN THE SOUTH-EAST

The first threshing machine was destroyed at Lower Hardres, near Canterbury in East Kent, on the night of 28 August 1830. The precise date is worth recording, as the breaking of machines was to become the characteristic feature of the labourers' movement of 1830, which, starting in Kent, spread over a score of counties in the next three months. And yet machine-breaking, while the most significant, was only one of the numerous forms that the labourers' movement assumed. Arson; threatening (or "Swing") letters; wages meetings; attacks on justices and overseers; riotous assemblies to extract money or provisions, or to enforce a reduction in rents or tithes—or even of taxes—all played their part. Properly speaking, in Kent alone, where the movement not only started but persisted longest, it may be divided into five distinctive phases: first, fires in the north-west, reaching into the neighbouring county of Surrey; second, the wrecking of threshing machines in East Kent around Dover, Sandwich and Canterbury; third, late in October, wages meetings accompanied by Radical agitation against sinecures, rents and tithes around Maidstone; in early November, wages meetings and machine-breaking in West Kent, reaching into the Sussex Weald; and, after mid-November, a further round of fires, tithe-riots and machine-breaking in East Kent.

The fires began with the destruction of farmer Mosyer's ricks and barn at Orpington on 1 June. It was at Orpington, too, that, seven weeks earlier, a mysterious incident had taken place at the corn mill used by the overseers to employ the parish poor: it may, or may not, have had any connection with the sustained labourers' movement that developed soon after. Here machinery was "feloniously" damaged by a parish pauper, William Eldridge, who was sentenced to 9 months' jail at the Easter sessions at Maidstone.[1]

Further fires followed in the first week of June: one at Vowles' farm at Orpington and three more in the neighbourhood of Bromley. By the end of September, a total of twenty incendiary fires had been reported in the district around Bromley, Sevenoaks and Orpington.[2] Meanwhile, there had been a fire attended by strange circumstances at Portley Farm, near Caterham in Surrey, on the night of 2–3 August.

The whole farm was reduced to ashes, but it was noted that it was the thatch of the barn housing the threshing machine that had first been set alight. Conflicting rumours had it that the fire was a reprisal for the employment of Irish labourers and, alternatively, that it was the Irish labourers themselves who had fired the barn. To add to the mystery, the previous occupant of the farm, a former business man said to be highly respected in the neighbourhood, was the only suspect actually brought to trial; but this was several months later. He was discharged for lack of evidence at the Surrey Summer assizes in 1831.[3]

So far there had been considerable alarm expressed at the spread of incendiary fires in this corner of Kent and Surrey, but arson was a weapon of rural protest that was already familiar to farmers and magistrates alike, and had certainly been practised even in this part of England, as at Northiam in 1828[4]. However, the attack on threshing machines in East Kent at the end of August came as a bolt from the blue. It was a form of activity that had not been experienced on any scale in Kent, and it took time before its significance was fully realised. The first assault was made on the night of Saturday, 28 August, when a machine hired from John Collick by Cooper Inge was destroyed in Lower Hardres. The next day one hired from John Hambrook was destroyed at Newington, near Hythe, again by the same party—mainly of Elham men, joined by those from Lyminge and later Stelling, who formed the corps of activists at this stage.[5] These early incidents went comparatively unnoticed at the time: county opinion was far more concerned with the incendiaries in the north-west corner of the county. However, they seem to have been the culmination of an embittered local conflict over the spread of machines, which had been regarded as provisionally settled by a parish decision to discontinue their use. A minority of farmers, unable to resist the temptation of stealing a march on their competitors, refused to abide by the decision of the community and continued to hire machines. (Those broken in August and September appear to have been of the kind hired rather than bought by farmers. Incidentally, at this stage farmers who promised not to use them, kept their own machines unscathed.)[6] There was a brief lull in the machine-breaking during the first fortnight in September, but on the 18th—also a Saturday, presumably after the closing of the inns—two further machines were broken on William Dodd's farm in Upper Hardres and nine further machines—all in the Canterbury-Folkestone-Hythe area—in the next days. By the third week in October something like one hundred machines were reported destroyed, mainly in East Kent.[7]

"These acts", wrote a justice to the Home Office from Canterbury, "appear to have been committed at midnight by a desperate gang amounting to upwards of 200 persons."[8] They were not. The size of the original gangs—presumably from Elham, Stelling and Lyminge, the first major centres—seems to have been about 20, though later they increased to something like 50.[9] Desperate or not, the seven rioters brought to trial for these offences at the East Kent sessions at Canterbury four weeks later, made no bones about their activities and, prompted by a sympathetic magistrate, publicly confessed their guilt.[10] They rightly felt that they had little to hide and that public opinion was on their side. They made no demands of any kind except to discontinue machine-threshing. They asked, at this stage, neither for higher wages nor for gifts of money from the rich. No element of politics is discernible in the original centres of agricultural Luddism.

Meanwhile, incendiarism continued in West Kent. During August, Jonathan Thompson, a retired tradesman of Hendon Farm, near Sevenoaks, had suffered four fires on his property in the course of which all his barns, outbuildings and farming implements were destroyed; five more fires were to occur on his premises before the end of September.[11] On 2 September, Mr. Manning, a local justice described as having been active in tracking down smugglers and poachers, had his barn and corn stacks destroyed at Orpington. Other victims during this first week of September were Mrs. Elizabeth Minette, a middle-aged "lady of fortune", of Havers Wood, near Brastead; Mr. Love, of Shoreham; Mr. Jessop, of Otford; and the Rev. Thomas Harvey, of Cowden. *The Times* reported on 17 September that "scarcely a night passes without some farmer having a corn stack or barn set fire to. It is really dreadful."[12] A disquieting feature was that many labourers not directly involved in the attacks appeared to condone the activities of the incendiaries. From Orpington came a message to *The Times* that, after a barn had been set alight, labourers standing by said calmly, "D—n it, let it burn, I wish it was the house; we can warm ourselves now; we only want some potatoes: there is a nice fire to cook them by". Elsewhere, fire engines were rendered useless by bystanders who slashed the hoses or leather pipes.[13] Meanwhile, threatening letters were being received by some of the intended victims: one recipient was Mrs. Hubble, a "poor widow" of Ide Hill; others were Peter Nouaille and William Morphet, a linen draper, both of Sevenoaks. These were the first of the "Swing" letters, soon to become a common feature of the labourers' movement, both in Kent and other counties.[14]

There appears at this stage to have been a lull in West Kent, but machine-breaking in the eastern part of the county around Canterbury and Dover continued with unabated vigour: in fact, *The Times*, with perhaps pardonable exaggeration in view of the paucity of accurate reports, described the destruction of machines as having extended "throughout the county of Kent".[15]

In early October, the movement spread to the Dover area, west ot Canterbury, and to the Isle of Thanet, and now for the first time arson and machine-breaking appeared in the same district and appeared as elements in a joint operation: *The Times* of 14 October wrote of an "organised system of stack-burning and machine-breaking". Early that month, there was a riot at Lyminge followed by arrests; and the Rev. Ralph Price, one of the magistrates concerned, had his ricks burned as an evident reprisal. Another victim was Michael Becker, a justice and overseer of the poor, whose property at Ash was gutted: a correspondent wrote to the Home Office that this was an act of vengeance for his "unfeeling conduct" towards the poor. The same letter reported a fire at Ramsgate on the 10th, and that at midnight on 6 October, immediately after the fires at Lyminge and Ash, a dozen men, three of them "well dressed", had visited Major Garret's farm at Margate and threatened to destroy his threshing machines. Farmers were becoming alarmed and, in order to save themselves from these nocturnal visits, were taking the initiative by voluntarily destroying their own machines. This was so, the same correspondent wrote, even at places like Wingham which had as yet received no visits; and he added that a prime mover in this work of voluntary destruction was a local landlord of substance, the Earl of Guildford.[15] Commenting on the ambivalent attitude of many farmers towards the machines, *The Times* gave the following interesting explanation of their conduct: "It is understood (it wrote) the farmers whose thrashing machines have been broken do not intend to renew them"; for (it added) "farmers do not consider thrashing machines of much advantage; seeing that they throw the labourers out of work, and consequently upon the parish".[17] One of Sir Robert Peel's correspondents, a class-conscious clerical magistrate of Farningham, took a somewhat less sanguine view. "If this state of things should continue" (he wrote—and he underlined the final words of the sentence), "the

Peasantry will learn *the secret of their own physical strength*." Armed bands were to be expected "in the dark nights of winter" and "an organisation for far more desperate measures of plunder & revenge"; and, to avert these dangers, he begged the government to "sanction the arming of the Bourgeois classes" by re-establishing the Yeomanry Corps or by other similar methods.[18]

Fires continued in October and the movement swung back from east to west across the centre of the county. An inflammatory poster appeared at Dover on the 6th; there were fires at Boughton Hill, west of Canterbury, on the 8th and between Wrotham and Farningham on the 11th. On the night of the 14th, 100 quarters of wheat, the property of a wealthy farmer, were burned out at West Peckham, between Sevenoaks and Maidstone. There were further fires at Otford on the 17th; at Borden, near Sittingbourne, on the 21st; at Upstreet and Ash on the 22nd; near Sandwich and at Shipbourne Green on the 23rd; at Selling Court and at Cobham Hall, the Earl of Darnley's seat, on the 24th; and once more at Boughton Hill and (reputedly) on the Isle of Sheppey on the 28th. Arson had re-appeared across the Surrey boundary; and, on 22 October, the barns and outhouses of Mr. Thompson and Mrs. Ford had been destroyed at Oxted. Reporting these last two incidents, *The Times* expressed surprise that Mr. Thompson's property, at least, should have been attacked, "as it seems he neither used a thrashing machine nor ever employed strangers to work in his employment—two circumstances which might be supposed to have operated favourably for him, as it is well known that the employment of machines, and also of strangers, in that part of the country as well as in Kent, has given rise to much discontent amongst the labouring classes in these places".[19]

Meanwhile, the first machine-breakers had been brought to trial. Their case was heard before the East Kent quarter sessions at Canterbury on 22 October, when, to the surprise of all concerned, the presiding magistrate, Sir Edward Knatchbull, discharged his seven prisoners with a caution and a three-days' prison sentence. In doing so, he hoped "that the kindness and moderation evinced this day by the magistrates would be met by a corresponding feeling among the people".[20] The effect was scarcely what he had hoped for. The same night, a threshing machine was destroyed at Hartlip, five miles from Sittingbourne: it was the first operation of the kind in that part of the county, and it was observed that the assailants had "blackened faces". The next day, the movement swung back east, and four further machines were destroyed on farms at Bekesbourne, near Canterbury, and Sandwich. The press reported that large bodies of men had been seen marching, armed with bludgeons, on the roads near Ash and Rainham, others at Charing and Lenham. What is more interesting, for the first time we observe a distinct influence of political radicalism. A tricolour was hoisted at Newington, the chief local centre in the Sittingbourne area, and indeed tricolours (in one or two cases combined with black flags) were also seen in various villages in the Sittingbourne–Faversham–Maidstone area, through which a band led by an evidently Jacobin and Republican naval deserter, Robert Price, passed.[21] It was now noted, too, that the attacks were made "in open day", as if the labourers now felt more confident of public support and more conscious of the justice of their cause.[22]

The movement now swung to the centre of the county and entered upon a new and more radical phase. It was no longer a case of isolated attacks on ricks or machines at dead of night. Labourers were beginning to assemble in large numbers in broad daylight to demand a higher rate of wages: the usual demand in Kent was for a minimum of 2s. 3d. in winter and 2s. 6d. in summer. Farmers and landowners were being asked to make contributions in money or in kind, and the agitation of Radical groups was beginning to permeate the labourers' movement. This new development first appeared in great assemblies of labourers at farms, rectories and country houses at Hollingbourne, Langley and East Sutton, near Maidstone, on 28 and 29 October.[23] The following account of the events at Langley and East Sutton is taken from the Treasury Solicitor's brief in the case of John Adams, a Radical journeyman shoemaker of Maidstone, who played a leading part in the affair:

> On Friday the 29th of October last about 4 o'clock in the afternoon a Mob of about 300 persons, many of them armed with short sticks, came to the Revd Sir John Filmer of East Sutton Park. Sir John Filmer being informed that they were coming went to them in company with the Revd William Wright Wilcocks to the farm yard gate at the back of the house and inquired what they wanted. No answer was returned but some of them made a sign as if to some person to advance, and the def(endan)t who appeared to be their leader came in front and said he hoped the Gentlemen would go hand in hand with the Labouring Classes to get the expenses of Government reduced. He was answered that this was what all

wished. After some further parley about the grievances and distresses of the Labouring Classes which lasted for about ten minutes and in which no one of the Mob spoke but himself, some others came round Sir John Filmer and hemmed him in. Sir John then asked Defendant whether he had any thing more to say. He replied no, but some of the men had come from afar and wanted refreshment and something from Sir John would be acceptable. Sir John made no reply but gave Def(endan)t two sovereigns. Those that stood round Sir John then withdrew and the Mob went away in the direction of Sutton Valence across a field belonging to Sir John, where they appeared to form a ring and one man seemed to be addressing them.

On the same evening about 6 o'clock, a Mob . . . headed by Defendant and amounting to about 200 appeared at the house of the Rev[d] James Edward Gambier, Rector of Langley, a neighbouring parish to East Sutton. Mr. William Henry Gambier, his son, went to them and asked them what they wanted. Def(endan)t was spokesman as before and answered that he must be aware of the dreadful state of the poor, that they were starving . . . and that they were going about from house to house to ask assistance to better their condition. I (Mr. Gambier) enquired in what way. They answered there were many sinecures. I told them that the present King was desirous of doing all that could be done and that I had no doubt Parliament had the same disposition and that they should wait until Parliament had met. . . . He said all the country were in the same state and ready tho' the Government had sent troops into the North where they were in the same state. That they were going round the country peaceably to all the Gentlemen to procure their assistance in obtaining their rights, but if they did not succeed in that they would bedew the country with blood and pull down the house which had thoroughly got the dry rot and build up the new with honest materials and would not use one of the old. . . . Towards the latter part of the conversation the crowd became impatient and cried, "Sum it up, come to the point"; & then he said to sum it up, "These people want money". . . . After their waiting a little time longer I gave Adams a sovereign. . . . During the conversation they repeatedly said they did not mean to hurt my person or to crush a flower.[24]

In the first days of November, further wages meetings were reported from East Malling, near Maidstone, and Faversham and Boughton Street in East Kent. An eyewitness of the events at Faversham on 2 November wrote to *The Times* that a dozen labourers came into his yard and said "it was their intention to go to the different farmers ... with a view to get their wages raised to 2s. 6d. a day which, I believe, they accomplished. When they parted last night at Boughton Street, it was supposed they amounted to 400 men. They are going round the parishes in the neighbourhood tomorrow, and intend meeting the farmers at a vestry to be held at the church in the afternoon. I shall not be surprised to see 500 men. They are very quiet, and all they require is more wages. They say the next thing they intend doing is to go to the landlords and make them lower their rents."[25]

So a new issue had arisen; and there seems little doubt that the need to reduce rents—and also tithes—had in the first place been suggested to the labourers by the farmers; for how else could they afford to raise their wages? This emphasis on rents and tithes—and even on taxes—became the more insistent as the movement spread in early November into the Kentish and Sussex Weald. Now, for the time being, arson and machine-breaking tended to fall into the background and the stress to be all on wages and allowances and, through them, on tithes and rents and, more occasionally, taxes. This phase of the movement no doubt drew much of its inspiration from what had already taken place around Canterbury and Maidstone; but its immediate springboard lay not so much in eastern or central Kent as the district round Battle and Rye in East Sussex. Rye was already established as a centre of Radical agitation and, at the time of the elections held earlier that year, it had been the scene of violent popular riots in protest against the return of an unpopular Tory MP.[26] Cobbett had lectured at Battle on 16 October, as he had lectured two days earlier at Maidstone; and it was confidently believed by some that he had deliberately incited his audience to arson and riot and had, in particular, "much excited the feelings of the paupers".[27] However this might be, the opening phase of the movement in the Sussex Weald took the form of a series of attacks on the local overseers of the poor. Already on the night of 17 October, a barn belonging to a blacksmith and assistant overseer was fired at Hartfield. On 3 November, there was a fire at the George Inn at Battle, whose occupant, Charles Emery, was a local overseer. Further fires followed at Battle and Icklesham on the 4th; and, the same evening, at the village of Brede nearby there took place a meeting of labourers, which launched a local movement against the overseers of the poor that assumed considerable proportions. That night, according to Joseph Bryant, one of the ringleaders arrested a fortnight later, some fifty paupers met at Thomas Noakes' house and decided to take firm measures against Mr. Abel, an assistant overseer, who had made himself obnoxious by his frequent use of the parish cart for conveying the poor. The next day, at a further meeting, the labourers appointed a deputation of four to negotiate with eight of the farmers and a local minister at the Red Lion Hotel, as the result of which the following extraordinary document was drawn up and signed by both parties:

> *Resolution* 1. The gentlemen agree to give to every able-bodied labourer with wife and two children 2s. 3d. per day from this day [5 November] to the 1st of March next, and from the 1st of March to the 1st of Oct. 2s. 6d. per day, and to have 1s. 3d. per week with three children, and so on according to their family.
>
> *Resolution* 2. The poor are determined to take the present overseer, Mr. Abell, out of the parish to any adjoining parish and to use him with civility.

The unfortunate Abel was duly wheeled out of the parish in the parish cart and dumped across the border by a crowd of labourers wearing ribands in their hats, led, it was said, largely by smugglers, and applauded by several of the farmers as well, who treated the labourers to beer to show their appreciation. Yet Joseph Bryant's account suggests that the farmers had no intention of meeting the labourers' demands without receiving some compensation in return at the expense of the parson. For he relates how he had been approached a few days before the rector's tithe audit by three farmers, who had begged him to attend the audit with several of the labourers and "see if we could get a little of the tithe off for them—but to behave very civil and only to show ourselves".[28] The events at Brede and Joseph Bryant's account of them have a two-fold interest and significance. On the one hand, they amply illustrate the collusion of the farmers with the labourers at the expense of the parson which was so marked a feature of the "Swing" movement, not only in the Weald but later in Norfolk, Sussex and other counties. Moreover, the Brede wages programme—not to mention the summary treatment meted out to Abel—became a model for other neighbouring parishes to emulate: the Brede method of expelling or threatening to expel overseers on a cart was copied in Burwash, Ticehurst, Fairlight, Warbleton and Brightling, Mayfield,

Heathfield, Ninfield and of course Battle.[29] At Ninfield, as in Brede, the crowd contained smugglers—a natural group of "activists" in this part of the world, who were even supposed to be armed with pistols.[30]

The events of Brede and Battle also gave an impetus to a wider wage-movement that extended over the whole of the Kent and Sussex Weald. It swung to and fro across the county boundary, sometimes appearing in one county, sometimes in the other; but it would seem to have had its starting-point in Sussex rather than Kent. A magistrate of Tunbridge Wells wrote on 10 November (two days after it began) that, being market day, they were expecting a "visit" from the labourers of Mayfield, Wadhurst and Ticehurst across the Sussex border.[31] There was a riot, following a fire, at Robertsbridge on 8 November. In this well-known centre of local Radical agitation the match which set the area alight seems to have been provided by the decision of local millers to give poor relief in the form of two gallons of bad flour, which the paupers were forced to resell to finance their other purchases. As usual in this area, the farmers refused to be sworn in as special constables.[32] On the same day a Sussex landowner wrote to Sir Robert Peel that "a message has been sent from the labourers assembled at Battle to those assembled at Sedlescombe [3 miles east of Battle] & to the labourers in other adjoining parishes inviting them to join in organising a force for resisting the military which had just come down to Battle", and indeed the arrival of the troops seems to have sparked off a general explosion of mass meetings and other forms of action in at least twenty-four parishes of this part of East Sussex, in many of which the Brede programme, or something like it, was accepted by the farmers.[33] The leaders of the movement seem to have been largely artisans and shopkeepers: a butcher, a baker and two labourers in Wadhurst–Frant, a publican, a wheelwright and a carpenter in Rotherfield, though in a few instances we observe a formal refusal to recognise any leaders, which may reflect either fear of public exposure or a primitive egalitarianism. Thus in Ringmer (where the men met in church after the service) and in Lewes, they "deny having a captain and form a ring" saying "we are all as one". The letter containing their demands was then thrown into the ring. At Hurst Green also the rioters formed a ring round the rector's house.

The movement spread quickly across the Kentish border, and we read of wages meetings and "tumultuous assemblies"—sometimes accompanied by the smashing of threshing machines—at Hawkhurst and Goudhurst on the 9th; at Goudhurst again on the 10th and 15th;

at Cranbrook on the 11th; at Headcorn on the 12th; at Benenden, Rolvenden, Lamberhurst and Sandhurst on the 13th; and, reaching deeper into the county, at Hadlow, Nettlestead, Yalding, and East and West Peckham, near Maidstone, between 12 and 17 November.[34]

One of the earliest villages to be touched by this movement on the Kentish side was Hawkhurst; and we read that "this Mob was originally begun to be formed . . . so early as 1 o'clock a.m. of the Tuesday [9 November]. They were seen about that time at Hawkhurst engaged in perambulating and calling up journeymen & labouring men. . . . Between 2 & 3 the numbers amounted to about an 100 when they said they were going to Longhurst to break the threshing machine. They were seen to proceed to Hawkhurst Moor which is the direct road to Longhurst and thence towards Longhurst." Here they arrived at about 6.30, having "pressed the labourers into their service" as they went; and "when they reached Longhurst Farm, (they) proceeded to an oast house in which a threshing machine was deposited, having previously been taken to pieces. The machine was taken out and destroyed by means of saws, hatchets and axes."[35]

Goudhurst, which lies north-west of Hawkhurst on the road to Tunbridge Wells, was drawn into the movement on the same day; but here it assumed different forms, was more protracted and bore more evident signs of a Radical inspiration. "On this day (runs a Treasury Solicitor's brief) a body of men . . . proceeded generally over the parish, compelling labourers to join them by force where unwilling, and calling at the houses of the respectable inhabitants, asking 'for Charity', complaining of taxes, tithes and rents as grievances, airing their knowledge that many individuals were receiving from the State incomes of £30,000 and £40,000 a year; declaring that this should not continue, and that tithes should not be paid, etc. The following day, Wednesday the 10th, there was a similar assemblage and similar proceedings took place and an endeavour was made to excite a friendly feeling, if not cooperation, on the part of the farmers by telling them that tithes should be no longer paid—that if the farmers would raise the wages, they (the Mob) would stop the tithes, etc.—and they proceeded not only about the parish of Goudhurst but even into adjoining parishes, thus endeavouring to effect a general tumult." These approaches appear to have failed; but, on 15 November, the Goudhurst labourers, having won recruits in neighbouring farms, "pressed" the local owner of the rectorial tithes to join them, and marched back into the town to discuss their grievances at a meeting with the farmers and principal inhabitants. They were eventually dispersed by a troop of twenty-five dragoons who arrived on the scene with a magistrate from Cranbrook; the Riot Act was read and the leaders were taken into custody.[36]

Meanwhile, similar disturbances were spreading through the villages of the Sussex Weald. In addition to those already cited from the Hammonds, we may note Bodiam, Frant, Hurstfield, Newenden, Northiam, Salehurst and Wadhurst on 9 November; Rotherfield on the 11th; Warbleton (a protest against an overseer) on the 12th; and, beyond the Weald to the west, there were outbreaks at Herstmonceux, Ringmer and Lewes on the 15th and, on the same day, at Buxted, Crowborough, Mayfield, Withyham and Rotherfield—all villages lying on the edge of the Ashdown Forest. In some of these villages the labourers won immediate concessions, in others they failed. Among the latter, it would seem from the account set out in the Treasury Solicitor's brief relating to the affair, were those adjoining the Ashdown Forest. "Large mobs assembled in the neighbouring parishes of Mayfield and Rotherfield and, on the 15th of November last, between 50 and 60 persons who had previously assembled at Crowboro' Lodge in Rotherfield went to Mr. Howis's." . . . Mr. Howis was the owner of a large experimental farm between Rotherfield and Buxted; he employed a large body of labourers and was known to use threshing machines. The labourers ordered these to be destroyed and, having "pressed" several of Howis's men, made off towards the nearby village of Withyham. On the way, being challenged by the Earl de la Warr's steward (they were passing through the Earl's woods at the time), they told him "they were going down to the parsons to lower their tithes and to the farmers to raise their wages"; while one said he "must go down to Withyham because our Master is going to meet us there and 500 men are ready to join us from Wadhurst". More men were "pressed" in this district to the accompaniment of the slogan, "One and all, one and all, we'll stand by one another"; and they marched into Withyham 300 strong. But here the expected reinforcements failed to show up and, having demanded refreshment at the local poorhouse, they dispersed, "calling the labourers of Withyham a set of cowards who would not stand up for their rights".[37]

We have already noted the extreme variety of this phase of the labourers' movement, which, by mid-November, had spread over Kent and the western districts of Sussex: to quote the Hammonds' slightly exaggerated phrase—the labourers were by now "masters over almost all the triangle on the map, of which Maidstone is the apex and Hythe and Brighton the bases".[38] Arson still continued sporadically, sometimes as a prelude to a more highly concerted form of action, sometimes as an isolated act of individual reprisal. There were fires at Chatham on 3 November; at Caterham, in Surrey, on the 5th; at Northfleet, near Dartford, on the 7th; at Robertsbridge on the 8th; at Birchington and Rodmersham, in East Kent, on the 9th; at Bearsted and Thornham, by Maidstone, on the 10th; at Englefield, in Surrey, on the 11th; at Otham, near Maidstone, on the 12th; at Bexhill, in East Sussex, on the 13th; at Boughton Hill and near Hythe, in East Kent, and at Albury, Surrey, on the 14th; and there were further fires at Ockley, in Surrey, at Boughton Hill and Minster, and at Alland Court, on the Isle of Thanet, on the 15th.[39] The last of these was evidently no act of mere personal spite, as, a week later, the victim—a large farmer named George Hannam—had his two threshing machines broken by men with "faces blackened with soot". The same party went on to break "Mr. Pett's machine at Shuars in the parish of St. Nicholas Alwade; . . . from Shuars to Chamberwell, then to Gore Street, then to Monkton Parsonage and then to Sheriff's Court and broke in all six threshing machines".[40] It was the last large-scale operation of its kind in East Kent for several months.

Much of this activity, arson in particular, could hardly commend itself to the farmers, whether large or small. But there were, as we have seen, issues on which farmers and labourers could find common ground. At Brede and Battle, we have already noted the initiative taken by the farmers in the case of tithe; and, at Rochester, on 9 November, the East Kent farmers, when invited by Lord Clifton to enrol in the yeomanry, ignored the appeal and passed the following resolution:

> That, at the present alarming crisis, it is the duty of the landowners and clergy, by a liberal abatement of rent and tithes, to assist the farmers in bearing those additional burdens which the peculiar circumstances of the times necessarily impose upon them.

High taxes were another burden; and, three days later, farmers and labourers meeting at Headcorn, south of Maidstone, agreed jointly to petition Parliament for relief from the combined burdens of tithes, rents and taxes.[41] In the Sussex Weald, there were a number of protests against taxes and tax-collectors, sometimes promoted by the farmers while, at other times, the initiative might be taken by the labourers. As an example of the former we may cite the case of Dallington in the neighbourhood of Battle, 35 of whose rate-payers signed a petition (two of them by means of crosses) addressed to Sir Robert Peel and couched in the following terms:

> We the undersigned farmers, tradesmen and others, rate-payers in the small agricultural parish of Dallington in the county of Sussex, consider it our duty to make known to His Majesty and the Government through you, the Secretary of the Home Department, that altho' unable to bear it we have met the wishes of the magistrates of this district by *raising the wages of the labourers and the relief of the paupers* on a scale which we positively cannot continue for any length of time without bringing us all to one common ruin, and which we have done to prevent our property from being destroyed by incendiaries.
>
> We therefore implore His Majesty's Government, if they value the existence of the Middle Class of society, to take off all taxes which press on the industrious classes, otherwise there will be but two classes, the one most miserably poor and the other most extremely rich.[42]

At Crowhurst, also in the neighbourhood of Battle, the boot was on the other foot, and here it was the labourers that took the lead and set themselves up as the spokesmen for the village. "It appears" (again to quote from a Treasury Solicitor's brief) "that on the morning of the 18th day of Novr last at the parish of Crowhurst in this county several of the labourers met together for the avowed purpose of compelling one James Dengate, the collector of his Majesty's assessed taxes for the said parish, to return the money received by him (and which he was on that day going to pay over to the Receiver General, who was attending at the George Inn in Battle for that purpose) to those persons who had returned the same. It is supposed their object was to relieve the farmers from paying their taxes and by so doing enable them to pay their labourers higher wages." The movement, however, collapsed, as the farmers hesitated, when invited, to resort to an open act of rebellion and several of the labourers themselves decided, on further reflection, not to proceed with the plan as (to quote their own words) "it was the King's money and it wouldn't do".[43]

By mid-November the movement had crossed into West Sussex. On the 13th "Swing" letters were received at Horsham and there was a disturbance at the workhouse in Petworth; and two days later there were fires at Ashington and Watersfield, followed the next day by fires at Angmering and in the Horsham district. Possibly both Horsham and Brighton, centres of radicalism anxious to spread the agitation against aristocracy and corruption, may have acted as relay stations. Certainly the men knew that they were part of a widespread movement: "we know what they have done in Kent", they said at Pulborough.[44] The agitation now spread into an area in which both economic and political conditions were quite unlike the Weald and its immediate surroundings. Lord Egremont, who had been (rightly) doubtful of the possibility of raising a yeomanry in East Sussex—it was virtually impossible even to raise special constables—was now on home ground, where the farmers were more readily separated from the labourers.

The immediate impetus for the West Sussex movement may have come from the villages around Lewes. Here the lead appears to have been taken by the men of Ringmer, who paraded the countryside, demanding higher wages and the dismantling of all threshing machines. On 15 November, Lord Gage, the largest landowner in the neighbourhood, negotiated with a vast assembly of Ringmer labourers and accepted their principal demands: in summer, wages of 2s. 6d. for married men and 2s. for single; in winter, 2s. 3d. and 1s. 9d. It was further requested—and granted—"that the permanent overseers of the neighbouring parishes may be directly discharged, particularly Finch, the governor of Ringmer poorhouse and overseer of the parish".[45]

As the movement spread west of Lewes, threshing machines became once more the main target. From Chichester it was reported that, on 15 November, the labourers of Arundel, Bersted, Bognor, Felpham and Yapton had combined to destroy all threshing machines and to have their wages raised from the present 10s. to 14s. a week. As they marched from farm to farm, they recruited new forces by intimidation or persuasion, demanded money, food and beer and compelled farmers to agree to increase their wages. Meanwhile, ran the report, "almost every machine is broke up". The following day was market day at Chichester, and here 1,000 labourers assembled to meet the justices and principal farmers, who accepted their terms. Other labourers assembled at Pagham and Goodwood, but dispersed in good order when met by the justices and special constables, who promised to consider their claims.[46]

Horsham, like Chichester, was a market town that was invaded by labourers seeking redress of their grievances; but at Horsham, which was a lively centre of Radicalism ("a hot-bed of sedition", one magistrate called it), it appears to have been the town as much as the countryside that took the initiative. The climax was a riotous meeting in the parish church, when the labourers forced the assembled householders and gentry to accept their demands for lower tithes and a basic wage of 2s. 6d. a day; but it had been preceded, or was accompanied, by fires, threatening letters, and the circulation of Radical handbills which extended beyond Horsham to places as far afield as Dorking.[47] The labourers had allies among the farmers, who, the county's High Sheriff wrote to Peel, "are known secretly to be promoting the assembling of the people". A lurid and horrified account of what took place in the vestry on the afternoon of 18 November was given by a local lady in a letter sent the next day to a young correspondent:

> A vestry was appointed to be held in the afternoon, but early in the morning a large party assembled, and strengthened their numbers by *forcing* work people of every description to join them, both from this and the adjoining parishes, and at 3 o'clock they went in an immense body to the Church, where they insisted on being met by Mr. Simpson & the land owners. They went in a large body for Mr. Hurst (who holds the great tithes), and as he endeavoured to excuse himself they seized a chariot from the King's Head yard and dragged it up to his house, but luckily he had just set off, supported by his 2 sons. All these gentlemen were stationed at the altar to receive the demands of this lawless multitude, who I suppose occupied every tenable place within the walls, and by their shouts & threatening language shewing (!) their total disregard for the sanctity of the place. I am ashamed to say the farmers encouraged the labouring classes who required to be paid 2s. 6d. pr day, while the farmers called for a reduction of their rents & the tithes one half. Mr. Simpson in a very proper manner gave an account of the revenues of his living, and after shewing that he did not clear more than £400 per ann^{m} promised to meet the gentlemen & farmers, & to make such a reduction as they could reasonably expect. Mr. Hurst held out so long that it was feared blood would be shed. The doors were shut till the demands were granted; no lights were allowed, the iron railing that surrounds the monuments torn up, and the sacred boundary between the chancel & altar overleaped

> before he would yield; at last the 3 points were gained & happily without any personal injury. The Church is much disfigured. Money was afterwards demanded at different houses for refreshment &, if not obtained with ease, the windows were broken. . . . Today the Mob is gone to Shipley & Rusper.[48]

The Horsham events had repercussions across the Surrey border. On 19 November, *The Times* reported, "an immense multitude of peasantry" assembled at Wotton to compel the rector, The Rev. J. E. Boscawen, to reduce his tithes. Some of the demonstrators claimed to have been forced to do what they did by men from Horsham "whom they durst not disobey".[49] A part of the crowd then moved off, it was alleged, towards Dorking following a leader "dressed in a smock frock"; and the riots that followed three days later at Dorking and Walton, when the justices were besieged and assaulted in a public house,[50] appear to have been inspired from the same quarter.*

The labourers' movement, meanwhile, had also driven westwards through Petworth, Arundel and Chichester. On 17 November, west of Chichester, threshing machines were destroyed at Emsworth, Funtington and Westbourne, while "a desperate gang" levied contributions from householders and broke machines at Bosham and Fishbourne. Further north, wages meetings were held and machines were broken around Chithurst and Rogate on the Hampshire boundary. It was from these two points that the movement entered Hampshire on 18 November.[51] It appeared, almost simultaneously, in Berkshire, and in Wiltshire on the 19th and Oxfordshire on the 21st. Yet it had by no means exhausted itself in either Kent or Sussex; but from now on it became a generalised movement in the southern, western and Home counties, soon to be followed by similar outbreaks in the midlands and East Anglia. It had also acquired a greatly increased momentum. In Kent, the county of its birth, it had lingered for more than two months before spreading into the Sussex Weald. In the Weald and East Sussex it had continued for another fortnight before passing into West Sussex. And this it had crossed in a bare three days.

Notes to Chapter 5

1. *Maidstone Gazette*, 27 April 1830.
2. H.O. 52/8 (letters of 7 June, 1–2 August, 31 August and 8 October 1830); *The Times*, 8 September 1830.

* See Appendix III below.

3. *The Times*, 18 April, 10 August 1831.
4. *Extracts from the Information Received by H.M. Commissioners ... of the Poor Law* (London 1833), p. 35.
5. *The Times*, 6 September 1830.
6. M. Dutt, *The Agricultural Labourers' Revolt in Kent, Surrey and Sussex* (unpublished London Ph.D. 1966), chapter IV, pp. 127–8, 132–8.
7. *The Times*, 25 October 1830.
8. H.O. 52/8 (letter of 22 September 1830).
9. Fifty machine-breakers from Elham voluntarily surrendered to the justices in East Kent in early October (Dutt, p. 137).
10. *The Times*, 25 October 1830.
11. *The Times*, 8 September, 17 September, 15 October 1830.
12. *The Times*, 17 September 1830.
13. *The Times*, 17 September 1830; H.O. 52/8 (letter of 8 October 1830).
14. The first mention of "Swing" in *The Times* is on 21 October.
15. *The Times*, 27 October 1830.
16. H.O. 52/8 (letter of 17 October 1830); J. L. and B. Hammond, *The Village Labourer* (2 vols., Guild Books, 1948), II, p. 46.
17. *The Times*, 14 October 1830.
18. H.O. 52/8 (letter of 8 October 1830).
19. *The Times*, 16, 21, 23, 27, 30 October 1830; H.O. 52/8 (letters of 12 and 25 October 1830).
20. *The Times*, 25 October 1830.
21. Dutt, *op. cit.*, pp. 146–7, 156.
22. H.O. 52/8 (letters of 23, 25, 27 October 1830); *The Times*, 27, 30 October 1830. The 9 victims of 25 October are given by *The Times* as Adley, Culmer, Donce and Fox, of Stourminster; Southee, of Goldstone; Petley, of Overland; Spain, of St. Bartholomew Farm; and Nethersole, near Sandwich.
23. Cobbett had lectured at Maidstone on 14 October.
24. T.S. 11/5035.
25. *The Times*, 4 November 1830.
26. H.O. 52/10 (letter of 9 May 1830).
27. H.O. 52/10 (letter of 3 November 1830); T.S. 11/4051; *The Times*, 13 November 1830.
28. H.O. 52/10 (report of 19 November 1830); Hammonds, II, pp. 50–51.
29. *Ibid.*, p. 51.
30. Dutt, *op. cit.*, pp. 189, 199. Armed smugglers are also reported from Newington (Kent) as accompanying machine-breaking gangs (*ibid.*, p. 143).
31. H.O. 52/8 (letter of 10 November 1830).
32. Dutt, *op. cit.*, pp. 290–1.
33. H.O. 52/10 (letter of 9 November 1830).
34. *The Times*, 11, 12, 13, 15, 16, 17, 18 November 1830; T.S. 11/943, 4051.
35. T.S. 11/943.
36. *Ibid.*
37. T.S. 11/4051.
38. Hammonds, II, p. 48.
39. *The Times*, November 1830, *passim*.
40. T.S. 11/943.

41. *The Times*, 13, 18 November 1830.
42. H.O. 52/10 (letter of 18 November 1830).
43. T.S. 11/4051.
44. *Brighton Guardian*, 17 November.
45. Hammonds, II, pp. 52–3; *The Times*, 25 November 1830.
46. *The Times*, 19, 20 November 1830.
47. H.O. 52/10 (police report and printed "Notice" of 28 December 1830).
48. H.O. 52/10 (letters of 18, 19, 21 November 1830); Hammonds, II, p. 59.
49. *The Times*, 22 November 1830.
50. *The Times*, 27 November 1830; *Cambridge Chronicle*, 7 January 1831.
51. H.O. 52/10 (letter of 18 November 1830); *The Times*, 22 November 1830.

6

IN HAMPSHIRE AND THE WEST COUNTRY

It was in Hampshire and Wiltshire that the movement, as it drove westwards, became the most widely dispersed and attained its greatest momentum. When the riots were all over, there were 300 or more prisoners awaiting trial in each county, compared with a little over 160 in Berkshire and in Buckingham and a little over 100 in Kent. Yet in both the riots were remarkably short-lived, the main period of rioting being limited to a little over a week in either case. Once more, we find the same wide variety of issues raised and the same multiformity of disturbance: a law officer's return sent from Winchester on 9 December 1830 divides the 356 depositions already received into the following categories: arson, demolishing buildings and machinery, burglary, larceny, robbery, "felony under the Act", breaking threshing machines, threatening letters, and riot of every kind.[1] Yet new elements entered in and the forms that the riots took were not identical with those taking place in the south-eastern counties. On the one hand, there was less arson, considerably less than in Surrey and Kent; there was on the whole less pre-occupation with tithes and rents and, in proportion, a less marked degree of co-operation between farmers and labourers. On the other hand, there was a greater emphasis on machine-breaking, particularly in Wiltshire; a greater degree of levying money and food as rewards for services rendered, particularly in Hampshire; and, in both, a new tendency of the rioters to attack not only agricultural machinery (including iron ploughs, and winnowing and chaff-cutting as well as threshing machines) but also industrial machinery.[2]

In Hampshire, as in Kent and Sussex, there were certain preliminary warning signals before there was any continuous or concerted movement. "Swing" letters began to be received in the Portsmouth area about 10 November, some warning against the use of threshing machines. A letter addressed to the Home Office on 12 November warns of pending disaster for which the farmer is roundly blamed, for having, "by a grinding system of grudging economy, wickedly thrown his labourers on the Poor Law".[3] On 13 November, there had been a second meeting of local reformers—farmers, labourers and freeholders—at the Swan Inn at Sutton Scotney, near Winchester, to sign a petition addressed to Parliament: among its signatories were a number of persons who were later implicated in the riots.[4] There were fires on the Stoke road near Gosport on the 11th, on the Duke of Wellington's estate at Strathfieldsaye on the 15th, and at Wallington, near Fareham, on the 16th.[5] The next day, it was reported from Petersfield, the labourers of Harting and Rogate from just across the Sussex border joined forces to visit farms, demand higher wages and levy money and provisions. On the 18th, ricks were fired at Wadwick and St. Mary Bourne and a first wave of rioting swept into the south-east corner of the county. A Petersfield report relates how a "mob", a thousand strong, "passing thru' Chichester and Emsworth" and destroying all the machinery it could find, crossed the border north of Gosport, swept through Fareham, and headed for Horndean on the road to Petersfield.[6]

The same evening, a riot broke out at Havant, in Hampshire and a few miles from the Sussex villages of Emsworth and Westbourne. Nine threshing machines were broken "in open day" at Havant, Warblington and neighbouring farms, and beer and money were demanded. A further report relates how the Havant men, having accomplished their task, crossed the Sussex border and went—or returned?—to Westbourne, where nine of them were promptly taken prisoner.[7] For, adds a *Times* report, the "mob" operating in these districts had their "committee" at Westbourne.[8] All of which suggests that there was some form of organised collaboration between the villages on both sides of the border.

After this initial break-through, the Hampshire riots spread with remarkable speed both northwards, by-passing Petersfield along the Sussex border, and north-westwards into the neighbourhood of Winchester. On the 18th, there were already reports of wages meetings and levies on householders and passers-by at Micheldever and Overton, in the centre and north-centre of the county. At Overton, several hundred labourers paraded the streets of the town demanding money and food and higher wages, saying that they had been starving too long on a diet of potatoes and bread. They withdrew after receiving money and food from the shopkeepers and promises of redress from the farmers, but returned in greater numbers the next day, armed with flails, staves and sticks. At this stage, a dramatic twist was given to the incident by the appearance on the scene of Henry Hunt, the Radical leader and a former resident of the town, who had arrived by stagecoach on a west-country tour. According to a *Times* report he was invited by the farmers to act as arbitrator between themselves and the labourers and proposed that wages should be raised from 9s. to 12s. a week, that the farmers should pay their labourers' house-rents and, furthermore and as an earnest of their good intentions, should pay them forthwith 2s. for the two days lost from work. The labourers, for their part, should quietly disperse to their villages. The advice appears to have been well received by both sides and was followed by cheers and mutual expressions of good will; and, within ten minutes (so runs the report), the market place was empty and every man had returned to his work.[9]

The same evening, fifty men armed with sticks arrived at Down Grange, Cassandra Hankey's farm at Basingstoke. When they were asked what they wanted, "the answer was some money to support them, and then they were to rise in a body to have their wages risen". The owner was so flustered by the encounter that she later confessed that she did not know whether she gave the leaders, with whom she parleyed in her kitchen, one or two sovereigns to make them go away. Meanwhile, her winnowing machine was smashed. "They said it must go, as it was a machine; and it was broke to pieces."[10]

By this time, the labourers' movement had already crossed the county and had appeared close to the Wiltshire border. On the 19th, there was a riot at Alexander Baring's mansion at Alresford, and threshing machines were destroyed at Warnford, West Meon, Micheldever and on Sir Thomas Baring's estate at East Stratton. Beyond Stockbridge, at the Wallops, all work stopped while farmers and men met in a field to discuss the labourers' wages. A compromise was reached, whereby the current 8s. wage should be raised to 10s., provided the labourers helped to secure a reduction in taxes, tithes and rents. The agreement was followed by a visit to James Blunt, proprietor of the great tithe, who, at first reluctant, ended by yielding to the labourers' threats, which it was only too evident that the farmers were willing to exploit, and consented under protest to reduce his tithes by one-third.[11]

More sensational than these events was the outbreak at Andover and the neighbouring village of Clatford. Beginning on 19 November, the Andover riots lasted for several days. Summing up their results a week after they started, a local magistrate wrote to Lord Melbourne (by then Home Secretary in the new Whig Government) that "the Peasantry have not only dictated a rate of wages, not only destroyed all agricultural machinery, and demolished iron foundries, but have proceeded in formidable bodies to private dwellings to extort money and provisions—in fact, have established a system of pillage".[12] It began with the destruction of a threshing machine in a village near Andover. A prisoner was taken and escorted to Andover jail, where he was followed by a "huge multitude" who compelled shopkeepers to close their doors and bolt their windows and who, according to one account, broke open the prison gates, released the prisoner and carried him in triumph through the streets. Hunt happened once more to be on the scene and (according to this same account, but refuted by another), when called upon to address the crowd, replied: "Let the mayor and corporation, who have raised the storm, quell it." On the next day, a large party set out for Tasker's Waterloo Foundry at Upper Clatford, two miles away, and demolished its machinery, valued at £2,000. "The pretext for this outrage," the Andover magistrates wrote the same day to the Home Office, "was that the proprietor of the foundry in question has been in the habit of manufacturing iron work for threshing machines." The whole town and its neighbourhood continued (further to quote these justices) "in a state of the greatest agitation & alarm" until 22 November, when a troop of the 9th Lancers arrived on the scene and took several prisoners; after which, order was restored and all was "peace and penitence".[13]

At Steep, near Petersfield, on the Sussex border, the labourers were ordered to meet on 23 November—by persons, it was said, "calling themselves delegates from the general committee". The farmers were invited to sign a paper addressed to them by the labourers; it ran:

> Our complaint is that we have not a suficient maintance to suport our famleys, and as theare a geving more wages in the joining Parishes we do request that you will consent and sine your hands to this Paper that all labering men mairred and singel abel to do a day's work to have 2s. per day, and all lads over 16 yers of age to have 1s. per day, and all boys that works under 16 years of age to have 6d. per day, and refuse to pay tythes and taxes, and we will stand your frends and asist you old men that have a wife to Ceep to have 1s. 6d. per day.[14]

It was in the same district that the workhouses were demolished at Selborne and Headley on 22 and 23 November. This was really a combined operation with threshing machines, tithes and the overseers of the poor as its targets, in which farmers as well as labourers appear to have taken part. The rioters first went to Mr. Cobbold, the vicar of Selborne, and demanded that he should reduce his tithe by a half: "we think £300 a year quite enough for you ... £4 a week is quite enough". Having extracted a written consent from Cobbold, they went on to Headley whose vicar gave a similar undertaking. Meanwhile, they broke a threshing machine at Kingsley, and "pulled down" the workhouses in both parishes after politely giving the masters and their families notice of their intention. They showed considerable discrimination. "There was not a room left entire," the workhouse master of Headley testified later, "except that in which the sick children were. These were removed into the yard on two beds, and covered over, and kept from harm all the time. They were left there because there was no room for them in the sick ward. The sick ward was full of infirm old paupers. It was not touched, but of all the rest of the place not a room was left entire."[15]

In some places, the prompt action of a local justice or magnate nipped a disturbance in the bud or prevented a riot from gaining momentum. At Liphook, on the Sussex border, Dr. Quarry, a resolute magistrate, broke up a wages meeting by smartly arresting a "stranger" who had come to address them; and he appears, too, to have dissuaded many labourers from attending a larger meeting that was due to be held at Petersfield on market day, 24 November. The Duke of Buckingham organised something resembling a feudal levy to beat back the rioters from the villages of Itchen Abbas, Avington and Easton, a part of the county that was described as being "almost wholly (his) property". When labourers from the Winchester area began to break the threshing machines on his estate at Avington House, His Grace sent the rector into action at the head of 100 of his tenants and labourers organised as "specials"; they took between forty and fifty prisoners and put the rest to flight.[16]

About 23 November, a new wave of rioting spread into Hampshire from Hungerford, Kintbury and West Woodhay in Berkshire.* That day, threshing machines were destroyed and money was levied at Highclere, East Woodhay and Burghclere in the northern part of the county. The labourers of the neighbouring village of Ashmansworth had already "risen" on 22 November and had, that night, compelled the rector to pay them two sovereigns; but, in reporting these events, he relates how a greater ferment ensued the next day when "many

* See pp. 137–8 below.

have joined the parties which have come from over the hills".[17] It was yet another case of an inter-county operation.

By this time, the greater part of the county, excluding the New Forest and the Isle of Wight, had been drawn into the movement. The last areas to be seriously hit were the Southampton district and such places as Fordingbridge, Ringwood and Fawley, lying on the edge of the Forest. This all happened in the last week of November. Southampton itself had received threatening letters and, on the night of the 23rd–24th, a great commotion was caused by the firing of Charles Baker's extensive sawmills near the centre of the city. Following repeated warnings, guards had been posted at strategic points; so the panic was all the greater when flames were seen to rise from a timber shed adjoining the main building. Within three hours, the whole building, including its rich stock of circular saws, had gone up in flames to an estimated loss of £7,000.[18]

Near Southampton, there was a minor riot at Redbridge on 24 November; and, on the outskirts of the New Forest, there were riots at Fawley and Ringwood on the 25th and at Exbury on the 26th; at Ringwood, there was talk of "wandering hordes from the borders of the county" (i.e. Dorset).[19] But the last riots of any substance in the county were those that broke out at Fordingbridge, on the boundary of Dorset, on the 23rd and 24th. This was a major operation conducted by a man of resolution, James Thomas Cooper, a 33-year-old ostler of East Grimstead in Wiltshire, who rode on a white horse and was styled "Captain Hunt"; he became an almost legendary figure and was one of the two Hampshire men who were executed for their part in the riots. After burning threshing machines from six to eight miles around, some 300 labourers marched into the town, demanded money and beer and broke all the machinery at two nearby mills—the one Samuel Thompson's sacking manufactory at East Mill, the other William Shepherd's threshing-machine factory at Stuckton. At the first, £1,000 of damage was said to have been done and Cooper was reported to have boasted that "they had come from 20 miles above London, and were going as far down the country as there was any machinery, to destroy it".[20]

After these incidents, the movement in Hampshire tapered off and ended, as it had begun, in a round of fires and threatening letters. These were mainly on the Isle of Wight: there were fires at Newport on 25 November, at Rookley on the 28th and at Freshwater on the 29th. There was a strike of unemployed labourers near Newport on the 25th. On 28 November, the rector of Freshwater received a letter threatening him and the farmers and gentry with summary vengeance if they did not raise their labourers' wages.[21] Finally, as a parting shot, it was reported from Lymington across the water that "there has been what is termed a 'strike for wages' in almost every village hereabout, but unattended with anything like outrage".[22]

In Wiltshire, the first recorded disturbance was an assault that took place at Wilcot, a few miles south of Marlborough, on 19 November.[23] It was an isolated case and preceded by two days anything like a concerted outbreak in the county as a whole. Even before this, however, there had been the usual preparatory "softening-up" by threatening letters and incendiary fires. "Swing" letters were received by farmers at Codford St. Peter, between Wilton and Warminster, and at Horton, near Devizes, on or about 15 November. The same day, there was a fire at Knook, near Codford; and fires were reported at Collingbourne and Ludgershall, near the Hampshire border, on the 18th; at Oare, south of Marlborough, on the 19th; and others in the Marlborough district between the 17th and 22nd. And before the riots really got under way, further fires occurred at Stanton St. Barnard on the 20th and at Amesbury, Everleigh, Winterslow, and again at Stanton, on the 21st. (The victim of the second fire at Stanton had, it was reported, three or four threshing machines in operation.)[24] Already farmers were taking alarm and crowding into Salisbury to take out insurance policies against arson; but these, *The Times* noted grimly, the Fire Offices "prudently" refused to consider.[25]

The Wiltshire labourers, like those of other counties, were drawn into the movement by the "contagion" emanating from their neighbours: in this case, their fellow-labourers in Hampshire and Berkshire. But they had also their own particular scores to settle and local grievances that served as an immediate spur to action. Wages in Wiltshire were notoriously low, lower by far than wages in Kent and even lower than those in Sussex and Hampshire. The normal wage for an able-bodied man in full employment was 7s. or 8s. in winter and 8s. or 9s. in summer; occasionally, it might rise to 10s., but this was the exception rather than the rule. A letter addressed to *The Times* from Melksham at the end of November even claimed that there were fifty poor men in the parish, without wife or children, who were working for 8d. a day.[26] Demands for improvements were already being loudly voiced before the riots started; and Henry Hunt, as he travelled through the Wiltshire villages, related how the labourers told him (it was now

20 November): "We don't want to do any mischief, but we want that poor children when they go to bed should have a belly full of tatoes instead of crying with half a belly full."[27] Given such conditions and given the example set by Kent and their Hampshire and Berkshire neighbours, the labourers' attention settled on the threshing machines; and, in Wiltshire more than in any other county, this became the rioters' main target. In fact, when it was all over and more than 300 Wiltshire labourers and craftsmen were brought to court, no fewer than 92 of the 160 indictments proffered concerned the destruction of agricultural machinery.[28]

The first threshing machines were destroyed at All Cannings, east of Devizes, and at Hippenscombe, on the Hampshire border, on 21 November. The machine-breaking at All Cannings, which lay several miles from the Berkshire border, may have been associated more closely with the fires at the adjoining villages of Oare and Stanton than with any "contagion" from outside. But the position of Hippenscombe, lying in an enclave a few miles west of Andover, suggests that in this case the inspiration may have come from Hampshire. The presumption becomes the stronger when we read in an Andover report of 21 November that there was a plan afoot for the labourers of Fyfield (Hampshire) and those of Ludgershall (in Wiltshire, adjoining Hippenscombe) to join forces on the morrow.[29]

This was, however, only a small beginning. The next day—it was the day that Lord Grey's Whig Ministry took office—the riots spread and developed with explosive force. They broke out almost simultaneously in three main sectors, all in the east and all significantly close to the borders of Hampshire and Berkshire: in the area south of Marlborough, stretching south from Ramsbury as far as Collingbourne; in the centre, in the villages lying on the eastern fringe of the Salisbury Plain along the Avon between Everleigh and Amesbury; and, in the south, in a number of the villages south-east of Salisbury. A score of villages appear in the indictments, and cases of machine-breaking are recorded in all but seven. In the Devizes district the impact was such that farmers were already "busy in removing or totally destroying" their machines and hastening to comply with the labourers' demands—in some cases, a report added, aided by their own workpeople "without riot or disorder". The same report enclosed an appeal addressed to the "Labourers of Wiltshire" by "a sincere well-wisher", issued that day and widely distributed around Devizes, Pewsey and Marlborough, which bore the solemn injunction: "Beware of men who are going about the county to make you do what you will soon be sorry for. The times are bad. BUT WILL BURNING CORN MAKE YOUR SITUATION MORE COMFORTABLE OR GIVE YOU BREAD?"[30]

On the 23rd, the riots reached their greatest intensity. Twenty-five Wiltshire towns and villages appear in the indictments; and disturbances spread north to the area outside Swindon; to further villages along the Hampshire border; and, above all, they now penetrated more deeply into the interior of the county around Marlborough and Salisbury. From Salisbury, it was reported early that morning that all threshing machines in the neighbourhood had been destroyed and that, in anticipation of an imminent attack, the city's shops had been closed and their windows barred. It was the first day of the riots across the border at Fordingbridge, and it was feared that the example of industrial machine-breaking set by "Captain Hunt" and his men might be repeated in the woollen manufactories at Milford and Harnham close by and in the iron foundry at Salisbury itself, whose owner had already received threatening letters.[31]

From Devizes came a horrifying account of the demolition of a farm-house at Alton, near Pewsey, and the murder of its occupant. It proved to be a false alarm; the labourers there were no more murderously inclined than anywhere else. It appears that a body of men, who had assembled at Pewsey the previous day and levied £5 on Sir Edward Poore, a local magistrate, had gone on to Alton and destroyed two threshing machines. Whereupon, a third intended victim, Robert Pile, had seized a musket and wounded a number of his assailants. His furniture had been destroyed and £10 had been extorted from him by way of retribution; but, far from being murdered, he had been carried into the house for safety by Bullock, one of the rioters' leaders.[32]

It was at this point that the Devizes justices resolved

1. That "they would not accede to any demands made by any persons urging such demands in a tumultuous and riotous manner"; and
2. That, "when order and quiet should have been restored, *and not till then*, they would consider the labourers' grievances and demands".

However, this display of apparent firmness was somewhat tempered by their recommendation to owners and occupiers of land to "advance forthwith" their able-bodied labourers' wage to 10s. a week. This drew from the farmers an almost inevitable retort: a week later, 84 of them humbly requested "that the proprietors and tithe owners will openly and candidly declare what REDUCTION they intend to MAKE to their tenants, without which they cannot possibly accede to their wishes".[33]

The riots continued, and, on 24 November, they extended in two further directions—north of Swindon towards the Gloucestershire border and, in the south, west and south-west of Salisbury. At Newton Tony, near Amesbury, a farmer, James Judd, tried to save his threshing machines by bargaining with his assailants. "If you will disperse and go to work and protect our property when others come to destroy it, I will give you beer and money and anything else in reason." However, his price was not high enough and the rioters forced their way into his barn, "and in five minutes afterwards his threshing machine was broken to pieces". At Wilton, west of Salisbury, considerably more damage was done to John Brasher's manufactory for woollen cloth: 500 men arrived at his mill that afternoon and announced that they would break his machinery "in order to make more work for the poor people". They stayed an hour and broke five engines to pieces; the owner later estimated his loss at £500.[34]

The most sensational, and the most bloody, of the Wiltshire riots was that which took place at the Pyt House, John Benett's estate in the parish of Tisbury, on 25 November. Tisbury lies west of Salisbury, a few miles north of Cranborne Chase, and it may be that this phase of the riots received its impetus from the Fordingbridge events and those that followed at Handley in the northern part of Dorset.* There were conflicting reports concerning its local origins. *The Times* put out a story that it had started with fourteen quarrymen, whose wages had sunk to 3½d. a day and who "blamed the threshing machines for this low price"; but Benett, who was the County Member, denied this and claimed that the riots spread to Tisbury from Ansty, towards the Dorset border.[35] However it was, there were riots and machine-breaking that day in this corner of the county at Boyton, Hindon, Tisbury, Tollard Royal, Fonthill Gifford and Fonthill Bishop; and, according to Benett's own account, he was roused by his steward at seven or eight in the morning with a report that the rioters were approaching the Pyt House from Hindon, three miles away, "with the avowed purpose of destroying a factory and also threshing machines". He rode to meet them and found some 400 labourers at Fonthill Gifford, where, having armed themselves with bludgeons and crow-

* See p. 128 below.

bars taken from a blacksmith's shop, they smashed three threshing machines in local farms. He himself owned two large machines—the one at Pyt House worked by six horses, the other worked by water at his Linley Farm close by; and they told him that they wanted 2s. a day in wages and that "they would break all the threshing machines, and mine among the rest". He tried to divide them by threats and appeals; and he read out a Royal proclamation against rioting, newly issued, and warned that "any man by informing against 10 of you will obtain at once £500". It served no purpose; his barns were broken into and both his machines were destroyed before a troop of yeomanry cavalry arrived from Hindon and engaged the rioters in the wood adjoining the Pyt House farm. A battle followed in which the labourers fought it out with hatchets, hammers, pick-axes, sticks and stones against the yeomen's muskets. One labourer, John Hardy of Tisbury, was shot dead, several were wounded, and twenty-five were arrested.[36]

On that day also the yeomanry fought a running engagement with bodies of rioters who had destroyed threshing-machines in the Vale of Wylye, and who were sufficiently combative to barricade the road to Warminster in order to rescue the prisoners who were being taken there; with some difficulty, "owing to the turbulent spirit of the town". The "mobs" from Tisbury, Knoyle and Mere, on the Somerset border, were reported to be ready to attack the machines at the Deverills, "but their fortunate defeat simultaneous with that at Heytesbury seems for the present to have paralysed their future movements", as the Clerk to the Warminster magistrates wrote.[37]

This was the climax to the Wiltshire riots, as the Fordingbridge affair had been the climax to those in Hampshire. From now on, they took the form of a series of scattered skirmishes and isolated fires rather than of an organised or continuous movement. By 26 November, the riots had spread over wide areas of the county, particularly south and east of Marlborough, all around Salisbury and in the Devizes district. There were two large patches of the county left largely untouched: in the centre, Salisbury Plain, all but its eastern sector; and, in the west, the old traditional riotous centres of woollen manufacture in and around Trowbridge, Westbury and Bradford-on-Avon. Fears were expressed that Warminster would be attacked: it seemed all the more plausible in view of the reported presence there of the ubiquitous Henry Hunt; and, in demanding that troops be sent to these towns, magistrates rightly insisted that "if once (insubordination) reach the manufacturing districts, no man can foresee the consequences". But, as *The Times* was able to add reassuringly a few days later, "our manufacturing districts are unaffected by the surrounding commotions and the workpeople are in full employ and remunerative wages".[38] The "Swing" movement was to continue, as it had begun, as a movement of the country and not of the towns, of agricultural labourers and not of urban or industrial workers.

On 28 November, the two senior army officers sent by the Whig government to command and supervise the pacification of the western counties made their separate comments and evaluations. Lt.-Colonel Mair wrote from Salisbury that "the labourers are returning to their work and everything is becoming tranquil"; and from Warminster his colleague, Colonel Brotherton, wrote that the "spirit of insurrection" had been checked by two factors: the energetic measures taken by a few—but only by *a few*—magistrates, and the widespread compliance with the labourers' demands. He discounted the wild alarms and rumours that were still circulating and added that "the insurrectionary movement seems to be directed by no plan or system, but merely actuated by the spontaneous feeling of the peasantry & quite at random".[39]

Meanwhile, the disturbances had spread to south Gloucestershire and the eastern districts of Dorset. The first was exposed to the "contagion" of the Wiltshire towns and villages north of Swindon, the second to a pincer movement which had Salisbury as one of its epicentres and the Fordingbridge–Ringwood area in Hampshire as the other. In Dorset, there were two main areas of disturbance, and these were interlinked: the eastern inland plain stretching eastwards from Dorchester to Wimborne with Bere Regis at its centre; and the north-eastern "frontier" area between Cranborne and Stalbridge, passing through Cranborne Chase and Shaftesbury along the southern boundaries of Wiltshire and Somerset. Perhaps surprisingly, eyewitness accounts suggest that it was in the first rather than in the second of these sectors that the first disturbances occurred. One such eyewitness, a zealous magistrate of Moreton, whose faith in "the very orderly and quiet manner in which the labourers in Dorsetshire had always conducted themselves" had recently been shaken, set out on 22 November to enrol special constables in Dorchester and other towns. From his account it appears that labourers were already assembling to demand a 10s. weekly wage at Winterborne Kingston and Bere Regis; and that, during the next few days, the movement extended to villages around Wareham (24th), Puddletown (25th),

Winfrith and Knighton (27th) and Castle Hill, east of Dorchester (29th). This generally took the form of "illegal assemblies" for wages, but these were interspersed with outbreaks of arson (as at Hinsford, Bere, Puddletown and Preston) and the breaking of threshing machines (at Wolland, Lytchett and Castle Hill).[40]

The main centre of disturbance, however, lay in the "frontier" area in and around Cranborne Chase, more directly exposed to the riots already taking place in the neighbouring counties. On the 23rd, there was a case of "robbery" at Cranborne, close to the Hampshire border. The next day, a far more serious outbreak occurred at Handley, described by a local justice as "a singular place" with "a wild dissolute population of poachers, smugglers & deer stealers" and one "from whence our principal rioters have issued". But he shared with his neighbouring magistrates the view that the main impetus had come from Wiltshire. "The progress of the disorder," he wrote, "was from Salisbury. On Tuesday last [23 November], after the dispersion of the large mob there, they seem to have broken up into two grand divisions, one of which marched on Fordingbridge & the other on Handley. At Handley the rioters were increased by the junction of almost all the labourers of that village, and the thrashing machines & the machines of the neighbouring farmers were all destroyed."[41] The movement spread southwards towards Blandford and westwards towards Shaftesbury and the Somerset border. Threshing machines were destroyed at Buckland Newton on the 27th, and at East Stour, Stour Provost and Cann on the 29th; the next day, there was a riot at Shaftesbury and five prisoners were released. In all, 71 persons were committed for trial, eight or ten of them from Handley. But a certain discrimination appears to have been shown in their selection; for, as the magistrate concerned in the Handley affair wrote to the Home Office, "had we committed for participating in & aiding the burning of machinery, we might have committed two-thirds of the labouring population of the district".[42]

In Gloucestershire, the labourers' movement was more concentrated than in any other major area of disturbance. Later, there were cases of arson at Deerhouse, Dumbleton, Winchcombe and Moreton-in-the-Marsh in the north and at Aust in the west of the county;[43] but these had no apparant connection with the machine-breaking and "riotous assemblies" that were limited to a dozen parishes lying to the east and west of Cirencester along the north Wiltshire border. Fairford, where the first outbreak occurred on 26 November, was singularly exposed, lying a few miles north of Cricklade, where threshing machines had been destroyed two days before, and close to Lechlade, which lay at the junction of four counties, including Berkshire and Wiltshire. The labourers destroyed the threshing and haymaking machines at four farms and did damage later computed at £300. As in Dorset, there were now fears expressed of "large assemblages of people on the borders of this county, in Wiltshire & Berkshire, spreading over the borders". Moreover, it was reported that the labourers of Fairford, having achieved their initial success, were planning to join with those of Quinnington, Hatherop, Coln and Southrop to destroy further machines and, if need be, "fight to the last".[44] It proved to be a reasonably accurate forecast, as, in the immediate neighbourhood, machines were broken at Eastleach, Coln St. Aldwyn and Quinnington on 27 November; at Bibury and Coln Rogers on the 29th; and there was a riot at Southrop on the same day.[45]

Meanwhile, on the very day of the Fairford outbreak, the focus of rioting had moved west of Cirencester to Tetbury, which also lay along the Wiltshire border but considerably further from the machine-breaking villages in the north of that county. Threshing machines were broken on the same day at Tetbury, Horsley and Beverstone. At Tetbury, there were rumours of "strangers" on horseback who had asked suspicious questions and then were seen no more.[46] It seems far-fetched and we shall find reasons in a later chapter to discount such rumours in general; yet there is the possibility that these villages were visited by emissaries from Wiltshire or, perhaps more likely, from Fairford itself. At least, the possibilities of a combined movement were sufficient to alarm the magistrates and, at about this time, Lord Sherborne and his fellow-justices of Cirencester issued an appeal "To the Peasantry of the County of Gloucester", promising to "afford all just and reasonable redress" of their grievances, while imploring them to return quietly to their jobs.[47] It was followed by a massive arrest of labourers, 90 of whom were lodged in Gloucester jail.

As the riots moved further west from Gloucester and Dorset, they lost their continuity and momentum and became a series of more or less scattered outbreaks reaching west into Herefordshire and south-westwards along the coast of Cornwall. Of these "marginal" counties, Somerset was the only one whose riots had any *physical* connection with those spreading west from Wiltshire and Dorset. At South Brewham, on the Wiltshire border, a minor riot took place on 26 November and threats were made to destroy a threshing machine.

The next day, "inflammatory" handbills appeared in Taunton, allegedly by order of a Radical parson, said to have been a former election agent of Henry Hunt. At Banwell, on 30 November, there was a paupers' riot at the poorhouse, followed by an attack on the lock-up and a release of prisoners. The same day, it was reported from Frome that a farmer had set fire to his own threshing machine which had cost him upwards of £100; and, on 1 December, Lord Egremont's steward wrote from Ilton that "for miles around, the farmers and owners have all taken down & destroyed all (threshing machines) that are in the neighbourhood". Yet the only actual case of machine-breaking by labourers occurred the same day, when two threshing machines were destroyed at the two neighbouring villages of Yenston and Henstridge. It was the day of the Stalbridge riot, a bare mile across the Dorset border.[48]

In Devon, there was a scattered crop of outbreaks, most of them around Torquay and Newton Abbot. "Swing" letters were received by farmers near Exeter and at Axmouth in late November and at Ilfracombe, in North Devon, in early December; and there was the inevitable report that "that bad man Henry Hunt" had passed through Exeter and was stirring up the "lower classes". There was a tithe riot at Swimbridge, in North Devon, on 10 December, and a wages riot at Castle Hill. But the most frequent type of disturbance was a number of incendiary raids on isolated farms in which threshing machines were known to be kept. There were half-a-dozen such incidents at Abbotskerswell, Newton Abbot, Cockington and Highweek in the last fortnight of December.[49]

In Cornwall, there were food riots at Mevagissey and Fowey in November; others followed at Penzance and Helston in February 1831. But this was the traditional small consumers' protest of the Cornish miners and had no connection whatsoever with the agricultural labourers' movement. Lord Melbourne had been assured that "only strangers could create disturbance in peaceful Cornwall", where employment was plentiful and wages were relatively high. Yet there were parishes in the eastern parts of the county, around Callington and Launceston, where wages were said to be "shamefully low"; and here there were wages riots in mid-December, followed soon after by threatening letters against tithes and threshing machines at Morval and St. Neot. A disturbing feature (wrote the Vice-Lieutenant to Lord Melbourne) was "that in all instances the farmers have been the instigators and that they are very generally inclined to excite the labourers to disturbance with the hope of by that means forcing a reduction of rent and tithe".[50]

In Worcestershire, disturbance had its own peculiar pattern, much of it no doubt unrelated to the labourers' movement. There had been riots by carpet weavers at Kidderminster in August and, in early December, it was feared that weavers would burn the machinery at Worcester. At Redditch, on 6 December, workers destroyed four needle-stamps and presses. Meanwhile, on 1 December, two threshing machines had been broken by labourers at Redmarsh and Hanley Williams; and, a week later, a machine was broken at Wadberrow, near Pershore; the rioters followed this up by demanding food and money in the villages around. That there may, in this case, have been some connection between the urban and the rural movements is suggested by the wording of a seditious placard displayed in Evesham at about this time:

> Be not afraid of Evesham new police for they're nothing but thieves and robbers.
> Down with machinery and A free trade in Corn.[51]

Finally, on the extreme north-western fringe of the riots, there was the county of Hereford. Wages were similar to those paid in Wiltshire: 7s. to 10s. a week; and a correspondent writing to *The Times* at the end of November noted "a spirit of discontent" among the country labourers that required but a spark to erupt. No general eruption followed, no doubt because of the isolation of the county from the main centres of disturbance. But there were threatening letters sent to farmers and, on 25 November, when a fire broke out at a farm near Kenchester, "adjoining a barn where a threshing machine had worked all day", many of the labourers standing by refused to lend a hand. "You may take the engine home and mend it (some said), for it will not be long before it is wanted again." And among the "Swing" letters was one addressed on 17 November to a large farmer of Whitney that was clearly of more than purely local inspiration; it ran:

> Remember in Kent they have set ("with fire") all that would not submit and you we will serve the same for we are determined to make you support the Poor better than they have been soppored yet for they are all starving at present so pull down your Thrashing Maschine or els Bread or Fire without delay. For we are 5 thousand men and will not be stopt.[52]

It was written by a journeyman tailor, said to be a "ranting" preacher who was later transported to New South Wales. It had taken three months for the Kentish message to reach the borders of the Welsh hills, the extreme western outpost of the labourers' movement.

Notes to Chapter 6

1. H.O. 40/27, fo. 629.
2. H.O. 40/27 fos. 561–6; see also Appendix I.
3. H.O. 52/7 (letter of 12 November 1830).
4. A. M. Colson, *The Revolt of the Hampshire Agricultural Labourers and its Causes, 1812–1831* (unpub. M.A. thesis, Univ. of London, 1937).
5. *The Times*, 23 November 1830.
6. H.O. 52/7 (letters of 18, 19 November 1830).
7. H.O. 52/10 (letters of 18–20 November 1830); *The Times*, 23 November 1830.
8. *The Times*, 23 November 1830.
9. *The Times*, 22 November 1830.
10. H.O. 52/7 (depositions of 25 November 1830).
11. *The Times*, 23 November 1830.
12. H.O. 52/7 (letter of 26 November 1830).
13. *The Times*, 18, 22, 23, 25 November 1830; H.O. 52/7 (letter of 20 November 1830).
14. *The Times*, 30 November 1830. For a similar paper ("the document") presented by the Romsey labourers to farmers the same day, see Colson, *op. cit.*, pp. 89–90.
15. *The Times*, 30 November and 24 December 1830; Hammonds, II, pp. 61–2.
16. *The Times*, 25 and 30 November 1830.
17. H.O. 52/6 (letter of 23 November 1830).
18. *The Times*, 29 November 1830.
19. *The Times*, 27, 29, 30 November 1830.
20. *The Times*, 21–22 December 1830; H.O. 52/7 (letter of 26 November 1830); Hammonds, II, p. 61.
21. H.O. 52/7 (letter of 29 November 1830).
22. *The Times*, 6 December 1830.
23. Assizes 25/21 Wilts. H. Graham, *The Yeomanry Cavalry of Wiltshire* (Liverpool 1886), p. 72, reports burnings at Knock and Collingbourne that day, but gives no source.
24. H.O. 52/10 (letter of 22 November 1830).
25. *The Times*, 23 November 1830.
26. *The Times*, 2, 3 December 1830.
27. *The Times*, 23 November 1830.
28. P.R.O. Assizes 25/21 (Indictments).
29. H.O. 52/7 (letter of 21 November 1830).
30. H.O. 52/11 (letter of 22 November 1830, and printed poster).
31. H.O. 52/11 (letter of 23 November 1830).

32. *Ibid.*; *The Times*, 27, 30 November 1830.
33. H.O. 52/11 (printed poster of 23 November 1830); H.O. 40/27, fo. 184. The Calne J.P.s meeting on 25 November, forestalled this objection: they called for (1) a rise in wages from 8s. to 10s. in the winter and 9s. to 12s. in the summer; and (2) a proportionate reduction in rent and tithe (*The Times*, 1 December 1830).
34. *The Times*, 5, 6 January 1831; Hammonds, II, p. 62.
35. *The Times*, 10, 15 December 1830.
36. H.O. 40/27, fos. 415–16; H.O. 52/11 (letter of 26 November 1830); *The Times*, 30 November 1830, 3 January 1831.
37. Graham, *op. cit.* 82–3; R. Cobb, Correspondence, 27 November 1830.
38. H.O. 52/11 (letters of 26, 28 November 1830); H.O. 40/27, fos. 453–9; *The Times*, 1 December 1830. There were, however, two belated outbreaks of machine-breaking in this region: on 29 November, 2 threshing machines were destroyed at Wingfield (2 miles from Trowbridge) and one at Winsley (near Bradford) (H.O. 52/11 (letter of 1 December 1830)).
39. H.O. 40/27, fo. 449; H.O. 52/11 (letter of 28 November 1830).
40. Dorset R.O., "Account of the Regiment of Dorset Yeomanry Cavalry raised in the Year 1830" (n.d.); *The Times*, 30 November 1830. See also W. H. Parry Okedon, "The Agricultural Riots in Dorset in 1830" (*Proceedings of the Dorset Nat. Hist. and Arch. Soc.*, LXXXIV (1962), pp. 158–77.
41. H.O. 52/7 (letters of 26, 28 November 1830).
42. H.O. 40/27, fos. 51–2; H.O. 52/7 (letter of 28 November 1830).
43. *The Times*, 11, 14 November 1830; 22 January 1831.
44. H.O. 52/7 (letters of 27, 28 November 1830).
45. This appears to have developed out of a wages riot at Langford, Oxon., earlier that morning (T.S. 11/1849).
46. H.O. 52/7 (letter of 28 November 1830).
47. H.O. 52/7 (printed address, n.d.).
48. H.O. 40/25, fos. 595–8, 607–10; H.O. 52/7 (letter of 2 December 1830). *The Times*, 4 December 1830; *Reading Mercury*, 22 November 1830; *Dorset Chronicle*, 6, 13 January 1831. Somerset R.O., Calendar of Prisoners, Epiphany Sessions, Wells, 3 January 1831; DD/WY, Box 134: Earl of Egremont's Correspondence relating to his Ilton Estates.
49. H.O. 52/6 (letters of November–December 1830); H.O. 40/27, fos. 371–2, 390; *The Times*, 26 November, 27, 29 December 1830, 3 January 1831.
50. *The Times*, 23, 30 November, 28 December 1830; H.O. 52/6 (letters of 16, 21, 25 December 1830).
51. H.O. 52/11 (letters of 30 August, 3 December 1830); H.O. 52/15 (correspondence of 6 January–1 February 1831); *The Times*, 8, 13, 14 December 1830; *Worcester Herald*, 8 January 1831; Worcester R.O., Q.S. Order Books, XII (1831), pp. 144–5.
52. *The Times*, 29 November 1830; *Worcester Herald*, 14 January 1831; Hereford R.O., Q.S. records, Epiphany 1831.

7

IN THE HOME COUNTIES AND MIDLANDS

The labourers' movement in the Home Counties began in Berkshire in the middle of November. It had two separate starting points, neither of which appears to have been directly connected with the disturbances in the southern counties. The one was the village of Thatcham, in south Berkshire east of Newbury, which became the epicentre for the riots that followed in the central, western and northern districts of the county. The other lay in the extreme eastern part of the county, adjoining Windsor Forest and skirting the neighbouring counties of Surrey, Middlesex and Buckingham. It was admirably suited for the solitary incendiary raid and the terror that might be struck by the dissemination of threatening letters. And such letters were received by farmers at Holyport (Berks.) and Colnbrook (Bucks.) around 10 November, followed by others at Hounslow (Middlesex) and at Bray and Windsor on the 16th; and there were fires at Bedfont (Middlesex) on the 9th, at Englefield Green (across the Surrey border) on the 11th, at Hurst (in Berkshire) on the 16th, and at Holyport on the 19th.[1] Farmers at Hounslow and Windsor were already offering large rewards for tracking down incendiaries and, on 19 November, a Forest Association was formed at Wokingham for the express purpose of combating arson.[2]

Yet this part of the "Swing" movement in Berkshire, though thoroughly alarming to all concerned, was largely still-born; and as Norman Gash showed thirty years ago, the fires, of which a great proportion were confined to this eastern forest sector, were, in the main, isolated from the chief centres of disturbance in the county.[3] Only two cases of "robbery" or machine-breaking occurred in this region, and both were the work of the same band of labourers: the first at Waltham St. Lawrence on 20 November and the second, a night later, at Binfield. The first is perhaps of the greater interest, as Solomon Allen, who led the expedition, told the farmer's wife from whom he demanded beer and victuals for his men that "they were 40 sworn men come out of Kent; that I had heard what had been done there; they had come thro' London & were going thro' England to regulate the country. They then said we are determined to break all the Threshing Machines."[4] But these men were quickly rounded up and, after this, there were fires in this district but no other "Swing" activities.

The Thatcham incident, that touched off the main body of rioting in Berkshire, began on 15 November as a simple issue of higher wages and work for the unemployed. This bears out the opinion of the Deputy Lieutenant of the county who, writing to the Home Office a week later, attributed the Berkshire riots to "the success of a revolt in favour of wages in other counties";[5] while the churchwardens and overseers of the parish, in sending their observations to the Poor Law Commissioners in 1832, saw the underlying causes of this local, initiating outbreak as "the example of the Kentish labourers, and the excitement of the labourers' minds caused by reading certain violent publications in beer shops".[6] It may be, too, that a local tradition of labour militancy played a part; for, thirty years before, there had been a three-days' wages dispute of the Thatcham labourers that led to riots around Newbury and spread its influence deep into the Hampshire countryside.[7]

The opening stages of the disturbances of 1830 are thus described in the *Reading Mercury*:

> On Monday last [15 November] the labourers of Thatcham parish began to assemble at an early hour, for the purpose of inducing their employers to raise their wages. A sufficient number of them gathered together, they marched off (preceded by one of their company blowing a horn) to visit each of the farms, for the purpose of compelling the labourers to unite with them. By this means their numbers increased, and at noon they amounted to two or three hundred. They then marched into the churchyard and, the select vestry being convened, presented to the gentlemen assembled a verbal request that they might be provided with work, and have their wages advanced. To the former of these requests a favourable answer was returned, but no hope was held out of an improvement in the latter. Throughout the whole of these proceedings the men were quite peaceable, excepting forcing some who felt no inclination to join them.[8]

At this point the press reports become a little confused. The *Mercury*, in one issue (the one from which we have just quoted) relates how the Thatcham men reassembled on the Tuesday (the 16th) and "during that day, Wednesday and Thursday, destroyed the machines of the farmers and gentlemen (without respect of persons) at Bucklebury, Bradfield, Stanford Dingley and Beenham"; while a later report has it that the Thatcham labourers reassembled "on Wednesday (i.e. the 17th) and commenced destroying the threshing machines in Bucklebury and surrounding parishes".[9] Neither account is strictly accurate, though the second is likely to be more so than the first.

It appears, in fact, from the Treasury Solicitor's brief relating to the whole affair, that a two-days' lull followed the wages demonstration on the Monday; and that it was only on the night of Wednesday, 17 November, that the movement initiated by the villagers of Thatcham was taken over, and transformed in the process, by the labourers of Bradfield, Bucklebury and Stanford Dingley. They marched from farm to farm, demanding higher wages and "pressing" supporters, and proceeded to destroy machines at Beenham and other villages nearby. According to a Bradfield farmer, who received a visit "between one and two o'clock Wednesday night the 17th Nov^{r}", the labourers demanded food and drink and wages of 2s. a day, and one told him that "if I would not come to their terms they would have blood for supper". He had already taken the precaution to destroy his threshing machine; so, having accepted his money and removed some hammers and a broad axe from his workshop, they left him and went on, presumably, to Beenham. For here the Treasury Solicitor's notes are quite specific and set out in full detail the time-table of the events that followed. First to Beenham, where three threshing machines were destroyed on three separate farms at 7, 9 and 10 o'clock. The same night, they broke a machine at Aldermaston at eleven and stole a side of beef at Woolhampton at midnight. They returned to Aldermaston the next morning and, between ten and two, visited five farms, collected money and destroyed machines. The notes continue: "They went through all the adjoining parishes levying contributions from 2/6 to a sovereign, destroying every machine in the circuit & making the labourers leave their masters' horses at plough"; and, mustering their forces that afternoon in Aldermaston Park, they boasted of having destroyed 33 machines in as many hours.[10]

They continued their advance through Wasing, Shalford and Brimpton. At Colthrop, near Thatcham, they destroyed the machinery in a paper mill; but that afternoon at Brimpton Common they met their match in the shape of a resolute magistrate, the Rev. E. Cove, vicar of Brimpton, who had collected a large body of tradesmen and constables to meet them. The Riot Act was read and a battle ensued,

TO THE

Labouring Classes

THE Gentlemen, Yeomanry, Farmers, and others, having made known to you their intention of increasing your Wages to a satisfactory extent; and it having been resolved that Threshing Machines shall not be again used; it is referred to your good Sense that it will be most beneficial to your own permanent Interests to return to your usual honest occupations, and to withdraw yourselves from practices which tend to destroy the Property from whence the very means of your additional Wages are to be supplied.

Hungerford, 22nd November, 1830.

EMBERLIN AND HAROLD, PRINTERS, BOOKSELLERS, DRUGGISTS, &c. STAMP-OFFICE, MARLBOROUGH.

Notice issued by Berkshire magistrates, November 1830

at the end of which eleven rioters were arrested and taken to Reading jail.[11] It was the last disturbance in that district.

The next day, the unemployed of Speen, near Newbury, demanded a rise in wages and went from farm to farm to organise support. The select vestry met that afternoon and agreed to raise wages from 9s. to 10s. a week for both married and unmarried men, and to pay the price of a gallon loaf for each child over the second. The terms were accepted by the labourers, "whose conduct [ran a report] was almost without exception marked by forbearance and civility".

A more violent wave of rioting began, eight miles westwards, at Hungerford on the Wiltshire border on 22 November. The Hungerford men went round the neighbouring farms, destroying machines at Welford, Avington, Boxford, Chieveley and other places. Returning to Hungerford, they found their neighbours of Kintbury, a large village on the road to Newbury, in possession of the streets. The Kintbury outbreak had started the day before with an attack on the "Cage", or Blind House, to release a beggar who had been committed for abusing a magistrate who had refused him relief. The labourers had then proceeded, that evening and the next morning, to break machines and levy money at Kintbury and the neighbouring villages of Inkpen, Hampstead Marshall and West Woodhay. They went on to Hungerford, where they destroyed all the machinery and wrought iron at Richard Gibbons' iron foundry, "destroying to about the value of £260".[12] Faced with this double menace, the Hungerford justices invited both parties to appoint five delegates to meet them and discuss their grievances at the Town Hall. The Hungerford men asked for a 12s. weekly wage, a reduction in house rents and the destruction of all machines; and dispersed quietly when the first of the points was conceded and some promises were made with regard to the third.

The Kintbury delegates, however, were made of considerably tougher mettle. Unlike their Hungerford colleagues, they had come to the meeting armed with hammers and bludgeons and refused to be bought off with fair words or half measures. Their principal spokesman, William Oakley, a wheelwright, now addressed the startled magistrates as follows:

> You have not such damned flats to deal with as you had before. We will have 2s. a day till Ladyday and half a crown afterwards for labourers, and 3s. 6d. for tradesmen, and as we are here, we will have £5 before we go out of the place or be damned if we don't smash it. You and the gentlemen have been living upon all the good things for the last ten years. We have suffered enough, and now is our time, and we will now have it. You only speak to us now because you are afraid and intimidated.

And they departed with £5 in their pockets.[13]

But this was not the end of the affair. Other villages, whose inhabitants who had no doubt heard of the outcome of the Hungerford confrontation, sent a deputation that night to the Kintbury labourers to invite them to join in a combined operation. So the next day the riots continued at West Woodhay, Inkpen, Enborne, Wickfield and at Lord Craven's residence, Hampstead Lodge. There was even the threat of a great march on Newbury. By this time, the Kintbury men had appointed a treasurer, Francis Norris, a bricklayer (most of their leaders were tradesmen), who, at the time of his arrest, was found in possession of £100 in contributions. Lord Craven was made to pay £10, others paid £3 or £5; but the usual fee demanded after the smashing of a threshing machine was 40s. When Richard Harben's farm was attacked at Wickfield on 23 November, his bailiff was told "it was their congregation rules to have £2 a machine". Yet there were exceptions made. At Kintbury, when Joseph Randall refused to pay more than half the price that had been asked for, "Captain" Winterbourne, the rioters' leader, accepted it with the words, "he will take half price here because he has stood like a man". And a Kintbury manufacturer, William Squire, saved his machinery from destruction by consenting to pay the rioters 40s. in silver and four 10s. notes for beer at the Lion and Ball public house.[14]

The Kintbury men were rounded up the next day, large numbers were arrested, and their remarkable exploits ended as abruptly as they had started; but not before their example had, at Ramsbury and elsewhere, been carried across the Wiltshire border.* But, meanwhile, in Berkshire, a new focus of disturbance had appeared at Yattendon, only a few miles north of Thatcham, where the riots had started. The villagers assembled in the churchyard at daybreak on 22 November and went round the parishes of Yattendon, Frilsham and Hampstead Norris, "pressing the labourers at work and compelling the farmers to agree to higher wages". At Burnt Hill Common they stopped to drink beer—"40 quarts at each of the two public houses in the parish" —and joined forces with a party from Ashampstead. This combined force now went round the cottages and farms of Ashampstead, Aldworth and Streatley, collecting hammers, demanding higher wages, breaking machines and levying contributions. "The party were preceded by a horn, the rear was kept up by whippers-in as at a hunt"; and we learn that the standard fee for breaking a threshing machine was 5s., a modest sum indeed when compared with the Kintbury men's £2. At Streatley, some went home while others went on to break further machines at Basildon. But, at this point, they were so reduced in numbers that one farmer, when asked for beer-money, refused to give more than 2s. 6d. as "he said they had not half a mob". Soon after, they were surprised by a troop of soldiers sent from Reading, who took eleven prisoners and dispersed the remainder.[15]

Early that morning, riots broke out north of Hungerford in a chain of villages stretching north-east from Newbury into the Berkshire Downs. A threshing machine was broken at Lambourn; and from there the movement spread south to Eastbury and East Garston, where money was collected and several machines were destroyed. Once more, the price demanded by the rioters, no doubt in imitation of

* See p. 123 above.

those of Kintbury, was 40s. a machine. At East Garston, Thomas Palmer recognised Henry Mackrell, a Lambourn hurdle-maker, among those who came to his farm. "Hallo, Harry," he said (according to his deposition), "what beest thee come for, what beest thee want?" He was told: "To break the machine all to pieces & have two sovereigns—the same as he had had in other places; or otherwise he would pull down the buildings." At Eastbury there was a fight with the special constables, always a target of the labourers' hostility. Ten machines in all were broken in the valley; and foraging parties went as far as Boxford, four miles from Newbury, and over the Downs to the hamlet of Fawley.[16]

Meanwhile, machine-breaking had broken out east of Wallingford in a group of Oxfordshire villages; and it is possible that it was from this quarter that the immediate impetus came for the next phase of rioting in Berkshire, in the Vale of the White Horse and along the Upper Thames. It began at Hagbourne, near Wallingford, on 22 November, as a wages strike which compelled farmers to consent to raise weekly wages from 9s. to 12s. and to pay their labourers 2s. a day for the two days lost from work. At Aston Tirrold, on the 23rd, labourers paraded to cries of "We want more wages. We want 12s. a week and we will have them". A threshing machine was broken at Aston Upthorpe, but it was an isolated act and one condemned by the rioters' leader. Here, at least, it was wages and not machines that appear to have been the sole issue at stake.[17]

The last phase of the Berkshire riots took place on 24 November in a number of villages spread along the Vale from Wantage towards the Wiltshire and Gloucestershire borders. Two of these disturbances were minor affairs. At Balking, between Wantage and Faringdon, rioters dispersed when given bread and cheese; at Stanford, there was a wages riot and talk of breaking threshing machines; but it came to little beyond a farmers' promise to raise wages from 8s. to 10s. a week. At Wantage rioting took a more serious turn. A magistrate, in a letter to the Home Office, related how "about an hundred of the worst description of labourers from Wantage sallied forth to destroy any thrashing machines they might find in the townships of E. Challow and the parishes of Childrey and Sparsholt". They were dispersed by a large force of yeomanry and "specials"; but, the same afternoon, "a large party of the same fellows" broke a number of threshing and haymaking machines at an iron founder's in the town. Eight men were arrested and taken, two days later, to Abingdon to be committed to the Bridewell. But here a large election crowd had gathered to hear the results of a local mayoral contest. "The party spirit [runs a report] was tremendous on both sides"; and there were shouts of "No prison, they are only machine breakers". So the Wantage men were promptly released from their captors, made themselves scarce, and never appeared for trial.[38]

In Oxfordshire, rioting started at Crowmarsh and Benson (or Bensington), across the Berkshire border from Wallingford, on 21 November and quickly spread to a number of villages nearby. As an immediate prelude to the outbreak, a number of "Swing" letters were received by farmers in the neighbourhood of Henley-on-Thames, but nobody seemed to know by whom. "All persons talk of them," wrote a Home Office informant, "yet I cannot obtain or see any. When first received they are shown, afterwards they pass from hand to hand and cannot be found."[19] The underlying cause of rioting, according to this correspondent, was low wages: 7s. a week (he wrote) "even before harvest"; and, as in Berkshire, the most frequently voiced demands were for higher wages—either of 2s. or 2s. 3d. a day —and the destruction of agricultural machinery. Yet the smallholders' hostility to enclosure appears also to have played a part. Between Charlton and Islip on Otmoor there had been violent enclosure riots at the end of August and the beginning of September, when "large bodies of men in disguise" recruited from "the lower classes in the adjoining parishes" had torn down fences, hedgerows and buildings erected by Lord Abingdon and other landlords. The Oxfordshire Yeomanry Cavalry had been brought in and secured a large number of prisoners, but more than 40 of them had been released by a rioting crowd at St. Giles's Fair at Oxford as they were being escorted to the Castle. The affair had caused a great commotion in the county: an anonymous letter-writer, signing himself "Philo Fayette", had even compared the "liberties" of Otmoor with those proclaimed on the Paris barricades in July of the same year.[20]

The connection between enclosure and machine-breaking in the Oxford riots is not particularly clear, but that some such link existed is suggested by the fact that the first of the rioters' victims, Thomas Newton, a large farmer of Crowmarsh, was known to be about to make a further attempt—the last of many—to obtain an Enclosure Act for the neighbouring parish of Benson; and it was argued by defence counsel when the matter came to court that the large crowd assembled in the churchyard that morning (it was Sunday, 21 November) had gathered "not with the premeditated purpose of machine-breaking, but on account of Mr. Newton being about to give notice of applying to Parliament for an Act to enclose the parish of Benson".[21]

However that may be, the issue appears to have been lost sight of as the riots, no doubt further stimulated by the example of the Berkshire labourers, developed and spread to other parishes. According to Newton's own account:

> His premises [at Crowmarsh] were attacked first yesterday morning Sunday about 2 o'clock by about 30 men who said they had been sent to his house to destroy his threshing machine. His men who were watching did not know them as they had disguised their faces, but they thought they knew their voices. They however after a time got them to go away; but after they had got a few hundred yards they sounded a horn. About eleven in the day, a large mob of upwards of 200 persons returned to the premises, broke open the barn, and entirely destroyed the machine.

"From thence," he continued, "they went to several of the adjoining villages—at Benson, Ewelme, Berrick, Warborough & Shillingford, and did similar acts, and extorted money from the farmers." However, we probably get a more accurate picture from a report issued after the event by the local magistrates: from this it appears that machine-breaking spread from Crowmarsh, Ewelme and Rofford on the 21st to Burcot, near Dorchester, on the 22nd and 23rd; to Little Milton on the 23rd; to Barton on the 24th; and to Lord Granville Somerset's and other properties at Heythrop on the 26th. At Burcot, according to a witness, "there was huzzaing, blowing of horns, and shouting", and a rioter observed, "there had been fires and would be more". At Heythrop, 70 or 80 men marched into the servants' hall, demanded beer and money, broke into the barns and smashed machines of every sort, and uttered the traditional, ferocious threat: "Bread or Blood." Their leader, Thomas Hollis, a ploughman whom his followers called "The King", later claimed that they had been incited by "a gentleman groom" to smash machines, demand a wage of 2s. 3d. a day, and generally to assert their "rights".[22]

After a lull there were further scattered riots in the county, but without forming part of any consistent or continuous pattern. On 29 November, a machine was broken at Faulkner's farm at Broadwell, south of Burford and close to the Gloucester border. It was an isolated incident and appears to have had no sequel.[23]

The same day, a more remarkable series of events began at Banbury, in north Oxfordshire and far removed from the other centres of disturbance. It seems that, in this instance, the initiative to destroy machines came from the town, for it was here that crowds formed and marched out to break machines in the neighbouring villages. The affair began, according to a justice's report, with the burning of an unpopular citizen (whose identity we are not told) in effigy. There was a threat to burn a local factory; and, that night, a party went out to Neithrop and destroyed a threshing machine, the property of Joseph Paine. The next day, a machine was burned at John Wilson's farm at Bodicote; and two further machines were burned at Tadmarton on 1 December.

> About nine o'clock in the evening of that day [runs a Treasury Solicitor's brief] a mob of persons collected, it is believed, principally in Banbury, arrived at his (the prosecutor's) premises. They brought with them a hay-making machine which they had taken from the same hamlet named Kilby. They went by a back road to the farm yard of a Mr. Austin of the same village, & stole from thence a parcel of straw; a tinder box and matches they brought with them. With these means they set fire to both machines.

A significant feature of this affair was the prominent role played in it by the small tradesmen and craftsmen of the town: among twenty persons later brought to trial there were two weavers, a wool sorter, a canal builder, a basket maker, a coal dealer, a sawyer, a millwright, a shoemaker, and a chimney sweep, several of whom were residents of Banbury. Philip Green, the chimney sweep and a one-time sailor, was described, moreover, as "a great admirer of Cobbett, whose productions he is in the habit of quoting in the public houses he frequents". The case is suggestive, too, of some deeper animosity between town and countryside, prompted perhaps by political divisions between farmers and urban craftsmen; for we find appended to a Banbury magistrate's report on the week's events a cryptic note on "threats from the countryside to rise in large numbers to revenge themselves on the town".[24]

Meanwhile, a more violent set of riots had broken out in Buckinghamshire. Here, as in Berkshire, the first signs of disturbance had come from around the Windsor district. In the second week in November, there were reports of "Swing" letters at Colnbrook and Langley; and, at Marlow and High Wycombe, farmers and paper-makers began to be besieged with letters threatening to destroy their crops and buildings if their machines were not removed. Among the recipients were Lord Carrington, who owned a 4-h.p. threshing machine at Daws Hill Farm, near Wycombe Abbey; Richard Webb, a farmer of Marlow Bottom; and Joseph Biddle of Church Lane, Wycombe. Biddle's letter, dated 11 November, ran: "This is to acquaint you that if your threshing machines are not destroyed by you directly, we shall commence our labours. Signed on behalf of the whole SWING." Some farmers took the hint and began to dismantle their machines; and, in some of the paper mills, the erection of new machinery was suspended. The magistrates in turn were beginning to react; and, at a meeting of clergy, landowners and farmers held at Salt Hill, near Burnham, on 17 November, it was decided to take firm steps "in order to put a stop to the Horrid Attempts of some Diabolical Miscreants to injure Property and produce Confusion in this Country". Moreover, magistrates had a shrewd notion of the quarter from which the expected blow would come; and, on 23 November, the Duke of Buckingham and Chandos, Lord Lieutenant of the county, wrote to Melbourne that, in his view, "the outrages now committing in Berkshire will extend into Buckinghamshire in the south".[25]

But, even with these warnings and anticipations, the form that the initial outbreak took must have come as somewhat of a surprise. For the attack, when it came, was directed only marginally against threshing machines and almost exclusively against the machinery installed in half a dozen paper mills along the three-mile stretch between Loudwater and West (then Chepping) Wycombe. On 24 November came a more specific warning that the paper workers themselves, 300 of whom were said to be unemployed, would march on the mills and destroy the machinery. Two days later, on market day, a great meeting of paper workers took place on the Rye, half a mile out of High Wycombe, to protest against the continued use of machinery; and from there "an immense multitude" (to quote *The Times*) marched into the town, invaded the hall where the justices and householders were assembled, and turned their meeting into a bedlam. The Riot Act was read to no avail, and the presiding magistrate was even persuaded to send the Buckinghamshire Yeomanry Cavalry away in order to appease the crowd. Some rioters collected hammers and began to march on Messrs. Lane's paper mill with the intention of destroying the machinery forthwith. The attempt, however, failed and the operation was postponed until another day.[26]

On 29 November, from 5 o'clock in the morning, paper workers and labourers began to assemble to the sound of a horn on Flackwell Heath, some four miles east of High Wycombe; many were armed with sledge-hammers, sticks and crow-bars. Again the Riot Act was read, but the justices were overwhelmed and the High Sheriff was wounded by a stone. The rioters marched on to High Wycombe through Wooburn and Loudwater, picking up supporters on the way, and at 9 o'clock made their first stop at John and Joseph Lane's paper mill on the far side of the town, on the outskirts of West Wycombe. Two shots were fired and four gallons of vitriol were hurled at the assailants; but they soon broke in and destroyed the machinery, while the vitriol-thrower was ducked in a pond. After this, they went back to the town and levied contributions on the shopkeepers before retracing their steps towards Loudwater, destroying Zachary Alnutt's machinery at Marsh Green and John Hay's machinery a mile beyond. Next to Hay's mill stood Lansdale's farm, and here a threshing machine was smashed. The rioters now halted for refreshment at the Red Lion public house before going on to Loudwater a mile beyond, where they completed their work by breaking paper machines at Richard Plaistow's and Robert Davis's mills. But by now the forces of law and order had been thoroughly alerted; the Buckinghamshire Yeomanry arrived on the scene, supported by a party of red-coated huntsmen, mainly composed of local gentry, who joined in the affray. The rioters by this time were exhausted, while some were the worse for drink; and 45 prisoners were taken and committed; the rest dispersed. The damage done, at first computed by *The Times* at £12,000, was scaled down in a magistrate's report to the more modest figure of £3,265.[27]

A further sequel to the affair was the panic that it caused across the Hertfordshire border at Rickmansworth and Hemel Hempstead. In an urgent message the local justices begged Melbourne to send troops, as, following the High Wycombe example, they were hourly expecting an attack by "incendiaries" or by "above a Thousand Desparadoes" on the paper mills along the "Chesham stream" at Abbot's Langley and Chorley Wood.[28]

There were three other centres of disturbance in the county, but the outbreaks were pitched on an altogether lower key. The first took the form of burning agricultural machinery in the two neighbouring parishes of Waddesdon and Upper Winchenden, a few miles west of Aylesbury. Waddesdon, where the movement started, is described in a Treasury Solicitor's brief as a large parish "for a long time past much burthened with its numerous poor, & the latter have been for some time considered an unruly & a lawless set of people". We are told, too, that the Waddesdon men had for some weeks been stirred by "the diabolical fires & destruction of machinery, etc. perpetrated in other counties" and chose a moment for their outbreak when the Buckinghamshire Yeomanry had been withdrawn from the Aylesbury area and dispatched to meet the danger in the south. It began on the evening of 26 November, when the labourers went to draw their weekly allowances from the overseer at Waddesdon. After which, a party went to Stephen Page's farm at Upper Winchenden and set fire to his threshing machine; and from there they went on to other farms and broke and set fire to a number of drilling and threshing machines and draining ploughs. At one farm a rioter said, "I will have the machine broke for it will do as much work in one day as a Man will do in two". Two of their intended victims, however, saved their machines by treating their attackers to 85 pints of ale.[29]

A few miles south of Waddesdon, a threshing machine was destroyed at Stone on 27 November; two days later, a winnowing machine was broken to pieces at Long Crendon, close to the Oxford border. On 1 December, there was renewed rioting in the south: this time at Iver and Shredding Green, where labourers went round armed with bludgeons and compelled householders to give them food and drink and money. It caused some alarm at Uxbridge and Heston, as magistrates feared that the example might be followed across the Middlesex border.[30] Riots now moved north to the area enclosed by the towns of Bletchley, Wolverton and Newport Pagnell. On 1 December, threshing machines were burned at Little Brickhill and Fenny Stratford; and there was a final round of riots over wages at Stony Stratford on the 3rd, Newport Pagnell on the 4th, and Fenny Stratford on 9 December.[31]

Long before this, however, rioting had spread to the midlands counties of Bedford, Huntingdon and Northampton. Huntingdon, though the furthest removed from the major counties of disturbance, was the first to be affected and, in the space of three days, had a remarkable crop of machine-breaking outbreaks. As with so many counties, there was an opening phase of fires and threatening letters. At Bluntisham, on the Cambridge border, owners of threshing machines were warned to lay them aside as early as 10 October. Reprisals followed and, five weeks later, a corn stack and a barn were fired on a Bluntisham farm where a threshing machine was in use. There was another fire at Somersham, a few miles north, on 21 November. But the machine-breaking riots that followed two days later were on the opposite side of the county. They started at Sawtry and Conington on the 24th and moved southwards, reaching Alconbury Hill on the 25th, and Buckden, Buckworth, Hamerton, Old Weston and the two Stukeleys on the 26th. The same day, a "Swing" letter was received by a parson at Kimbolton, further south towards the Bedford border.[32]

The next morning, rioting broke out again north of Sawtry and spread north to the boundary of Lincoln and west into Northamptonshire. An early victim was a farmer of Morborne whose threshing machine was broken at 5.30 in the morning. Soon after, a machine was destroyed and money was demanded at John Trailwyn's farm at Alwalton, adjoining the Soke of Peterborough. One of the rioters'

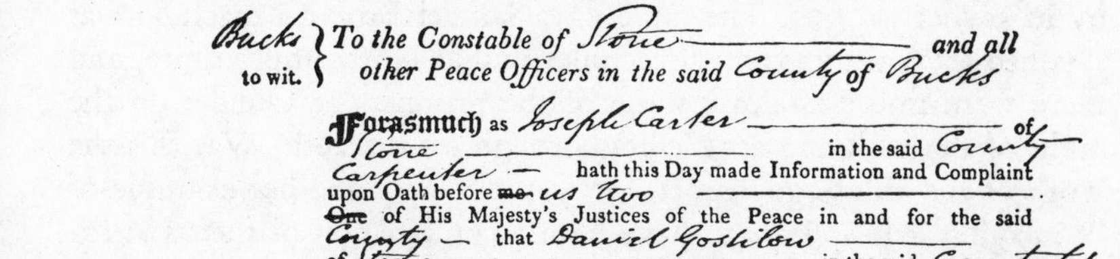

Bucks to wit. } *To the Constable of* Stone *and all other Peace Officers in the said* County *of* Bucks

Forasmuch as Joseph Carter of Stone in the said County Carpenter hath this Day made Information and Complaint upon Oath before ~~me~~ us two ~~One~~ of His Majesty's Justices of the Peace in and for the said County that Daniel Goslibow of Stone in the said County labourer on the 27th Day of November ~~at~~ instant at Stone in the said County together with divers other persons to the number of one hundred and more unlawfully and maliciously did break damage and destroy a certain Machine or Engine called a ~~Winnowing~~ Thrashing Machine

These are, therefore, to command you, in His Majesty's Name, forthwith to apprehend and bring before ~~me~~ us, or some other of His Majesty's Justices of the Peace in and for the said County the Body of the said Daniel Goslibow to answer unto the said Complaint, and to be further dealt withal according to Law. Herein fail not.

Given under ~~my~~ our Hand and Seal, the 28th Day of November in the Year of our Lord One Thousand Eight Hundred and thirty

W. Rickford   R. Ludgate

Warrant, 2.—C.   Sold by SHAW & SONS, 137, Fetter Lane, London.

Warrant for the arrest of Daniel Goslibow of Stone, Bucks.,
27 November, 1830

leaders, Thomas Stapleton, a labourer of Sawtry, is reported to have told the farmer:

> They should go to Haddon and break a machine—also to Yaxley and break another, and then proceed to Norman Cross to refresh themselves. After which, they shd break another at Holme, and that wd finish the week's work: should rest on the Sunday. On the following Monday thre wd be another party, who wd knock down butchers' and bakers' shops.

Whether such a programme was intended or whether such words were spoken it is impossible to verify by any other means. But, if the farmer's testimony is accurate, it is curious that the rioters should, after breaking a machine at Haddon, apparently have taken quite another course. Instead of moving south-east to Yaxley and Norman Cross, they turned west towards Northamptonshire. They stopped at Elton on the border and destroyed James Hayes' machine, later valued by its owner at £90. The same day, Samuel Brown's machine was smashed at Warmington, three miles within Northamptonshire, and there were riots to release some of the prisoners at Oundle on the night of the 28th and at Wellingborough on the 29th. Was this the work of the Huntingdon men, or was it merely another example of "contagion"? It appears to have been a combination of the two; for among the Northamptonshire quarter sessions records of 1830 there is the remnant of a torn-up poster, offering a £20 reward for the recapture of two escaped prisoners—

> Thomas Marriott, of Washingley, Huntingdonshire, Labourer, and William Gass, of Lutton, Northamptonshire, Labourer, (who) escaped this day from the custody of the Peace Officers at Wellingborough, who were conveying them to the gaol at Northampton, under a commitment for feloniously breaking a thrashing machine at Warmington.[33]

The "contagion" from Huntingdon was also felt in Lincolnshire; and the Stamford magistrates wrote to Melbourne expressing their fears that the Huntingdon example might provoke riots in that corner of their county.[34]

In Lincoln, these fears were never realised;* but in Northamptonshire disturbances continued, though not in the district where they had begun. At Finedon, south-east of Kettering, on 30 November, the

* See p. 167 below.

town crier was persuaded to go round the parish, ringing his bell and announcing that "no labourer should go to work next morning for less than 2s. 3d. a day". The same day, some labourers removed William Page's threshing machine "and carried it to a place called Mulso-square, where it was broken to pieces in the presence of a crowd of about 200 persons". A strange feature of the case was that Page himself later admitted having said "that he did not care about his machine being broken as he would not use it again, and would take no proceedings against any persons who would break it". Further incidents were scattered around the county. On 30 November, a hay-making machine was destroyed at King's Sutton: it was the day of the machine-breaking at Bodicote, near Banbury, a few miles across the Oxford border. Three days later, a threshing machine was burned at Upper Boddington, on the borders of Warwickshire; and, on 8 December, rioters broke a machine at Moulton, in the centre of the county.[35]

In Bedfordshire, there were fires, threats to parsons and wages riots, but no machines were broken. On 27 November, the day of a large fire at Wootton Pillinge, six miles from Bedford, the justices were warned by a group of householders "that tumult and riot are likely to take place within the county". They followed soon after but were limited to a couple of parishes widely separated from one another. The first and the most serious was a two-days' wages riot at Stotfold, towards Baldock on the Hertfordshire border. On 1 December, the labourers assembled to demand wages of 2s. 6d. a day, but dispersed when assured that a vestry would consider their claim the next morning. Early that day, the whole village turned out: one man (*The Times* reported) who stole away to work was "cudgelled for disobedience" and brought back by twenty others. The vestry met and accepted two of the labourers' demands: that labourers should be exempt from the payment of all taxes and that an unpopular assistant overseer should be dismissed; but their demand for a 2s. 6d. minimum wage was turned down flat. So the riots continued: there was a threat to burn down F. G. Fordham's corn and seed mill across the Hertford border, and householders refusing to give the labourers bread had their houses broken into; a large fire was lit in a nearby field "in order to raise an alarm of fire", and punitive measures were threatened against tithe-owners and parsons. At this stage, the labourers decided to return to work, while threatening further reprisals if at its meeting two days later the vestry refused them satisfaction. In consequence, the justices had time to rally support from both sides of the border: in fact, it was a Hertfordshire magistrate, the Rev. John Lafont, Rector of Hinxworth, who claimed to have played the largest part in their repression.[36]

The movement now shifted, briefly, to the other side of the county —to Flitwick, a village close to Woburn and opposite that corner of Buckinghamshire that had wages riots in the first days of December. The Flitwick riot began early on the morning of 6 December and was quickly over. It appears that thirty or forty men armed with sticks and bludgeons went round the parish, asking the farmers for "more money" and threatening to drag the labourers who refused to join them "thru' the pond". The rioters were quickly rounded up; and four of them—all men of excellent character and one a special constable recently enrolled—were later brought to trial.[37]

Meanwhile, in Hertfordshire, there were more alarms and half a dozen fires; but there were no riots or disturbances. Yet the threat was real enough and the Hinxworth magistrate, who had ridden across the border to lend a hand at Stotfold, wrote to Melbourne that, had that punitive action not been taken when it was, "seven or eight populous parishes would have joined during Sunday & Monday morning". On 3 December, an "itinerant Irishman", presumed to be a dangerous character, was arrested at Bishop's Stortford; and, from Stortford, too, went out a printed notice that "SPIES and INFORMERS are travelling about from place to place, endeavouring to induce others to commit disorderly acts, in order to obtain rewards by giving information against them. The writer of this is anxious to warn his Fellow Countrymen against the acts of such infamous wretches, who seek to enrich themselves with the price of other men's blood. BEWARE OF STRANGERS!"[38]

So, in one way or another, Hertfordshire, like Middlesex, remained relatively unscathed.

NOTES TO CHAPTER 7

1. *The Times*, 15, 22 November 1830.
2. H.O. 52/6 (letter of 28 November 1830, and printed handbill).
3. Norman Gash, *The Rural Unrest in England in 1830 with Special Reference to Berkshire* (Unpub. B.Litt. thesis, Univ. of Oxford, 1934), pp. 56–8. We are indebted to Mr. Gash for much that follows in our account of Berkshire.
4. H.O. 52/6 (letter of 28 November 1830, and enclosure).
5. H.O. 52/6 (letter of 22 November 1830).
6. Cited by Gash, *op. cit.*, p. 42.
7. *Reading Mercury*, 16 June 1800; cit. by A. S. Humphreys, *Bucklebury. A Berkshire Parish: the Home of Bolingbroke, 1701–1715* (1932), pp. 377–8.

8. *Reading Mercury*, 22 November 1830; cit. by Humphreys, *op. cit.*, pp. 378–9.
9. *Ibid.*, pp. 378–9.
10. T.S. 11/849.
11. *The Times*, 23 November 1830; *Reading Mercury*, 6 December 1830; Gash, *op. cit.*, p. 46.
12. T.S. 11/849.
13. Gash, *op. cit.*, pp. 47–9, 61–3; H.O. 52/6 (letter of 28 November 1830).
14. T.S. 11/849.
15. *Ibid.*
16. T.S. 11/849; Gash, *op. cit.*, pp. 50–1.
17. Gash, *op. cit.*, pp. 51–2.
18. H.O. 52/6 (letter of 26 November 1830); *The Times*, 30 November 1830; Gash, *op. cit.*, pp. 52–3.
19. H.O. 52/9 (letter of 26 November 1830).
20. H.O. 52/9 (letters of 3, 6, 7, 8, 14 September, 19 October 1830); *Jackson's Oxford Journal*, 5 March 1831.
21. *Jackson's Oxford Journal*, 8 January 1831. See also Hammonds, II, p. 70.
22. H.O. 52/9 (letter of 28 October 1830); *Jackson's Oxford Journal*, 8 January, 5 March 1831.
23. *Jackson's Oxford Journal*, 8 January 1831.
24. *Jackson's Oxford Journal*, 5 March 1831; H.O. 52/9 (letters of 29 November, 1, 12 December 1830); T.S. 11/1031. See also Pamela Horn, Banbury and the Riots of 1830 (*Cake and Cockhorse*, Autumn 1967, pp. 176–9).
25. *The Times*, 15, 22 November 1830; H.O. 52/6 (letter of 23 November 1830, and printed poster); H.O. 52/7 (Hunts., letter of 16 November 1830).
26. *The Times*, 29 November 1830.
27. *The Times*, 1, 8 December 1830; H.O. 52/6 (letter of 30 November 1830). Actually, the millowners received only £719 12s. in damages (see p. 227 below).
28. H.O. 52/7 (letter of 29 November 1830); H.O. 40/25, fos. 591–4.
29. T.S. 11/865.
30. *The Times*, 6 December 1830; H.O. 40/27, fos. 595–8; H.O. 52/8 (letters of 1, 2 December 1830).
31. *The Times*, 13 December 1830; H.O. 40/27, fos. 1–2.
32. H.O. 52/7 (letters of 16, 26 November 1830); *The Times*, 17 November, 1 December 1830.
33. *Cambridge Chronicle*, 18 March 1831; *Northampton Mercury*, 5 March 1831; *The Times*, 1 December 1830, 13 March 1831; Huntingdon R.O., Q.S. records, 1830; Northants. R.O., Q.S. records: letters, 1830 (misc.).
34. H.O. 52/8 (letter of 26 November 1830).
35. *Northampton Mercury*, 8 January, 19 February 1831; *The Times*, 3 March 1831; H.O. 52/9 (letters of 28–9 November 1830).
36. H.O. 52/6 (letter of 25 November 1830); *The Times*, 6 December 1830; Beds. R.O., Q.S. records, 1830 (misc.).
37. Beds. R.O., QSM 30 (transcript), p. 185; QSR 502 (transcript); *Cambridge Chronicle*, 14 January 1831.
38. H.O. 52/7 (letters of 27 November, 3 December 1830, and printed handbill).

8

IN EAST ANGLIA AND THE NORTH

In East Anglia, the disturbances had their own distinctive pattern. In these counties, unlike Kent, there had been a recent history of opposition to threshing machines; and, in this sense, there was a certain continuity between the events of 1830 and those of 1816 and 1822.[1] Moreover, the long-standing antagonism of farmers to tithe was strongly reflected in the East Anglian movement, particularly in south-east Norfolk and East Suffolk, where tithe-and-wages riots probably eclipsed all other forms of protest. And, side by side with this concern for tithe, went the association of labourers and farmers which, in these two counties, was closer and in greater evidence than in any other area of disturbance. In fact, the farmers' hostility to parsons—and less frequently to landlords—and their consequent collusion with the labourers were the subject of repeated comment by observers. From Boxford, Colonel Brotherton noted in December: "The collusion between farmers and labourers [in Suffolk] appears more & more evident. We have proof of it—amounting almost to a case of conspiracy"; and, from Long Melford, he remarked on the "evidence of the farmers' use of the labourers' movement to promote their own ends by reducing tithes".[2]

Lord Suffield, for his part, observed that "they [the farmers and yeomanry] have in some instances been supposed to incite & encourage the late outrageous proceedings, to have suggested the outcry against Tithes & Rents"; and from East Suffolk it was reported that "the farmer is more the complainant than the labourer, tho' each are suffering".[3]

In all three East Anglian counties, arson played a certain role as a curtain-raiser to disturbance, and the riots themselves were interspersed with occasional incendiary outbreaks; but generally, as in Hampshire and Wiltshire, they marked the tail-end rather than the full flood of the movement, while the labourers were described as being "very hostile to incendiaries".

In Norfolk, stacks were fired at Melton Constable, a later centre of disturbance, on 10 November; three days before, a farm at North Cove, near Beccles in East Suffolk, suffered fire-damage to an amount of nearly £1,000; and the Essex riots were preceded by a fire at Rayleigh, near Southend, on 5 November. Yet it is perhaps more significant that between 10 December, when the disturbances were all but over, and mid-January there were at least three fires in Essex, four in Suffolk and eight in Norfolk.[4]

The movement started in the north-eastern corner of Norfolk, in an area more remote than any other from all previous centres of disturbance. On 19 November, seventy men from neighbouring parishes marched in to North Walsham, where the justices were meeting, and demanded that all threshing machines in the district should be destroyed or laid aside; and they assured them that the county as a whole would follow their example. Having delivered this ultimatum, they retired to a beer-house for refreshment and then "marched back in the same order in which they came—the magistrates not thinking it advisable to interfere with them".[5] The first machine was broken by the labourers that night at Paston, a few miles from North Walsham; and from there machine-breaking spread west to Briston, Holt, Melton Constable and Hindolveston on 22 November; back to the north-eastern coastal area at Walcot, North Walsham, Honing and Southrepps between the 22nd and 25th; and south to Themelthorpe on the 23rd and to Foulsham, Field Dalling, Cawston and Whitwell on the 24th and 25th. The labourers armed themselves everywhere with sledge-hammers and bludgeons and set about their work as though they expected to meet with little opposition; in fact, the farmers were generally submissive and showed little inclination to resist. At Honing, a rioter, when asked what he was up to, said simply: "we are not going to do any harm to any one, we are only breaking a threshing machine"; and, at Cawston, where one farmer refused to break his own machine, another, when informed of the rioters' intentions, "told his men to take the machine to pieces and bury it if they thought it was the cause of distress".[6]

Yet there were some departures from this pattern. On 25 November, threats were made to "pull down" the workhouse at Smallbrugh;[7] and the first wages-and-tithe riot began at Edingthorpe, three miles from North Walsham, on the 22nd. Both labourers and farmers—including some of the largest tithe-payers in the parish—were involved. That evening, as the rector, the Rev. Richard Adams, later recollected, "a vast number of people went past my gateway, some halloing & laughing, and making other noises". Two days later, the labourers returned "and asked me an advance of wages, and I said I would give them 2s.

per day from Michaelmas to Lady, and 1s. 6d. per day from Lady to Michaelmas—1s. 6d. per coomb for threshing wheat, 1s. for barley, and 9d. for pease and oats, at which they were very well satisfied". But this was only one side of the affair; for on the morning of the 23rd, the day after the labourers' first demonstration, the following encounter (as related by the rector) took place between himself and the farmers:

> At ten o'clock, Bush came into my kitchen while I was finishing my breakfast; . . . he said he came for a reduction of tithes. I replied, it appears very extraordinary that you should now require a reduction, for when you and Turner came through my yard last Sunday you told me you were satisfied. I saw all the farmers together afterwards. Bareham [the farmers' leader] asked if I would make a reduction of tithe, to which I replied, as I have been taking up your tithe it can be no concern of yours; and Bareham then said, he would not cast his tithe again or pay it. I said, if it were reasonable and right, and the neighbourhood would reduce their tithe, I would do so. Abusive language was used after this observation; Boreham said they would have the tithe, but that I should have nothing at all if they did not please.[8]

This first phase of rioting in the north-eastern coastal area was over by 26 November; and, the next day, Colonel John Wodehouse, chairman of the Bench at North Walsham, reported to Lord Melbourne that "tranquillity" had been restored and thirty prisoners had been taken, some by mounted "specials" armed with cutlasses.[9] But far from showing undue severity and a lack of sympathy for the labourers, these and the other Norfolk justices displayed a degree of indulgence that was later to bring them a severe reprimand from Lord Melbourne.* The "Public Notice" issued by the North Walsham magistrates on 24 November is so remarkable that we reproduce it here in full:

> The *Magistrates* in the Hundreds of *Tunstead* and *Happing*, in the County of Norfolk, having taken into consideration the disturbed state of the said Hundreds and the Country in general, wish to make it publicly known that *it is their opinion* that such disturbances principally arise from the use of Threshing Machines, and to the insufficient Wages of the Labourers. The Magistrates therefore beg

* See p. 235 below.

> to *recommend* to the Owners and Occupiers of Land in these Hundreds to *discontinue the use of Threshing Machines, and to increase the Wages of Labour* to Ten Shillings a week for able bodied men, and that when task work is preferred, that it should be put out at such a rate as to enable an industrious man to earn Two Shillings per day.
>
> The Magistrates are determined to enforce the Laws against all tumultuous Rioters and Incendiaries, and they look for support to all the respectable and well disposed part of the Community; at the same time they feel a full Conviction that *no severe measures will be necessary*, if the proprietors of Land will give proper employment to the Poor on their own Occupations, and encourage their Tenants to do the same.[10]

Nor was this an isolated expression of opinion; for, nine days later, we find the combined committee of magistrates, set up at Norwich "for the purpose of concerting Measures for the Preservation of the Peace in the County of Norfolk", issuing an address that firmly recommended "the general disuse of THRESHING MACHINES as a friendly concession on the part of the Proprietors to public opinion, and as a proof of their anxiety to remove as far as possible every pretext for the violation of the laws". This attitude of the magistrates certainly did not escape comment; and, already on 25 November, an anonymous observer, writing to Lord Melbourne from Aylsham (in the heart of the disturbed area), commented shrewdly on the causes and course of the disturbances, and on the half-hearted efforts of farmers and magistrates to suppress them: the "liberal gentry", he wrote, were "inclined to stress the sufferings of the poor" and were therefore "weak in putting down disturbance and (tend) to remain inactive".[11]

Machine-breaking had, meanwhile, moved south towards Norwich. Threshing machines were destroyed at Taverham and Colton, west of Norwich, on 27 November. At Colton, it was alleged that John Kay, the farmer concerned, had given "the mob leave to break his machine, and not to make more noise than they could help, as Mrs. Kay was very unwell"; but this he denied.[12] At Taverham, an attack was also made on Robert Hawkes & Co.'s paper mill, where machinery was destroyed to the value of nearly £500; another paper mill was attacked and further machinery was destroyed at Lyng, five miles to the west. Two days later, there was a similar outbreak east of Norwich. Sawyers assembled on St. Catherine's Plain, on the city's outskirts, to discuss their wages; they moved on to the Gray Hills and destroyed

PUBLIC
NOTICE.

THE *Magistrates* in the Hundreds of *Tunstead* and *Happing*, in the County of Norfolk, having taken into consideration the disturbed state of the said Hundreds and the Country in general, wish to make it publicly known that *it is their opinion* that such disturbances principally arise from the use of Threshing Machines, and to the insufficient Wages of the Labourers. The Magistrates therefore beg to *recommend* to the Owners and Occupiers of Land in these Hundreds, to *discontinue the use of Threshing Machines, and to increase the Wages of Labour* to Ten Shillings a week for able bodied men, and that when task work is preferred, that it should be put out at such a rate as to enable an industrious man to earn Two Shillings per day.

The Magistrates are determined to enforce the Laws against all tumultuous Rioters and Incendiaries, and they look for support to all the respectable and well disposed part of the Community; at the same time they feel a full Conviction, that *no severe measures will be necessary*, if the proprietors of Land will give proper employment to the Poor on their own Occupations, and encourage their Tenants to do the same.

SIGNED,

JOHN WODEHOUSE.
W. R. ROUS.
J. PETRE.
GEORGE CUBITT.
WILLIAM GUNN.
W. F. WILKINSON.
BENJAMIN CUBITT.
H. ATKINSON.

North Walsham,
***24th November* 1830.**

J. PLUMBLY, PRINTER, NORTH WALSHAM.

Notice issued by Norfolk magistrates, November 1830

machinery at Robert Calver's saw-mill at Catton; the mill itself was set alight. A week later, Norwich itself was attacked. On 6 December, silk weavers rioted at Henry & Edward Willett's bombasine (silk) manufactory in St. Martin's parish and cut the silk in twenty-six looms, causing damage on which £262 9s. 4d. was later paid as compensation to the owners. Was this a case of a weaver-labourer combination, as the labourers and paper-workers had combined at High Wycombe in Buckinghamshire a week before? It seems unlikely, as the Norwich weavers had already rioted for higher wages in January 1830. Moreover, we have the evidence of Jasper Howes Tipple, a textile manufacturer employing 600–700 workers at Wymondham, who, writing to Lord Melbourne on 2 December, assured him that 6,000 local weavers were "ready to repulse the agricultural labourers if they entered the town".[13]

However that may be, industrial machine-breaking lay, at most, on the fringe of the Norfolk labourers' riots. More typical was the outbreak of agricultural machine-breaking and rioting over tithes that took place on 29–30 November in a score of towns and villages in the areas south and west of Norwich and along the northern coastline. There were wages riots and attacks on threshing machines at Binham, Docking, Southrepps, Roughton, Burnham Overy and Burnham Thorpe in the north; and at Sparham, Thurgarton, Weston and Whinburgh to the west and north-west of Norwich. At Burnham Overy, William Brett's threshing machine was broken to shouts of "Break it! don't let him take it away, it keeps an honest man from getting work." At East Tuddenham, two threshing machines were broken: the rioters included a woman, Jane Taylor, who was later brought to trial; and they claimed (so it was reported) that "they had a paper from the magistrates authorising them to break machines". At Roughton, Lee Amis, a small farmer occupying eight-to-ten acres of land, accompanied the labourers to another farmer's to demand a rise in wages; and he was said to have urged them on by saying, "they were fools to let him escape; now was the time to stand up for their rights—viz. one stone of meal a day for each".[14]

The tithe-and-wages riots were centred mainly south and south-east of Norwich, reaching towards the East Suffolk border: the exception was Saxlingham in the North Walsham district, where a nascent riot was nipped in the bud by the arrival of troops.[15] There were outbreaks at Forncett, Stoke Holy Cross, Moulton and Long Stratton on the 29th; and at Toft and Haddiscoe on 30 November. These were followed, in turn, by similar disturbances at Banham on 2 December, at Burgh and Bressingham on the 3rd, at Attleborough between the 4th and 5th, and at Surlingham soon after. The pattern was generally the same: a demand for higher wages by the labourers; acceptance by the farmers made conditional on a reduction of tithes; and then (at the explicit or implicit instigation of the farmers) "mobbing" of the tithe-owner (usually a parson) by the labourers, with the farmers standing by. At Stoke Holy Cross, the farmers agreed to raise wages by one-fifth, provided tithes and rents were reduced in proportion—viz. tithes by a quarter and rents by one-sixth. This package-deal was rejected by Sir Robert Harvey, the largest landowner and tithe-impropriator of the district; but, after the farmers had refused to enrol as "specials" and the labourers had launched a threatening demonstration, he agreed to submit the dispute to arbitration—"which" (wrote *The Times*) "satisfied the labourers". At Haddiscoe, the Rev. Thomas Elliston was besieged in the Crown Inn, where he had gone to receive his tithes, by "an assembly of persons" carrying a red flag and blowing a horn, who said "that they wanted a reduction of the tithe, so that their masters might pay them more wages". He was asked to reduce his tithes by one-third; and when he refused he was kept locked in a room, and only released when he made a substantial concession. At Burgh, there was a clear case of farmer-labourer collusion. When the labourers visited the rector, the Rev. W. Boycatt, they said to him (to quote his own words) that "they were too low paid, that the farmers told them they were so oppressed by me they could not pay them and that I must reduce my tithe". Meanwhile, he was assured by the farmers that whatever he refunded in tithe would be divided among the labourers in wages.

In some of these encounters, issues other than tithes and wages were raised by the rioting labourers. At Forncett, when the minister, the Rev. Mr. Jack, eluded his assailants, they made for the poor-house which they partly "pulled down". The Attleborough affair was more complex and protracted. In the course of three-days' rioting, the labourers marched on the workhouse and forced the governor to give them bread and cheese; destroyed four drills and a chaff-cutting machine at neighbouring farms; demanded money and drinks with menaces from householders and passers-by; and compelled the vestry to assemble to discuss their claims for a 2s. daily wage and the reduction by one-third of the rector's tithe. According to one account of the affair, the rector was "dragged thru' the pond", while another claimed he was threatened but not seriously molested. But on one point all eyewitnesses agreed: that the farmers had a hand in the proceedings. "The reduction of tithes," said one, "was required by the farmers in the first instance"; and others saw "a concert between the farmers and the labourers".[16]

In Suffolk, the labourers' movement began on the last day of November. That same morning, the Duke of Grafton, the Lord Lieutenant, sent Lord Melbourne a report. He noted the absence of riots in the western part of the county where the labourers were "fully employed" and where the farmers had the good sense to lay their threshing machines aside rather than wait for the labourers to break them. But even in the eastern region, where there was greater distress and there were frequent complaints that the clergy had not reduced their tithes in response "to the injury of bad harvests", there had as yet been "no outrages".[17] The riots began the same day in the eastern sector, close to the Norfolk border yet, at first, without any clear connection with the disturbances taking place in the north. They took the form of "tumultuous" wages meetings, held at Wortham, Cotton, Kettleborough, Bacton, Bramfield, Bungay, Harleston, Thrandeston and Wickham Skeith; the demands were for higher wages and lower tithes, but no violence was committed. At Wortham, where some labourers had been working for 9d. a day without allowances for wet weather, they demanded to be paid 2s. daily, wet or fine; and the labourers' "respectful" conduct was matched by that of the rector, who invited them to attend his tithe-audit the same night. At Wickham Skeith, many married men returned to work when their wages, previously never more than 18d., were raised to 1s. 8d.; others went to Bacton, three miles away, where the rector's tithe-day was being held.[18]

Two days later, at Redgrave, on the West Suffolk and Norfolk borders, the farmers' complicity in the movement became more obviously apparent. The labourers besieging the rectory that night claimed that they had been incited by their employers to demand a reduction of the tithe; and when the justices arrived on the scene the next day, they were confronted with a joint meeting of the labourers and farmers. "It was in vain [they later reported to Melbourne] to persuade the farmers to separate the two questions between the Rector & themselves and the labourers & themselves." In the event, the negotiations proved highly successful. The rector agreed to refund 25 per cent on his current tithe and to abate 23 per cent on the next;

and the farmers, for their part, promised to increase wages from 8s. or 9s. to 10s. a week: both concessions, it appears, merely brought Redgrave into line with what had already been agreed in the neighbouring parishes. But for the Duke of Grafton the outcome was not a happy one: he wrote angrily to Melbourne that the rector had been compelled through intimidation "to yield to the demands of one Flowerdene, a considerable farmer, backed by an assembly of people, led & influenced by him to reduce his tithes in future".[19]

A few days later, there was a similar outbreak near Bury St. Edmunds, in the western half of the county. The Stanningfield labourers, like those of Redgrave, told the vicar, the Rev. Thomas Image, that they had come at the instigation of the farmers; for these had said, when asked for higher wages, "that they could do nothing for them unless Mr. Image reduced his tithes". The vicar, though protesting at this "extortion & robbery" by the farmers, promised to do as they wished and gave them money for drink. They went on to the estate of Thomas Halifax, a large landowner of the district; but by this time their forces were depleted and, when asked to leave, they quietly dispersed.[20]

But, in West Suffolk, this appears to have been an isolated affair. In this part of the county, as in neighbouring Essex, the issue was most often a straight one of higher wages between the labourers and their employers, in which that convenient scapegoat, the tithe-owning parson, played no particular role. On 6 December, there was a wages strike by the labourers of Withersfield, which lay significantly near both the Essex and Cambridgeshire borders, where similar movements had already begun.* The labourers threatened to remove the farmers' corn from the fields and broke threshing machines—the only recorded case of its kind in the county. The movement spread the same day to Great Thurlow, near Haverhill, and, on the next, to Chevington, Whepstead, Ixworth, and Stanningfield Green. Further east, at Hadleigh, there was a wages strike of the unemployed poor; and the local postmaster, in reporting the affair to the Home Office, proposed that Cobbett's works, "one great cause of these disturbances", should be suppressed.[21]

At Rushmere Heath, near Ipswich, villagers from miles around were summoned to attend a meeting to discuss the labourers' wages on 6 December. The justices banned the meeting, troops were called in, and the attendance was disappointing. Yet the incident has a special

* See pp. 162, 166 below.

interest, as it was followed by the arrest and prosecution of three Ipswich craftsmen—two tailors and an upholsterer—for inciting the labourers to engage in "illegal" assemblies.[22] But the more usual pattern in East Suffolk continued as before: tithe-and-wages riots in which the tithe-owner rather than the farmer was the labourers' natural target. There were disturbances of this kind between North Cove and Beccles on the 7th, and at Walpole, near Halesworth, on the 8th; others followed at Hoxne, near the Norfolk border, on the 13th, and at Bacton (where the first outbreak had begun) as late as 29 December. In the earliest of these affairs, the villagers of North Cove, Ellough and Beccles joined forces and marched into Beccles, where the tithe-audit was being held. Their spokesman demanded "that the Tithes should be reduced and the Rents be reduced and more wages for the labourers . . . or it would be the worse"; and the labourers insisted that a 1s. receipt stamp be affixed to the tithe-receiver's undertaking to attend a meeting to reduce the rents. At Walpole, the issue was somewhat different. A meeting called to enrol special constables to combat the riots broke up in pandemonium when the labourers (incited, it would appear, by the farmers) began to shout, "Do you want to be sworn in to starve one another?"; "Down with the tithes!"; "Reduce the taxes and rents!"; and "Let the poor man have wages that he can live on!" At the Swan Inn, Hoxne, a small farmer was among the rioters that disturbed the Rev. George Clarke Doughty's tithe-dinner. He is supposed to have shouted: "Now, my boys, is the time to stick up for your rights and get 2s. and half-a-crown a day, as I pay my labourers!"[23]

But, in Suffolk, perhaps the greatest commotion of all was caused by the arrest on 16 December at Stradishall of a man who was widely and confidently believed to be the notorious "Swing" himself. He was John Saville, a well-dressed, middle-aged straw-plait merchant from Luton, Bedfordshire, who enjoyed an excellent reputation for good works in his home parish. He had been travelling in a green gig all over the eastern counties and was found in possession of £580 in notes and a large quantity of "inflammatory" notices, all signed "Swing". One of them read: "Oh ye church of England Parsins, who strain at a knat and swallor a cammell, woe woe woe be unto you, ye shall one day have you reward"; and another: "Will you farmers and Parsons pay us better for our labour, if you wont we will put you in bodily fear." He was evidently a Radical and probably a "ranter", who had exploited the occasion to vent his feelings against the Established Church and men of wealth; but the courts took him seriously enough to sentence him to a £50-fine and a 12-months' term in prison.[24]

In Essex, disturbances were distributed over three main districts and, with few exceptions, took the form of simple wages riots. The first group were centred in the north-west corner near the meeting of the boundaries of Suffolk, Cambridgeshire and Hertford. They began on 1 December with a three-days' riot at Ridgewell, Birdbrook and Stambourne, near the Suffolk border. The Ridgewell labourers, who initiated the affair, visited farmers in the three villages, "pressed" their neighbours into service, and demanded pork, bread and beer and a 2s. daily wage. On the third day, the farmers offered a small increase in wages, which the labourers accepted and quietly dispersed. "Specials" were enrolled to meet them, but no arrests were made.[25]

Other outbreaks in this district generally followed the same non-violent pattern. On 6 December, at Sheering, near Harlow, the labourers visited farmers and enquired after threshing machines; but when offered beer and given assurances that no machines were in use, they quietly departed. Along the Hertfordshire border, there were further wages movements: at Great Dunmow (where a plough was broken) on 9 December, at Henham and Arkesden on the 10th, at Clavering on the 11th; and there was a final outbreak at Finchingfield, east of Thaxted, on 14 December.[26]

The second centre of disturbance in Essex was the area around Colchester and, more particularly, along the coastal strip between Harwich and Clacton. West of Colchester, at Coggeshall, there had been a riot at the poor-house on 22 November, when the overseer's windows were broken in protest against the levying of a new poor rate; but this presumably had nothing to do with the labourers' movement.[27] The wages riots began with a large meeting of labourers on Mile End Heath, outside Colchester, on 5 December. The meeting was dispersed and eleven prisoners were taken; but it served as a jumping-off point for two separate movements. One spread north across the Suffolk border, where similar meetings took place the next day at Polstead, eight miles from Mile End Heath, and Rushmere, near Ipswich (as we have already noted). The other spread east of Colchester and developed from wages riots at Mile End and St. Michael into the widespread destruction of threshing machines at Ramsey, Walton-le-Soken, and Little and Great Clacton, on 7 and 8 December. At Mile End and St. Michael, disturbance followed the familiar pattern we have observed since the first wages riots began in East Kent at the end of October. Labourers went from farm to farm, "pressing" for reinforcements as they went and presenting the farmers with a paper which, in this instance, ran as follows: "We wish to have 2s. a day and beer, up to Lady-day; it is all we wish to have. We will have it by fair means or foul." Farmers protested their inability to pay, but signed none the less; and the rioters dispersed after Sir Henry Smith, Bart., a local landowner, had met them at the head of a force of magistrates and "specials" and promised "to consider the matter with his friends".[28]

At Ramsey, arson and machine-breaking appear to have been closely related. Osborne Palmer's stacks were fired on 7 December, and soldiers attended the same evening to investigate and make arrests. After the soldiers had left (we learn from a Home Office correspondent) a threshing machine was pulled out of the farmer's barn by labourers who "broke it up". At Walton-le-Soken, rioters who, on 8 December, smashed Samuel Wilson's machine swore to have "blood for blood" and to tear the "preventive force", if it were mobilised to oppose them, limb from limb. But the greatest destruction was done at Great Clacton, where eight threshing machines were broken.[29]

In addition, there was a small isolated pocket of disturbance south of Chelmsford and near the present Southend-on-Sea. In this area, we have already noted a fire at Rayleigh, which consumed a small farmer's corn stacks on 5 November. There was another fire close by at Basildon on 2 January; and at Hawkwell, on 10 December, Daniel Brockies, bailiff to Jeremiah Kesterman, a landed proprietor, received the following threatening message:

> Mr. Brockis, I send this to you to let you know that if you Do not give 100 Shillins A Day EVrey thing shall come to Ashes We have come from Kent in that inteniton And so we mene to go through Essex We brought this to yore dore Becaus we Dont like to put you to No exspence And we ment to Burn up the Pash Nige up first.

But the only direct threat to the "Pash Nige" as such that appears in the Essex riots was a letter addressed to the Rev. N. M. Hurlock, M.A., of Dedham (significantly close to the East Sussex border) on 14 December. He had refused to reduce his tithe by £15 per cent, as requested by the farmers, and the latter bore the phrase: "There is not a farmer in the Parish but what hates you." But this was presumably the work of a farmer rather than a labourer.[30]

£50 REWARD.

THE **TRUSTEES** of the **CHARITIES** in **DEDHAM**, having received Information, that a most scandalous and disgusting Letter has been sent to the Rev. W. M. HURLOCK, Lecturer of that Parish, **THREATENING** him, and the Premises in his Occupation, with

DESTRUCTION,

DO HEREBY OFFER A REWARD OF

Fifty Pounds

TO ANY PERSON

who will give such Information as shall ensure the **CONVICTION** of the **WRITER** of the above-mentioned Letter.

DEC. 13th, 1830.

PRINTED BY SWINBORNE, WALTER, AND TAYLOR, COLCHESTER.

Reward offered in Sussex, December 1830

There remain two further major counties of disturbance: Cambridgeshire and Lincoln. Here, too, we find that the labourers' movement bore features that, in both cases, were quite distinct from those that marked its progress in Kent, Wiltshire, Berkshire and the East Anglian counties. In Cambridgeshire, it was compounded (apart from minor deviations) of arson, wages riots and machine-breaking; and these tended to occur in different regions and at different periods. The fires came first, and they were mainly located north and north-west of Cambridge, in the Isle of Ely and along the Huntingdon border. There was a fire at Byddal Chambers' farm at Coveney, near Ely, on 17 November: this was, perhaps significantly, the nearest point reached by the "Swing" movement to the main centres of disturbance in the Isle of Ely riots of 1816.[31] Four days later, there came a far more serious conflagration at Willingham, further south towards Cambridge. It burned down five farm-houses, ten cottages, and vast quantities of wheat, barley, oats and hay, including the properties of some of the largest farmers in the district, the local overseer among them. "The consternation was terrible", wrote *The Times*, which judged the damage at first at £8,000, and later at £4,000.[32] A week later, there was a further fire at March, in the Isle of Ely; and, on 2 December, thirty stacks of hay and corn were consumed at Richard Dinzer's farm at Coton, two miles west of Cambridge. It caused some alarm, being so near to the county capital, and the Earl of Hardwicke, the Lord Lieutenant, sent Melbourne a "cloak-and-dagger" report on a suspect who said "he had been where the fires had been, in Kent, Sussex, Norfolk, Suffolk and Yorkshire" and had subsequently taken the road to Baldock—"and on that day (his Lordship added) there was a disturbance at Stotfold near Baldock".[33] Moreover, he summoned a meeting of magistrates at Cambridge the next day, where it was resolved

> That in order to allay the irritation which appears to exist at the present time in the minds of many of the Labouring Classes, and which has been increased and fomented by the representations of evil-disposed persons, the Magistrates for the County of Cambridge will immediately make particular ENQUIRY into the actual STATE and CONDITION of the Poor in every parish in the County.

He went further; and, on 4 December, he issued a stirring proclamation to the county, calling on every public-spirited citizen to enrol in a

"General Union of all Classes . . . for the preservation of Property and the Detection of Incendiaries".[34]

But the fires went on; and, on the evening of 6 December, two men were detected in the act of setting fire to a stack of oats at Pampisford, on the Essex border. Their descriptions were posted: "One a tall Man, about 5 feet 10 in. high, sandy whiskers, large red nose, apparently between 50 and sixty years of age"; while "The other Man was apparently about 5 feet 4 inches, and between 30 and 40 years of age; had large black full whiskers, extending under the chin." A Harlow magistrate added: "There can be no doubt that they are 2 of the principals in the incendiary system." A reward of £100 was offered; but that was the last that was ever heard of them.[35]

Meanwhile, wages riots had begun in the villages lying north, east and south of Cambridge, towards the Suffolk, Essex and Hertfordshire borders. The city itself appeared to be threatened and, on 4 December (a market day), there were rumours of an impending "general rising of the people".[36] A justice sent a long report to the Home Office, in which he related "that the labourers of Cherry Hinton, Bottisham, Gt. and Little Shelford intended, on their pay-day (Friday, 3 December) to demand of their respective farmers an increase of wages—e.g. from 10s. to 12s. per week day-work, & task work in proportion; &, in case of refusal, to meet all together on Sat^y, our market day & justice-meeting day, & proceed in a body to Cambridge, joining with them in their way the men of Barnwell parish, a very populous place, & full of bad characters of all descriptions". In the event, the week-end passed off peacefully enough and Cambridge market was held "in perfect tranquillity" (possibly due to a massive enrolment of special constables in the city); but, on 6 December, the labourers of Balsham, Horseheath and Abbington Pigots went round in bodies to the farmers and parsons, impressing their workers and demanding higher wages. At Balsham, the rector was asked, in addition, to lower his rents to enable his tenants to pay them. At Shingay, when a farmer refused to give the rioters beer, they threatened to "pull down" his house and swore to destroy his threshing machine and, finding it already dismantled, they "nearly destroyed his privy".[37]

This first wave of wages riots was over by 7 December. It was followed, a fortnight later, by a second, which appears to have been confined to the village of Fowlmere, a few miles north of the Hertfordshire border. The labourers struck for higher wages and, for two days, assembled in groups in the streets; they assaulted a constable but committed no other violence. Justices and "specials" were summoned from Royston, the Riot Act was read, and five prisoners were secured and locked up in the Castle at Cambridge.[38]

After this, there were further fires at Chatteris and Barrowmoor, near March, in the Isle of Ely; and, a whole year later, the unemployed of Bassingbourne rioted against a new work scheme that was being imported from Baldock. The Baldock overseer, who had come to supervise its introduction, was driven back across the Hertford border. But even this was not the end of "Swing" in Cambridgeshire, where his activities persisted long after they had been stamped out or died a natural death elsewhere. For the first and only outbreak of machine-breaking in the county took place on 3 September 1832, as the result of which 15 labourers of Croydon, near the Bedford border, were charged and sentenced for "feloniously breaking to pieces and destroying part of a threshing machine, the property of James King, of Tadlow, in this county, farmer".[39]

In Lincolnshire, the movement was remarkably one-sided. There were no attacks on poor-houses or overseers, and no machines were broken.[40] Apart from a few scattered threatening letters, the emphasis was all on arson; and there appears to be a certain continuity between the Lincoln fires and those in the adjoining areas of west Norfolk (around King's Lynn) and northern Cambridgeshire.* Most of these fires (and we have counted 28 between mid-November 1830 and mid-March 1831) occurred along the coastal strip between Louth and Boston.[41] Seventeen were reported in a single month and are conveniently set out in a table (overleaf) sent to the Home Office on 20 December.[42]

There remain the marginally affected counties, lying west and north of Lincoln. In Leicester, memories of "General Ludd" were still sufficiently fresh for magistrates to feel concern that the stocking weavers might revive their old activities in imitation of the labourers.[43] These fears appeared to be realised when, on 6 December, the Loughborough weavers struck for higher wages and threatened to burn down the houses of two master hosiers. Troops quickly dispersed them and the Loughborough justices found no direct connection between this event and "the outrages in other counties"; yet they added, in reporting the affair, that the weavers' language "certainly showed that they were emboldened by the present public excitement".[44]

There were scattered incidents in other nearby counties that suggest

* See map on p. 199.

Incendiarism in Lincolnshire, 1830

Place	Owner	Date	Observations
Stickford	John Wilson	19th November	50 qrs of Beans and two Stacks of Hay burnt.
South Reston	Mawer	27th November	Corn Stacks &c damage £600.
Moncton	——	28th ——	Corn Stacks.
Irby	——	Do. ——	Do. ——
Swaby	Kemp	Do. ——	Do. ——
Burwell	Hand	——	Do. and great loss.
Easton near Stamford	Thomas Woodroffe	29th ——	A large Stack yard but stopped with only one Stack.
Spalding	The Revd Dr. Johnson	29th ——	Hay Stock worth £30 placed amongst others.
Donington	Josepf Glead Esqre	1st December	Corn Stacks attempted and the Incendiary wounded but escaped.
Wothorpe	The Marquis of Exeter	——	A large Stack yard attempted but men escaped
Long Sutton	Redmoor Allenby	6th December	Corn Stacks and three Men committed for the Offence.
Moulton	William Benner	— November	Wheat Stack.
Deeping Fen	Johnson	6th December	Wood Stack and Straw Stack.
Deeping Fen	Philips Sanderson	9th December	Stack of Wheat and two Stacks of Oats.
Bowen	William Hardwicke	10th ——	Hay Stack and Straw Stack.
Do. ——	Henry Austin	Do. ——	Straw Stack and Hay saved.
Deeping Fen Stow Gate	Clarke	18th ——	Above 200 qrs of Wheat; large Rick of Beans cont'g several qrs; 4 Horses and 13 fat Beasts burnt, besides several pigs & sows some of them 30 stone each. . . . Total loss at Stow Gate between £1500 & £2000.[42]

a similar "contagion". In December, a threshing machine was broken at Edgehill in Warwickshire. Threatening letters were received in Staffordshire, Derbyshire, Lancashire, Shropshire, Cheshire, Nottingham, Yorkshire and Cumberland. In the North Riding, a Richmond parson was ordered to reduce his tithe and three Whitby farmers to lay aside their threshing machines. Among the numerous northern and midlands counties afflicted by rick-burning were Cheshire, Shropshire, Leicester, Derby, Warwick, Stafford, Cumberland, and the East and West Ridings of Yorkshire. At York, the magistrates met on 9 December and warned the inhabitants of the dire penalties imposed by Statute on all who burned ricks, destroyed threshing machines, and sent "Swing" or threatening letters.[45]

The most northerly point reached was Carlisle, in Cumberland. On 30 November, two ricks were fired at separate farms on the outskirts of the city. It appears to have been an act of political reprisal; and three weavers—described as Radicals—were arrested and lodged in Caldewgate. Shortly after, handbill was posted near by, offering "£1,000 reward, in the apprehension of Borough-mongers, Stock-jobbers, Tax-eaters, Monopolizers, Special Constables, and the Extinguishers of freedom—by order of the SWING UNION".[46] Couched in a less formal literary style was a letter addressed by "Sargin Swen" to his "dear friends" of "the compony", urging attendance at a meeting "persisly at 6 a clock on monday evining", for "we are determined to release these three men that is in the gate". And, a month later, the city's clerk of the peace was warned by "Swing" in the name of his "committee" that "your house & other property shall be burnt to ashes from the bad character you have with the people of Carlisle".[47] The whole incident had presumably nothing to do with the labourers' movement; yet it points to the pervasive influence of "Swing".

We return briefly to what lay at the core of the whole "Swing" movement: the breaking of threshing machines. Continuous machine-breaking went on from the end of August, when the first machines were broken in East Kent, to early December, when machines were broken in Essex, Worcester, Buckingham and Warwick. There followed the massive retribution exacted by Special Commission, assizes and quarter sessions in the form of hangings, imprisonment and transportation to Australia.* Yet, when all this was over, there was a brief revival of machine-breaking in some of the counties most affected by the earlier disturbances. On 11 January, a bare week after the main body of Gloucester rioters had been tried and sentenced, a solitary threshing machine was broken at the small village of Bromsbarrow. More significant were the outbreaks in Kent and Norfolk in the late summer of 1831. In East Kent, on 31 July, a machine was broken at Patrixbourne, which lay remarkably close to Lower Hardres, where machine-breaking had first started almost a year before. In early August, there were "illegal assemblies" over wages at Halstead and Sittingbourne; and a machine was broken at Ripple on the 5th.

* See pp. 262–3 below.

The destruction of two machines followed, two days later, on Romney Marsh; and the magistrates felt impelled to post a cautionary notice, warning the labourers against a prevalent notion "that persons guilty of breaking threshing machines are not liable to punishment".[48] On 6 September, a machine was destroyed at Dilham, in Norfolk; this, too, lay significantly close to the starting-point of 1830. Yet, in this case, the argument was new; for a rioter, later sentenced to two years' prison, claimed that "in destroying machinery, I am doing God a service".[49]

But the last recorded episode in the whole "Swing" movement was yet to come. This was, as we have seen, the destruction of a threshing machine at Tadlow, a Cambridgeshire village near the Bedford border, in September 1832.

RIOTS: DURATION AND SPREAD 1830.

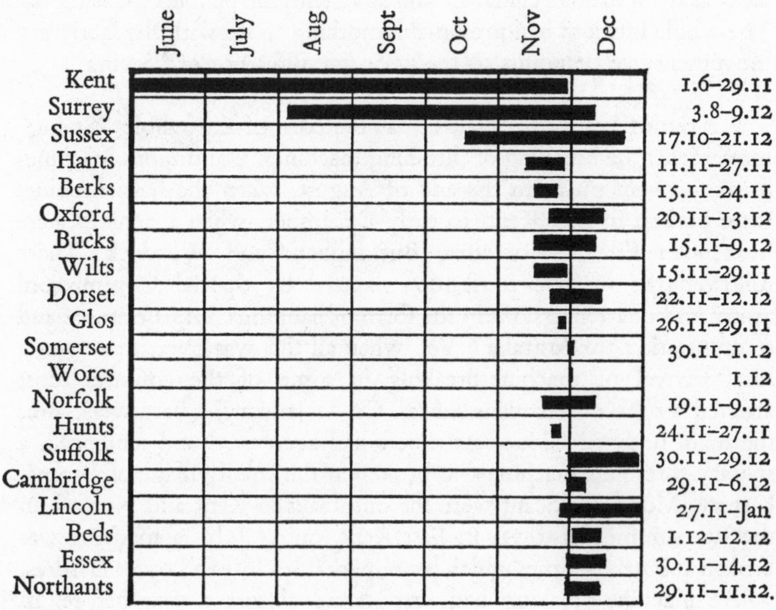

Notes to Chapter 8

1. See pp. 83–4 above.
2. H.O. 40/27, fos. 162–3, 166–9.
3. H.O. 52/10 (letters of 27, 30 November 1830).
4. *The Times*, 16, 22 November, 16 December 1830; 15, 17, 19, 21 January 1831. H.O. 52/10 (letter of 30 November 1830); H.O. 52/14 (letters of 23 November 1830, 26 November 1831).
5. *The Times*, 25 November 1830.
6. H.O. 52/14 (letter of 23 November 1830); H.O. 52/9 (letters of 24, 26 November 1830); *East Anglian*, 11 January 1831.
7. H.O. 52/9 (letter of 26 November 1830).
8. *Norwich Mercury*, 30 July 1831.
9. H.O. 52/9 (letter of 27 November 1830).
10. H.O. 52/9 (printed poster of 24 November 1830).
11. H.O. 52/9 (printed poster of 3 December 1830, letter of 25 November 1830).
12. *East Anglian*, 11 January 1831.
13. *The Times*, 2, 6, 10 December 1830; H.O. 52/9 (letters of 25, 30 November 1830); Norfolk R.O., City of Norwich Q.S., Minute Book, 1830–32.
14. *East Anglian*, 11 January 1831.
15. *The Times*, 6 December 1830.
16. *East Anglian*, 11 January 1831; *The Times*, 6 December 1830; H.O. 52/9 (letter of 7 December 1830).
17. H.O. 52/10 (letter of 30 November 1830).
18. *Ipswich Journal*, 4 December 1830; H.O. 52/9 (letter of 30 November 1830); H.O. 52/10 (letter of 2 December 1830).
19. H.O. 52/9 (letter of 3 December 1830); H.O. 52/10 (letter of 15 December 1830).
20. H.O. 52/10 (letter of 6 December 1830).
21. H.O. 52/10 (letters of 6, 7 December 1830); *Ipswich Journal*, 11 December 1830, 15 January 1831.
22. *The Times*, 6, 8 December 1830; *Ipswich Journal*, 4 December 1830.
23. H.O. 52/10 ("information" of 8 December 1830); *The Times*, 10, 23 December 1830; *Ipswich Journal*, 15 January 1831.
24. H.O. 52/10 (letter of 16 December 1830); *The Times*, 23 December 1830; P. Singleton, "Captain Swing in East Anglia", *Bull. for the Study of Lab. History*, August 1964, pp. 13–14.
25. H.O. 52/7 (letters of 3, 7 December 1830).
26. H.O. 52/7 (letter of 7 December 1830); Essex R.O., Q/SPb 20, pp. 248–64; Q/SR 1028.
27. *The Times*, 1 December 1830.
28. H.O. 52/7 (letters of 7, 8 December 1830); *The Times*, 11 December 1830.
29. H.O. 52/7 (letter of 8 December 1830); *The Times*, 13 December 1830.
30. H.O. 52/7 (letters of 15 December 1830, 2 January 1831); Essex R.O., Q/SR 1028.
31. See A. J. Peacock, *Bread or Blood. The Agrarian Riots in East Anglia: 1816* (1965), p. 133.

32. *The Times*, 23, 24, 25 November 1830.
33. H.O. 52/6 (letter of 5 December 1830).
34. H.O. 40/52, fo. 639; H.O. 52/6 (printed poster of 4 December 1830).
35. H.O. 52/10 (poster [n.d.]); *The Times*, 10 December 1830.
36. *The Times*, 6 December 1830.
37. H.O. 52/12 (letter of 7 December 1830); *The Times*, 17 March 1831; Cambs. R.O., Q.S. Rolls, Epiphany 1831.
38. *The Times*, 27 December 1830.
39. *Cambridge and Hertford Independent Press*, 17 March, 27 October 1832.
40. For *threats* to break machinery, see H.O. 52/14 (letter of 12 January 1831)
41. *The Times*, 1, 2, 10, 13, 16 December 1830; 1, 6, 8, 22, 29 January 1831. H.O. 52/8 (correspondence of 19 November–20 December 1830); H.O. 52/14 (letters of 8, 12 January, 9 March 1831).
42. H.O. 52/8 (enclosure of 20 December 1830).
43. See H.O. 52/8 (letter of 30 November 1830).
44. Leicester County R.O., Q.S. 31/1/3 (letter of 7 December 1830).
45. H.O. 40/26, fo. 376.
46. *The Times*, 7, 20, 29 December 1830.
47. Cumberland R.O., Carlisle City Corp.: correspondence of 5 December 1830, 4 January 1831.
48. *Kent Herald*, 27 October 1831; H.O. 52/13 (poster of 19 August 1831).
49. *East Anglian*, 25 October 1831.

9

THE DISTRIBUTION OF RIOTS

When the historian surveys the entire area from Lincolnshire to Dorset across which the labourers' rising passed in a matter of six to eight weeks, he is bound to ask himself what determined the spread and geographical distribution of the movement. That is to say, (1) what determined the general area of unrest as distinct from those parts of England which were not seriously affected, (2) what determined the regional distribution of the movement within the riotous sector of the country, (3) what determined within a given county or hundred whether a village rioted or remained quiet. These questions may require different kinds of answers, and in so far as answers can be given to them, they will be more speculative in one case than in another. There is another question which is also relevant to the enquiry into the geographical distribution of the 1830 rising. Along what lines of communication did the unrest spread from one area to the next? The present chapter tries to deal with these problems. As we shall see, it is often impossible to give firm answers to them. We can merely indicate which explanations sound more, which less plausible.

The broad *national* pattern of the rising can be most easily explained. As we have seen, agricultural England could in the 19th century be divided into a grain-growing South and East and a mainly pastoral North and West, but also into a comparatively high-wage North and a low-wage South. The Swing movement, for reasons which should be clear to any reader of the first two chapters, occurred essentially in the region in which cereal farming was combined with low wages. This does not mean that it was entirely confined to this area. An immense movement of this kind generates its own momentum, and there is no reason to be surprised because it overflowed its "natural" geographical boundaries—into the high-wage corn-growing zones of Lincolnshire and the East Riding of Yorkshire or into the pastoral counties of the West. The power of geography is nevertheless evident. In Dorset, for instance, the line between corn and pastoral zones pretty clearly divides the riotous from the quiescent area, and in neighbouring Wiltshire the "chalk" part of the county (to use the convenient short-hand term) was riotous, the "cheese" part on the whole tranquil. As for the average wage-level, there is no question that the rioting counties were the poorer ones. The mean wage-level of 27 counties as given by Caird was 9s. 7d. a week, but that of the 14 counties on his list which were heavily involved in the 1830 riots was only 8s. 4d. Only two of the riotous counties (Kent and Sussex) reached or exceeded the global average; all the rest were clearly below it. If we want the most general answer to the question about the geographical distribution of the riots, it is still the old and simple statement that they occurred where corn and low wages combined.

Nevertheless, within this large area the unrest was clearly not equally widespread, explosive or intense. In a ring surrounding the metropolis of London the movement seems to have remained distinctly weak. We find some initial arson in North-west Kent, Surrey and Middlesex, but the movement either died down or remained at the level of more or less sporadic incendiarism, except where (as in the Dorking area of Surrey) more ambitious types of mass activity were imported from adjoining areas remote from London. Hertfordshire remained remarkably quiet throughout, and the movement reached Essex late, and from the north. The parts of Berkshire and Buckinghamshire nearest to London were also the least disturbed, or at any rate they saw nothing much more than some incendiarism. Speaking broadly, the area within a radius of perhaps twenty-five miles of London was immune to the rising. This is all the more surprising because, as we have seen, some of the earliest manifestations of discontent occurred there.

Why was there so little rioting round London? We cannot say for sure, but at any rate there are some plausible reasons. Geography may have played its part here and there, by multiplying common, waste and heath in Surrey, woodlands in Essex. However, the main reasons must have been the effect of London's demand on the structure of home counties agriculture, and of the London labour market on its wage-level. The immense metropolitan demand for meat, dairy products, vegetables, fruit, and hay (for the horses which were still the major engines of transport) can be most clearly seen in Middlesex, where the arable acreage (14,000 acres) was almost equalled by that of market gardens and nurseries (11,500) and vastly exceeded by that of pastures (70,000). However, it is known that not only Middlesex, but parts of Surrey, Essex, Kent and Berkshire were similarly affected by the pull of the London market.[1] And even where this was plainly not so, as in Essex and Herts., where tillage largely prevailed over animal husbandry or other forms of agriculture, except in the areas closest to London, there was the effect on wages and employment of the vicinity of the metropolis, observed by contemporaries.[2] In one way or another, therefore, London provided a prophylactic against too much unrest in its surroundings.

However, there is a more puzzling phenomenon. There was evidently a fairly general social conflagration in Kent, Sussex, Hampshire, Berkshire and Wiltshire, and another obviously explosive area in Norfolk and perhaps Huntingdonshire. However, in the broad belt of counties stretching from the Thames to Norfolk, the outburst of unrest was curiously patchy. Most of Buckinghamshire, Bedfordshire, Cambridgeshire, and large parts of East Anglia outside the main centre of riot in Norfolk, not to mention the adjoining Midland counties, formed a zone of partial rather than of general insurrection. This was plainly not because the labourers were less discontented. Certainly counties like Bedfordshire, which came at the top of the tables of both poor law expenditure and illiteracy, had plenty to be discontented about. In any case, it was precisely in this "grey" zone of unrest—Suffolk, Bedfordshire, Cambridgeshire, Essex—that incendiarism became most persistent and remained most threatening *after* 1830, as we shall see in Chapter 15. In the present state of our knowledge we can only speculate about the reasons for this. How far was it due to the absence of those discontented small farmers who formed so powerful a reinforcement and stimulus for labourers in parts of Norfolk and Kent? How far to the prevalence of large estates? How far to the brutal suppression of the relatively early unrest of 1816 in parts of this area, which may have cowed the poor? We do not know. Perhaps we cannot even guess with any profit, but merely note the phenomenon as one which future research must try to explain.

Regional generalisations should not allow us to overlook the interesting relation to unrest of certain types of cultivation. Presumably those most likely to produce discontent were crops with very large fluctuations in their demand for labour (i.e. which required either the maintenance of a large reserve of unemployed against the peak season or large seasonal immigration), and those with large fluctuations in price and prosperity. Wheat is the obvious example of such a crop. Hops is another. It happened to be largely localised in Kent and East Sussex, and where it was important, there were riots. The following table shows this:

Rioting and Hop cultivation in Kent and Sussex

Parishes cultivating more than	Total	Rioting	Non-rioting
400 acres	12	12	0
300–399 acres	9	5	4
200–299 acres	19	13	7
100–199 acres	46	3	3

Source: An account of the total number of acres of land in Great Britain under cultivation of hops in the year 1831. Parl P. XXXV of 1833.

As Dr. M. Dutt has pointed out, both within Kent and Sussex the distribution of the riots shows a concentration on the areas of corn-farming and hops, while certain other areas—notably those engaged in forestry and pure pastoral farming (like the Romney Marshes)—remained quiet, at least at the time of the major unrest.

This leaves us with the intractable problem of the uneven *local* distribution of unrest. Why, in other words, did one village riot whereas its neighbour did not? We can, alas, never be certain of our answers. A village is a subtle complex of past and present, of the permanent and the changing, of nature, technique, social and economic organisation, men and communications. What happens in it depends on the landscape and the soil which condition the nature of its agriculture at the given levels of knowledge and skill; on its geographical situation which determines its place in the larger social division of labour; on the size and structure of its human settlement, the pattern of its landownership and occupation and the social relations of production of its agriculture. It depends on the nature and the interests of its ruling groups, or those who create the framework of administration and politics in which it functions, on the nature and dispositions of its own leaders and activists, and on the pattern of its communications with the neighbouring villages and the wider world. And it depends not only on what these things are *now*, but on their changes: on whether population is rising or falling and at what rate; whether poverty has increased, is diminishing, and by how much; on whether labourers are in the process of losing their land, their status and security, and how suddenly or dramatically; on whether a new road is opened or an old one by-passed. What happens in a village depends on all these factors simultaneously, and on various others also. Though we may have a shrewd idea which of them are likely to be—other things equal—more important, we can never exclude the possibility that at certain times or in particular cases their actual conjunction may be different from the theoretically probable one. Or that in individual cases purely local and personal factors may prevail.

We can nevertheless go some of the way towards an answer by comparing and contrasting villages in respect of their various characteristics, separating the riotous ones from the tranquil ones.[3] Fortunately, thanks in large part to the insatiable demand of Parliament for statistical or other "returns" and some material in the archives of government, we have at our disposal enough comparable information about all the parishes in the country to construct a virtual "profile" of each of them, if we so choose. These data have their weaknesses, of which the absence of comparable information for all parishes for the same date (ideally not later than 1830–31) is the least; for we can use comparable data for earlier or later years so long as there has been no major change in the ranking order of the parishes in respect of the factor measured, or of such vital factors as landownership and land-use; i.e. up to about 1850. The unreliability of the local worthies who puzzled over the numerous London questionnaires, often interpreting them in various ways, sometimes giving vague or even invented answers, is more damaging, but cannot be helped. Lastly, no amount of ingenuity can recover relevant information which is simply not there. Thus neither illiteracy nor criminal statistics are generally available below the level of the county or "hundred" (or similar subdivision), although here and there some local writer extracted them, presumably from local officials.

Of course it is impossible for two individuals, even with some research assistance, to compile and analyse this information for all parishes of some 15–25 counties, though perhaps one day this may be done. We have therefore been eclectic. A few "hundreds" have been very fully analysed, several more partially investigated, while on some specific points information has been drawn from an even wider sample. In the main, our sample, which covers between 130 and 230 parishes, depending on the question, is drawn from Norfolk, Suffolk, Hampshire and Wiltshire, and covers areas of heavy, medium and light rioting. The main sources for our analysis have been the following:

For demographic data we have used the 1821 and 1831 censuses. This includes also such occupational data as the number of families engaged in agricultural and non-agricultural pursuits; the number of farmers employing labour, of those not employing hired labour, and of farm-labourers; the number of resident persons of wealth, and of male and female servants. For landownership we have analysed the land-tax returns for two hundreds (Hartismere, Suffolk and Eynsford, Norfolk) and consulted county directories, mostly not available before the 1840s.[4] Directories also supplement the censuses' occupational information. Additional information about the distribution of property and income can be taken from various parliamentary returns about rates, and for pauperism the numerous parliamentary papers on this gloomy topic.[5] For the communal structure of the parish (the pattern of settlement, inns, the "seats" of gentlemen, commons, town estates, etc.) we have relied on directories and gazetteers as well as maps, and for the record of enclosures on the various handlists of enclosure Acts and awards published in more modern times.[6] For the vexed question of "open" and "close" villages we have had to collect our information, which is necessarily partial and not too reliable, from a variety of sources, often of the later 19th century.[7] For the place of the parish in the system of communications—transport, the presence or absence of markets, fairs, court sessions, etc., and of professional and trading elements indicating a centre of services—we have relied on directories, on the *Law List* for 1830 (country attorneys), and the *Provincial Medical Directory* (1st edn., 1847). For the presence of a local middle-class or politically active nucleus, in addition to directories, on *Poll Books*. For religion, the 1851 Census, directories and denominational sources must guide us, but only some of these take us as low as the parish. For literacy, the *Registrar-General's Report* for 1840 gives the data by hundreds, but not, alas, by parishes. Nor are criminal statistics often available on this basis.[8]

The work of collating all this material is laborious and its results far from certain. Nevertheless it is essential, for without it we are likely to be misled. Let us take, for instance, the problem of *enclosures*. General surveys have suggested that they can have had no significance for the riots, since these occurred in regions of recent enclosure and in those which had never known common fields, in villages without common lands and in those with an unusually high proportion of them. Thus in Suffolk the most disturbed Hundred (Hartismere) was also the one possessing the highest remaining proportion of commons. Yet closer analysis reveals a distinct connexion. In Eynsford four out of the nine parishes enclosed since 1800 rioted; yet only nine out of 31 parishes were disturbed.[9] In Erpingham South three out of the five parishes enclosed since 1800 rioted; yet only six out of 38 parishes were disturbed. In Hartismere half the four parishes recently (since

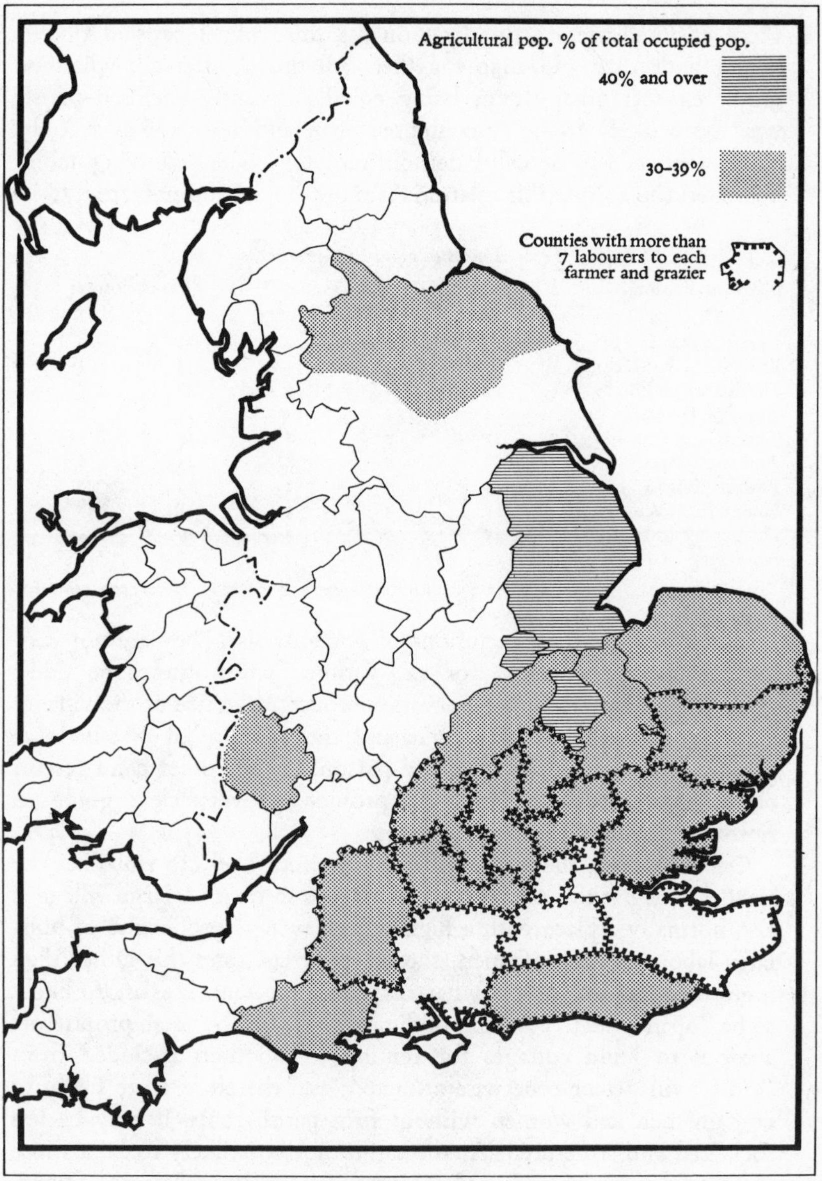

AGRICULTURAL POPULATION, 1841

1800) enclosed were active; yet only a third of all parishes rioted, taking both 1822 and 1830 together. All this is, after all, what we might expect: other things being equal a recently enclosed parish was more likely to be discontented than another. However, only closer analysis can actually demonstrate this. The following table, however, shows that this relation does not hold good universally:

Table: Enclosures and Riot-proneness

Name of division	Number of parishes	Enclosures Total	Enclosures Rioting	Non-enclosures Total	Non-enclosures Rioting
Eynsford (Norfolk)	31	9	4	22	5
Erpingham S. (Norfolk)	38	5	3	33	3
Hartismere (Suffolk)	32	4	2	28	8
Alton N. (Hants.)	14	1	1	13	0
Thorngate (Hants.)	13	2	1	11	4–5
Andover (Hants.)	17	2	2	15	6
Pewsey (Wilts.)	23	9	4	14	8
Hungerford (Wilts.)	11	3	3	8	5
Devizes (Wilts.)	25	6	2	19	3
Amesbury	23	7	2	16	3

Both Enclosure Acts and private enclosures, awards since 1800, have been counted.

What then are the conclusions of our analysis? They are not easy to present systematically, for the various factors cannot be tidily isolated. The three major observations concern the size of the village, its relations with its landowners and the presence of certain local groups, independent of squire and parson. On the other hand certain other factors, curiously enough, provide no very clear guide to riotousness. Pauperism is one of these.

On the whole, the larger village was more likely to riot than the smaller.[10] What this means is by no means so clear. A large village is also normally a place with a higher than average proportion of non-farm-labourers, of craftsmen, shopkeepers, etc., and this rather than mere demographic size is what may be important. It is more likely to be "open", i.e. to contain building land owned by small proprietors anxious to build cottages for renting to labourers excluded from "close" villages or otherwise attracted; and therefore more likely to contain men and women without firm parish roots. It may be less socialised and structured. At the same time it is likely to be a more important centre of trade and communications, and therefore of news, discussion and action, and as such setting the tone for surrounding smaller settlements. (We are here thinking of genuine but large villages like Kintbury in Berks. or Ramsbury in Wilts., not of small provincial towns or market centres whose social and economic structure is rather different, if only because they are clearly dominated by the non-farming element, even when they are economically dependent on farming.) Not that sheer numerical size is negligible. It is hardly surprising that the 299 farm labourers of Great Bedwin (Wilts.) should find it easier to form an activist mob than the 108 of Little Bedwin, which did not riot in 1830.

Can we isolate the element of mere numbers from the others with which it is so often combined?

Large or not, there is a little evidence that the riotous villages were sometimes less purely agricultural than the tranquil ones:

Percentage of agricultural population in riotous and tranquil villages

Division	Parishes		Number in which agric. families were			
	Total	Riotous	50 per cent or less		75 per cent and over	
			All	Riot	All	Riot
Eynsford	29	7	2	1	10	3
Erpingham N.	32	4	9	2	11	0
Diss (Norfolk)	15	4	3	0	6	1
Hartismere	32	10	5	4	10	0
Potterne & Ramsbury (Wilts.)	9	2	2	1	3	0
Selkley (Wilts.)	12	3	1	1	8	2

However, as the above table shows, there was sufficient rioting among highly agricultural parishes (those with 75 per cent or more of their families dependent on farming) to make any generalisation, however cautious, impossible. On the other hand it is extremely probable that the riotous village contained a higher proportion of village craftsmen than the rest. If we take the shoemakers as an index (which is both suitable because of their notorious radicalism, and convenient because of their inclusion in county directories), this point may be very vividly illustrated in the following table:

Average number of shoemakers in riotous and tranquil parishes

Division	Riotous parishes	Non-riotous parishes
Eynsford	4.5	just under 1
Erpingham S.	3.5	1.9*
Hartismere	2.2	0.9
Andover	4.0 (1.3†)	0.5
Barton Stacey (Hants.)	2.0	0.25
Thorngate	1.8	0.5
Evingar (Hants.)	4	2.5‡

* in spite of tranquillity of Aylsham (19 shoemakers).
† excluding Andover (20 shoemakers).
‡ including Whitchurch (12 shoemakers).

This leaves virtually no room for doubt. The average riotous parish had from double to four times as many shoemakers as the average tranquil one!

It is also probable that there is a relation between the village's role as a centre of communication and trade, and its disposition to unrest. If we use the presence of a market, a fair, or a resident attorney (which may indicate a centre of legal and commercial transactions)[11] as a guide we find that riots tended to occur there, as witness the following table:

Markets, Fairs, Resident Lawyers and Riotousness

Division	Places with...............					
	Markets		Fairs		Lawyers	
	All	Riots	All	Riots	All	Riots
Eynsford	1	1	3	3	2	2
Erpingham S.	1	0	4	2	1	0
Hartismere	1	1	7	3	1	1
Potterne & R.	0	0	0	0	1	1
Evingar	1	0	1	0	1	0
Andover	1	1	3	2	2	2
Barton Stacey	0	0	1	1	0	0
Thorngate	0	0	1	1	1	1
King's Somborne	1	1	2	2	2	2

However, too few villages were centres of communication and trade for this factor to be generally significant.

The second aspect of our analysis concerns the village's relations with its landlords and farmers. This problem is sometimes presented simply as that of "close" as against "open" villages, but this elementary dichotomy is not very helpful, partly because it is much harder to apply in practice than some students think,[12] partly because it gives us only one dimension of landownership, partly because much of the riotous area was dominated by large landed property anyway. The important differences in such areas must be those *within* the pattern of large property.

In any case the simple distinction between "open" and "close" villages is insufficient. It is true that we may occasionally encounter (*a*) genuine monopoly villages owned entirely by one landlord, or villages so dominated by one or two landlords as to make the description "close" quite realistic. It is also true that in practice this may not be a very different situation from type (*b*) which may be described as *oligarchy*—i.e. a parish dominated by a group of gentry and noble families none of which singly owns an overwhelming proportion of it. Such oligarchies were common in some parts of East Anglia (possibly the result of the familiar medieval multi-manor villages in that region). Thus in Hartismere Hundred, Suffolk, some combination of Henniker, Wilson, Kerrison, Frere, Adair, Tomline, Cobbold, etc. dominated perhaps 17 out of 34 parishes, though only five could be described as "close" in the narrower sense. But how much ownership was needed to "dominate"? And what of type (*c*) in which a strongly established landlord or oligarchy coexists with a fair number of small owner-occupiers? For instance (to use Hartismere Hundred once again as an illustration) the six parishes in which more than 30 per cent of the land-taxed properties were owner-occupied, while between 60 and 90 per cent of the tax was paid by one monopoly landlord or an oligarchy?

Such cases of *mixed* parishes may come close to type (*d*), the (rare) case of the "*open*" parish mainly in the hands of small owners, or the much more frequent case of a *village* within a parish whose building land was owned by small men—publicans, shopkeepers, artisans and the like, while the bulk of farming land was monopolised or owned by an oligarchy. This latter case is probably the one most often mentioned as the classical "open" village in the literature (e.g. Ixworth and Earl Soham in Suffolk, Pewsey and Ramsbury in Wiltshire) and was probably typical of the small rural township in most regions.

It would not be surprising if "open" parishes had been more riotous than others, since they were *par excellence* the rural slums, whence the surplus labour issued to work on the fields of their neighbouring parishes. And indeed there is some evidence that this was so. Thus in the Thingoe Union, Suffolk, the only three parishes out of 48 to riot were all open—i.e. three out of 11 open, none out of 27 close and none out of 10 mixed parishes. In the Ampthill and Woburn Unions of Bedford the only parishes to show unrest in 1830 and 1843–44 were five open ones (out of 35 parishes, none of the close ones rioted).[13] On the other hand in estimating the riotousness of these and similar parishes we must distinguish between two factors which are not always combined in them: the discontent of labourers in cottages not tied to farms, and the attitude of bodies of small owner-occupiers, who were concentrated there. This is not negligible. In the Hartismere Hundred of Suffolk (which we have analysed most fully) the disturbed parishes averaged 1·7 owner-farmers, the tranquil ones 1·1; and 4·5 farmers employing hired labour as against 2·6. Or, if we take the number of electors in the unreformed Parliament as a crude index of independence, in 1830 the disturbed parishes averaged between five and six, the tranquil ones 3·3.[14]

There may be good reasons for this. Any nucleus of persons, indeed any person in the village who was independent of squire and parson, was *ipso facto* an example to those who were not. The small yeoman, unlike the large farmer, belonged to "the people", as did the village artisan. He was indeed sometimes contemptuously described as "like a servant himself".[15]

However, before we draw too many conclusions, let us remember that our evidence is not overpowering (given the unreliability of the statistics), though probably enough to authorise a little confidence. Even in Hartismere, where the parishes in which more than a third of land-taxed properties were occupied by their owners did not riot in greater proportion than the rest—as elsewhere they often did—the mean percentage of owner-occupiers in riotous parishes was 29·6, in tranquil ones 25·9.[16]

At the other end of the scale, there seems to be some reason to suppose that parishes of types A and B were rather less inclined to riot than the rest, as witness the following table:

Riotousness of parishes with concentrated landownership

Area	Total parishes	Rioting parishes	Total A & B parishes	Rioting A & B parishes
1 Suffolk Hundred (*a*)	34	10	12	0
2 Norfolk Hundreds (*b*)	69	15	47	9
8 Hants. Hundreds (*c*)	113	39	38	10

(*a*) *Hartismere*; (*b*) *Eynsford*, Erpingham South; (*c*) Odiham, Kingsclere, Evingar, Pastrow, Selborne, Thorngate, Andover, King's Somborne. Data for hundreds italicised are taken from land tax returns, the others from (somewhat later) directories.

However, it is doubtful whether the ownership of land mattered very much to the labourers themselves, who certainly owned none and demanded none. From their point of view the presence or absence of the local squire or gentry might have been more relevant.

The table on page 185 shows the relations between riots and gentlemen's residence, defined as the presence of one or more "seats" of the nobility and gentry in the parish.[17]

The curious fact about this table is the lack of any general trend. If in the Wilts., Suffolk and perhaps Berkshire samples parishes with "seats" seem somewhat more immune to riot than the rest, in the Bedfordshire, Norfolk and Hants. samples they seem, if anything, to

Comparative riotousness of parishes with "seats"

Area	All parishes	Rioting parishes	All parishes with "seats"	Rioting parishes with "seats"
Bedford (*a*)	35	5	14	4
Berks. (*b*)	16	2	1	0
Hants. (*c*)	48	21	9	4
Norfolk (*d*)	127	22	38	7
Suffolk (*e*)	52	13	9	2
Wilts. (*f*)	37	19	4	1

(*a*) Ampthill and Woburn Unions; (*b*) Abingdon Union; (*c*) Andover, Thorngate, Evingar, Pastrow Hundreds; (*d*) Eynsford, Erpingham North and South, Diss Hundreds; (*e*) Hartismere, Cosford Hundreds; (*f*) Potterne and Ramsbury, Kinwardstone, Selkley Hundreds.

be more riot-prone. We have found no satisfactory explanation of these variations. If they indicate anything, it is that local factors determined the relations between labourers and gentry. These might be good. The complex of ten Norfolk villages belonging wholly or partly to Lord Suffield remained unaffected—except at the fringes—by the rioting which went on all around it.[18] On the other hand three out of the seven parishes in which G. Wilson owned land in Hartismere rioted, whereas in the same Hundred only one of the seven parishes in which Lord Henniker owned land did so. Half of the four parishes in Eynsford in which Sir Jacob Astley was a major landlord, were disturbed; but Messrs. Coke and Lombe, who were important in the same number of parishes, each confronted only one riot. The trouble at Pyt House, Wiltshire (see above, p. 125) shows us how much might depend on the character of one particular squire or his estate administration, and perhaps this is the point at which further research must be abandoned to local historians.*

The relations between labourer and landowner are obscure, perhaps because they were at best remote. Those between labourer and farmer

* But not without drawing the student's attention to a very curious phenomenon. If we take as our guide to the resident squirearchy not contemporary lists of resident noblemen and gentlemen, but later 19th century gazetteers (e.g. Bartholomew's), a different and much clearer picture emerges. It is, roughly, that in areas with a high density of "seats" (i.e. in which more than, say, 40 per cent of parishes are listed in the gazetteer as also having a "seat"), parishes with squires did not riot less and may have rioted more than others; in areas with a low density of seats (e.g. less than 30 per cent of all parishes), resident squires tended to protect the village against riotousness. Since this very striking correlation is based on quite anachronistic evidence, we shall not even bother to speculate about possible explanations. But is the evidence of later gazetteers to be entirely rejected? May not Messrs. Bartholomew, in singling out the seats named after villages and those prominently associated with them, express something like common opinion, and therefore some element of the permanent realities of parish structure?

are very much clearer. As we might expect, there is evidence that parishes with concentrated employment were more likely to riot than the rest, though as usual this was not invariably so. Still, as the following table shows, the correlation is very marked:

Proportion of employing farmers to labourers in parishes

Hundred	Rioting	Non-rioting
	Proportion of farmers to labourers	
Norfolk, Eynsford	1 to 8·5	1 to 5·8
Norfolk, Erpingham N.	1 to 6·6	1 to 6·1
Norfolk, Diss	1 to 6·6	1 to 5.8
Suffolk, Hartismere	1 to 6·2	1 to 5·4
Wilts., Potterne & Ramsbury	1 to 14·0	1 to 4·8
Wilts., Kinwardstone	1 to 10·4	1 to 8·5
Suffolk, Cosford	1 to 9·4	1 to 6·2

Source: 1831 Census.

Incidentally, these figures show how misleading the usual global estimates of farm employment are—for this period they usually suggest a proportion of about one farmer to 2·5 labourers.[19]

One final indication of riotousness may be mentioned here. There is an obvious correlation between local nonconformist strength and unrest, though it must not be misinterpreted. In Hartismere four of the eight villages with nonconformist congregations in 1845 rioted in 1822 or 1830. In Eynsford six out of 11 such parishes were active in 1830, i.e. almost all the actual centres of unrest had subsequent or contemporary nonconformist links; in Erpingham South four out of eight such centres, or two-thirds of the activist parishes. Taking seven Hants. Hundreds together we find:[20]

Parishes		Nonconformist congregations 1859	
Total	Rioting	Total	Rioting
68	25	27	18

We do not, of course, suggest a causal connection: this would be all the more foolish as several of these parishes did not even possess nonconformist congregations in 1830. Even for those which did, we are not entitled to assume that the religious dissenters initiated, inspired or led the movement. There is occasional evidence that they did (as in the case of James Alford of Tisbury, Wilts.), but nothing at all general, and as far as the Wesleyans are concerned, some evidence that they were conciliatory rather than activist. The most we can claim is, that here and there riot and dissent went together in too striking a manner to be wholly accidental. Thus in both 1829 and 1830 the North Walsham circuit of the Primitive Methodists was easily the largest of that connexion in East Anglia (with c. 20 per cent and 22 per cent of regional membership respectively).[21] This was also the area in which the rising began in 1830. Again, in Kent the Bible Christians, a similar sect which had migrated east from its original home in Devon and Cornwall (almost certainly *via* its seafaring or naval members, for it established itself primarily in seaports and dockyards) had penetrated to three inland places: Faversham (1827), Tenterden (1830) and the village of Elham in East Kent (1829), which has no claim to anyone's attention except one. It was there that the machine-breaking of 1830 began.[22] The fact that both Primitives and Bible Christians were later to have a marked connection with agricultural trade unionism is of course not relevant to what happened in 1830. Nevertheless, the coincidence is too good to be entirely fortuitous.

What we can say is this. A nonconformist congregation in a village is a clear indication of some group which wishes to assert its independence of squire and parson, for few more overt gestures of independence could then be conceived than the public refusal to attend the official church. It may be that the very existence of such a nucleus encouraged labourers to assert their rights. It may be that it furnished them with some sympathisers, perhaps among non-labourers. It may be that the mere fact of having risen in 1830 predisposed a village later to welcome religious dissidence. (As we shall see below, pp. 288–91, this is indeed extremely likely.) At all events, the connection seems established.

As against size of village and pattern of landownership and employment, poverty alone gives us no reliable clue to riotousness. That the disturbed parishes would normally be those with a high total expenditure on the poor is not in itself significant, for as we have seen larger parishes tended to be more riotous and they would, even for a similar proportion of paupers, have heavier total expenditure. Moreover, the difference in *per capita* poor law expenditure between disturbed and tranquil villages is so small that it would be unwise to regard it as significant, given the general unreliability of the figures; in four Hampshire hundreds it was £4 6s. per family for riotous parishes as against £4 2s. for passive ones.[23] Various other methods of investigating poverty—by tracing the changes of expenditure over the period 1828–30, by establishing the age-structure or mean family size of parishes,[24] produce equally uncertain results. At first sight this may be surprising, but it can be readily explained. Poverty was so general that it would not distinguish one village from the next very sharply, and poor law expenditure does not accurately measure its impact. (For instance, heavily pauperised parishes may be those in which the pressure of the poor or of public opinion imposed those high rates of expenditure against which the 1834 commissioners complained so often.) Perhaps if we knew the exact incidence of actual unemployment we might have a better guide, but our sources do not allow us to discover this for more than scattered and not necessarily typical areas in 1830.

It is regrettable that we have no comprehensive information about either education or crime, for there is some evidence that these factors played a part. Thus Hartismere Hundred, the most disturbed Suffolk area in 1830, was also the most illiterate. In 1848, 61 per cent of its bridegrooms signed with a mark. (The earliest official figures for 1841[25] do not distinguish between Hartismere and the hundreds of Bosmere, Claydon, Stowe and Horne, but this complex nevertheless had a markedly higher rate of illiteracy than the rest.) In 1848–52 it was one of the three Suffolk hundreds with the highest rate of criminality, ranking below Cosford and Wangford with one committed criminal to every 620 inhabitants, but considerably above its less riotous but otherwise not dissimilar neighbour Hoxne with one criminal per 780 inhabitants.* Its other "moral" statistics (to use the contemporary term) were less illuminating. Nonconformity seems to have been weak—in 1841 non-Anglican marriages amounted to about 9 per cent of Anglican ones in the Hartismere, Bosmere, etc. complex—but its church attendance in 1851 was low—just over one-third of the population—though no lower than in other parts of the country.

Can we now begin to draw a provisional "profile" of the village disposed to riot? It would tend to be above average in size, to contain a higher ratio of labourers to employing farmers than the average,[26] and a distinctly higher number of local artisans; perhaps also of such members of rural society as were economically, socially and ideologically independent of squire, parson and large farmer: small family cultivators, shopkeepers and the like. Certainly the potentially riotous village also contained groups with a greater than average disposition to religious independence. So far as landownership is concerned, it

* However, this may merely be another way of expressing Hartismere militancy. Of the 191 rural prisoners in the Bury and Ipswich jails at that time no less than 72 were serving sentences for arson, an exclusively "social" crime. Glyde, *op. cit.*, p. 144.

was more likely to be "open" or mixed than the rest. Local centres of communication such as markets and fairs were more likely to riot than others, but there were too few of these to explain the prevalence of unrest. It might well contain rather more pauperism and unemployment than the tranquil village, but there is no reason to assume that it was normally *much* more miserable than its miserable neighbours. We need hardly add that it was more likely to be engaged in tillage and especially grain farming, or in the production of specialised crops with a highly fluctuating demand for labour, and less likely to be engaged in pastoral farming. If it had a history of local disputes—most likely over enclosures, perhaps also over local politics and administration—this would increase its propensity to riot; and in some cases, for which no generalisations are possible, it might actually become one of those local centres of militancy whence riot radiated out over the surrounding region.

These are neither dramatic nor unexpected findings, and they are subject to much local variation. Thus, and most obviously, in an area of general rioting (such as the Kinwardstone Hundred of Wilts. in which 12 out of 17 parishes, including 80 per cent of the population, rioted) the sheer effect of "contagion" would spread the movement to centres which might otherwise have been unaffected. Conversely, in otherwise largely tranquil regions only exceptional centres with exceptional conditions or an unusual history would move. Hence our findings are based primarily on the intermediate regions in which the differences between the riotous and the tranquil parishes are least overlaid by such general factors.

There remains the problem of how the riots spread. One thing can be said with some confidence: they were essentially a *rural* and local phenomenon. That is to say that their diffusion had nothing to do with national lines of communication, and very little to do even with the local towns. Over most of Sussex, Hants. and Wilts., for instance, the movement spread across such main roads as there were from London to the coast or from one town to another. The most obvious exceptions, such as the extension of the Sussex rioting northwards into the Dorking area of Surrey, were due to anomalies, e.g. the deliberate attempts by the Radicals of Horsham, i.e. by *city* people, to propagate the movement. The towns were relatively untouched. Canterbury, for instance, surrounded by riot, merely observed it quietly. Norwich (a much more militant city), Winchester, Portsmouth, Southampton, Salisbury, Devizes, Reading or Chichester, did not budge. There were exceptions: as we have seen Maidstone and Horsham, for instance, were involved in the movement, as was Brighton. On the whole, however, the towns were out of the movement, and even the most active among them had much less effect than they might have imagined. Thus there is no doubt about the determination of the Radicals in Horsham and Brighton to take part in the labourers' insurrection. Yet the earliest riots in West Sussex developed on either side of the Downs, broadly speaking in the area where the Adur pierces the hills, and if anything moved east towards the line Horsham–Shoreham later: the initiative came not from the radical town, but from the a-political village.

The path of the rising therefore followed not the main arteries of national or even county circulation, but the complex system of smaller veins and capillaries which linked each parish to its neighbours and to its local centres. Thus in Kent the machine-breaking began in the triangle enclosed by Canterbury, Ashford and Dover, and the tracks which linked such places as Upper and Lower Hardres, Barham and Elham, were of much greater importance to its diffusion than either Watling Street or Stane Street.

Notes to Chapter 9

1. Cf. J. Middleton, *Gen. V. Agric. Middlesex* (1807), pp. 158, 287, 326, 336, 342; A. Young, *Gen. V. Agric. Essex* (1807), p. 95; J. Malcolm, *A Compendium of Modern Husbandry* (1805), I, pp. 350, 361, 452.
2. A. Young, *Gen. V. Agric. Herts.* (1804), p. 221.
3. This is not as easy as it sounds. Our sources—essentially legal records, newspaper and other reports—may give us a slightly misleading distribution map of unrest, for four reasons: (*a*) because they may omit parishes in which unrest was headed off by timely concessions, (*b*) because they may not list the origin of crowds from various parishes attracting the attention of the authorities in only one place, (*c*) because they may fail to note that some activities taking place in several parishes (notably machine-breaking) may be the work of gangs from only one or two, and (*d*) because they may fail to distinguish, more generally, between those acts which imply some sort of mass mobilisation and those which do not, e.g. between different types of incendiarism. At the level of parish analysis these uncertainties may be troublesome. We have, nevertheless, chosen to regard as "riotous" any village in or near which one of the incidents listed in Appendix III are recorded (and in some cases also those in which such incidents are recorded for earlier periods such as 1822), and as "tranquil" all the others.

4. White's *Histories*, etc. for Norfolk, Suffolk (1844, 1845) and Hants. (1859) are the most useful.
5. We may mention the returns on poor relief for each parish in XI of 1830— and XVII of 1835, LIII of 1847–48, XLVII of 1849 (Lancashire, Suffolk, Hants. and Gloucester) and XXVII of 1850 (several counties).
6. Notably the list in R. Hindry Mason, *The History of Norfolk* (1884), p. 619; in *Suffolk Review*, II (1959–64), p. 188: W. E. Tate, Sussex Enclosure Awards (*Sussex Antiq. Collections*, LXXXVIII), p. 115: W. E. Tate, A Handlist of Wiltshire Enclosure Acts and Awards (*Wilts. Arch. and Nat. Hist. Mag.*, LI (1947), p. 127; L. E. Tavener, *The Common Lands of Hampshire* (Hants. County Council, 1957).
7. Rural Question 16, of the 1834 *Poor Law Commission*, gives a rough picture of the distribution of landed property. (For the degree of coverage of this enquiry, see M. Blaug, The Poor Law Report Reconsidered, in *Jnl. Econ. Hist.*, XXIV, 1964, p. 229). The *Reports to the Poor Law Board on the Laws of Settlement and Removal of the Poor* (Parl. P. XXVII of 1850) contain lists of open and close parishes for certain Poor Law Unions (e.g. Abingdon, Ampthill, Woburn) and much scattered information. The *Report on Agricultural Labour* for the R.C. on Labour (XXXV of 1893–94) contains similar lists (e.g. Wantage, Thingoe, Pewsey Unions); and, in addition to directories, certain local studies (e.g. J. Glyde, *Suffolk in the 19th Century*, 1856, p. 326) provide comprehensive material.
8. Unfortunately certain valuable sources, such as the data collected in connection with Tithe Awards in the 1830s and 1840s, were far too bulky for us, and have not therefore been consulted.
9. Or 7 out of 29, if Kerdiston and Whitwell are counted together as one with Reepham.
10. This point was first made by N. Gash in his monograph on Berkshire, and we have confirmed it by an analysis of ten Hundreds in Norfolk, Suffolk, Hants., and Wilts. (177 parishes), of which all but one confirm it so obviously that we shall not trouble to print the statistics. The Hundreds concerned are: Eynsford, Erpingham N., Diss (Norfolk), Hartismere (Suffolk), Potterne and Ramsbury, Selkley (Wilts.), Thorngate, Evingar, Andover, Pastrow (Hants.).
11. Or the presence of a very large estate administration which employed a lawyer.
12. Most lists of "close" or "open" parishes are based on observer's impressions, rather than on objective criteria. Thus we may find equally competent observers assigning the same villages to different categories, and any attempt to check this against quantitative documents, such as land tax returns, may well suggest that they can be assigned to neither. It should be remembered that the discussion of "open" and "close" parishes originally arose in connexion with the Poor Law, and was later kept alive by an interest in rural housing. The light it throws on our subject is therefore only oblique.
13. For lists of "open" and "close" parishes in Thingoe, Parl. P. XXXV of 1893–94, pp. 52–3; for Ampthill and Woburn, XXVII of 1850, *Rep. of the Poor Law Board on the Laws of Settlement.*
14. White's *History etc. of Suffolk* (1844); Census of 1831; Suffolk Poll Book, August 1830.

15. *S.C. on Agric.*, V of 1833, Q 9442.
16. Calculated from the land tax returns.
17. The list of "seats" has been taken from Samuel Tymms, *The Family Topographer, being a Compendium of the Ancient and Present State of the Counties of England* (London n.d. but clearly compiled in the 1820s and 1830s). Everything depends on the reliability of this list. Available county directories are generally much later, and, in Tymms' words, "from the frequent changes in the occupants—especially in the neighbourhood of the metropolis" make data from the 1840s and 1850s unreliable. However, for the sake of comparison, the following table illustrates the possible variations for some areas:

	Tymms			White	
	Seats	Rioting		Seats	Rioting
Suffolk, Hartismere	5	1	(1844)	7	1
Norfolk, Eynsford	13	3	(1845)	12	2
Norfolk, Erpingham S.	13	3	(1845)	10	1
Hants., Andover	6	3	(1859)	5	2
Hants., Thorngate*	0	0	(1859)	4	3
Hants., Evingar	3	1	(1859)	4	1
Hants., Pastrow*	0	0	(1859)	2	1

The hundreds marked with an * indicate the possibilities of error.

18. The list of Suffield parishes, was given by his Lordship's representative to the Lords Committee of 1831, p. 353.
19. For a recent critique of these estimates, see Barrington Moore Jr., *The Social Origins of Dictatorship and Democracy* (Boston 1966), pp. 514–17.
20. Hundreds of Selborne, Thorngate, Andover, Barton Stacey, King's Somborne, Evingar, Pastrow.
21. The figures are taken from the Primitive Methodist Conference Minutes.
22. Minutes of Bible Christians Conference. Both the Wealden centre and Faversham also have their interest for students of the labourers' rising.
23. Poor Law expenditure from XI of 1830–31 (H. o. C. 83), *Amount of money expended for the relief and maintenance of the poor in every parish* ... 1825–29. For the 1830 figures, Parl. P. XVII of 1835. I have chosen the 1829 figures, as 1830 was incomplete at the time of the rising.
24. On the assumption that mean family size signifies a somewhat higher proportion of the unmarried, who were by far the hardest-hit under the Speenhamland Poor Law.
25. J. Glyde, *Suffolk in the 19th century* (London 1856), p. 360; Fourth Report of the Registrar-General, Parl. P. XIX of 1842, p. 461.
26. This might indicate either the prevalence of large farmers, or the concentration of labourers who went out to work in other parishes, we cannot say which.

PART 3

THE ANATOMY OF SWING

10

THE PATTERN OF REVOLT

A remarkable feature of the labourers' movement of 1830, distinguishing it from many others of its kind, was its multiformity. As we have seen, arson, threatening letters, "inflammatory" handbills and posters, "robbery", wages meetings, assaults on overseers, parsons and landlords, and the destruction of different types of machinery all played their part. There were only three cases of rioting over enclosure, two of them in Oxfordshire; and food riots, still prevalent in the East Anglian riots of 1816, were now almost entirely confined to Cornwall, a last bastion of this traditional form of the small consumers' protest.[1]

Yet behind these multiform activities, the basic aims of the labourers were singularly consistent: to attain a minimum living wage and to end rural unemployment. To attain these objects, they resorted to means that varied with the occasion and the opportunities at hand. They might take the elementary course of meeting to determine the amount that should be asked for, drafting a "paper" or "document" for presentation to their employers and, should resistance be encountered, accompanying their demands by "illegal assemblies" and threats of violence: such cases were particularly frequent in the Kentish Weald, Berkshire, Hampshire, Essex, Suffolk, and both parts of Sussex. Yet, even here, there was considerable variety in both the procedures adopted and the rates demanded. Wages meetings were generally, in their inception at least, on a village basis; but they might easily spread to embrace groups of neighbouring villages, as in the Maidstone area and in the Kent and Sussex Weald; they might invade the select vestry of the parish or local market town; or the labourers might assemble in larger meetings like those convened at Rushmere Heath, near Ipswich, or at Mile End, near Colchester, on 5 and 6 December.

Again, the rates demanded varied from one county to another. In Kent and Sussex, where wages were relatively high, the wage demanded for an able-bodied married man was 2s. 6d. a day in summer and 2s. 3d. in winter. These rates were occasionally repeated elsewhere, as at Kintbury in Berkshire and at Stotfold in Bedfordshire. But, in other counties, the usual demand was for 2s. the whole year round, with lower rates for unmarried men and boys and allowances for children. Yet there were further local variations, such as the 2s. 3d. a day demanded at Finedon in Northamptonshire and the modest 8s. and 9s. a week claimed by two villages in Wiltshire; while Mr. Gash writes that, in Berkshire, "at Streatley, the demand was for 12s. a week for married, 9s. for unmarried men; at Hagbourne, for 12s. instead of 9s.; at Binfield, for 2s. a day; at Speen, for 10s. a week instead of 9s., together with the price of a gallon loaf for each child above two; at Aston Tirrold, for 2s. a day during winter, and for 2s. 6d. a day during summer".[2]

But this direct form of soliciting higher wages was by no means that most commonly adopted by the labourers: it was only in West Kent and Essex that it eclipsed all other forms of agitation. It was frequently accompanied or replaced by approaches to landlords and parsons to reduce rents and tithes in order to make it possible for the farmers to raise their wages; and the "mobbing" of the parson was, as we saw, a common feature of the riots in the Sussex Weald, in Norfolk and East Suffolk, while in other counties (Wiltshire is a notable example) it was hardly seen at all. On some occasions, the labourers drafted a comprehensive charter in which their claims on the farmer, landlord and parson were balanced in a common declaration. Such was the case

RIOTS GRAPH OF INCIDENTS: SOUTH.

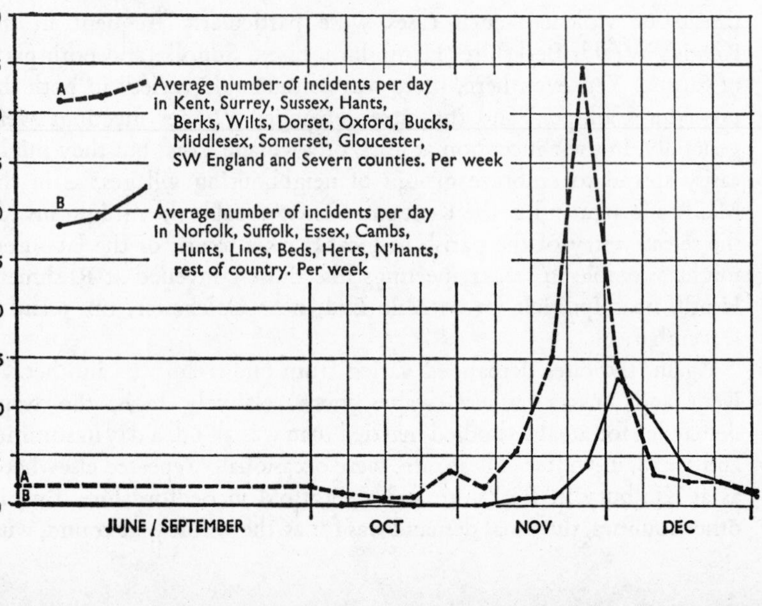

at Romsey in Hampshire, where the labourers issued a document which read:

> Gentlemen Farmers we do insist upon your paying every man in your parish 2 shillings per day for his labour—every single man between the ages of 16 and 20 eighteen pence per day—every child above 2—to receive a loaf and sixpence per week—the aged and infirm to receive 4s. per week. Landlords—we do also insist upon your reducing their rents so as to enable them to meet our demands. Rectors—you must also lower your tithes down to £100 per year in every parish but we wish to do away with the tithe altogether.[3]

Other forms of pressure to increase wages included attacks on overseers, justices and parsons, and far less frequently on farmers: these account for a large proportion of the cases appearing in the indictments as "riots". Of a different order altogether were the levies of money, beer and food on householders and passers-by. These played a large part in some counties, but not in others; and were most prevalent in Berkshire, Wiltshire and Hampshire. The first example of this type of rioting appears to have been at East Sutton, near Maidstone, at the end of October, when the Radical shoemaker, John Adams, persuaded Sir John Filmer to hand over two sovereigns, as his men "had come from afar and wanted refreshment". From this comparatively modest beginning such levies became a regular feature of the riots as they spread westwards. To some extent, too, they changed their purpose; and we saw how the Kintbury men demanded a fixed monetary contribution, not so much to buy food and drink as a direct payment for services rendered.

This type of "robbery" (as it is generally termed in the indictments) assumed considerable proportions, particularly in Hampshire, where more rioters were indicted on this charge than on any other.* But, even in these southern and midlands counties, it was not so much this form of disturbance, impressive as it was, as machine-breaking that set its stamp on the whole labourers' movement. In fact, the distinctive hall-mark of "Swing"—even more than arson or the threatening letter that gave the riots their name—was the breaking of agricultural machinery. It was by no means universal: there were no threshing machines broken in Bedfordshire, Lincoln or Surrey and only one machine was broken in Cambridgeshire, in Suffolk and in the Sussex Weald; but, taking the riots as a whole, it was the most

* See Appendix I and p. 258 below.

constant and the most frequent of the rioters' activities. Between 28 August 1830, when the first threshing machine was broken in East Kent, and 3 September 1832, when a final, solitary machine was destroyed in a Cambridgeshire village, we have counted a total of 387 threshing machines—and 26 other agricultural machines—in 22 counties.[4] The purpose, here too, was to force up wages and "make more work"; for the introduction of threshing machines in the Canterbury area in the summer of 1830 was seen by the Kentish labourers as the greatest single threat to their means of existence. As the riots spread west and into the midlands counties, other farming implements, such as cast iron ploughs, harvesters, chaff-cutters, hay-makers and seed and winnowing machines, were added to the labourers' targets: we have noted such cases in Hampshire, Wiltshire, Berkshire, Buckingham, Gloucester and Norfolk. And from the barns where the machines were housed it was natural that the rioters' attention should occasionally be diverted to the foundries and workshops where they were forged or manufactured. This accounts for the major part of the "industrial" machine-breaking that occurred in foundries and factories at Andover, Fordingbridge, Hungerford and Wantage. In addition, paper-machines were destroyed at High Wycombe, Colthorp, Taverham and Lyng, and other machines were destroyed by sawyers, needle-makers and weavers at Redditch, Loughborough and Norwich. Yet fears expressed that the labourers' initiative would release a general outbreak of industrial machine-breaking were never realised,[5] and as far as the labourers were concerned, it was the threshing machine, far more than any other, that was the symbol of injustice and the prime target of their fury.

Yet to many contemporary observers the most notable and memorable of "Swing" activities were the dispatch of threatening letters and incendiary attacks on farms, stacks and barns. There were good reasons for this: it was by such means that the movement began in the summer of 1830 around Sevenoaks and Orpington; they were widely reported, far more so than the destruction of machines; and, being carried on at dead of night and under conditions that made it easy to escape detection, they led to the wildest rumours and were followed by comparatively few prosecutions. Among such rumours was the constantly repeated tale that "gentlemen" or "strangers" were travelling round the countryside in "green gigs", making mysterious enquiries about wage-rates and threshing machines, distributing money and firing stacks with incendiary bullets, rockets, fire balls or other

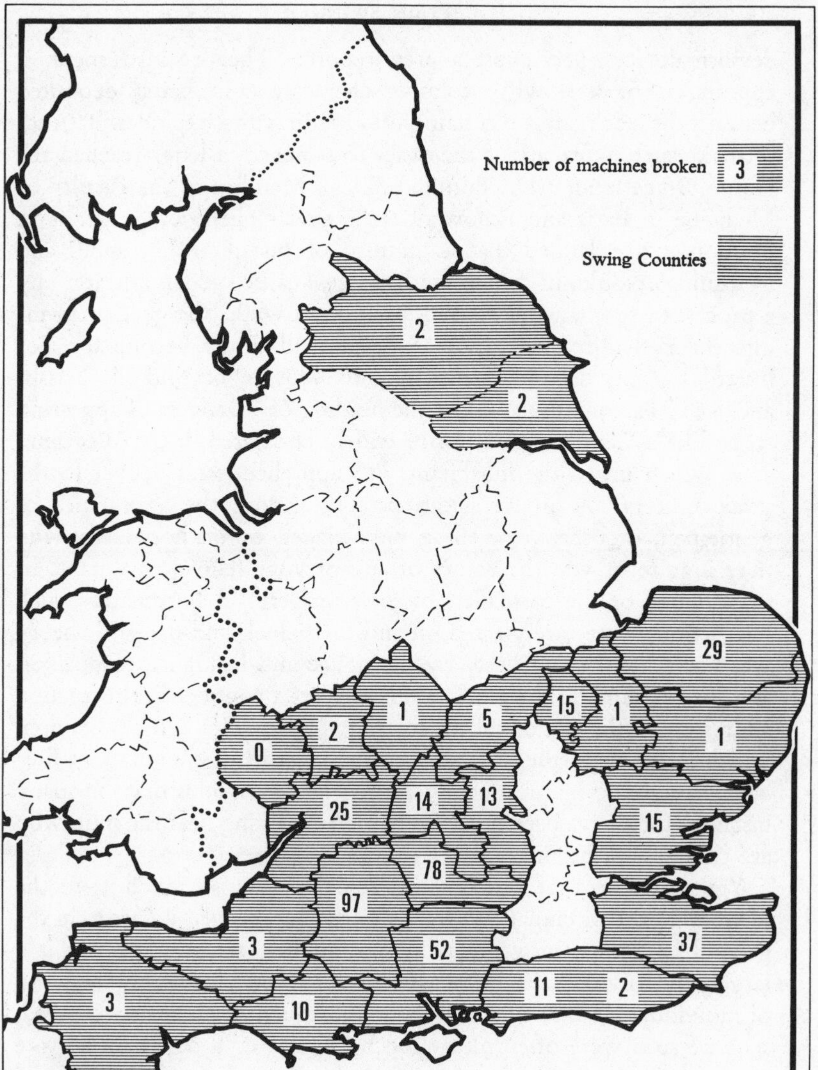

THRESHING MACHINES BROKEN—BY COUNTIES (1830–32)

devilish devices. (To quote a press report: "The fire instrument, it appears, is of a slowly explosive character, and being deposited beneath the stack, after a certain period ignites and explodes.")[6] And, to make such explanations the easier to stomach, a letter reached the Home Office from a Dr. Edmund Skiers, Member of the Faculty of Medicine in Paris and Fellow of the Royal College of Surgeons in London, who claimed that a mixture of phosphorus, sulphur and iron filings would, in contact with water, "cause sudden ignition" by a process of spontaneous combustion.[7] Meanwhile, the gentlemen-in-gigs theory had reached a point where it had almost become a major hazard for any seeming gentleman to venture beyond his parish; and *The Times* published under the heading of "Dangers of appearing to be like a Gentleman" a notice widely circulated in the Worthing area, which urged the inhabitants "to apprehend and deliver to the peace officers . . . all suspicious persons having the appearance of gentlemen, or others, travelling in carriages, or on horseback, who may inquire of you the names of any of your fellow-inhabitants or neighbours, or the particulars of their property".[8] Fortunately, such instructions were rarely acted on and the "cloak-and-dagger" theory was not taken too seriously by the police and insurance companies; and we find among the Home Office papers a confidential instruction addressed to the police officer for the County Fire Office, London, which insists that "the stories about strangers in gigs, and about fire-balls, have in no instance been realized" and even adds that "in many instances they have been invented by persons living near the spot, who are themselves the incendiaries".[9]

Yet an element of mystery still remains—not so much as to the identity of the incendiaries,* but as to the part played by arson in the general labourers' movement. Was it an integral part, or was it a largely intrusive or alien element? Fire-raising was inevitably the work of individuals and, as evidence at the subsequent trials clearly showed, such persons were often motivated by malice or a desire for private vengeance that was only remotely related to the problems of the labourers as a whole. Yet we have seen that in certain areas—though admittedly not in others—the labourers felt a bond of sympathy with the incendiaries,[10] and the repeated lamentations of the insurance offices over "the incendiary state of the country" are eloquent enough proof that incendiarism had reached proportions that were far beyond the normal.[11] Moreover, the fires in the majority of counties where

* See Chapter 12 below.

DESCRIPTION of TWO MEN detected in the act of SETTING FIRE to a STACK of OATS in the Parish of PAMPISFORD, in the County of Cambridge, about Eight o'clock in the evening of MONDAY the 6th of *December*, 1830.

One a tall Man, about 5 feet 10 in. high, sandy whiskers, large red nose, apparently between 50 and 60 years of age. Wore at the time a snuff-colored straight coat, light-colored pantaloons, and low shoes.

The other Man was apparently about 5 feet 4 inches, and between 30 and 40 years of age; had large black full whiskers, extending under the chin. He wore a blue straight coat, light colored breeches, and boots with cloth overall-tops.

Both the Men were seen at Pampisford at half-past twelve at noon on Monday, coming from Babraham, and probably from the Newmarket road.

Notice issued by Cambridgeshire magistrates, December 1830

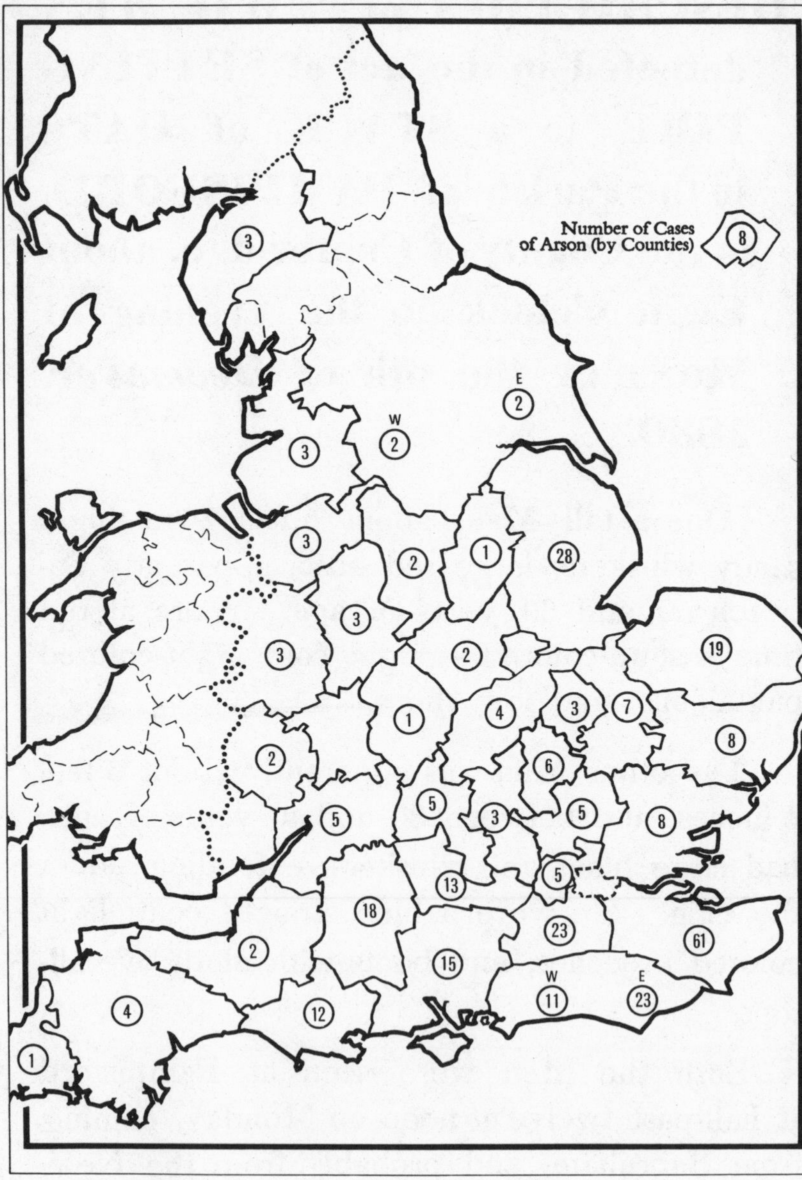

INCENDIARISM—BY COUNTIES (1830–31)

they occurred followed a pattern that links them more or less closely with the labourers' movement. It was not so much that arson and machine-breaking or wages movements generally ran side by side: this was so in the Wingham–Sandwich district of East Kent in October 1830 and there were cases, as in Yorkshire and Devon, of threshing machines being deliberately destroyed by fire; but more often we find the two forms of activity occurring in different places or at different times. Thus, broadly speaking, we may speak of *machine-breaking* counties and *incendiary* counties: thus, as shown on the maps on pages 199 and 202 the areas of intensive machine-breaking were East Kent, West Sussex, Hampshire, Berkshire, Wiltshire, parts of Huntingdon and Dorset, East Norfolk and some of the midlands counties, while the counties of intensive incendiarism were North and East Kent, Surrey, East Sussex, West Norfolk, Cambridgeshire and Lincoln. It is true that there was a fair sprinkling of fires in Berkshire, Hampshire and West Sussex, and that in Dorset and East Kent there were as many, or almost as many, incendiary attacks as there were attacks on threshing machines or wages movements. In some of these counties, as in Berkshire and Dorset, fires tended to occur in areas little touched by the general labourers' movement; while, in others, incendiarism served as a curtain-raiser or an aftermath and was less in evidence while the disturbances were at their height: we find *The Times*, for example, reporting from Kent and Sussex in mid-November that rick-burning was now on the decline and wages movements were on the increase.[12] The one exception was East Kent, where machine-breaking and arson appeared at times to be closely associated in both time and place. From all of which we may conclude that the role of arson varied from one county, and from one part of a county, to the next; that it rarely appeared where the mass movement was at full strength; and that, though a genuine expression of the labourers' grievance, it lay at the fringe rather than at the core of the movement.

In some respects, the "Swing" letter played a similar role. It was often, like arson, a prelude to a more general disturbance; it warned of the calamity that would befall its victim if he failed to comply with the sender's wishes, but the threatened reprisal was almost invariably that of arson. Like the incendiary attack, the anonymous letter was sometimes the work of a disgruntled individual, whose aim was to settle a personal score rather than to right a public wrong: it might be a disguised form of blackmail with the object of extorting money, or it might even, as in the case of the Eton scholars' protest against

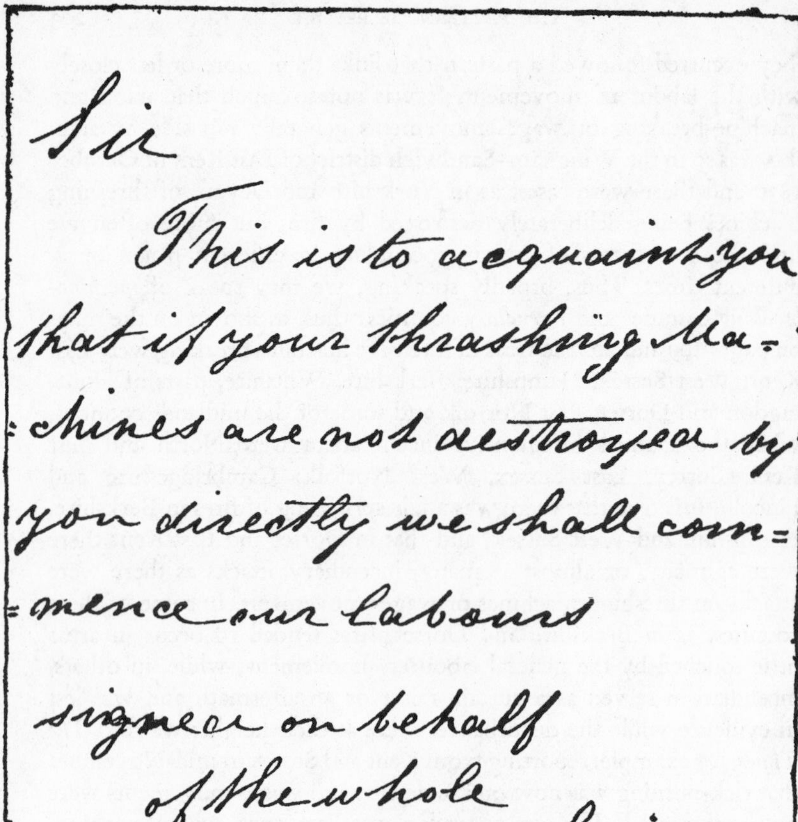

Sir

This is to acquaint you that if your thrashing Ma=
=chines are not destroyed by you directly we shall com=
=mence our labours

signed on behalf
of the whole

Swing

A "Swing" letter

the Head Master's use of the "thrashing machine",[13] be an obvious practical joke. Yet such cases were hardly typical, and we have found no case of a county where "Swing" letters circulated which was not touched in some other way by the labourers' movement. As with arson, the pattern varied. In some counties, as in Berkshire, Buckinghamshire and Hampshire, a spate of "Swing" letters was closely followed by a collective or organised outbreak. In others, the only close concordance appears to have been between the anonymous letter and arson; in others again, apart from the threat of reprisals, even these appear to be unrelated. Some letters were written by educated (not merely marginally literate) persons; others, as in the case of John Saville's in Suffolk, affected an illiterate style; while others may have been the work of the labourers themselves.* Some had a gay, lyrical quality like the one sent to a gentleman in Worthing: "Revenge for thee is on the Wing from thy determined Capt. Swing." Others were brutally terse, like the following received in Norfolk: "J. Deary mind your yards be not of a fire dam you D."[14] How many of them were genuine? how many were faked? We have no means of knowing, all the less so as remarkably few of the letter-writers were brought to justice.†

Arson and the writing of threatening letters were, then, individual acts and, even if related to the general labourers' movement, were rarely part of any organised plan. "Robbery", too, lent itself to a certain amount of unorganised free-booting, specially when carried out as a form of private enterprise by individuals who had strayed from their original group. There is the example of Thomas Willoughby of Hungerford, whose indictments record at least three occasions when he appeared alone at a house or farm and demanded money with the threat of bringing up "the mob".[15] But such undertakings, as also machine-breaking, wages riots and the "mobbing" of overseers and parsons, generally depended on numbers and, even if erupting spontaneously, quickly developed the nucleus of a local organisation. In most riots, the typical basic unit was a small village group, composed of neighbours or bound by families ties,[16] which took the initiative in organising their own and neighbouring villages for common action by persuasion, the force of example, or impressment. We have seen several examples of such focal or initiating villages: they include Lower Hardres in East Kent, which in a sense launched the whole

* For examples, see pp. 204, 206, 208, 210 below. † See Chapter 13 below.

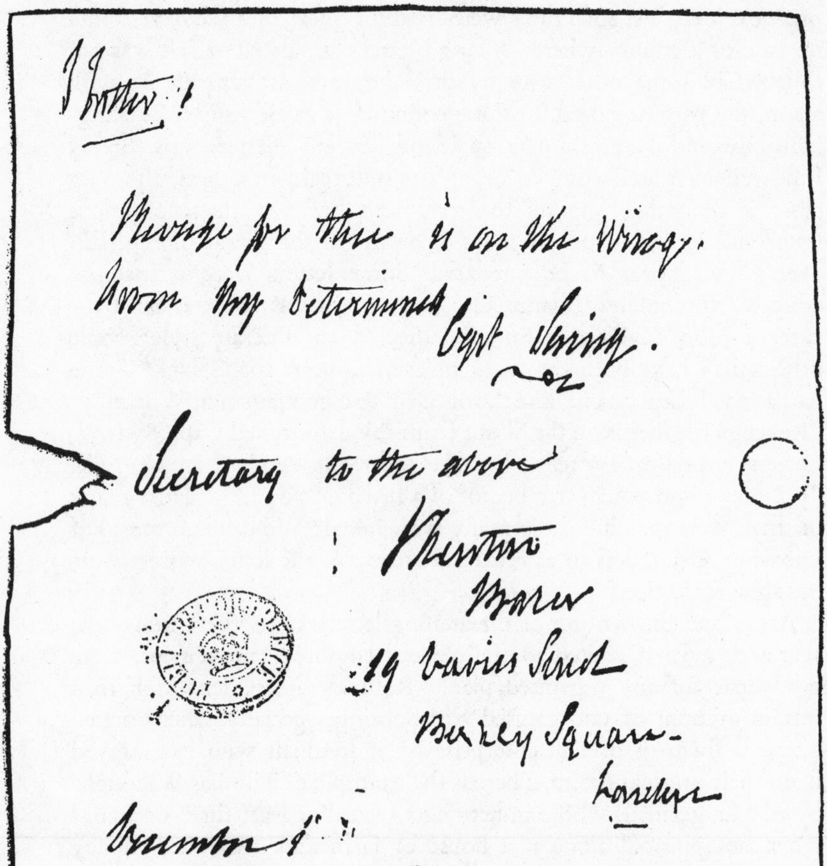

Brother !

Revenge for thee is on the Wing.
From thy Determined Capt Swing.

Secretary to the above

Thornton
Baker
19 Davies Street
Berkeley Square
London

December 1st
1830

Bathurst
Row

A *"Swing" letter received at Worthing*

labourers' collective movement; Robertsbridge, the starting-point for the wages movement in the Kent and Sussex Weald; Thatcham and Kintbury in Berkshire; Westbourne in West Sussex; Waddesdon in Buckinghamshire; and Micheldever, which initiated the Andover riots in Hampshire.

In all such village groups there was a recognised leader, either accepted as such for a single expedition or extending his authority over a longer period. At East Sutton and Langley, in central Kent, there was John Adams, the Radical cobbler of Maidstone. At Ash, in East Kent, also in October 1830, there was "Captain" Revell, while, a month later, "General" Moore, of Garlinge, led the labourers who destroyed machines at Alland Court on the Isle of Thanet. Richard Knockolds, who fired a stack of hay at Swanton Abbott, in Norfolk, in January 1831, was "head of an extensive body of men who gave him the title of 'Counsellor' ". Thomas Hollis, who took part in the Heythrop riot in Oxfordshire, was known as "The King". Among other "captains" there were "Captain" Charles Davis at Alton Barnes, in Wiltshire, and the famous "Captain" or "Lord" Hunt (alias James Thomas Cooper), who led the rioters at Fordingbridge and extended his operations into the neighbouring counties of Wiltshire and Dorset. The Kintbury men had three distinctive leaders: William Oakley, who harangued the magistrates at the Hungerford Town Hall meeting; "Captain" Thomas Winterbourne, who was indicted on sixteen separate counts; and Francis Norris, leader of several machine-breaking parties and treasurer of the group, who was found with £100 and a couple of receipts in his pocket when arrested by the troops.[17]

In many cases, the leader appears to have emerged by a natural process of selection, based on his personal initiative or his standing in the community; and it is certainly significant, though hardly surprising, that so many local leaders were blacksmiths, cobblers and other craftsmen.* In other cases, there may have been a more democratic method of election: at Kintbury, as we saw, it was "the congregation" (presumably a mass meeting), and not just the "captain", that determined the price to be levied on the farmers for the breaking of their machines. We have seen, too, the part played by "delegates" at the Hungerford Town Hall meeting; it was at the request of delegates from other villages that the Kintbury men were persuaded to resume their activities on 23 November; and, at the end of March 1831, when

* See Chapter 12 below.

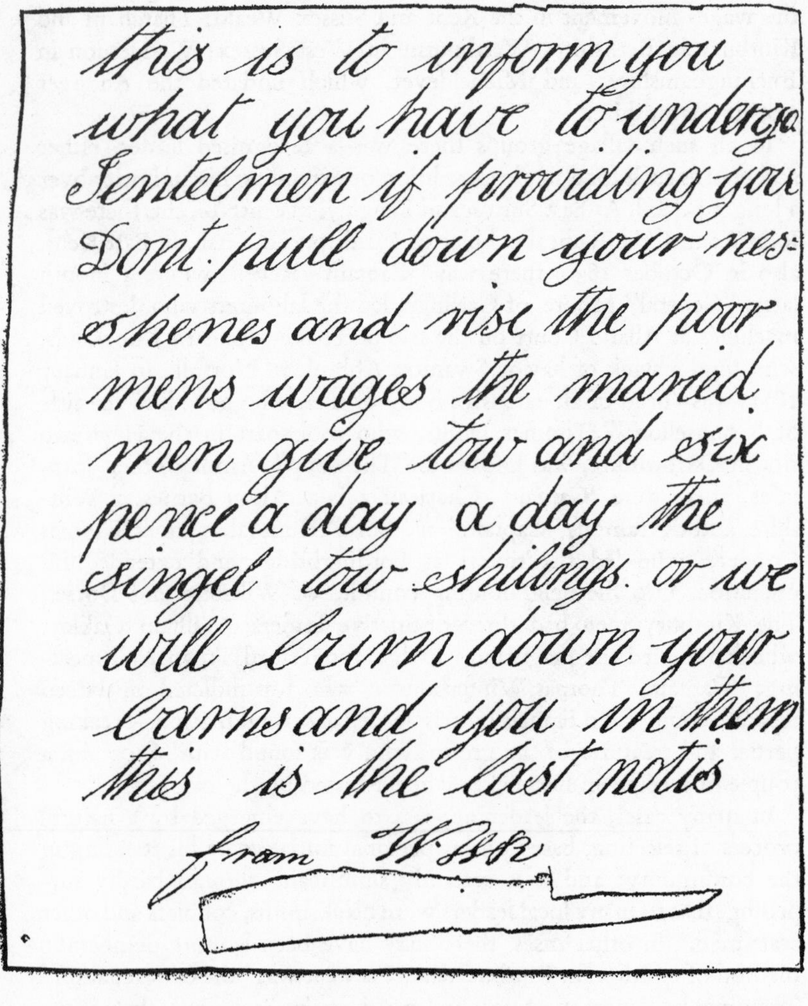
this is to inform you
what you have to underge
Gentelmen if providing you
Dont pull down your mes:
shenes and rise the poor
mens wages the maried
men give tow and six
pence a day a day the
singel tow shilings or we
will burn down your
barns and you in them
this is the last notis
from W.Bk

A "*Swing*" letter

the "bad spirit" of the labourers revived in the Rye and Battle area of Sussex, the magistrates reported to the Home Office that "delegates" from neighbouring parishes had been appointed to attend a central meeting.[18]

In some districts, committees were formed, presumably from delegates from the surrounding villages. Information on this point is sparse; but we hear reports of a committee at Westbourne, in West Sussex, which appears to have directed operations in the villages along the Sussex–Hampshire border. Again, at Steep, near Petersfield, a wages meeting held on 28 November was said to have been convened by persons "calling themselves delegates" from a "general committee"; and a Hampshire correspondent wrote to the Home Office that "the practice seems to be to form local combinations between contiguous parishes to force all reluctant persons into their schemes, and to threaten an unison of forces for the accomplishment of their purposes".[19] Beyond this, the documents are significantly silent, and we must assume that in other counties even such a district form of organisation was the exception rather than the rule: to quote *The Times* on the mid-November riots in Kent, Surrey and the Sussex Weald: "There is no ground for concluding that there has been an extensive concert amongst them. Each parish, generally speaking, has risen *per se*."[20] As for the existence of a higher form of organisation, based on a region or a county, this seems all the more unlikely in spite of all the reports and rumours concerning "itinerant incendiaries" and men "come out of Kent". The Kentishmen's example was real enough and was a factor of considerable importance; but there appears to be no evidence whatsoever for the existence of an operational high command based on Kent or London or any other centre.

To return to the village, the centre and starting-point of all "Swing's" multiform activities. It was here, as we have seen, that a nucleus of militants initiated action and built up support, by persuasion or intimidation, before putting their demands before the local parson or farmer. It was from here, too, that the local movement radiated outwards and swept up other villages as it gained impetus and momentum. The typical agent of propagation was the itinerant band, which marched from farm to farm, swelling its numbers by "pressing" the labourers working in the fields or in their cottages at night. One such case was that described by Samuel White, a labourer of Ashampstead, in Berkshire, who was "pressed" into service by the Yattendon "mob" on the night of 23 November:

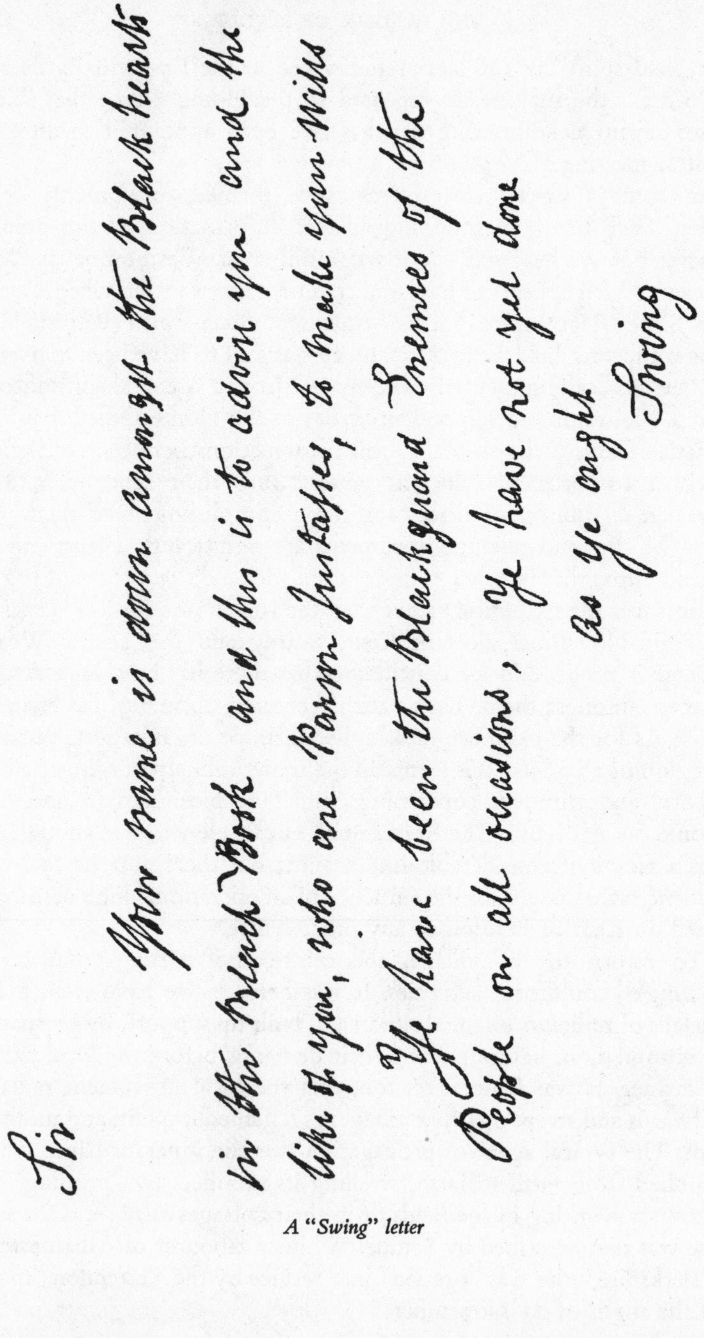

Sir

Your name is down amongst the Black hearts in the Black Book and this is to advise you and the like of you, who are Parson Justasses, to make your Wills

Ye have been the Blackguard Enemies of the People on all occasions, Ye have not yet done As ye ought

Swing

A "Swing" letter

> I live with my father in Ashampstead Street: my younger brother George who is younger than I am lives at home also. About three o'clock in the morning of yesterday week I was awakened by the blowing of a horn. Stephen Davies of Ashampstead Common came and called to us and said the Press Gang was coming; he is a cripple and rides on a donkey. Myself and brother got out of bed. I looked through the window: we have no upstairs. A great many persons came before the house and holloed to us to unlock the door or they would beat it open. I opened the door. Three or four came in. They said if we did not go with them they would draw us out. My brother and I went out with them into the Street. They stopped at Hunt's the next door, but the gate was locked and he did not get up. . . . They would not let my brother stay in doors to do up his shoes. One catched him by the arms and pulled him out and I went out and did up my shoes beyond the gate. . . . They waited for my father and then went on to Farmer Taylor's. . . . A horn was blown sometimes by one and sometimes by another. . . . All the houses were visited and the men in them pressed.[21]

There was always a certain ceremonial attending such operations. The leader might wear a white hat or ride on a white horse; flags were carried, and horns were blown (as in the case just quoted) to arouse the villagers and warn them of the rioters' approach. In the earlier (and later) days, when the militants were more inclined to fear detection, raiding parties might blacken their faces and do their work at night; but as the movement developed, riots took place in open day, and were public performances and at times assumed a festive air. There were frequent reports of the gaiety and good humour with which the labourers set about their work; and, in Dorset, Mary Frampton, the sister of a local justice, described the rioters at Winfrith "as being in general very fine-looking young men, and particularly well dressed as if they had put on their best clo' for the occasion".[22]

The atmosphere was, however, not always so light-hearted, and there are equally frequent reports of the violent, even ferocious, language used by rioting groups. Terms such as "blood for supper" or "blood for breakfast", or the more traditional threat of "bread or blood", were voiced on numerous occasions. "Captain" Winterbourne, the most prominent among the Kintbury leaders, was much given to such epithets and we find him telling a farmer: "If you don't give me a sovereign, I will spill blood on your house." Daniel Bates was reported to have said in a Wallingford pub: "Be damned if we would not beat the bloody place down"; and, one of his companions, William Champion, threatened the local "specials" in the following uncompromising terms: "Blast my eyes, I will smash the bloody Buggers' heads, six at a time."[23] Such violence, however, was largely limited to words and was rarely matched by commensurate violence to persons. "Though violent language was often held & formidable weapons carried round," wrote Sir John Denman, the Attorney General, from Wiltshire at the time of the Special Commission, "there has been such an absence of cruelty as to create general surprise."[24] To carry weapons, to bandy ferocious threats, and to destroy machinery was one thing; to shed blood was quite another. In fact, no single life was lost in the whole course of the riots among farmers, landlords, overseers, parsons or the guardians of law and order—not even among the "specials" for whom the labourers felt a particularly strong revulsion. Farmers were rarely molested, but there were occasional beatings-up of "specials", overseers and parsons. In tithe-and-wages riots in particular, parsons were frequently "mobbed"; and other labourers refusing the "press-gang"'s summons might be thrown in the pond, carried away by force, or otherwise manhandled.

"Pressing" was, in fact, an essential measure both to bring about a general stoppage of work and to muster a sufficiently imposing force; for it was only by a display of large numbers that many of the labourers' activities could be carried through. This was not true of the actual physical destruction of threshing machines, where the skilled hands of a few men (including preferably a blacksmith or a carpenter) armed with sledgehammers would be more effective than the clumsy efforts of a larger number: thus, in Wiltshire, the indictments show that a total of no more than 336 men were directly involved in destroying 98 machines.[25] But in the case of riots and wages meetings, visits to farmers and landlords, marches on workhouses or the "mobbing" of parsons, the position was very different. Here numbers counted and were an essential condition of success. In Hampshire, for example, 2,000 labourers rioted against the police at Ringwood, 1,000 marched to destroy the Headley poor-house, 700–800 were mustered for the various operations carried through at Micheldever, while in other, lesser, disturbances numbers varying between 100 and 300 were commonly reported.[26] In cases of "robbery" the size of a raiding party would be of even more directly calculable importance, as the contribution that might be levied would tend to rise or fall in proportion to the numbers engaged; and we noted the case of the Basildon (Berkshire) farmer who, confronted with a dwindling band of rioters from Yattendon, refused to give more than 2s. 6d. as beer-money on the perfectly intelligible grounds that they "had not half a mob".[27]

Again, numbers were one of the factors determining how far an itinerant band might safely wander from its base: in the case just quoted, the Yattendon men had clearly exceeded this limit by driving as far north as Streatley (7 miles from Yattendon) before crossing the river to Goring and Basildon, by which time their numbers (at one time 300) had sadly diminished. By this time, too, night had fallen and it was rare indeed (if it ever happened) for a party to camp out and not return to its base for the night. This would also place a limit on the scale of its operations. In some cases the evidence permits us to measure this with a fair degree of accuracy. In the neighbourhood of Maidstone, for example, John Adams and his band, having launched their movement at Hollingbourne on 28 October, extended their operations to East Sutton and Langley on the 29th; the round trip might be 15 miles. In Berkshire, we saw how the labourers of Bradfield, Bucklebury and Stanford Dingley, having taken over the initiative from those of Thatcham, in two days destroyed 33 threshing machines over a radius of some 20 to 25 miles. The men of Kintbury appear to have operated over a wider field: in one day's rioting they took in Inkpen, Hampstead Marshall, West Woodhay and Hungerford, and on a second West Woodhay, Inkpen, Enborne and Wickfield—a combined radius of 30 to 35 miles. The Sawtry (Huntingdon) labourers went further still. Having marched south on 24 and 26 November, they turned north on the 27th and, in one single day, extended their activities along the Lincoln and Northamptonshire border (if not into Northamptonshire itself) as far as Haddon, Morborne, Alwalton and Elton. Almost as ambitious were the Romney labourers taking part in a wages riot at Ruckinge on 16 November. According to a magistrate's report, they marched through Ham Street into Ruckinge (already 7 miles); and they had intended, if not stopped by the police from going further, to march on to Belsington, Mersham and Ashford: this, with the return trip to Romney, would have added up to 25 miles. And, had it not been for the police, they might have realised their objective, as they had adopted special means to avoid over-stretching their lines of communication. For the same report continues: "In their progress they take the men of the parish they have left with them; and, having finished their business in the second parish, they send back the men of the first parish and take the men of the second with the third parish and so on."[28]

By similar "waves" of rioting—involving both direct contact and the force of example or "contagion"—the disturbances in one county easily leapt across the borders of its neighbour. We have seen examples of direct contact in the "frontier" operations carried on by raiding bands along the Kent and Sussex Weald; between West Sussex and Hampshire, Berkshire and Hampshire, Hampshire and Dorset, Wiltshire and Dorset (and *vice versa*), Huntingdon and Northampton, Essex and Suffolk, and there is a fair presumption that "Captain Hunt" of Fordingbridge led raiding bands into the neighbouring counties of Wiltshire and Dorset.* A more specific case is that recorded by a farmer of Langford in Oxfordshire, who, having seen James Rowland and William Radway in a wages riot at Langford early in the morning of 29 November, saw them an hour later at Southrop across the Gloucester border "in a great mob, who were many of them armed with hammers, axes and bludgeons". An exceptional case, no doubt, was that of John and Robert Barrett, natives of Highworth (Wilts.), who, while taking part in the Wiltshire riots, threatened "to go into Buckinghamshire and join the rioters there".[29]

In other cases, rioting may have spread from one group of villages or from one county to another after the arrival of delegates or "strangers" (we have quoted the example of Tetbury in Gloucestershire), or by such intangible means as are generally termed "contagion". Among such "contagions" we may note the general "contagion" of Kent, which probably cast its spell over all the riotous counties; and the more localised "contagions" spreading from Hungerford into east Wiltshire, from Stotfold (Beds.) into Hertfordshire, from Norfolk into Suffolk, from Andover towards Salisbury, and from Salisbury and Fordingbridge into the Cranborne Chase along the Dorset–Hampshire–Wiltshire border.

Such factors as raiding parties, visiting "strangers" and a local or generalised "contagion" explain a great deal once the riots had got under way, and if one village was affected, it might need comparatively little persuasion for its neighbour to follow suit. But there were other factors, among them the basic underlying discontent over wages and allowances that needed a spark to set it alight. This spark was, no doubt, in most cases provided by the example or persuasion of neighbouring villages or counties; but there were also local "triggers" that

* See pp. 106, 117, 120, 121, 127–8, 148, 162 above.

played a large part in determining not only the starting-point, but the timing and nature of a local outbreak. At Hardres, in East Kent, as we have seen, it was the introduction of threshing machines that served as a "trigger" to disturbance. At Brede and Battle, in East Sussex, the example of Kent was given a keener edge by the particular grievances excited by the conduct of the local overseers. At Thatcham, in Berkshire, some days before the direct influence of Sussex or Hampshire could be felt, riots had broken out over the labourers' wages. At High Wycombe, the immediate local issue was unemployment among the paper workers; at Waddesdon, it was the allowances paid to the poor; at Tisbury, it may have been the quarrymen's wages or John Benett's treatment of his cottagers; while at Kintbury the movement was "triggered" by the committal of a beggar for abusing a penny-pinching magistrate. In nearly all these cases, the ensuing riots, by a process of transformation, developed forms that bore little direct relationship to the issues that had provoked them. The incidents at Brede and Battle led into the wide-spread wages movement in and around the Kent and Sussex Weald; around Thatcham, the local wages movement became transformed into a large-scale operation directed primarily against threshing machines; and the Kintbury men not only proceeded to break machines and levy contributions, but threatened to engulf the whole Hungerford and Newbury area in a general labourers' insurrection.

An important question still remains to be considered. How far were the riots influenced or propagated by outside agents, by so-called "strangers", Methodist preachers or Radical groups? Following the July revolution in Paris and the first incendiary fires in Kent and Surrey, the air became thick with rumours of French and Irish agents and "itinerant Radicals", travelling round the country in gigs, starting fires and inciting the labourers to break machines. Among the conflicting rumours circulating in Kent, the press reported, were that fires and riots originated "with the smugglers—with the Papists—with the agents of O'Connell—with the agents of Government—with the bigoted Protestants—with the Radicals—with foreign revolutionaries"; while another rumour had it that the fires in Kent were a "blind" to divert attention from the smuggling of spirits from France.[30] A Norfolk magistrate assured the Duke of Wellington that "the fires are entirely occasioned by foreign influences". From Surrey came a report of "an extraordinary demand for county maps by foreigners"; in Cornwall it was argued that but for "strangers" there would have been no rural disaffection; while from Berkshire a correspondent wrote that "agents of some vile conspiracy" were "travelling through the country to effect the work of destruction, and to incite the labourers to meet and commit depredations on all descriptions of property". From Egham, Surrey, came numerous "addresses", warning against "the artful and wicked designs of foreigners and strangers". One read:

> Awake from your trance! The enemies of England are at work actively to ruin us. Hordes of Frenchmen are employed doing the deeds of incendiaries, and inciting to acts of tumult. ... The fires of Normandy are revived in Kent, are spreading to Sussex and Surrey. ... Shall the conquerors of the Nile, of Trafalgar, and Waterloo be tricked by the arts and deceits of Frenchmen, or of base Englishmen, corrupt and infidel?

And in response to these "cloak-and-dagger" theories numbers of "strangers" were rounded up—among them one Vaundenbrooke, "stated to be a Frenchman", in Kent: four Italians, a Frenchman and an Irishman in Norfolk; a French-speaking Irishman in Datchet (Bucks.); and, in Sussex, a certain William Evans, who kept a mistress, travelled in a chaise, carried £40 in cash and receipts for £800 in Bank of England stock, and a recipe for "the preparation of combustible material".[31]

Most frequently, suspicion centred on Radicals and Non-conformists. Writing from Norfolk, "A.Z." stressed the influence being exercised on the labourers by "Republicans" and "the lower order of preachers". *The Times* reported on the part played by "Dissenting or Methodist teachers" in acting as spokesmen for the labourers in the Kentish Weald; and Job Hanson, a Wesleyan district preacher, was said to have acted as an intermediary between rioters and justices at Kintbury. A leading part in instigating "the peasantry of the West" was ascribed to Richard Alford, a congregationalist farmer of Tisbury; and Lord Arundel, Alford's landlord, felt impelled to protest at persistent local rumours that "Catholics and Dissenters have occasioned this (the Tisbury) disturbance". It was, however, the influence of the "radical scoundrels" (as a Berkshire justice termed them) that was generally thought to be the more pervasive. A close watch was kept on the Rotunda, the Radical meeting hall in Blackfriars Road, where Cobbett and Richard Carlisle spoke before large audiences: in early November, Peel was warned that "20,000 men will come up from Kent" to attend a meeting; and, a month later, a Hampshire magistrate expressed the view that "the origins of all these riots may be traced to the Rotunda". Cobbett's and Hunt's activities were viewed with particular suspicion. Cobbett, as we have seen, lectured at Maidstone and Battle in mid-October, and it was noted that riots and arson followed in both districts shortly after; moreover, Thomas Goodman, an East Sussex incendiary, actually saved his life by "confessing" that Cobbett's lectures had virtually "turned his head". Meanwhile, the worst possible construction was being put on Hunt's West Country travels. It seemed all the more credible that he was up to no good when it was learned that Cooper had borrowed Hunt's name at Fordingbridge and that a Dorset rioter had testified that "there was a gentleman rode through (the village) a few days before who said his name was Hunt and who told us that the Government wished people to break threshing-machines, and that they should be paid for their trouble". It was even suggested by a magistrate at Fordingbridge that Cooper had been a fellow-prisoner of Hunt's at Ilchester, and had become his servant and followed him to London.[32]

And certain of these explanations, at least in their less exaggerated form, seemed plausible enough. There had been a revolution in France, a mere twenty miles across the Straits of Dover; and Gibbon Wakefield, who discounted the tales of itinerant Papists, French Jacobins and Methodist preachers, firmly believed that the English poor were inspired by the "heroes of the barricades" in Paris, the news of whose exploits inflamed them "against those whom they justly consider as their oppressors". Already in August, Lieut.-Colonel Shaw wrote from Manchester: "The excitement caused by the Revolution in France is greater than I should have anticipated; they talk a great deal of their power of putting down the military and constables." In imitation of the French, Radicals and working men were parading with tricolour flags: cases were reported from Blackburn, Middleton and Carlisle in October, London in November, and Dukinfield (Lancashire) in December; and, in relating the East Kent disturbances in late October, *The Times* added: "In several instances, we hear the labourers have hoisted the tricoloured flag."[33]

Moreover, there were known centres of Radicalism in the heart of the disaffected counties. Maidstone was described as being "infested with Radicals" and Horsham as a "hot-bed of sedition"; and we have noted the case of Battle and Rye in Sussex, Sutton Scotney in Hampshire, Ipswich in Suffolk, and Banbury in Oxfordshire.* At Battle, a

* See pp. 104, 116–17, 143, 161 above.

certain Charles Inskipp was said to have worn a cap with tricoloured ribbons and displayed "a piece of paper with colour round the edges and said they were the things worn at the French Revolution on the 28th and 29th of July and, if they were of his mind, there would be a revolution here". At Kidderminster, in Worcestershire, a Political Council, pledged to radical reform, was active in November 1830; and, in January, it was reported to Melbourne that a branch of the Birmingham Political Union had been formed in Aylesbury and High Wycombe. At Horsham, at the time of the riots, local Radicals distributed a handbill, headed a *Conversation between Two Labourers residing in the County of Sussex*, in which the following exchange takes place:

> A. What, then, becomes of all this money they collect in Taxes?
>
> B. I'll tell you what that there shopkeeper said: That it was given to people who gave nothing in exchange for it, some fine ladies and gentlemen, who like to live without work, and all the time they make the working class pay the present amount of Taxes there will be no better times. He said a man the name of Grey was going to make a pretty big alteration, and if he done his duty and did not deceive us, we should have better times again.

Another handbill, *Englishmen Read! A Letter to the King for the People of England*, was widely distributed in Yorkshire and other counties. It was an attack on placemen and sinecures and complained:

> that the whole of the laws passed within the last forty years, specially within the last twenty years, present one unbroken series of endeavours to enrich and to augment the power of the aristocracy, and to empoverish and depress the middle and labouring part of the people.[34]

It was from handbills such as these, or from Cobbett's *Political Register*, that John Adams, the Maidstone cobbler, was citing when he told Sir John Filmer at East Sutton Park that "there were many sinecures" and that "the expenses of Government should be reduced". And there were other Radical craftsmen, tradesmen and small-holders among those arrested for participation in the riots. In Oxfordshire, there was Philip Green, a chimney sweep of Banbury, described as "a great admirer of Cobbett"; while, in Hampshire, there were the brothers Joseph and Robert Mason, Radical small-holders of Bullington, William Winkworth, shoemaker of Micheldever and reader of

Cobbett's *Register*, and no less than sixteen others who had signed the Reform petition at the Swan Inn at Sutton Scotney shortly before the riots started.[35]

Yet, if we consider the riots as a whole, all this amounts to comparatively little. It suggests that the labourers' movement was touched (but was it ever provoked?) by Radical agitation round Maidstone, Battle, Horsham, Banbury, Ipswich and Micheldever. It suggests, too, a certain concordance between Radicalism and wages and tithe-and-wages riots, but remarkably little (the one exception is Banbury) between Radicalism and machine-breaking: Berkshire and Wiltshire, it will be noted, the two counties in which more machines were broken than in any others, appear to have been singularly untouched by Radical agitation. As for Hunt's West Country travels, a Dorchester report suggests that he was "solely engaged on his own business" (he was a manufacturer of paints and powders). Cobbett evidently had readers among the craftsmen and small-holders of villages and market towns in the South; but he had many more among the industrial workers in the North and West: we read of nightly readings from his works before vast audiences of iron workers at Glamorgan in South Wales. Again, most of the reports of political meetings with "tricoloured flags" came from the northern industrial districts; and it is certainly significant that by the time the Radical agitation for reform reached its climax in the Derby, Nottingham, and Bristol riots of October 1831, the labourers' movement, apart from isolated outbreaks, had long been over. Moreover, we should note that a great deal of the Radical agitation, far from condoning or being sympathetic to "Swing's" activities, was actively opposed to them. One of the two labourers of Horsham, from whose "conversation" we have quoted, argued that a reduction of taxes "would put a stop to all that burning and mobbing that is going on at present"; and a Radical pamphleteer of Northamptonshire urged his readers to "give up all these petty outrages against property, so unworthy of you, and unite all for a Glorious Revolution"![36]

Perhaps there was a closer connection between the rioters and Dissent. We have seen the part played in Herefordshire and Suffolk by two "ranting" preachers—Henry Williams, journeyman tailor of Whitney, and John Saville, the Radical straw-plait merchant and self-styled "Swing" from Luton, Beds.* More significant, no doubt, was the existence of thriving Methodist groups in those districts of Norfolk

* See pp. 131–2, 161–2 above.

and Suffolk where tithe-and-wages riots and active hostility to Church of England parsons played so large a part in the labourers' activities.[37]

Yet, even allowing for these and similar intrusions, this was essentially a labourers' movement with essentially economic ends. This was the view of the more responsible of the government's agents in the countries, who were not greatly impressed by the stories of "strangers in gigs" and "itinerant" Radicals or incendiaries, and said as much. From East Kent Sir Edward Knatchbull wrote that he saw "no political association and no extending of insubordination outside the labourers' ranks". In East Sussex George Maule, legal adviser to the Home Office, could detect "no bad feeling among the peasantry against the Government". From Norfolk, Colonel Brotherton wrote that he could not "possibly conceive anything so inconceivable as a distinct corps of incendiaries gliding thru the country unperceived". In Wiltshire, a senior magistrate rejected all exaggerated reports "attributing the calamity to political incendiaries"; and Brotherton concluded that "the insurrectionary movement seems to be directed by no plan or system, but merely actuated by the spontaneous feeling of the peasants, and quite at random".[38] By and large, their verdict appears to be a just one.

Notes to Chapter 10

1. See A. J. Peacock, *Bread or Blood*, *passim*. See also Appendix I for the distribution of types of riot by counties.
2. See pp. 102, 105, 118–19, 136, 140–1, 149 above; H.O. 52.11 (letter of 29 November 1830); and Gash, *op. cit.*, p. 55.
3. H.O. 52/7; cited by Colson, *op. cit.*, pp. 89–90.
4. See Appendix I. This is certainly an under-estimate, for records are far from complete.
5. See H.O. 40/25, fos. 79–82 (report of 4 November 1830), for *London*; H.O. 52/8 (letters of 30 November and 13 December 1830), for *Leicestershire* and *Lancashire*; and H.O. 52/11 (letter of 3 December 1830), for *Worcestershire*.
6. *Gentleman's Magazine*, C (July–December 1830), p. 362.
7. H.O. 52/10 (letter of 19 November 1830).
8. *The Times*, 25 November 1830.
9. H.O. 40/25, fos. 904–5 (note of 24 December 1830).
10. For conflicting attitudes of labourers towards incendiarism in various counties, see chaps. 5, 6 and 7 above, and see Gash, *op. cit.*, pp. 56, 58–9.
11. See, for example, a letter of 22 November 1830, suspending insurance on water-driven corn-mills in Hampshire (Guildhall Lib., Hand-in-Hand Fire Office, General Letter Books, 1752–1842, p. 128).

12. *The Times*, 18 November 1830.
13. *The Times*, 29 November 1830.
14. H.O. 52/10 (enclosure of 3 December 1830); *Norwich Mercury*, 15 January 1831.
15. T.S. 11/849.
16. Examples are Andover, Micheldever, Owslebury, St. Mary Bourne (Hants.); Boxford, Hungerford, Kintbury (Berks.); Fowlmere (Cambs.); Finedon (Northants.); Wrotham (E. Kent); Highworth, Tisbury (Wilts.); Stone (Bucks.).
17. T.S. 11/943, 849; *The Times*, 27 November, 21 December 1830; *Camb. Chron.*, 1 April 1831; *Jackson's Oxf. Journ.*, 5 March 1831. Norris's receipts are in Berks. R.O., D/EPg OI/5.
18. H.O. 52/15 (letter of 28 March 1831).
19. *The Times*, 23, 30 November 1830; H.O. 52/7 (letter of November 1830).
20. *The Times*, 17 November 1830.
21. T.S. 11/849.
22. W. H. Parry Okedon, "The Agricultural Riots in Dorset in 1830", *Proceedings of the Dorset Nat. Hist. and Arch. Soc.*, LII (1930), pp. 90–3.
23. T.S. 11/849; and see Gash, *op. cit.*, pp. 61–2.
24. H.O. 40/27, fo. 552.
25. Assizes 25/21 (indictments). See also the case at Alconbury (Hunts.) where "most (of mob) looked on while breakers confined to a few" (*The Times*, 27 November 1830).
26. Hants. R.O., *Calendar of Prisoners for Trial at the Special Commission of Assize held at the Castle of Winchester on Saturday, 18 December 1830.*
27. T.S. 11/849. Mr. Gash goes on to argue that, in Berkshire at least, "the area of riot corresponded with the area of big villages" and that "in every instance the nucleus of a large population was necessary for a successful revolt" (*op. cit.*, pp. 42–3).
28. T.S. 11/849, 943; H.O. 40/27, fos. 39–40; H.O. 52/6 (letter of 28 November 1830); *The Times*, 17 November 1830; *Camb. Chron.*, 18 March 1831; Gash, *op. cit.*, pp. 47–9, 61–3.
29. Bucks. R.O., Letter (n.d.) to Clerk of Petty Sessions, Buckingham, in Correspondence, 1830.
30. *The Times*, 6 November 1830; H.O. 40/25, fo. 575.
31. H.O. 40/27, fos. 141–3; H.O. 52/6 (letters of 30 November, 16 December 1830); H.O. 52/9 (letter of 29 November 1830); H.O. 52/10 (letter of 6 December 1830); *The Times*, 22, 23, 29 November 1830.
32. H.O. 52/9 (letter of 25 November 1830); *The Times*, 17 November 1830; H.O. 52/6 (letter of 22 November 1830); H.O. 40/27, fo. 456; H.O. 52/11 (letter of 6 December 1830); H.O. 52/6 (letter of 5 December 1830); H.O. 40/25 (report of 8 November 1830); H.O. 52/11 (letter of 3 December 1830); *The Times*, 24 December 1830, 13 January 1831.
33. E. Gibbon Wakefield, *Swing Unmasked, or the Causes of Rural Incendiarism* (London 1831), pp. 6–7, 24–5; H.O. 40/26, fos. 63–6, 340; H.O. 40/27, fos. 535–8; H.O. 40/25 (report of 7 November 1830); H.O. 52/8 (letter of 21 December 1830); *The Times*, 30 October 1830.

34. T.S. 11/4051; H.O. 52/10 (report of 1 December 1830); H.O. 40/27, fos. 505–6; H.O. 52/10 (December 1830); H.O. 40/26, fo. 340.
35. T.S. 11/1031; A. M. Colson, *op. cit.*, pp. 144–60; H.O. 52/7 (letter of 15 December 1830); *The Times*, 3 January 1831.
36. H.O. 40/27, fos. 150–1, 431, 377–8; H.O. 52/12 (Derby and Bristol), H.O. 52/15 (Notts.); H.O. 52/14 (letter of 2 January 1831).
37. See above, pp. 157–8.
38. H.O. 40/27, fos. 146–7, 162–3; H.O. 52/8 (letter of 6 October 1830); H.O. 52/11 (letters of 20, 28 November 1830).

11

SWING'S VICTIMS AND ALLIES

It was Gibbon Wakefield's belief that, in these riots, the aims of labourers and farmers were basically the same, that they were both equally hostile to squire and parson, and that it was they rather than the farmers who were the principal targets and victims of the labourers' activities.[1] From what we have already seen there may appear to be some truth in this claim; but before we discuss the nature of "Swing"'s allies, we must consider the losses incurred by his victims.

The greatest damage to property was done not by machine-breaking or riot but by arson. To cite some examples. The estimated loss suffered through the burning of Charles Baker's sawmills at Southampton, with their expensive machinery and outhouses, was £7,000; and the first estimates made of the damage to the farm-houses, cottages and stacks of wheat, barley, oats and hay at Willingham, in Cambridgeshire, ranged between £4,000 and £8,000.[2] These were extreme cases, but even the destruction of single farm-houses or barns, particularly when filled with stocks of farm produce, would involve their owners, even if partially insured against fire, in considerable financial loss. Thus, Elizabeth Minett's farm stock at Brasted in Kent, destroyed by fire in October 1830, was insured for £2,000. A farm at Borden, near Sittingbourne, fired in the night of 21 October, was valued at £1,500 to £2,000. A barn at Selling Court in East Kent, which was burned down three days later, was valued at £1,000. In November, a fire at North Cove, in Suffolk, seen for thirty miles around, burned out a stackyard whose contents were estimated at £1,700 (of which £700 were covered by insurance). A fire in Lincolnshire did damage to wheat and livestock assessed at £1,500 to £2,000. Farm buildings and corn stacks at the Priory Farm, near Dover, fired in January 1831, were valued at £1,200; and, in March, four barns at Steventon, near Abingdon in Berkshire, were destroyed at a loss of £2,000, two-thirds of which were covered by insurance.[3]

These dozen cases, involving the properties of landowners, large farmers and overseers, are admittedly not typical of "Swing"'s victims among the rural community as a whole. The more usual figure, as given in *The Times* or the Home Office correspondence, ranges between £100 and £800. From these it is quite impossible to estimate with a high degree of accuracy the gross damage done by arson; but if we assume the number of incendiary fires to have been around 350 to 400 over the whole period of "Swing"'s activities, we may arrive at a total sum of rather more than £100,000.

In the case of industrial machine-breaking, we are on far more certain ground. According to the records, there were between 20 and 25 cases of this kind. They varied considerably in importance: at the two extremes, we have the 170 panes of glass broken at a tanner's at Hungerford and the 14s.-worth of iron bars destroyed at Owslebury on the one hand, and the destruction of Tasker's iron foundry near Andover and of the five paper mills at High Wycombe on the other. The most widespread and costly destruction was done at High Wycombe: *The Times* at first estimated the damage at £12,000, the local justices more modestly (and certainly more accurately) at £3,265. In the Andover riots, the damage was assessed at sums varying between £2,000 and £3,000; at Fordingbridge (two factories), around £1,500; at Colthorp, near Thatcham, at £1,000; at Wilton, in Wiltshire, at £500; at Lyng and Taverham (Norfolk), between £2,700 and £5,000; at Norwich, between £260 and £400; at Barford St. Martin (Wilts.), at £185 15s.; while Richard Gibbons of Hungerford, whose foundry was attacked by the Kintbury men on 22 November, claimed £261 8s. for damage done to his furnace, crane, mill patterns and iron bars.[4] If we add to these the smaller amounts of damage incurred at Redditch, Catton (Norfolk), Wantage, West Harnham (Wilts.) and elsewhere, we may reach a total of some £13,000.

We know something, too, of the amounts claimed or paid out for damage caused by riot, involving the destruction of private property, lock-ups and prisons at Banwell (Somerset), Wymondham (Norfolk), Wellingborough and Watford (Northants.), and to John Benett's and Robert Pile's barns and outhouses at Tisbury and Alton Barnes.[5] These amount to some £600; to which must be added the cost of repairing or rebuilding the workhouses at Headley and Selborne, in Hampshire; but on these the records are completely silent.

The owners of threshing machines suffered losses that defy any accurate assessment. It depended on the size and type of the machine. Some, like John Benett's at the Pyt House, were driven by half-a-dozen horses or by water-power: the value of such a machine might be £100 or more. At Elton (Hunts.), a machine destroyed by the Sawtry labourers was valued by its owner at £90. These were exceptional, as was the £150 claimed on a threshing machine and a chaff-cutter at Bibury after the riot of 29 November. At Bibury, too, the price placed on a threshing machine, a chaff-cutter and a seed-machine, all destroyed on the same occasion, was also £150. For a similar combination of machines a farmer at Upper Winchenden, in Buckinghamshire, claimed only £55. More commonly, a large machine was valued at £50, as at Stone and Blackgrove (Bucks.), Beverstone (Glos.), Heythrop (Oxon.) and Great Clacton (Essex). Below this, prices varied according to the size of the machine and the damage done to it in the course of riots: we find £45 claimed at Little Clacton; £40 at Beverstone and in five cases at Clacton; £30 at Redmarsh (Worcestershire); £20 at Little Brickhill (Bucks.); and numerous examples of £5 and £10—and even one of £2—of which £10 appears to have been the most frequently quoted figure for the smaller type of machine.[6] If we now assume that some 400 agricultural machines were destroyed—admittedly an under-estimate—and assume a mean price of £20 for a machine, we arrive at a total loss to machine-owners of £8,000.

In practice, of course, a varying proportion of these losses was offset by the compensation recovered from insurance, private donations, local authorities or government rewards. The most fortunate, in this respect, were those owners or occupiers whose property was fully covered against arson. These, however, were comparatively few: farm buildings and stock might be insured, but not the dwelling house, and vice versa. Again, insurance companies might not be as liberal in their assessments as the press, or even the more cautious of the magistrates. To take one example from the dozen cited earlier: James Lamming, occupier of the farm at North Cove in Suffolk, which was fired on 13 November, was reported to have suffered a gross loss of £1,700; but only the farm buildings (assessed at £700) were insured, and the actual amount recovered from the Norwich Union Fire Insurance Society was only £450.[7]

More serious was the fact that, faced with the spread of incendiarism, insurance offices were refusing to accept new policies covering farming stock in the disaffected counties, or were steeply raising their premiums. We have seen how the Wiltshire farmers, who, in mid-November, crowded into Salisbury to insure their wheat stacks against arson, had met with a blank refusal from the companies.[8] And such restrictions had, by then, been in operation for the past two months. As early as 10 September, the Committee of Fire of London Insurance had given a lead by resolving that

> in consequence of the numerous Fires that have occurred in the neighbourhood of Sevenoaks, the policy of £2,000 on farming stock, the property of the late John Lewis Minet Esq., which will become due at Michaelmas, be not restored, and that for the present no insurance upon Farming Stock in that part of the country be accepted.

This rigorous policy however was, six weeks later, modified to one of conditional acceptance when it was learned that "other Offices had shown inclination to extend this business at the Company's expense": in fact, the Norwich Union, in reply to anxious queries from its agents in East Kent, had instructed them "to continue taking insurance as usual, but to use discretion in so doing". By November, as arson and rioting spread westwards, other companies had begun to decline all insurance on farming stock and buildings "except under very peculiar circumstances". The Hand-in-Hand Fire Office declined new policies in Kent, Sussex and Hampshire and raised its premiums on others. The Phoenix ordered its agents to charge double premiums on all farming policies in Kent, Surrey and Sussex; and, a few weeks later, the Norwich Union went further. Alarmed by the advent of machine-breaking in their own county of Norfolk, the Directors decided on 22 November

> to refuse insuring all Farming Stock & Farm Buildings of parties who possess or who use Threshing Machines, & to discontinue all existing policies under such circumstances.

The insurance companies thus gave what Lord Melbourne would certainly have considered an incitement to riot, and continued to do so for a considerable time thereafter.[9]

Victims of arson who failed to obtain redress from insurance might recoup some of their losses by private subscription; or, if they were lucky, they might qualify for a share in one of the £500 awards offered to persons bringing rioters or incendiaries to justice in Lord Melbourne's Proclamation of 23 November 1830. This proved in most cases to be poor comfort, as comparatively few incendiaries were tried and far fewer were convicted; moreover, claims were generally entertained only if the damage had been done before 23 November;[10] in consequence, only a handful of the numerous payments made were made in respect of arson. Among these fortunate few were: in Surrey, James Franks, owner of a mill at Albury, who was awarded £190; in Sussex, Henry Alderton, who owned a farm at Battle, awarded £100; and, in Northamptonshire, the owner of a farm at Shutlanger, Lord Pomfret, and its occupier, Thomas Horn, who received respectively £180 and £80.[11]

Owners of workshops or industrial machinery proved to be somewhat more fortunate. Apart from the occasional rewards made under the terms of the Proclamation, the normal means of redress lay through claims lodged with the appropriate hundred in the counties, as provided for by an Act of 1827. According to the terms of this Act (7 & 8 Geo. 4th, cap. 31), owners of chapels, mills, mines, houses, stables, barns, shops, offices, warehouses, or industrial machines ("whether fixed or moveable") physically destroyed—but not *burned*—in riots, might lodge a claim within seven days of the disturbance and were entitled to such compensation from the hundred as the justices in petty sessions might determine. Under these provisions, a large number of claims were heard, mainly in the spring and summer of 1831, and several counties paid out considerable sums in damages. The county of Norfolk, besides spending some £2,500 on lawyers' fees and the employment of special constables and troops, put aside some £900 for prosecutions on this score. The city of Norwich paid out £262 9s. 4d. as compensation for the damage done to Messrs. Willett's silk mill. In Buckinghamshire, the owners of three of the High Wycombe paper mills destroyed in the November riots were paid off with £719 12s. In Worcestershire, two needle-manufacturers, whose presses had been damaged or destroyed, received £26 10s. as compensation and £56 3s. in costs. In Northamptonshire, sums of £5 19s. 3d., £11 14s. and £32 10s. were paid to the victims of riots at Kettering, Watford and Wellingborough. In Essex, two claimants received sums of £26 2s. 10d. and £16 0s. 11d. for windows broken at the workhouse at Great Coggeshall. Far larger payments were authorised by the justices in Hampshire and Wiltshire. In Hampshire, compensation of £1,273 15s. 11d. was paid, including nearly £850 at Fordingbridge alone; and in Wiltshire, £1,361 15s. 11d of which John Benett received £353 2s. 5d. for the damage done to his farm buildings at Tisbury.[12]

Owners of threshing machines and other agricultural machinery destroyed in the riots were not so fortunate. Their claims on the hundreds were rejected in every case as falling outside the provisions of the Act, presumably as such machines were not employed "in any Trade or Manufacture or any Branch thereof". There was, however, no lack of claims submitted. William Page claimed on a machine destroyed at Finedon "that had cost him £80"; James Hayes on one destroyed at Elton (Hunts.), valued at £90. From Pewsey (Wilts.) and Wakefield (Yorks.) came pleas for a revision of the law; and a West Sussex woman, who had been refused redress in her own county, asserted (wrongly) that such claims had been met in Hampshire. A Huntingdon farmer protested that, though denied redress on his own machine, he might, through the county rate, have to contribute to the restoration of his neighbour's mill. Even the threshing-machine manufacturers of Fairford, whose machines had been broken in their shops, were only able to recover £40 on one of their claims and an additional £60 through private subscription—a poor compensation for damage estimated at £300.[13]

Yet, failing the Act, there were other means of obtaining some redress. One was by qualifying for a government reward; the other was by receiving compensation from one's county in the form of costs awarded in successful prosecutions. In Worcestershire, James Fretwell, whose threshing machine had been destroyed on his landlord's instruction, recovered £19 in this way, and John Groatman recovered £6 12s. 6d. on a machine valued at £30. The Norfolk magistrates, who by March 1831 had paid out £700 in similar cases, quite deliberately chose this means of making up for the deficiencies of the 1827 Act; for they stressed "the importance of paying the costs of prosecutions in full, as many of these had already suffered severe damage for which the law allows no compensation".[14] But, outside Norfolk, the sums paid out appear to have amounted to very little.

The second course was to apply for a share in one of the government's £500 rewards. Records show that such rewards were made as the result of 188 successful prosecutions of rioters and incendiaries in twenty-three counties. But the number of persons receiving payments was far greater, as the pressure of claimants compelled the Treasury to subdivide the rewards, sometimes into £50 shares, but often into far smaller amounts. In Buckinghamshire, for example, the High Wycombe affair led to the payment of a total of £639 to 88 applicants and, in Bedfordshire, no fewer than 266 persons shared in the £500 awarded following the riot at Stotfold. Frequently, as with county awards, rewards were used as a means of compensating the owners of threshing machines, denied redress under the Act of 1827; and we find cases of machine-owners being rewarded as informers in Berkshire, Dorset, Gloucester, Hampshire, Huntingdon, Norfolk,

Northamptonshire and Wiltshire. Sums received varied between £20 or £30 at one end of the scale and £100, or even £130, at the other. There were perhaps fifty such cases in all; but it is doubtful if the owners of threshing machines were compensated for more than one quarter of their losses in this way.[15]

If we put all these facts and figures together, we can get some idea of the scale of damage and net losses suffered by "Swing"'s victims; but we shall not yet have discovered which of these victims—the landlord, overseer, parson, farmer or manufacturer—bore the main brunt. If we discount the manufacturer—who provided at most an occasional target—does it appear that the labourers were selective or indiscriminate in their attacks on landlords, parsons and farmers? Some observers wrote as though their blows were directed without any discrimination whatsoever against "all descriptions of property" and "without respect of persons".[16] Others, like Gibbon Wakefield, took a directly contrary view. According to Wakefield, the labourers quite deliberately spared the farmers, as their quarrel was not with them but with their common enemy, the squire and the parson. And he goes on to argue that even the firing of farming stock did little injury to the farmers, who were generally insured, whereas tithe-stacks were rarely covered against arson and the insurance companies refused to insure the property of the "peasant-hated rural aristocracy".[17]

This is certainly an exaggeration, and the last point, in particular, finds no support in the records that we have consulted. There might appear to be more truth in the claim that the parson (if not the landlord) was the most consistent among the labourers' victims and that the farmer was less frequently the target than eye-witness and newspaper accounts would seem to indicate. We have seen that farmers (unless they also happened to be overseers) were rarely manhandled by the labourers and that, in certain districts, as in the Weald and along the Norfolk–Suffolk border, parsons were more often the victims of attack than any other group. Yet if we consider the riots as a whole, the picture will look somewhat different. In cases of arson, there is little doubt that farmers suffered most. In 202 cases, in which we have with some degree of certainty been able to establish the victim's identity, there were 36 involving landlords, justices and gentry; 12 involving parsons; 9 involving overseers; 21 involving tradesmen; and 132—two-thirds of the whole—involving farmers.[18] In cases of agricultural machine-breaking and "robbery", the proportion of all the victims formed by the farmers was certainly as great, and probably far greater. They also had their fair share of threatening letters, though these were more evenly distributed: among 82 letters whose recipients we have noted, 16 were addressed to landlords, 19 to parsons (the number is significant), two to overseers, 12 to tradesmen and 33 to farmers.

In wages riots, the farmers probably did somewhat better and the parsons almost certainly did worse. In demanding higher wages, the labourers addressed their demands with equal insistence to all their employers, whether farmers, parsons, overseers or landlords. The farmers generally acquiesced; but we have seen that it was often on the understanding that the parson—if not the landlord—should really foot the bill. In many cases rents, and far more frequently tithes, were in fact reduced to meet the farmers' and labourers' demands;[19] but were they commensurate with the rise in wages? It seems extremely unlikely, as wages rose appreciably in all the disaffected counties whereas reductions in rent and tithe were by no means universal and were based as much on promise as on performance. Thus, here too, the farmers (like other rural employers) were called on to make some immediate sacrifice; yet, in this case, at least, it was only a temporary one, as, once the riots were over, wages might often tend to slip back towards their former level.[20]

It would seem therefore that the farmers, whatever the labourers' intentions, were in practice as much the victims of the riots as the parsons or the country gentry. But though this invalidates one part of Wakefield's argument, does it invalidate the other? Does it mean that the farmers stood in the same relationship to the riotous labourers as the squire and parson and viewed the disturbances with a similar hostility, indifference or apprehension? If it were so, it would make nonsense of all the reports of collusion between the farmers and labourers, of which we have quoted examples from East Anglia and the Kent and Sussex Weald. Was this a general feature of the riots or was it restricted to this handful of counties?

There were certainly exceptions. Thus, in Wiltshire, it was noted that farmers tended to be "men of substance";[21] and here, probably more than in any other county, the labourers met with organised resistance and found comparatively little support from the farming community. In Berkshire, too, reports spoke of "the total want of feeling of the farmers towards the common labourers" and of the close collaboration of farmers and gentry to suppress the riots.[22] At the other end of the scale were those counties and districts where small farmers predominated or were able to make their voices heard. In the Weald, for example, the labourers' movement compelled the small farmers ("the great majority of our Weald agriculturalists"), in defending their own livelihood, to take a firm line with the landlords and clergy. The *Brighton Herald* thus reports the situation:

> The middle class of farmers, thus pressed on the one hand by their starving labourers, and on the other by the landlords and clergy, will, unless speedily rescued from their painful dilemma, be compelled to make common cause with the former, whom they must consider as fellow-sufferers, while the latter they must look on as exactors and oppressors.

The high level of rates was another bone of contention: we have seen the case of Dallington, near Battle; and, at Ringmer, where Lord Gage negotiated with his tenants and labourers on 17 November, it was reported that, among the farmers, "one of the smock-frock working example" gave strong support to the labourers' claims and protested against under-paid farm-workers being forced on to the parish rates. In West Sussex, even before the riots started, a small farmer complained that he was paying 11s. a week in tithe and poor rate. In Surrey, a major source of disturbance was said to be "the small farmers, who are disposed to urge their poorer neighbours to the commission of excesses, in the hope that by such means they may succeed in getting rid of tithes, and diminishing the amount of rent". In Wiltshire, it was said of the small farmers that, even if they did not actually take part in the riots, they "are glad to see the labourers at work"; and, on the Sussex–Hampshire border, the small farmers were "bankrupt" and, in one instance, "told the Mob to burn away", as "the farms were not their property".[23] And, in some counties, small farmers were actually arrested, charged with active participation in the riots: we shall find examples in Dorset, Hampshire, Suffolk, Surrey and Norfolk.*

But, if large farmers tended more often to oppose the labourers and small farmers to support them, this is only a part of the picture. There is plenty of evidence to suggest that, between these extremes, the farming community as a whole (except in parts of Wiltshire and Berkshire) tended to become passive, if not active, allies in the labour-

* See p. 244 below.

ers' cause. Most often, it was a simple matter of attempting to make the landlords and clergy bear the costs of the labourers' demands. Typical examples of this are provided by such meetings as took place at Wallop in Hampshire and Stoke Holy Cross in Norfolk. At Wallop, the farmers offered to increase wages from 8s. to 10s. provided that rents, tithes and taxes should be lowered in proportion; at Stoke Holy Cross, they agreed to raise wages by one-fifth provided that tithes were reduced by one-quarter and rents by one-sixth. At Headcorn, in Kent, farmers and labourers signed a joint petition to Parliament, requesting relief from tithes and taxes and parliamentary reform; at Lewes, they put forward a combined demand for higher wages for the labourers and reduced tithes and taxes for the farmers. At Ugborough, in Devon, the farmers issued what amounted to a general tenants' manifesto. Meeting on 6 December, they unanimously

> RESOLVED—That the difficulty of supporting themselves and families, without sacrificing their Capital—which the Renting Farmers of this Parish have experienced during the last several years, occasioned in a great degree by the disproportion of Rents and Tithes to the price of Farm Produce—has been the immediate cause of that want of employment and consequent distress of the Labourers.
>
> RESOLVED—That such diminution of Agricultural Capital and Farm Labour is highly detrimental to the Interests of all Classes of the community.
>
> RESOLVED—That the non-residence of many of the principal Landholders of this Parish, and the extracting from it, in the shape of Rent and Tithes, upwards of two thirds of the whole amount of the annual Rent, without expending any portion of the same in its immediate Neighbourhood, is a grievous injury to the Inhabitants generally, and especially to the Labouring Classes.
>
> RESOLVED—That the evasive answers and positive refusals which many of us have received from our Superiors, when individually applying for Reduction of Rent, or Tithes Composition, and seeing, notwithstanding, our unremitting exertions—our Capital and means of employing the Labourer daily diminishing—and the consequent increase of pauperism and distress, from causes over which individually we have no control, we feel it a duty which we owe to ourselves, our families, and our dependants, to present our united request—That the Landowners and Tithe-

holders of this Parish do meet the Occupiers at the SHIP INN, in Ugborough, on TUESDAY, the 21st of DECEMBER, 1830, at ELEVEN o'clock in the Forenoon, for the purpose of conferring with them, and advising the most satisfactory and effectual modes of relieving the existing Distress, and enabling the Tenant Farmer to employ the Labourer on his Farm, at wages adequate to the support of his Family; which, it is the opinion of this meeting, can only be affected by a corresponding reduction of Rents, Tithes, and Taxes, in proportion to the exigences of the present time.[24]

Inevitably, such an agitation by the farmers, coming at such a time, exposed them to the charge—often fully justified—that they were deliberate instigators of disturbance. This was particularly the case in East Anglia, and the *Norfolk Mercury* reported that "in the great majority of instances the labourers were as much the instrument of proferring the complaints of the farmers as of their own". At Wrotham, in East Kent, where the labourers "mobbed" the rector to compel him to reduce his tithe, it was said that "the farmers . . . were not unconnected with the assembly". At Horsham, a correspondent wrote that the farmers "were known secretly to be promoting the assembling of the people". At Tisbury, labourers who had taken part in the assault on the Pyt House claimed that "the farmers were at the bottom of it: that they gave them beer and urged them to excesses". In Cornwall, it was even said that the farmers "are generally inclined to excite their labourers to disturbance with the hope of by that means forcing a reduction of rent and tithe". Such a charge would seem plausible enough in the case of the Callington farmers who, in calling on the rector to reduce his rent, wrote that "otherwise (they could) not answer for the peaceable conduct of the labourers".[25]

In the matter of threshing machines, the farmers' attitude was somewhat different from what it was on wages, rent and tithe. Yet it was, to say the least, ambivalent and might, here too, on occasion be construed as a direct encouragement to the labourers' activities. There were remarkably few occasions when farmers resisted the rioters and stoutly defended their machines. Such efforts, where they were made, were almost universally half-hearted, and every press reporter and correspondent commented on the speed and ease with which the machine-breakers achieved their purpose. This was as true of Kent and Sussex as it was of Hampshire, Berkshire, Wiltshire, Gloucestershire,

Devon, Huntingdon and Norfolk; and, even in counties like Yorkshire, West Suffolk, Nottingham and Lincoln, where there was strictly speaking no machine-breaking movement, farmers hastened to comply with the labourers' wishes and destroyed their own machines at the mere rumour or prospect of impending riot.[26] Of course, in some districts it may have been a case of discretion proving the better part of valour, and threshing-machine owners, even if disposed to protect their property, may have decided that resistance would expose them to even greater dangers. So *The Times*, in reporting the mid-November events in Kent and Sussex, commented that farmers universally agreed to the labourers' demands—to raise wages and dismantle their machines, as they were not foolish enough "to refuse requests not unreasonable in themselves & put to them by 300–400 men after a barn or two had been fired and each farmer had an incendiary letter addressed to him in his pocket".[27]

Thus the element of compulsion in itself played an important part; for why else should the machines have been introduced in the first place or not have been put aside before the riots started? Yet the farmers' "over-zeal" (as one reporter termed it) to comply with the labourers' demands had more to it than that. Some farmers' zeal was such that they not only put aside, but destroyed, their own machines before the rioters appeared in their districts; and, at the last machine-breaking of the whole "Swing" movement, Thomas Faircloth, a Cambridgeshire farmer, told the labourers (or so it was reported), "I suppose you have come to break the machine, and there it is, break it"; and such incidents were not infrequent.[28] It could be, as in this particular instance, that the farmer in question, having hired the machine, would not himself be the loser. In other cases, even if the owner, he might expect (before the Act of 1827 had been put to the test) to receive adequate compensation for its loss. But there were other reasons, such as that put forward in a *Times* report on the first machine-breaking riots in East Kent:

> It is understood [it ran] the farmers whose thrashing machines have been broken do not intend to renew them. So far, therefore the objects of the riots will be answered. . . . Farmers do not consider thrashing machines of much advantage, seeing that they throw the labourers out of work, and consequently upon the parish.[29]

Besides, there was a widespread feeling—and it was shared by many outside the farming and labouring community—that the thrashing machine was a socially dangerous, if not an immoral, innovation. We have seen the speed with which the Norfolk magistrates acted in recommending "the general disuse of threshing machines as a friendly concession ... to public opinion".* In Kent, the Earl of Guildford required his tenants to lay aside their machines; and in Somerset, the Marquess of Bath ordered the farmers to destroy them. At Blockley, in Worcestershire, Lord Northwick actually sent his bailiff and a constable to break his tenant's, Thomas Fretwell's, machine when he refused to do so himself.[30] And we have noted the remarkable leniency of Sir Edward Knatchbull, who sentenced the first machine-breakers in East Kent to a three-days' term in prison.†

Such views and actions were explicitly condemned in a Circular issued by Lord Melbourne on 8 December. He sharply rebuked magistrates who, in certain districts, had approved uniform wage rates (a practice long fallen into general disuse and specifically forbidden by an Act of 1813) and who had recommended "the Discontinuance of the Employment of Machines used for thrashing out Corn and for other purposes". "These Machines", he continued,

> are as much entitled to the Protection of the Law as any other Description of Property, and ... the course which has been taken of prescribing or recommending the Discontinuance of them is, in fact, to connive at, or rather to assist in the Establishment of a Tyranny of the most oppressive Character.

Several of Melbourne's correspondents thought otherwise and remained unrepentant. On the very day of the Circular, a Dorset magistrate was proposing that owners of threshing machines who refused to destroy them should be penalised by only receiving half the insured value of their corn in the event of arson. Others, while not going quite so far as that, thought that the law, in offering its protection, should distinguish between threshing machines and other forms of machinery. A Berkshire magistrate, commenting on the destruction of Mr. Goddard's ploughs and machines at Templeton, stressed the fact that "the rioters did not confine themselves to threshing machines, *the use of which might be doubtful*, but destroyed ploughs & other useful instruments of husbandry of acknowledged use". And from London a correspondent wrote in direct reply to Melbourne:

> Threshing machines cannot be defended on the same principle as machinery in Manufactures, because the ability to supply the home

* See p. 155 above.

† See p. 101 above.

> or foreign market does not in any degree depend on them, and (I) will undertake to prove if called upon that they are *on the whole* a great *disadvantage* to the farming interest . . . I can excuse the farmers giving low wages on the score of their own poverty, but can any excuse be offered for men who are so deaf to humanity & blind to their own *permanent* interest as to substitute Horse power for manual labour & leave the population born on the soil to subsist on a miserable pittance in idleness or unproductively employed on the roads?[31]

It was undoubtedly because they shared similar views that many farmers were so half-hearted in their defence of their machines, and thereby they made the labourers' task an easier one. Their hostility to tithe and rent went deeper and led them, on occasion, as we have seen, to become not merely passive spectators, but active accomplices in the labourers' movement. Yet, taking them as a whole, they were uncertain and hesitant allies and it was only a minority that responded to Cobbett's appeal "to make common cause with your labourers in obtaining a removal of the cause of their sufferings".[32] Had it been otherwise, the events of 1830 and 1831 might have had very different results.

Notes to Chapter 11

1. E. Gibbon Wakefield, *Swing Unmasked*, pp. 20–24, 28–31.
2. *The Times*, 29 November, 23–25 November 1830.
3. *The Times*, 30 October, 20 November 1830; 17 January 1831; H.O. 52/8 (Kent); H.O. 52/12 (Berks.).
4. *The Times*, 21, 22 November; 1, 2, 8, 18 December 1830. H.O. 52/7 (Hants.); H.O. 52/9 (Norfolk); T.S. 11/849; T. 1/4193. Norfolk R.O., Norwich Q.S. Minute Book, 1830–32; Hants. R.O., *Calendar of Prisoners . . . 1830*; Wilts. R.O., Treasurer's Account Book, 1831–32; Q.S. Draft Minute Book, 1830–32.
5. T. 1/4194; Wilts. R.O., Treasurer's Account Book, 1830–32; Northants. R.O., Treasurer's Account Book (Western Division), 1830–31.
6. Values are taken from Prison Calendars and Q.S. records.
7. *The Times*, 16, 20 November 1830; Norwich Union Fire Insurance Society, Board of Directors' Minute Book, March 1826–October 1831, p. 73.
8. *The Times*, 23 November 1830.
9. London Assurance, Minutes of the Committee of Fire, June 1827–31 December 1831 (Minute of 10 September 1830); Minutes of the Court of Directors, XXV (1829–32), pp. 164, 175, 288. Hand-in-Hand Fire and Life Insurance Society, General Minute Book, 1826–33 (Guild. Lib., MS. 8666/34),

pp. 288–98; General Letter Book, 1752–1842 (Guild. Lib. MS. 8670), pp. 107, 128. *The Times*, 21 October; 10, 29 November 1830. Norwich Union Fire Ins. Soc., Board of Directors' Minute Book, 1826–31, pp. 59, 75–9, 82, 88. See also H.O. 52/9 [Norfolk] (letter and enclosure of 12 December 1830). See also Sun Fire papers (Guild. Lib. MSS. 11,931–7), Globe Insurance papers (Guild. Lib. MSS. 11,657–8).

Unlike other Companies, Royal Exchange Assurance does not seem to have raised its premiums: see Royal Exchange Assurance Co., Fire Policy Registers: (*a*) Agents' Books, 1826–33 (Guild. Lib., MSS. 7253/93–98; (*b*) Head Office, 1828–34 (Guild. Lib., MSS. 7254/64–66).

The usual premiums on farming stock appear to have been restored by early December. Yet London Assurance was still instructing its agents in Kent and Sussex, as late as August 1831, to refer all new insurance on farming stock to Head Office for approval (Minutes of the Court of Directors, XXV (1829–32), 175, 288).

10. See H.O. 36/22, Treasury Entry Books General, 1829–35, p. 170; and H.O. 52/7 [Essex] (letter of 9 December 1830).
11. T. 1/4194 (Northants., Sussex); see also H.O. 36/22.
12. Norfolk R.O., Q.S. Minute Book, 1827–32, pp. 225–7; Norwich Q.S. Minute Book, 1830–32 (entry for 9 March 1831). Worcester R.O., Q.S. Order Books, XII (Mich. 1830–Easter 1833), 145, 149, 172–3. Northants. R.O., Treasurer's Account Book, Easter 1830–Easter 1832 ("incidental expenses"). Essex R.O., Treasurer's Accounts, Midsummer Q.S. 1829–Summer Q.S. 1831 (accounts for Winter 1831). Hants. R.O., Treasurer's General Account Books, no. 28, entries for 28 June–18 October 1831, 3 January–28 March and 3 July–22 September 1832. Wilts. R.O., Treasurer's Account Book, 1831–32, entries 89–100; Q.S. Draft Minute Book, 1830–32.
13. Northants. R.O., Kettering Petty Sessions, Draft Minute Book, October 1830–July 1832 (entry for 3 January 1831). Hunts. R.O., Q.S. 1830: depositions. H.O. 52/11 (letter of 3 December 1830); H.O. 40/26, fos. 431–4; T. 1/4193 (Essex); H.O. 52/13 (letter of 9 March 1831); H.O. 52/12 [Glos.] (n.d.). *The Times*, 5 March 1831.
14. Worcester R.O., Q.S. Order Books, XII, 144–5, 152; Norfolk R.O., Q.S. Minute Book, 1827–32, pp. 225–7.
15. T. 1/4193–4. Amounts vary between £20, £30, £40, £50, £100, £130.
16. *The Times*, 22 November 1830.
17. E. G. Wakefield, *op. cit.*, pp. 28–31.
18. For these and subsequent figures, see Appendix III. Of these 132 cases, 24 appear to relate to *large* and 6 (less certainly) to *small* farmers.
19. For examples, see *The Times*, 30 November (Surrey), 6 December (Bucks.), 7 December (Berks.), 9 December (Glos.), 13 December 1830 (Oxon., Sussex, Norfolk, Notts.); *Ipswich Journal*, 4 December 1830 (Suffolk); *Cobbett's Two-Penny Trash* (3 vols., London 1831–32), I, 143 (Kent).
20. *The Times*, 10 December 1830 (Northants.); 22, 28 January 1831 (Glos., Sussex). H.O. 40/27, fos. 396–7 (Hants.); Gash, *op. cit.*, pp. 82–3 (Berks.). But see below, p. 298.
21. *The Times*, 4 December 1830.

22. H.O. 52/6 (letter of 28 November 1830). For high tithes and taxes and (less certainly) rents in Berkshire, see *The Times*, 27 November 1830.
23. *The Times*, 13 December, 25 November, 13 November, 22 November 1830; H.O. 52/11 (letter of 26 November 1830); H.O. 52/7 (letter of 21 November 1830).
24. *The Times*, 18, 23, 25 November 1830; 6 December 1831. H.O. 52/12 (6 December 1830).
25. *The Times*, 3, 25, 28 December 1830; H.O. 40/27, fos. 119–20; H.O. 52/11 (letter of 21 November 1830); H.O. 52/6 (letter of 25 November 1830).
26. See *The Times*, 16, 17, 22, 23, 29 November; 1, 4 December 1830. H.O. 52/8 (letter of 17 October 1830); H.O. 52/11 (letter of 22 November 1830); H.O. 52/9 (letter of 25 November 1830); H.O. 52/7 (letter of 1 December 1830).
27. *The Times*, 17 November 1830.
28. *Cambridge & Hertford Independent Press*, 27 November 1832; and see *The Times*, 5 March 1831, for William Page, farmer of Finedon (Northants.).
29. *The Times*, 6 September 1830.
30. H.O. 52/8 (letter of 17 October 1830); *The Times*, 29 November 1830; H.O. 52/15 (correspondence of 6 January–1 February 1831).
31. *The Times*, 9 December 1830; H.O. 40/25, fos. 667–70 (8 December 1830); Berks. R.O., D/EPg 01/5; H.O. 40/27, fos. 363–4 (10 December 1830).
32. *Cobbett's Two-Penny Trash*, I, 143.

12

WHO WAS "SWING"?

Observers were inclined to draw a sharp distinction between "Swing" the incendiary and "Swing" the machine-breaker. Once the movement got under way, it became customary to label the rioters as "peasants" —in 1830, still the most common synonym for farm labourers. There were exceptions, as in Kent, where there was at first a disposition to see the machine-breakers purely as "smugglers" or "poachers"; and, on the Wiltshire–Dorset border, a magistrate of Cranborne Chase described the Handley rioters as the product of "a wild and dissolute population of poachers, smugglers & deer-stealers".[1] But, usually, opinion was quick to realise that the rioters who held wages meetings, marched on workhouses, broke threshing machines, and held farmers and householders to ransom—often in open daylight—were more generally typical of the village labourers, or "paupers", who worked for the farmers and drew relief from the overseers of the poor.

Regarding the incendiaries, however, observers were not so level-headed and—as in the case of the anonymous letter-writers—were prone to indulge in more extravagant speculations. It was natural, too, that men who operated at dead of night should appear to be outsiders or "strangers", divorced from the local rural population. It seemed all the more likely as the machine-breaking labourers—as in Berkshire, Wiltshire, Suffolk and Lincoln—frequently condemned the incendiary and disassociated themselves from his activities.[2] So he might appear in the guise of a down-at-heel vagrant, like the "itinerant Irishman, who vends leather straps" and carried a luridly-phrased "Swing" message from one "Johnny Bonny", who was arrested at Bishop's Stortford. But, more often, he was thought to be a "stranger" of a more respectable appearance. After a fire at Otham, in Kent, on 12 November, the incendiary is described as "a stranger, dressed in shabby genteel, but of manners apparently above the ordinary class". At Stanton, in Wiltshire, two men were seen to wear "great drab coats"; a third appeared to be "a stranger" and "a respectable-dressed man". At Wotton Pillinge (Bedfordshire), two "gentlemanly-looking men" were the strongest suspects; at Preston (Middlesex), it was "a prosperous stranger". At Heythrop, in Oxfordshire, "two well-dressed men in a green gig" had been seen to be watching the ricks. At Holyport, in Berkshire, the chief suspects were two "Jew-looking fellows"—presumably from London.[3] And so we could go on.

Other observers were equally convinced that the incendiaries had no connection with the local labouring population. At Egham, a householders' meeting decided that the fires in Surrey were "the work of distant & foreign incendiaries". Similar reports appeared in *The Times* from its correspondents at Battle and at Uckfield, in West Sussex; while, in Bedfordshire, following a spate of fires in late November and early December, opinion was divided: "It is generally supposed [ran a report] that the fires are not the work of the peasantry, though there are many exceptions to the general belief."[4]

A Rye correspondent thought, however, that there, at least, there was "no doubt" that the fires "were contrived by the labourers". And this was certainly by now becoming the view of the more responsible observers. Gibbon Wakefield, who had the advantage of writing after the riots were all but over, insisted that the incendiaries were simple labourers or "paupers". He distinguishes between two kinds: the weak, degraded pauper and the sturdy, intelligent labourer. "Who", he asks rhetorically, "is that defective being, with calfless legs and stooping shoulders, weak in body and mind, inert, pusillanimous, and stupid, whose premature wrinkles and furtive glance tell of misery and degradation? That is an English pauper." The other class of "pauper" he describes as "strong, intelligent, upright . . ., but driven to poaching & smuggling by the futility of the Poor Law". And "Swing", whom he sees essentially as an incendiary, is compounded of the two.

A more specific picture is that presented in a confidential report to the Police Officer for the County Fire Office, in London. It firmly discards all "the stories about strangers in gigs and . . . fire-balls" and concludes that "in almost every instance, wherein conviction has taken place, the culprit has been a servant of the sufferer or person living near to him, acting under some motive of revenge".[5]

And this is precisely the picture that emerges from a study of the police and prison records. There were 96 persons tried for arson in 24 counties between the autumn of 1830 and the summer of 1831. There is no "stranger" and hardly a "gentleman" among them. They include seven women, of whom two were convicted—Sarah Wheeler, who was sentenced to a year in prison by the Wiltshire Summer

Assizes of 1831, and Elizabeth Studham, transported to Tasmania for setting fire to an East Kent workhouse. Of the 39 whose occupations are given, two were farmers: an Essex tenant farmer, charged with firing his house to defraud the Equitable Insurance Office, and a one-time merchant, suspected of firing a Surrey farm-house from motives of revenge; but neither of these was convicted. There were five described as weavers, including two Cumberland Radicals, charged with burning wheat stacks at Carlisle. Four of these were discharged: the exception was Richard Knockolds, a Norwich weaver, who was capitally convicted for firing stacks at Swanton Abbott. The rest were all farm servants—a hurdle-maker, a carter, and 30 labourers and ploughmen. All except one (a "vagrant") was a local man; many had been employed by the landlord or farmer whose stacks or buildings they burned down; and in only one case was it seriously suggested that the means employed was anything more pyrotechnical than a box of matches or a labourer's pipe.[6]

We know less about those tried or convicted for writing threatening letters. Forty-six names appear in the trial records of 22 counties. Five of them were women, one of them described as "decently dressed": we know nothing about the others. Only 13 people were convicted, six of them to varying terms of transportation. Unfortunately, occupations appear only in one quarter of the cases that came before the courts. Unlike the incendiaries, they are evenly divided between labourers and others, and include four labourers, a gardener, two schoolmasters, an attorney's clerk, a journeyman tailor, and a straw-plait manufacturer.[7]

How did the machine-breakers and wages-rioters differ from these smaller groups? In their case, as we have seen, press reports and the descriptions of Home Office correspondents tended to be more sober and objective. Occasionally, as we should expect, there are angry accounts of "desperate gangs", of "strangers dressed as labourers", or of "the lowest description of persons"; and there is more than a touch of social prejudice in a Berkshire magistrate's picture of the Bucklebury and Aldermaston rioters as "men of indifferent character, well-known in the neighbourhood, and chiefly unmarried men", and of their leader as "an old offender, a desperate fellow, a kind of half-gypsy".[8]

But such ill-tempered expletives are comparatively rare, and contemporary observers give us a far more convincing picture of the "Swing"-rioters than their forbears would have done, on similar occasions, half a century before. In these accounts, a distinction is often made (as by Wakefield) between the underfed paupers and better-paid labourers, and also between labourers and craftsmen, between leaders and followers, and between the rioters in one region and those in another. Of the Hungerford riots we read that those engaged were "the lowest class of the poor" and that, at Wantage, they were "the worst (or lowest) description of labourers". On the other hand, a correspondent wrote of the Heythrop men that "none appear to be in distress or workless"; and of the Pershore rioters in Worcestershire it was said that "their hearty, hale appearance and decent attire bespoke anything but indigence". Colonel Mair, who attended the Special Commission at Winchester, remarked on the relative affluence of the Hampshire prisoners: they appeared generally (he wrote) to be "free from the pressure of want"; and he noted in particular the large number of "carpenters, blacksmiths & other mechanics", earning wages between 14s. and 30s. Others noted differences between the leaders and their followers. A witness of a midnight visit to a farm on the Isle of Thanet distinguished between "3 men well dressed on the lawn in front of the House" and "9 men in rear of the House who were countrymen & strangers". Leaders were often seen to be craftsmen. Such observations are particularly frequent at Maidstone, Horsham and the Sussex Weald, where the urban craftsmen were widely held to be politically disaffected. Maidstone was said to be "infested with radicals, chiefly journeymen artificers". At Lewes, the journeymen tailors are described as being "a class of Artisans who we have private information are very active in promoting discontent and tumult"; while, from Brighton, a magistrate wrote of the riots in the Kent and Sussex Weald: "The Mechanics throughout the whole business have been the worst, the leaders & plotters of the whole mischief. They were all well paid & are nearly all disaffected."[9]

For a fuller and more rounded picture we must turn to the prison and judicial records. These relate to nearly 2,000 persons who were tried in some thirty counties, and a quarter of whom were later transported to the Australian colonies.[10] They fully confirm that the machine-breakers and other rioters were predominantly "peasants" or country labourers. This is so in nearly every county in which disturbances took place: among prisoners, the proportion varies between 70 per cent in Hampshire, Oxfordshire and Berkshire and about 95 per cent in Huntingdon, Bedfordshire and Essex. The one exception is Buckinghamshire, where, in view of the nature of the local riots, it is hardly surprising that the prisoners were almost equally divided—if we except a handful of craftsmen—between labourers and paper-makers. Yet the distinction between the two is not as sharp as it might appear; for several paper-makers were also village labourers, some labourers were former paper-workers, and, in the records of those transported, we find numerous instances of paper-makers whose sisters or daughters were married to farm-labourers, and vice-versa.[11]

But the term "labourer" was a generic one applied to a variety of village occupations. Most frequently, these labourers were ploughmen; but we also find among them reapers, mowers, milkmen, herdsmen, shepherds, shearers, carters, carriers, waggoners, ostlers, grooms, stable-boys, jockeys, horse-breakers, porters, waiters, footmen, house servants, hop-planters, spadesmen, "navigators" (or road-makers), stone-breakers, kitchen and market gardeners, well-diggers, builders' labourers, or simply "paupers" or "out of work". Sometimes a labourer combined farm-work with another occupation: so we find among the Wiltshire prisoners one ploughman who was also a butcher, another who was a chimney-sweep, and a third who was a "jobber in pigs and chickens".

Were these labourers relatively prosperous or were they among the poorest of the poor? It depended partly on the county, but far more on whether a man was fully or partly employed, or wholly dependent on the miserable allowance paid by the overseer of the poor; and on such facts as these the records tell us very little. In Kent, a fully employed farm-worker would be earning, even before the riots started, up to 12s. 6d. weekly and a thrasher (if not already superseded by machinery) perhaps 3s. more. Among the Hampshire prisoners, Colonel Mair claimed that many labourers were earning 12s. or even 15s.; and, at Shingay, in Cambridgeshire, the justices reported that "the most violent" of the rioters, who were demanding an increase in allowances, "in nearly every case were earning good and, in some cases, high wages".[12] But such cases were quite exceptional. In most of the southern counties, wages were not above 10s. weekly, and this is the figure most commonly cited (in the few instances where one appears at all) in the records of prisoners in full employment. In Wiltshire, wages were considerably lower, and Lord Arundel, in making a return of the Tisbury and Fonthill Gifford men who had been in his employment, notes that every one of the labourers was earning 7s. a week. A partly employed or unemployed man might earn as little as half that sum. Among the High Wycombe prisoners was a paper-maker, whose weekly wage was a mere 5s.; and some "paupers" among the rioters were drawing allowances of 3s. 6d. and 6s. a week. Prison and conviction inevitably brought greater hardships; and it appears that nearly one in three of the married men transported to Tasmania (in those cases where the facts are known) left their wives and children "on the parish".[13]

Yet, as noted by observers, the labourers in these riots were often accompanied, or led, by men of other occupations or other social groups. Apart from craftsmen and farmers, who deserve a special mention, there were among the Hampshire prisoners a mill-worker, a worker in a tin-yard, a road surveyor, a gypsy razor-grinder, a house-property owner, and an attorney's clerk. In Berkshire, they included a paper-maker and a publican; in Huntingdon, a miller; in Northamptonshire, a pedlar and an Army officer; in Oxfordshire, a wool-sorter, a shag-weaver, a basket-maker, a chimney-sweep and a coal-dealer; in Wiltshire, three brick-makers, a leather-cutter and a carpet-weaver; in Buckinghamshire, a beer-house keeper, a miller and a needle-maker; in Cambridgeshire, a shopkeeper; in Somerset, a horse-dealer; and, in Sussex, an ex-policeman. But more significant were a small number of farmers and small-holders, who carried their hostility to squire and parson, or to the government itself, to the point of directly participating in the riots. In Hampshire, there were the two Radical small-holders, James and Robert Mason, who played a leading part in the riots around Micheldever and were transported to New South Wales. A small Hampshire farmer was John Boyes, who was convicted of demanding money with menaces at Owslebury. His brother, William Boyes, though acquitted of this charge, came up for later trial with two other farmers, Thomas Deacle and John Hoar, on a charge of having conspired together to compel "certain landlords and tithe-owners to reduce their tithes and rents, and increase the wages of the labourers in their employment"; they were acquitted. In Dorset, John Dore, a farmer of Stower Provost, was bound over for two years for participation in a riot. In Norfolk, Lee Amis, who occupied a small farm at Roughton, was acquitted of a charge of inciting labourers to demand higher wages; and, at Hoxne, in Suffolk, Robert Watling, another small farmer, was alleged (though here again the case was dismissed) to have played a leading part in a tithe-and-wages riot.[14]

But these farmers were only a handful: generally, as we have seen, the farmers' activity lay at the fringe rather than at the centre of the labourers' movement. Far more important was the role played within it by the town and village craftsmen, who appeared in considerably greater numbers than the farmers among the rioters themselves. It was of these that Mr. Justice Parke, a presiding judge at Winchester and Salisbury, was speaking when he commented sourly on the frequent participation in the riots of men "whose wages were such as to place them far above the reach of want"; and he picked out for special mention "blacksmiths, carpenters and artisans—men who were in a somewhat superior condition of life".[15] There were, of course, significant variations as between one county and another. Among 133 Hampshire prisoners whose occupations we have noted, there were 30 craftsmen: bricklayers, carpenters, blacksmiths, wheelwrights, sawyers, tailors, shoemakers, tanners, hoop-makers and thatchers. In Wiltshire, there were 25 craftsmen out of 147; in Berkshire and Sussex, they were nearly one in four; in Oxford, Norfolk and Somerset, two in seven; in Kent, one in six; in Dorset, one in seven. In some counties, the proportion was considerably lower: one in 29 in Buckingham, one in 31 in Cambridgeshire, one in 57 in Huntingdon, and, in Essex, only one in 86. In all, we have counted 142 craftsmen among 1,000 prisoners whose occupations appear in the records of 19 counties.

But the real significance of the craftsmen's participation was far greater than a bare recital of such numbers as these might indicate. To quote Mr. Justice Parke at Salisbury: "[They] have been the foremost in the destruction of threshing machinery and in the violent and often felonious acts which the Mob, in the pursuit of that purpose, have so often committed." To the judges it seemed inconceivable that men so placed should have had anything but the most dishonourable motives for behaving in such a way. At Ramsbury, among those convicted were a carpenter, a blacksmith, and a woodman: "They belonged to a class of persons (the judge commented) who had not even the vain pretence that these machines could affect them in any manner." And the judge thus addressed a man convicted of having broken a machine at Whiteparish: "You, William Hayter, are a clock-maker. You had nothing to do with thrashing-machines. What assignable motive, but an improper one, could you have for joining the mob for their destruction?"[16]

Yet their conduct was by no means inexplicable. Blacksmiths, carpenters, sawyers, millwrights and wheelwrights, in particular, had skills that could be easily turned to the dismantling of machines.

Possessing such skills and being owners of saws and hammers, they were naturally sought out by the labourers as allies—or, if need be, as "pressed" men—to do a useful job. So we find frequent examples of these tradesmen among the prisoners: 16 in Wiltshire, seven in Berkshire, four in Oxford, three in Sussex, and two in Dorset, Norfolk, Surrey and Worcester. In one single incident at Bosham, in Sussex, those arrested included, in addition to a butcher, a bricklayer and a brick-and-tile-maker, two sawyers and a carpenter; and, at the Pyt House riot in Wiltshire, we read of Edmund White, a blacksmith, that "he had a sledge-hammer and was hammering on a cast-iron roller".[17]

There were other reasons equally, if not more, compelling that prompted craftsmen to join the labourers' cause. They were tied to them by the bonds of the village community; they were the more literate and educated of the workers in the villages and country towns; and when Radical groups were formed and Radical press and pamphlets circulated, it was they rather than the labourers who became the purveyors of the new ideas. As such, it is not unexpected that they should often emerge as the natural, or appointed, spokesmen of the village as a whole. Of the Kintbury leaders, Norris and Winterbourne were bricklayers and William Oakley, the chief spokesman at the Hungerford Town Hall meeting, was a carpenter and wheelwright. Among the Hampshire Radicals who played a leading part in the riots about Micheldever was William Winkworth, a shoemaker and former constable, who was said to have read Cobbett's *Register* aloud to "a small party of Hampshire bumpkins" on Saturday nights. At East Wellow, the rioters were led by William Reeves, a publican and blacksmith, who was reported to have told the farmers, "we have come from over yonder to regulate the tithes and wages".[18] At Goudhurst, in the Kentish Weald, the leaders included Richard Catbush, a labourer; Stephen Eves, a sawyer; and William Standen, a glover, said to be earning 30s. to 40s. a week. And we have already seen the part played at the Rushmere wages meeting in Suffolk by three Ipswich craftsmen—two tailors and an upholsterer; and the activities of the Radical cobbler, John Adams, in the riots around Maidstone.*[19]

It is perhaps not surprising that women played so small a part in this movement: had the issue of food-prices risen more sharply it might not have been so. Yet there were 22 women arrested and tried in a dozen counties, four of them by the Special Commission at

* See pp. 102, 160–1 above.

Salisbury and Dorchester. The charge was generally one of arson or of writing "Swing" letters, but five were charged with breaking agricultural machinery. Only eight were convicted; and of these two were transported to Tasmania: Elizabeth Studham, of Birchington (East Kent), for arson; and Elizabeth Parker, of Gloucestershire, originally sentenced to seven years for machine-breaking, reprieved and subsequently sentenced to life for larceny.

The rioters were generally young men or men of early-middle years: it was comparatively rare to find boys or old men among them, Of 1,238 persons whose ages appear in the prison records, only 32 were younger than 18, and 35 were over 50; overwhelmingly, they were in their 20's or 30's. The average age of the prisoners sent to New South Wales was a little over 27, and of the larger number sent to Tasmania it was 29: this is significantly higher than the average age of all convicts transported to the Australian colonies (which was 25·9).[20] In Gloucestershire and Dorset, the average age of all prisoners brought to trial was 27 years and 4 months in the first case and 27 years 6 months in the second. This appears to be the usual pattern, though there were (no doubt significant) variations as between one riot and another. In the Chevington (Suffolk), Pershore (Worcester) and Tadlow (Cambridge) riots, for example, the average age of prisoners ranged between 26 years 9 months and 28; whereas at Hardres and Newington (East Kent) it was 33½ and at Stotfold (Bedford) it was 34. Accordingly, the proportion of married men among the rioters was also high. In Wiltshire, the point was noted by a correspondent of *The Times*.[21] Of those transported to Australia, over one in two were married, which is 50 per cent. or more above the usual convict average.[22]

All this suggests a relatively high degree of stability and "respectability" among the rioters as a whole. Such a general impression is amply confirmed by a study of the records. Reading them, one is struck by the frequent reference to the good characters and high moral qualities of these labourers and craftsmen. Reporting on the trial of the Wiltshire rioters, *The Times* commented on the excellent characters given them by witnesses and by their own employers: Lord Arundel, for one, highly praised the labourers who had worked for him. Among others receiving good characters, and consequently recommended to some degree of mercy, were James Goddard and William Webb, the two arsonists convicted in Hertfordshire; the eight machine-breakers sentenced for the Finedon riot in Northamptonshire; and all fifteen of the labourers tried at Cambridge for breaking a threshing machine at Tadlow.[23]

For a more detailed picture, we must turn once more to the records of the men transported. Colonel Arthur, the Governor of Tasmania, wrote to his superiors at home of the "most exemplary conduct" of the main body of prisoners sent to Hobart; and, six years later, when giving evidence before the Select Committee on Transportation, he picked them out for special mention as convicts of "the better sort". His views were shared by the Directors of the Van Diemen's Land Company, who selected a couple of dozen men (and would, if they had had the chance, have taken several more) for work on their estates in the northern part of the island; and by John Capper, the Superintendent of Convicts at London Docks, who said "he never saw a finer set of men".

To this descriptive evidence we may add that of the prisoners' conduct records. They were markedly better than those of the general run of convicts. Of the men sent to Tasmania, only one in three had served previous prison sentences—mainly for short terms and for typically "rural" offences such as poaching, trespass, bastardy, cutting fences, assault, petty larceny, or leaving their master's service. Of the smaller number transported to New South Wales, only one in twelve had previous offences recorded against them. With this we may compare the general record of all male convicts transported to Australia, six in every ten of whom had committed one or more offences before their shipment overseas. Equally instructive is the comparative record of offences committed in the colony itself. In the case of Tasmania, the normal average crime-rate was, up to 1840, as high as six per man, whereas the "machine-breakers'" rate was only 1·7. There are no comparable figures for New South Wales; but only one in thirteen of the labourers sent there appear in the local prison records, and when free pardons were offered by Governor Gipps in 1836–38, only six were specifically excluded as being "unworthy of indulgence for their colonial offences".[24]

But, naturally, there was a minority whose records were not quite so unblemished. The two women, for example, who were sent to Tasmania: the one for arson and the other for machine-breaking and larceny. Elizabeth Studham, though "well behaved and orderly" on the outward journey, was "supposed (ran the ship's report) to be of loose habits". In the colony, she was sentenced for ten offences, mainly for bad language and disorderly behaviour, but in two cases for theft, for which she received two years' hard labour on the first count and twelve months on the second. Elizabeth Parker had, on her own admission, been "on the town" for 2½ years before sailing to Australia; and, after her arrival, she was convicted on 18 separate occasions on charges ranging from drunkenness and assault to indecent exposure and being found "in bed in a disorderly house after hours".[25] Of the men, some dozen had served sentences in England of six, nine or twelve months, or more, for relatively serious offences: John Ingram, an Essex ploughman, for example, had spent three years and four months of a seven-year sentence in prison for stealing a watch. In New South Wales, Alfred Darling, one of the Kintbury leaders, served a twelve-months' sentence for an attempted rape; Joseph Arney, a Hampshire wheelwright, was sent to the penal settlement on Norfolk Island for eight years for cattle-stealing; Henry Williams, the "ranting" tailor of Whitney, passed twelve years on the island, and four others spent a year in the chain-gang in an island prison. The Tasmanians' record was somewhat worse. Forty-eight men (or nearly one-third of those convicted of colonial offences) were found guilty of serious misdemeanours; and of these a dozen had substantial criminal records, involving sentences of two, seven or fourteen years' hard labour; one even served a life sentence for "breaking and entering".

So they were not all "village Hampdens". But these were a small minority; and what should surprise us is not that there were so many, but so few, who took to crime under the brutalising influence of the transportation system. By and large, the labourers of 1830 fully deserved the good reputations that their employers and neighbours gave them. They were not criminals: comparatively few had even the mildest form of prison record behind them. But they believed in "natural right"—the right to work and to earn a living wage—and refused to accept that machines, which robbed them of this right, should receive the protection of the law. On occasion, they invoked the authority of the justice, or government—and even of the King and God himself—to justify their views and actions.[26] For like most "primitive rebels", and like Sir John Hampden 200 years before, they were firmly convinced that justice—and even the law—was on their side.

Notes to Chapter 12

1. *The Times*, 23 October, 6 November 1830; H.O. 52/7 (letter of 28 November 1830).

2. See Gash, *op. cit.*, pp. 56, 59 (Berks.); *The Times*, 2 December 1830 (Lincoln), 7 January 1831 (Wilts.); H.O. 52/10 (letter of 30 November 1830) [Suffolk].
3. H.O. 52/7 (letter of 3 December 1830) [Herts.]; *The Times*, 19, 24 November and 1, 4 December 1830; *Reading Mercury*, 22 November 1830; H.O. 52/9 (letter of 27 November 1830) [Oxon].
4. *The Times*, 12, 22, 29 November; 14 December 1830.
5. *The Times*, 24 November 1830; E. G. Wakefield, *Swing Unmasked*, pp. 8–13; H.O. 40/25, fos. 904–5 (24 December 1830).
6. From *The Times* and provincial press, Q.S. records, prison and transportation records.
7. *Ibid.*
8. *The Times*, 22 November 1830.
9. H.O. 52/6 (letters of 23, 26 November 1830); *The Times*, 30 November 1830, 17 March 1831; H.O. 52/9 (letter of 27 November 1830); *Worcester Herald*, 8 January 1831; H.O. 40/27, fos. 494–7, 150–1; H.O. 52/8 (letter of 17 October 1830); H.O. 52/10 (letters of 30, 22 November 1830).
10. For what follows, see mainly Prison Calendars; Assizes 33/11 (Gaol Books); Criminal Register, 1830–1 (H.O. 27/39–42); Australian convict records.
11. Tasmanian Arch., acc. no. 53/4328.
12. H.O. 40/27, fos. 444–7; *The Times*, 17 March 1831.
13. H.O. 40/27, fos. 509–10; Tas. Arch., acc. nos. 2/132–178, 53/4328.
14. *The Times*, 7 March 1831; *East Anglian*, 11 January 1831; *Ipswich Journal*, 15 January 1831.
15. *The Times*, 3 January 1831.
16. *The Times*, 7 January 1831.
17. *The Times*, 1 January 1831.
18. *The Times*, 3 January 1831; Colson, *op. cit.*, p. 90.
19. It should be noted, however, that there were probably as many labourers as craftsmen among local leaders: one of the Kintbury leaders was Alfred Darling, a spadesman; Thomas Hollis ("the King"), at Heythrop, and George Williams (known as "Staffordshire Jack"), at Aldermaston, were labourers; Charles Davis, "Captain" at Alton Barnes, was a ploughman; and Charles Jerrard, one of the Tisbury leaders, was a carter.
20. L. L. Robson, *The Convict Settlers of Australia* (Melbourne, 1965), p. 182.
21. *The Times*, 3 December 1830.
22. Robson, *op. cit.*, p. 183.
23. *The Times*, 3 December 1830; H.O. 40/27, fos. 509–10; *Cambridge Chronicle*, 11 March 1831; *The Times*, 5 March 1831; *Camb. & Hertford Indep. Press*, 27 October 1832. See also, for rioters at Flitwick (Beds.) and Old Weston (Hunts.), *Camb. Chron.*, 14 February, 18 March 1831.
24. See G. Rudé, " 'Captain Swing' in Van Diemen's Land", *Tasmanian Hist. Assoc. Papers & Proceedings*, October 1964, pp. 6–24; " 'Captain Swing' in New South Wales", *Historical Studies Australia and New Zealand*, April 1965, pp. 467–80; and Robson, *op. cit.*, pp. 177, 101.
25. Tas. Arch., CON 40/9, p. 105; CON 40/7, p. 48.
26. See, e.g., *The Times*, 13 January, 9 February 1831; *East Anglian*, 11 January 25 October 1831.

PART 4

REPRESSION AND AFTERMATH

13

REPRESSION

To stop the riots, the authorities adopted a series of expedients—some military, others judicial or political; some repressive, others conciliatory. It is an open question which of these means proved the more effective. But there is certainly a strong probability that, in some of the counties, the riots, having run their course, died a natural death and were little affected one way or the other by the active intervention of the government or magistrates.

However, it seems likely that, in Kent at least, the disturbances would not have lasted as long, and subsequently spread with such momentum into other counties, if the government had had the means, and the farmers and justices the means or the will, to check them. But local administration was still in the hands of a small privileged class of landed gentry and Church of England parsons, who had neither the energy nor the means at their disposal to take effective action in an emergency of the kind. The farmers could not be relied upon to give more than half-hearted support to justices who, to them, represented the main obstacle to their own hopes and aspirations. The "new" Police had hardly begun to operate except in London and a few of the largest provincial cities. Many of the corps of Yeomanry Cavalry had been disbanded since the Napoleonic Wars—to the regret, it was said, of many farmers.[1] "It is vain now", wrote a Berkshire magistrate, "to lament the dismissal of the Yeomanry force in this county. If it had existed, all these insurrectionary movements would have been easily controlled."[2] Possibly. But in Wiltshire, where the Yeomanry rode round the county with great zeal, and received the right to call themselves "Royal" for their efforts, it would seem that they made the rioters more embittered, if anything.[3] There was always the regular army, but it was a small force and, in peace-time, was widely scattered between the ports, the capital and the main provincial centres. Moreover, in 1830, there were two further considerations that made the government hesitate to commit more than a skeleton force against the labourers: the political developments in France and Belgium and the rumbling discontent and agitation in the large industrial towns.

In consequence, Wellington's Tory Ministry found itself, in the summer and autumn of 1830, incapable of dealing swiftly and effectively with the rural outbreaks in Kent and Surrey. After the first machines had been broken near Canterbury, Sir Robert Peel, at the Home Office, took alarm. He was appalled by the leniency displayed by Sir Edward Knatchbull at the East Kent Assizes; and, a few days later, when Lord Camden, the Lord Lieutenant, urged to take firmer action, had replied, "I do not think the delay of a few days . . . will be important", he appended to the letter the angry comment: "I am quite of a different opinion. The delay may defeat everything."[4] Yet it was not until the riots spread into the Kent and Sussex Weald that the government itself took any positive action. Two troops of cavalry were dispatched to Cranbrook on 11 November, and General Dalbiac was sent to Battle in command of a force composed of "every disponible Cavalry soldier". By mid-November, the 7th Dragoon Guards had established headquarters at Canterbury; a squadron of the 2nd Dragoons was centred on Chatham; and, in the Weald, single troops of the 5th Dragoons were stationed at Grinstead, Uckfield and Mansfield, Rotherfield and Mayfield, and Battle, with headquarters at Tunbridge Wells. A few days later, when requested by the Horsham magistrates to send troops into West Sussex, Peel agreed to dispatch 100 men from Portsmouth: they could not come from anywhere else, as "the only cavalry force in the West of England (was) stationed at Dorchester". As the riots spread into Hampshire, further units were sent to Andover and Basingstoke.[5]

Such forces served as a deterrent and a warning against future disorder; they rarely affected the issue in a riot that had served as the pretext for their dispatch. By the very nature of things, they were inclined to arrive too late to do much else: this was as true of Battle as it was of Horsham and Andover. Moreover, they were intended to guard towns rather than villages or farms: as Peel had written to the Horsham magistrates, the protection of individual properties was their responsibility, not his; and, for the purpose, he urged them to enrol "specials", form voluntary associations and, even if they wished, revive the old corps of Yeomanry Cavalry.[6] So, outside a few strategic centres, the justices were left largely to fend for themselves. Their initiative took a number of forms. At Rochester, on 9 November, Lord Clifton invited farmers to enrol in the yeomanry, but his audience neatly sidestepped the issue by calling for "a liberal abatement of rents and tithes" instead.[7] As the riots spread, a similar reluctance to enrol as "specials" proved, even where magistrates themselves showed some degree of resolution, to be a major stumbling-block to success. Such cases were reported from nearly every riotous district: from Ashford and Tonbridge and most of the towns of the Kentish Weald; from Horsham and Arundel in Sussex; from Fairford in Gloucester; from North Stoneham in Hampshire; from Halesworth in Suffolk; from Houghton in Northants.; from Salisbury and Shaftesbury; and, fairly generally, from Somerset and Norfolk.[8]

Yet a variety of supplementary devices were found. The Spelthorne (Middlesex) magistrates, meeting at Bedfont, set up a nightly watch on farming property and raised subscriptions to combat arson. At Windsor and Wokingham, Forest Associations were formed; and, at Salt Hill, in south Bucks., the Duke of Buckingham and Chandos headed a list of subscribers to a fund "for the protection of property". In Berkshire, the Sheriff summoned "all Knights, Gentlemen, Yeomen, Husbandmen, Labourers, Tradesmen, Servants, and Apprentices, and all persons above the age of fifteen years, and able to travel" to rally to preserve "the King's peace"; and, at Hungerford, the inhabitants formed a mutual protection society. At Carlisle, "all Masters and Heads of Families (were) requested to prevent their Servants, Apprentices, and Children, from being out in the Streets unnecessarily after Sunset". In Norfolk, Lord Suffield, finding "specials" hard to come by, enrolled his own private army of a hundred men, "32 of them old soldiers . . . actuated by a sort of feudal attachment".[9] We have seen, too, how the Duke of Buckingham organised a similar "feudal" force of labourers and tenants near Winchester;* and the Duke of Wellington later boasted of having hunted down Hampshire rioters like game or cattle:

> I induced the magistrates [he wrote] to put themselves on horseback, each at the head of his own servants and retainers, grooms, huntsmen, game-keepers, armed with horsewhips, pistols, fowling pieces and what they could get, and to attack in concert, if necessary, or singly, these mobs, disperse them, and take and put in confinement those who could not escape. This was done in a spirited manner, in many instances, and it is astonishing how soon the country was tranquillised, and that in the best way, by the activity and spirit of the gentlemen.[10]

Some magistrates resorted, and with no less success, to more orthodox methods. In Dorset, we saw how an energetic justice in the neighbour-

* See p. 120 above.

hood of Bere Regis anticipated disturbance and enrolled constables even before the riots had crossed his county's borders—in itself an unusual piece of initiative. But the most highly commended action of all was taken by the Duke of Richmond in the western part of Sussex. He enrolled a constabulary force of shopkeepers, yeomen and "respectable" labourers, organised them in sections and districts under local commanders, and sent them out as mobile units to occupy villages, whether already rebellious or likely to become so. The "Sussex Plan" was quickly adopted by Lord Gordon Lennox at Chichester, and it became a model for other counties to follow.[11]

Meanwhile, Lord Grey's Whigs had taken office and Lord Melbourne had succeeded Peel at the Home Office. The change was marked by a more resolute intervention in the suppression of disturbance. On 23 November—the day after he took up his post—Melbourne issued a Proclamation, offering rewards of £500 for bringing rioters and incendiaries to justice. It was followed, two days later, by a circular letter to magistrates, instructing them to act more energetically in enrolling constables and recommending them, in particular, to adopt the Duke of Richmond's "Sussex Plan". The response, in some counties, was reasonably satisfactory. During the following weeks, reassuring resolutions were passed by magistrates at Cirencester (Glos.), at Bridgwater and Chard, in Somerset; at Ramsbury, in Wiltshire; and at Doncaster and York. The "Sussex Plan", or something very similar, was adopted at Reading, Winchester, High Wycombe, Swindon, Stamford and Bridport (Dorset)—though, in all cases, after the riots were over. Some magistrates and overseers added their own rewards to those offered by the Treasury. In Wiltshire, the Yeomanry Cavalry was mobilized: Colonel Mair counted nine local units, including the Hindon troop of 48 men that helped to suppress the Pyt House riot. Large numbers of "specials" were sworn in at Newbury, Aylesbury, Banbury, Devizes, Marlborough, Poole and Wellingborough; and (after a considerable delay) in most of the large towns of Shropshire, Leicester and Northamptonshire.[12] Pensioners, too, were pressed into service. On 29 November, the Royal Hospital, Chelsea, called on its out-pensioners, residing in widely scattered provincial parishes and market towns, to volunteer as special constables; and, a few days later, Ordnance pensioners (numbering 6,811 men distributed over 159 stations) received similar instructions.[13]

The new government also showed more energy in organising and equipping the forces more directly under its own control. Military officers were sent into the counties to supervise the disposal of troops and to advise magistrates on the levying of local volunteers. Colonel Brotherton was sent to East Anglia, and later to Bristol and the west; Colonel Doherty to the Midlands; and Colonel Mair to Winchester and the south-west. But there is no evidence of any build-up of forces, and the plan of operations, though more methodically pursued, remained as before. Troops continued to be stationed in or near the cities—Norwich, Leicester, Bristol—and in the large manufacturing towns. From them "small mobile forces" (Colonel Brotherton's phrase) might be sent out to crush disturbance as the need arose. Once more, the strategy betrayed the government's overriding concern: the fear that "peasant" disturbance might touch off a far more dangerous conflagration among the industrial workers in the north and west.[14]

So the main onus, as before, rested on the local magistrates. But, in some counties they were too overwhelmed by riots in their localities to be very effective.[15] In others (Norfolk was a notable example), the justices had divided loyalties and were all too evidently dragging their feet. Out of concern for the labourers, they were more inclined to make concessions—by raising wages or advising the farmers to lay aside their machines—than to repress the disturbances by force. An extreme case was that of a magistrate of Holt, in Norfolk, who, on 2 December, wrote to Melbourne:

> If when the riots commenced on Monday the 22nd ult° at Beeston near this place, the magistrates had remonstrated with the people, and told them that their wages should be increased, Rents and Tythes reduced, and Thrashing Machines laid aside, they would have quietly dispersed, and committed no further violence.[16]

To Melbourne such sentiments were utterly repugnant; and it was in direct reply to arguments and actions such as these that he sent out his Circular of 8 December, of which some mention has been made in an earlier chapter. Having castigated those magistrates who had (illegally, he argued) fixed higher rates of wages and recommended the disuse of threshing machines, he concluded:

> It is my Duty therefore to recommend in the strongest Manner, that for the future all Justices of Peace, and other Magistrates, will oppose a firm Resistance to all Demands of the Nature above described, more especially when accompanied with Violence and

Menace; and that they will deem it their Duty to maintain and uphold the Rights of Property, of every Description, against Violence and Aggression.

Yet Melbourne's rigid orthodoxy and his narrow text-book concern to protect all types of property were not acceptable to all. Opinion remained divided and the Circular elicited, in addition to some we have already quoted, protesting answers from magistrates at Banbury and in Norfolk.[17] But, in any case, it is doubtful if, by this time, the outcome of the riots was affected in any way by the Circular of 8 December. It gave a foretaste of what the arrested rioters might expect at the hands of justice; but it came too late to alter the course of a movement which, virtually, was already over. In Colonel Brotherton's view, it was not force alone, but a combination of "energetic" and "conciliatory" measures that had brought the riots to an end:[18] he was writing of Wiltshire, but the observation was as true of other counties.

Repression, though uncertain and divided, had already filled, or overfilled, the prisons in more than twenty counties, where over 1,900 rioters were awaiting trial. Fearing the over-tenderness of local magistrates, the government decided to appoint a Special Commission to try the prisoners in certain of the major counties of disturbance—particularly in those where machine-breaking and damage to property had been most pronounced. The selected counties were Hampshire, Wiltshire, Berkshire, Dorset and Buckinghamshire; but not Kent or Sussex, where judicial proceedings had already started.

The first Special Commission opened at Winchester on 18 December. There were 285 prisoners up for trial, most of them charged with extorting money or with breaking machinery: 125 on the first charge and 95 on the second. Other indictments were on the score of having destroyed poorhouses (12), rioted (6), tumultuously or riotously assembled (respectively 6 and 19), conspired to raise wages (10), stolen (5), demanded a tithe reduction (5), and sent a threatening letter (1); there was no single case of arson. Several of these offences carried the death penalty under three Acts of 1827 and 1828. Any man who could be proved to have broken machinery (other than threshing machines) or destroyed barns or buildings, or to have "robbed" or extorted money by threats or simple riot, was liable to suffer death as a felon. Moreover, the same penalty applied to any person forming part of a crowd, whose collective action led to extortion, violence, or physical assault, whether he was a direct or willing participant or not. Under these savage laws, no fewer than 156 of the Hampshire prisoners were liable, if convicted, to be put to death—all 12 charged with "robbery", 13 of the machine-breakers (those charged with destroying property at Andover and Fordingbridge), all 12 charged with "pulling down" poorhouses at Selborne and Headley, at least one of two charged with assault, four of five charged with theft, and one or more of those charged with riot. The law, of course, was liable to interpretation; but the intention was to inspire terror and make an example, not to pick out extenuating circumstances and give the prisoners the benefit of the doubt. "We do not come here", said Mr. Justice Alderson, "to inquire into grievances. We come here to decide law."[19] In the event, 101 prisoners were capitally convicted, of whom six were left for execution, 69 of the 95 remaining being sentenced to transportation. Of the others, 68 were sent to prison, two were fined, and 96 were acquitted, discharged, or bound over.[20]

Having finished its work at Winchester, the Special Commission moved on to Reading (and later to Abingdon) on 27 December, to Salisbury on 1 January, and to Dorchester and Aylesbury on the 10th. The same three judges who had presided at Winchester headed the Commission that met at Salisbury. This time, there were 336 men and three women in the dock—the largest batch of prisoners to appear before a court in the wake of these disturbances. Two hundred and thirty-nine were charged with machine-breaking—all but 20 of them with breaking threshing machines; 66 with "robbery" and eight with riot. In all, some 90 prisoners were liable to the death sentence: less than at Winchester because the breaking of a threshing machine, which eclipsed all other charges, was only a transportable offence. On the whole, the judges showed more compassion than before and took more account of age and circumstances than they had done in Hampshire; but, as before, they were consistently severe to all craftsmen and others above the rank of common labourer. Some 50 men were capitally convicted, though only two (later reprieved) were left for execution. Of the rest, 150 were sentenced to transportation, 46 to prison, and 133 were acquitted or bound over.

At Dorchester, there were only 57 prisoners for trial: in Dorset the riots had been on a comparatively minor scale. Here again, the majority were charged with breaking threshing machines. Of seven men charged with "robbery", six were sentenced to death, but none was left for execution; 14 were sent to prison and no fewer than 30 were acquitted.

Dorset was a special case, but in Berkshire and Buckingham the riots had been on a scale and conducted with a violence to property comparable to those in Hampshire and Wiltshire. Yet the Commission, composed of a different set of judges, behaved without the vindictive ferocity that had marked the earlier trials. *The Times* noted the difference and remarked that the Berkshire Commission was "a merciful contrast" to that at Winchester; while the *Brighton Gazette*, commenting on "the uneven severity of the law", noted that at Aylesbury the lives of men were spared who had committed offences "of the same kind" as those who at Winchester were left for execution.[21]

In Berkshire, 162 prisoners were up for trial, three-quarters of them at Reading and a smaller number (mainly charged with less serious offences) at Abingdon. About 60 were liable to the death penalty for "robbery" (36 cases), riot (4), arson (2), and breaking machinery in an iron foundry at Hungerford (17). The Commission proceeded with the utmost severity against the Kintbury men: of 27 capitally convicted, all but one were from the village that had terrorised Hungerford and the surrounding countryside; and the three left for execution "without hope of reprieve" were three Kintbury leaders: Oakley, Darling and Winterbourne. But having gone so far, the prosecution entered into a bargain with the counsels for defence, and we find among the prosecutor's notes the following: "Those not yet tried to plead guilty on condition of their lives being spared."[22] At Aylesbury, a similar pattern was followed and a similar bargain was struck. At first, extreme severity was shown towards 49 men charged with destroying machinery in paper mills at High Wycombe: 44 of them were sentenced to death, though none was left for execution. Most of the agricultural-machine breakers, however, were allowed to plead guilty and to be discharged on their own recognisances; and 81 prisoners (half the total number) were acquitted.

When the Special Commissions wound up their work at Aylesbury, they had sat for almost four weeks. They had tried 992 cases. Of these, 378 had, virtually, been dismissed; 35 men had been sentenced to varying terms of transportation, some for life or fourteen years but most of them for seven years; 252 had been sent to prison, and two had been fined. Sentences of death had been passed on 227; but of these only 11 had been left for execution. For these men the hope of reprieve seemed a slim one, and it was on their behalf, and of the far larger number sentenced to long years of transportation, that a campaign for mercy now began. In Hampshire, petitions were sent to the Home Office, almost as soon as the trials were over, by the inhabitants of Gosport, Basingstoke, Portsmouth, Romsey and Whitchurch; and from Winchester came a petition signed by bankers, Low Church ministers (but not the Cathedral clergy), and "every tradesman in the town without exception". At Reading, within thirty-six hours of the Commission's sentence, a petition for reprieve had been signed by 15,000 residents, including several magistrates. At Shaftesbury, in Dorset, a town's meeting promoted a petition to the King that recalled that "in no instance, during the late riotous assembling, had it been the object of the distressed peasantry to shed the blood of their supposed oppressors". From Newcastle upon Tyne came a Radical petition for mercy for those "convicted of incendiarism", in which the hope was expressed that "a new administration, pledged . . . to *redress of grievances*, should not commence their rule, with evil auspices, by measures of *severity*".[23]

The campaign had its effect, and in mid-January it was announced that the lives of eight of the eleven had been spared. They included four Hampshire men: John Gilmore, of Andover; Robert Holdaway, of Headley; Henry Eldridge, of Fordingbridge; and James Annals, of Barton Stacey; the two Wiltshire men: James Lush, of Broad Chalke; and Peter Withers, of Rockley; and, in Berkshire, two of the Kintbury leaders, Oakley and Darling. In their case, the death sentence was commuted to one of transportation for life. There remained the less fortunate three. Winterbourne was executed at Reading on 11 January, and Henry Cook and James Thomas Cooper at Winchester four days later.

But justice was as yet far from having completed its work. Nearly 1,000 cases were still outstanding. The assizes and quarter sessions had still their toll to take—in Gloucester, Kent, Sussex and Norfolk and other major counties of disturbance. In Kent, as we have seen, the first machine-breakers were already up for trial in October 1830. In East Kent a Special Quarter Sessions followed in November, succeeded in turn by the East Kent Special Winter Assizes and the Dover Gaol Delivery in December. The last Kentish machine-breaker was tried at the Romney Marshes Quarter Sessions in 1832. By that time, 102 prisoners had been tried in various parts of the county by twelve separate courts: 25 had been acquitted (including John Adams, of

Maidstone), four had been executed (all for arson), 48 had been imprisoned and 52 transported.

In Sussex, too, prisoners had been brought to trial almost before the Special Commission began its work at Winchester. The East Sussex Winter Special Assizes opened at Lewes on 20 December, and from then on until the Easter Quarter Sessions of 1831, 52 men and women were tried by five separate courts in both parts of the county; here the toll was one execution (again for arson), 16 jail sentences, 17 sentenced to transportation, and 18 acquittals. In Gloucestershire, 94 were tried at quarter sessions; 41 were acquitted, 26 sent to prison, and 27 (of whom 25 actually sailed) were sentenced to transportation. In Norfolk, as might be expected from the temper of the magistrates, the toll of transportation was considerably lower: only 13 out of 129 cases brought to trial. In Essex, on the other hand, it was relatively high: 24 (of whom 23 sailed) out of 123 brought to trial, with only 31 acquittals. In Cambridgeshire again, the 49 prisoners were tried by a succession of courts: eight in all between the Lent Assizes of 1831 and the Michaelmas Quarter Sessions of 1832. Here, three men were sentenced to transportation (of whom only one man sailed) and 23 to prison, while 23 were acquitted. In some of these numerous county courts, as at Norwich, the prisoner might expect a more reasonable chance of an acquittal than in others. In several, the usual sentence for a machine-breaker was a few weeks or months in prison; in others, he was more likely to be transported for seven years. In none, however, was the same degree of bitter vindictiveness displayed as by the landowning jurors and judicial Commissioners at Winchester and Salisbury.

In all, 1,976 prisoners were tried by 90 courts sitting in 34 counties.* We may briefly tabulate the sum total of their sentences as follows:

Sentenced to death:	252	(of these 233 commuted, mainly to transportatin, some to prison).
Executed:	19	
Transported:	505	(of these only 481 sailed).
Prison:	644	
Fined:	7	
Whipped:	1	
Acquitted or bound over:	800[24]	

Taken as a whole, were these sentences peculiarly harsh? In terms of death sentences and executions, they followed the usual pattern of

* See Appendix II.

the times: there were 19 executions, but all but three of them for arson.[25] Yet in terms of men transported, they were quite remarkably severe. No less than 481 persons were wrested from their families, and shipped 12,000 miles away with virtually no hope of ever returning to their homes. In the south of England, there were whole communities that, for a generation, were stricken by the blow. From no other protest movement of the kind—from neither Luddites nor Chartists, nor trade unionists—was such a bitter price exacted.

Notes to Chapter 13

1. H.O. 52/7 (letter of 1 December 1830) [Northants.]; H.O. 52/9 (letter of 25 November 1830) [Norfolk].
2. H.O. 52/6 (letter of 22 November 1830) [Berks.].
3. H. Graham, *The Yeomanry Cavalry of Wiltshire* (Liverpool 1886), pp. 72–93.
4. H.O. 52/8 (letter of 27 November 1830).
5. H.O. 41/8, pp. 32–40, 50–51, 57–8, 91–3.
6. H.O. 41/8, p. 57 (18 November 1830).
7. *The Times*, 13 November 1830.
8. *The Times*, 24, 25 November; 6, 10, 23, 28 December 1830. H.O. 52/10 (letters of 18, 21 November 1830) [Sussex]; H.O. 52/9 (letters of 25 November 1830) [Norfolk, Northants.]; H.O. 52/7 (letters of 28 November 1830 [Dorset]; 26 November 1830 [Glos.]); H.O. 40/27, fo. 436 [Somerset].
9. H.O. 52/7 (15 November 1830) [Middlesex]; H.O. 52/6 (17, 20, 22 November 1830) [Bucks., Berks.]; H.O. 52/10 (letter of 27 November 1831) [Suffolk]. Cumberland R.O., correspondence 1830 (poster of 13 November 1830).
10. Cited by David Williams, *John Frost* (Cardiff, 1939), pp. 59–60.
11. *The Times*, 26 November 1830. There is a copy of the "Sussex Plan" as far north as Carlisle (Cumberland R.O., correspondence 1830).
12. H.O. 52/7 (Glos., Dorset), 52/8 (Lincs), 52/9 (Northants., Oxon., Somerset), 52/11 (Wilts.), 52/15 (Salop); H.O. 40/27, fo. 47 (Leicester); Bucks. R.O., correspondence 1830 (letter of 7 December 1830); *The Times*, 2 December 1830.
13. H.O. 50/444 (War Office and Chelsea Royal Hospital, 1830); H.O. 50/375 (1820–30)–376 (1831–39).
14. H.O. 40/27, fos. 1–54, 160–252, 367–576; and see H.O. 52/11 (Brotherton's dispatches from Wilts. of 26–28 November 1830).
15. See the *Correspondence* of J. Cobb, Clerk to the Magistrates at Salisbury (*Wilts. Arch. & Nat. Hist. Soc.* Library, Devizes).
16. H.O. 52/9 (letter of 2 December 1830).
17. H.O. 52/9 (letters of 16 December 1830) [Norfolk, Oxon].
18. H.O. 52/11 (letter of 28 November 1830).
19. *The Times*, 21 December 1830. For a fuller account of this and other trials by the Special Commissions, see *The Times*, 21 December 1830–17 January 1831, and Hammonds, II, 74–110.

20. H.O. 40/27, fo. 562; Hants. R.O., *Calendar of Prisoners . . . December* 1830; Criminal Register, 1830 (H.O. 27/40); Criminal Entry Books, December 1830–May 1831, H.O. 13/57. Similar records have been used for Bucks., Berks., Dorset, Wilts.
21. *The Times*, 1 January 1831; *Brighton Gazette*, 20 January 1831.
22. T.S. 11/849.
23. *The Times*, 8 January 1831 (cited by Hammonds, II, 91–2); Gash, *op. cit.*, p. 79; H.O. 52/12 (Dorset); H.O. 52/7 (Durham). For a London petition, see *The Times*, 6 January 1831.
24. These figures are considerably higher than those usually quoted (e.g. by the Hammonds, II, 111); but the usual estimates leave out of account trials held outside the major counties of disturbance and later trials held in Kent, Sussex, Wilts., Hants., Berks., Bucks., Norfolk and Essex.
25. In all counties of England and Wales (including London and Middlesex), 1,404 death sentences were passed in 1830. Forty-five executions (or 3·2 per cent of this total) followed: 5 for arson, others for murder, buggery, sodomy, burglary and housebreaking. (H.O. 26/36, 27/39–40.)

14
AUSTRALIA

During the next two years, the transported prisoners sailed to the Australian colonies. Six ships brought 144 men to New South Wales and ten brought 330 men and two women to Tasmania, then known as Van Diemen's Land. The bulk of the Sydney prisoners (133 men) sailed together on the convict ship *Eleanor*, which docked in Sydney Cove (Port Jackson), after a voyage of 126 days, on 26 June 1831; the rest followed, accompanied by thieves and other common law offenders, in the *Camden*, the *Surrey*, the *Portland*, the *Isabella* and the *Captain Cook*, the last of which arrived in Sydney on 6 May 1833. All but a handful of the Tasmanians sailed on two ships: the *Eliza* (the first ship of all to sail), which brought 224 men to Hobart on 25 May 1831; and the *Proteus*, which carried 98 "Swing" rioters and four other convicts to Hobart on 4 August of the same year. Eight men followed on board the *Larkins*, *Lord Lyndoch*, *Gilmore*, *England*, *Lord William Bentinck*, and *Lotus*. The *Lotus* was the last ship to arrive—on 16 May 1833—and, having travelled by Rio instead of the Cape, took 154 days instead of the usual 120 to make the trip. The two women arrived by separate ships: Elizabeth Studham on the *Mary* and Elizabeth Parker on the *Frances Charlotte*; these docked at Hobart respectively on 19 October 1831 and 10 January 1833.[1]

Before sailing, the convicts were taken from prison to the hulks at Portsmouth or in the Thames at Sheerness; and from there to the port of departure which was, in most cases, Portsmouth but might be London, the Downs, Sheerness or Plymouth. From Portsmouth Robert Mason wrote two letters—one to his prosecutor, the Rev. James Joliffe at Barton Stacey, and the other to his mother at Bullington. They both suggest that he, at least, had lost none of his militancy or Radical convictions from the experience of his trial and sentence. To Joliffe he wrote:

> I do think as to politics at the present time people are nearly all of one mind and that is "they want a change", but interest leads men —some men—to speak contrary to their opinions.

Through his mother he sent a message to an old Radical associate,

Enos Diddams, a shoemaker of Newton. If (he wrote) a reformed Parliament or a "revolution" came about, he hoped that the parishioners of Sutton Barton and Bullington would be the first to present a petition for the release of the transported convicts; for if the Government "blows up", they might expect an early return to England.[2]

On boarding the transports, the male prisoners were washed and issued with the regulation dress of jackets and waistcoats of blue cloth or jersey, duck trousers, check or coarse linen shirts, yarn stockings, and woollen caps; the women wore their own clothing but, before they disembarked in Australia, each was given a brown serge jacket and petticoat, a couple of linen shifts, a linen cap, a neckerchief, a pair of worsted stockings, and a pair of shoes. Food was generally considered to be adequate and of better quality than that served in the army or navy, though prisoners were easily exposed to being cheated of their prescribed rations by unscrupulous masters and stewards. "The rations are both good and abundant," wrote a ship's surgeon of the convict ships of the 1820s, "three-quarters of a pound of biscuit being the daily allowance of bread, while each day the convict sits down to dinner of either beef, pork or plum-pudding, having pea-soup four times a week, and a pot of gruel every morning, with sugar or butter in it. Vinegar is issued to the messes weekly, and as soon as the ship has been three weeks at sea, each man is served with an ounce of lime-juice and the same of sugar daily, to guard against scurvy, while two gallons of good Spanish red wine and 140 gallons of water are put on board for issuing to each likewise—three to four gills of wine weekly, and three quarts of water daily, being the general allowance."

The prisoners' quarters lay between-decks and consisted of two rows of sleeping-berths, one above the other, each 6 feet square and made to hold four convicts, so that each man had 18 inches of space to sleep in. The quarters were dark and gloomy, and the ventilation was almost invariably bad; and never so bad as when a ship was becalmed in the tropics or when, in stormy weather, the hatches were battened down and the prisoners, instead of taking their daily exercise on deck, were compelled to endure the foul atmosphere of the hold for hours, and even days, on end.

While exercising, the convicts were handcuffed together and secured by leg-irons. "Ironing" was also, next to flogging, the most common form of punishment for male prisoners. Women were also occasionally flogged; but more commonly their heads were shaved, or they were placed in a scold's bridle or in the coal-hole, or made to parade the deck in a tub. At other times, prisoners were put to pick oakum, or the more favoured might be allowed to assist in navigation or be selected as schoolmasters (as Robert Mason was) to teach their illiterate shipmates to read and write.

Generally, the journey was long and tedious, though it might be enlivened by disaster. In 1833, for example, the female transport *Amphitrite* was wrecked off Boulogne and 101 women and two children were drowned; and, two years later, 139 convicts out of a ship-load of 220 lost their lives when the *George the Third* struck a rock on the approaches to Hobart. The *Surrey*, which brought two of the transported labourers to Sydney, had, on an earlier voyage, lost 51 men through an epidemic of typhus. But, this time, all but one of the sixteen ships had a comparatively uneventful journey. The mortality was rather lower than the average, except on the *Frances Charlotte*, on which five women out of the hundred she carried died on the voyage. Some of the *Eliza* men caught a chill while crossing the line, as the result of which (it was believed) two young labourers died of consumption shortly after their arrival in Tasmania. But only the *Isabella* had anything like a dramatic experience. Ten weeks out from England, a sailor refused to obey orders and was clapped in irons; several of the crew mutinied, and the ship arrived in Hobart with fourteen men in chains. The convicts were not involved: in fact, some helped the officers, the ship's carpenter, the boatswain and the remaining seamen to bring the vessel into port.[3]

On arrival at their destination, the prisoners were kept on board until their "particulars" had been taken and they and the ship had been cleared by the Port Health Officer: at Hobart, this might take two or three days, but at Port Jackson a week or more. Only then were they taken ashore and assigned for service with the colonial government or private employers. After 1840, prisoners were sent on arrival to "probation" stations, from which they were gradually released for employment with free settlers according to their record of behaviour. But, in the 1830s, the "assignment system" was still in operation. It had the advantage of providing the prisoner with immediate productive employment, though he might be exposed to the whims of an unsympathetic master, who was empowered to send him before a magistrate on the slightest hint of misconduct or insubordination. Punishments were frequent and often savage: even for comparatively slight offences men might be sentenced to 25 or 50 lashes; while more serious offenders were put to work in chain-gangs on roads and bridges and might become subject to even more drastic penalties. But, by the 1830s, the system had begun to become more humane, and comparatively few convicts (and a mere handful of the "Swing" prisoners) found their way to the penal hells of Port Arthur in Tasmania and Norfolk Island, off the coast of New South Wales.[4]

So, on setting foot on shore, the machine-breakers were mustered and assigned for service. For New South Wales, the assignment lists and muster rolls of this time are remarkably complete; and, in the case of the *Eleanor* men and the few who followed them to Sydney, it is therefore possible to present a fairly accurate picture of how and where and to whom they were assigned and where they were residing six years later.[5] In view of the large proportion of rural craftsmen among these convicts (nearly one in three of those transported to New South Wales), it is surprising how few of them, either at this time or later, were assigned to government service. Only one man, James Pumphrey, a road surveyor who had signed the Radical petition at Sutton Scotney, was immediately placed "at the Governor's disposal"; and, in December 1837, the muster records him as working for the government at Newcastle, a hundred miles north along the coast from Sydney. By this time, four others had found their way into government employment: Abraham House, of Dorset, at Goulburn; Isaac Cole, of Wilton in Wiltshire, at Liverpool; and two Hampshire men, William Stanford and Isaac Manns, the first at Bungonia, the second in the Vale of Clwydd in the neighbourhood of Bathurst. Another Hampshire craftsman, Thomas Warwick, a shoeing smith, was assigned for service with the Australian Agricultural Company near Port Stephen. The rest were scattered widely over the whole colony—the largest number in the wealthy Cumberland Plain in and around Sydney, and smaller groups in the Hunter River Valley, along the coast and in the western plains near Bathurst. They were put to work for a variety of employers: some as indoor servants at the homes and offices of doctors, lawyers, parsons, merchants and magistrates in Sydney and numerous country towns; but more often as farm servants or herdsmen to farmers, graziers and owners of large estates. It was rare for two men (and never for three) to be sent to work for the same employer). Among old associates who were separated in this way were the two Masons of Bullington. Robert Mason, the younger of the two, was assigned for service with Benjamin Sullavan, the Resident Magistrate at Port Macquarie; while James went to work for Henry McArthur, a Member of the Council, at Parramatta.

Six years later, we learn further of their whereabouts from the muster rolls of 1837. By this time, some had changed masters, but few (Robert Mason was one) had moved from their original point of settlement. A number had already died. Charles Davis, the former riot-"captain" at Alton Barnes, died soon after his arrival in the colony at the age of 33; he was buried at Liverpool, near Sydney, on 30 August 1831. Another Wiltshire labourer, William Lewis, aged 31, was burned to death at Parramatta while in the service of John Blaxland of Newington. An older man, Abraham Childs, a Hampshire indoor servant, died at Bathurst in January 1833. Albert Cook, a Wiltshire farm-worker, died at Goulburn in February 1834, and Albert Thorne, a Dorset milkman, in Bathurst Hospital a few months later. A year after, Thomas Warwick, the Hampshire shoeing smith, was drowned in the Karuah River and buried at Port Stephen; and Robert West, a Norfolk gardener who had come to Sydney with the *Portland*, died at Port Macquarie on 4 December 1837.

Meanwhile, the Tasmanian prisoners had undergone a similar experience. In their case, there are comparatively few "appropriation" or "assignment" lists, and we often have to depend on the more casual evidence of the Governor's returns and entries on the convicts' records to find where they settled and where they moved during the next half a dozen years. In June 1831, Colonel Arthur, the Governor, reported to the Colonial Office that, of the 224 men who had arrived on the *Eliza*, thirty had been retained for service as craftsmen with various government departments, twenty-five had been sent to Launceston to work at the various depots of the Van Diemen's Land Company, three had gone to Norfolk Plains for work with the Van Diemen's Land Establishment, and the rest were being assigned to farmers, landowners and other private employers. In August, after the arrival of the *Proteus*, he reported that only two were to be employed on public works, while the remainder would be farmed out to the settlers. After this, except in the case of those who fell consistently foul of their employers, the records give us only an occasional picture of the men's activities and whereabouts during the following years. But we catch fleeting glimpses of them as postal messengers, constables, watchmen and overseers (these are the selected few); as servants at the Female Orphan School or at Giblin's private school at New Town; working for merchants and drapers at Launceston or for auctioneers at Hobart; employed by parsons, doctors and Army officers, or serving their time on road-parties, building the bridge at Ross, or in a chain-gang. Most, however, worked on farms and agricultural estates—for Thomas Reiby at "Entally" on the South Esk River; for Roderick O'Connor (Feargus's elder half-brother) near Oatlands; for the Archers and Bryans near Launceston; for Deprose in Epping Forest, Youl near Campbell Town, De Gillern and Desailly at Richmond, Hobler at Launceston, Roadknight and Trott at Hamilton, and Captain Vicary at Triabunna.

The selection of the twenty-five men for service with the Van Diemen's Land Company in the north of the island had been something of a comedy of errors. Like many colonial employers, the Company was suffering from an acute shortage of suitable labour. The "agricultural convicts" (as they called them) seemed to provide an admirable solution. The Directors were well placed to get their pick, as two of them were Members of Parliament in disaffected counties and one of these, Joseph Cripps, was also Chairman of the Gloucester Quarter Sessions that sentenced twenty-four rioters to transportation. Their aim was to get fifty men or more, mainly farm-workers but also blacksmiths and carpenters, put them on board the *Eliza* (the first ship to sail), and land them if possible at Launceston, which lay conveniently within reach of their estates. In return, they undertook to send out at their own expense three free servants for every five convicts they acquired. With this bait, they persuaded the Colonial Office to approve their quota of fifty men and they actually drew up a list of these men—fifteen from Wiltshire, eleven from Berkshire (where one of the Directors, John Pearse, was an M.P.), and all twenty-four of the Gloucestershire men, hand-picked straight from the dock.

But the plan miscarried. The Colonial Office would not hear of a prior selection in England: this must be left to the Governor, Colonel Arthur, who insisted, besides, that all ships must land at Hobart. And, to embarrass the Directors further, their own local agents found it difficult to absorb so many new recruits at once. So the Company ended up with half their quota, and of these only ten (all Gloucester men) were on their original list of fifty. The Directors felt a golden opportunity had been allowed to slip and spelled out the reasons for their disappointment in a revealing letter to their Launceston agent:

> Our object was to get, not the number of Convicts but the number of that description, 50 Agricultural Labourers who, with the exception of that Crime for which they were expatriated, were considered free from crime, *a description of Men which had never been*

sent in such numbers to your Colony, and consequently an opportunity of securing such labourers will never again occur.[6]

Moreover, a number of these men were already suffering from consumption, believed to have been contracted on the outward voyage, when they arrived at the Company's depots; and two of them—William Rogers (aged 20) of Wiltshire and George Jenman (aged 22) of Hampshire—died a few months later. Seven others, most of them young men, died the same year. One of them, John Moody, a Buckinghamshire ploughman, was accidentally killed on service at New Norfolk. In the other cases, the cause of death is not recorded, though Colonel Arthur had his own views on the matter. He wrote to Lord Goderich that several of the *Eliza* men "died immediately from disease induced apparently by despair"; and he told the Molesworth Committee in 1837 that "a great many of them died —due, he believed, to the despair and deep sense of shame and degradation".

Meanwhile, some of the prisoners, both in Sydney and Hobart, had accepted the Governor's offer to have their wives and children brought out to them from England at the government's expense. Yet considering the many family men among them, the number was remarkably small. In Tasmania we have found only six such cases and in New South Wales only three. They included George Carter, a Hampshire blacksmith, with six sons and four daughters; James Toomer, a ploughman of Hannington, Wiltshire, the father of five boys and three girls; and Charles Green, a Hungerford labourer, whose wife Sarah sailed for Sydney with a small daughter in May 1837.

Many more—and they were not all bachelors—found wives among the free or convict women of the colonies. There are about eighty such cases recorded in the marriage registers in Tasmania and a dozen or more in New South Wales. Among those who married in Tasmania were Thomas Goodman, who had been sentenced for firing stacks at Battle; Peter Withers, one of the two Wiltshire men who had been "left for execution"; and John Boyes, the Hampshire farmer who had been transported for "conspiring to raise wages". In New South Wales, there were four Wiltshire men that married: George Durman, William Francis, Henry Toombs and Thomas Whatley; and three Hampshire men, including Robert Mason, who married Lydia Mills, a "ticket-of-leave" convict woman, at Paterson, in November 1841.

Generally, the bachelors found little difficulty in securing the

Governor's consent to marry, though John Ford, a Wiltshire ploughman, was refused permission to marry a minor until he obtained her legal guardian's consent. Those whom their records showed to be already married were naturally in a somewhat different situation. Here the applicant was generally required to afford proof that his marriage had been annulled (an unlikely event at this time) or that his wife had died since his arrival in the colony. It is all the more remarkable to find no fewer than twenty-five allegedly "married" men among the eighty who married (or re-married) in Tasmania. Some presumably got away with bigamy. There was certainly one such case, though it took some time to be discovered. David Bartlett, an *Eliza* man from Wiltshire, described on his arrival as being married with one child, married Agnes Skewes at St. George's Sorell, on 31 January 1842; and, seventeen years later, in January 1859, was convicted of bigamy and sentenced to one year's hard labour at Port Arthur.

An interesting case is that of Charles Fay, a Hampshire tanner, who had been transported to New South Wales for his part in the Andover riots. In December 1837, he requested the Rev. Charles Dickinson at the Field of Mars Church, near Sydney, to publish the banns of his intended marriage to Jane Burrows, a 23-year-old spinster of Lane Cove. The request was refused as Fay, according to his indent, was already married to Harriet, *née* Arlett, of Andover. He claimed, however, that his wife had died since his departure from England and, to prove it, he produced a letter which was passed on to the Colonial Secretary with a testimonial from the minister to show that Fay was "a sober, honest, industrious man". The letter, addressed to Fay care of his former employer, William Charles Wentworth, at 21 George Street, Sydney, had been written at Andover by his mother-in-law, Mary Arlett, in March 1833. It is a moving document, perhaps unique of its kind in that it gives a graphic picture of the effects of transportation on family life in an English country town; for seven Andover men, in addition to Fay, had been transported to New South Wales. Fay's small son, it appears, believed that his father had "gone to fight the Blacks" and his wife, having received no news of him, thought him dead and died of a broken heart. The letter and the Rev. Charles Dickinson's testimonial served their purpose: the Colonial Secretary withdrew his objection and Fay was allowed to re-marry.

In her letter to her son-in-law, Mary Arlett had written of the energetic efforts being made to secure a pardon for the transported machine-breakers: "so if you behave well and keep a good Character you won't be their 7 years". Her prophesy proved to be substantially correct and Fay, although a "lifer", was among the first of the New South Welshmen to receive their absolute pardon at the end of 1836. The campaign to secure an amnesty for the prisoners had begun while they still lay in the hulks. Robert Mason had written about it to Enos Diddams from Portsmouth before he sailed. Two days later, Henry Hunt, newly elected Member for Preston, moved in the Commons for "a general pardon and amnesty to those unfortunate agricultural and other labourers who had been tried and convicted at the late special commissions"; but after a long debate he found only Joseph Hume to support him.[7] In the next three years, however, opinion changed and, in June 1834, Governor Arthur was directed to release John Boyes, the Hampshire farmer: he was the first of the "Swing" prisoners to receive a free pardon.[8] The next step was taken a year later when, in August 1835, Lord John Russell, who had succeeded Melbourne at the Home Office, announced that 264 machine-breakers were to be pardoned. They included 236 men who had been sent to Tasmania aboard the *Proteus* and *Eliza* (four of whom were already dead)—that is, all those sent to the island for seven years except ten who were serving current sentences. The remaining 18 amnestied prisoners were men who had come to Sydney on the *Eleanor*; but, although singled out in this way for early release, they proved in practice to be less fortunate than most of their companions. For, by some fantastic bureaucratic oversight, the warrants for their release were left blank and, by the time they reached the colony, there had been added to them, presumably in one or other of the offices in Whitehall, the names of eighteen men who had been sentenced to death for high treason in 1820 and had, after their reprieve, been transported not to Sydney but to Hobart. In consequence, these unfortunates, far from benefiting from an early release, had at first to satisfy themselves with "tickets-of-leave" and, omitted from the general pardon gradually extended to their fellows, obtained their freedom at various dates between 1837 and 1846, several having petitioned the Colonial Office in the meantime.

A second batch of pardons, issued in October 1836 and taking effect in New South Wales on 1 January 1837, followed. They applied to 45 of the *Eleanor* prisoners, including the rest of the seven-year men, several fourteen-year men, and a number of "lifers" among whom were Charles Fay, John Gilmore and Isaac Manns of Andover. A further 60 New South Welshmen and 31 Tasmanians were declared pardoned in October 1837; and, at the same time, the Governors were instructed to issue "conditional pardons" to the remainder (mainly "lifers"), except such as were serving sentences for offences committed in the colonies. By November 1838, all the *Eleanor* men in New South Wales had received their pardons except 25, which included the unfortunate eighteen whose warrants had gone astray and six hardened offenders (among them Alfred Darling, the Kintbury leader), who were considered from their records to be "unworthy of indulgence". Meanwhile, in Tasmania, bureaucracy had once more intervened, and 42 men—most of them from the *Proteus* and including nearly all the Suffolk, Norfolk and Buckinghamshire prisoners—were only released in stages after energetic intercession by the Governor.

As yet, nothing had been done for the prisoners who had come out on the dozen ships other than the *Eliza*, *Proteus* and *Eleanor*. Only a handful of these had been tried by the Special Commissions, or by the quarter session or assizes held at about the same time in Kent, Sussex, Gloucester, Essex, Suffolk and Norfolk. So they had either been forgotten or, as special cases, were not thought to be covered by the amnesty. Some of these, like James Goddard of Hertford, who came out to Hobart on the *Lord Lyndoch*, had already died; while his fellow-arsonist, William Webb, received a conditional pardon, entitling him to move freely about the Australian colonies, in July 1841. The two women—Elizabeth Parker and Elizabeth Studham—had records that would have disqualified them from the amnesty even if their names had been on the lists; they were both given conditional pardons in 1846.[9] In most other cases, the prisoners, provided their conduct had been reasonably good, merely served their allotted time before receiving their freedom "by servitude". This applied equally to New South Wales; but an exception was made in the case of four men who had been sentenced by the Special Commission at Winchester and had come to Sydney with the *Captain Cook*. Although all "lifers", they were conditionally pardoned as from the end of 1839—that is, those who still survived, as two had already died: Robert Cook in February 1834 and Jacob Wiltshire in January 1839. A few months earlier—the letter is dated 23 September 1838—Wiltshire had petitioned the Colonial Secretary for his release in the following terms:

To D. Thompson, Secretary, Sydney.

Mr. Thompson, Sir, pardon me for taking the Liberty of a Drass you but mi torobles calls me to do so. I rived by the Ship Captain

Cook in the Year 1833 Santanse Life for Riating & Meshan Braking. I saw the newspaper with menn that was triad with me the have goot ther Liberty. I have been in no troble since mi arivale. I hope you will be so kind as to in form me if theires anthing aganst me mi name Is Jacob Wilsher and it so far up the contry I have no ways of guting Down to make in qury I have a sined Sarvent to Mr. Thos BEATTS of Paramatta and is at Molongl[y?] in the Districk of Willington . . .

Your humble sarvent &&
Jacob Wiltsher.[10]

So, by the middle or late 1840s, all the prisoners, if we except a score who had died and perhaps a dozen "lifers", "incorrigibles" or "forgotten" men, had been released from transportation—that is, they were free (if freely pardoned) to go where they would or (if their pardon was "conditional") to move freely around Australia and New Zealand. But how many actually used their freedom to leave the colony or return to their homes in England? To return home was a costly business as free passages were not provided. Governor Arthur told the Molesworth Committee in 1837 that "very few indeed (and he was talking of convicts 'of the better sort') seek to return to England"; and, on an earlier occasion, he reported to the Colonial Office, that of 102 men to whom he had issued pardons between 1826 and 1833, only eight had left for England and four for Sydney. On the other hand, the Hammonds quote Hudson's remark in *A Shepherd's Life* that, in the case of the machine-breakers, "very few, not more than one in five or six, ever returned". Yet even this is probably an exaggeration and we have found the records of only two such cases. One was that of William Francis, a Wiltshire ploughman, who sailed (or was due to sail) with his employer, Major Thomas Livingstone, the Solicitor General of New South Wales, to England on the *Duchess of Northumberland* in February 1837. The other was John Tongs, a blacksmith of Timsbury, in Hampshire, who returned to England from Tasmania shortly after his free pardon in 1836. But he did not remain there long, and in January 1843, he re-appeared in Hobart as a free migrant with his wife, a daughter and three sons.[11]

Several others, however, moved to another part of Australia and, from there, they may have gone farther afield. Two of the Sydney men accompanied their masters to Tasmania while still serving their sentence: John Shergold, a Wiltshire labourer, sailed to Port Dalrymple at the end of 1832; and Solomon Allen, a Berkshire ploughman who had led the rioters at Waltham St. Lawrence and Binfield, followed him to Hobart a few weeks later. Charles Bennett, a servant of the Van Diemen's Land Company, found work at Western Port (in present-day Victoria) after his pardon in February 1836; and two other Tasmanians—Thomas Fisher, of Buckinghamshire, and Thomas Hardy, of Hampshire—almost certainly made for the mainland after absconding from their chain-gangs. Many more were tempted to seek their fortune in Victoria during the Gold Rush of the early 'fifties; and we have found the names of twenty *Proteus* and *Eliza* men among over 50,000 who sailed from George Town in Tasmania to Melbourne and adjacent ports between June 1848 and November 1854. Others must have sailed from Hobart, and many more from Sydney; but for these ports there are no detailed shipping lists to tell us.

However, it appears likely that the majority of the prisoners, having achieved their freedom, stayed on in the colony to which they had been sent and lived out their lives as farmers, tradesmen, craftsmen, stockmen and labourers of every kind. Of the later careers of the New South Welshmen we know absolutely nothing. Yet several were related as brothers, cousins, or father and son—such as the two Manns of Andover, the two Masons, the four Shergolds and two Stones of Wiltshire, the two Thornes and two Elkins of Dorset, and the two Bulpits and two Simms of Hampshire; others, like Fay, Myland, Gilmore and the two Manns, had a common bond in their home-town of Andover; and it might be supposed that some of these renewed old associations after their period of servitude was over, as was done by some of their fellows at Launceston and Hobart. Yet, for lack of records, this remains mere speculation.

In the case of several of the Tasmanians we are on more certain ground. A handful—perhaps three or four—are recorded as having bought small lots of government land during their first twenty years of freedom. Some twenty-five to thirty are listed in the censuses of 1842 and 1851 as lease-holders or owners of shops, pubs, farms, houses and cottages in different parts of the island. In some cases, old fellow-prisoners came together as joint-owners or occupiers of farms and homes: so, in 1842, we find Robert Blake and William North, both from Great Bedwin in Wiltshire, leasing a farm together in the Bothwell district; the brothers Joseph and Matthias Alexander sharing a wooden house at Carrick in the Norfolk Plains; while, in the same year, James Everett and William Horner, one-time shipmates on the

Proteus, were neighbours and shared a servant at Jerusalem, north-east of Hobart.

In the case of some, we know their later occupations. Four, at least, became publicans. John Eyres became licensee of the Cape of Good Hope Inn at Black Marsh, Oatlands, in October 1842; he appears to have passed it on in 1845 to an old shipmate, William North, who still held it six years later. John Boyes, the Hampshire farmer, was the publican of the Hog's Head Inn in Melville Street, Hobart, from October 1839 to May 1853.[12] Another Hampshire man, Isaac Isles, took over the Canterbury Inn, Hollow Tree Bottom, Colebrook, in October 1836. Later, he moved to Richmond; and, in 1842, he was living at Tee Tree Bush in this district with a wife and four young sons. By 1851, his children had become eight—seven sons and a daughter—and he was living at Brandy Bottom, Colebrook; as he still was in 1865, when he owned 100 acres valued at £25 per annum. He, at least, was not broken by his experiences, for he died on his property in September 1896 at the ripe old age of 95.[13]

Others became farmers; among these were Robert Blake, John East, William North, John Stannard, Thomas Vinen and John Weeks. Some found urban occupation; David Gee became a distiller, William Dove a butcher, William Snow a baker, John Shepherd a brickmaker, John Beale a "mechanic", and William Bloomfield and John Walduck shoemakers—all of them in Hobart. Another shoemaker was John Hart, who settled at Launceston, while James Town became an overseer at Spring Bay, along the eastern coast. Of those whose names appear in the census returns, most professed to be members of the Church of England. Among the exceptions were Robert Blake, John Silcock, Thomas Smith, John Tongs and John Walduck, who claimed to be Wesleyan Methodists; John Eyres, a Protestant dissenter; and Levi Millard, who is cited (surprisingly) as a "Mahomedan" or "Pagan". Some had wives of other denominations: three married (or appear to have married) Roman Catholics and one a member of the Church of Scotland.

But these are merely scraps of information. In two cases only has it been possible to piece together something like a consistent and continuous biography; and these two men came to Tasmania from the same Wiltshire village, sailed on the same ship, married sisters and, at one time (as we have seen), shared a farm at Bothwell.[13] William North, a 23-year-old ploughman, was sentenced to seven years' transportation by the Special Commission at Salisbury and arrived in the colony on the *Eliza* with his brothers, Daniel and Samuel, in May 1831. We hear of him living in Bothwell as early as April 1834. He committed no offences and received his free pardon on 3 February 1836. He became a farmer at Bothwell and it was there, shortly before we read of him sharing a farm with Robert Blake, that he married Sarah, 18-year-old daughter of Edward Bowden (also a former convict) at St. Luke's Church on 18 October 1841. A son, William, was born at Bothwell on 19 March 1845; and it was shortly after this that North became the licensee of the Cape of Good Hope Inn near Oatlands. He was still there in 1851, when he bought the 400-acres property of "Grantham" near Bothwell (once occupied by his father-in-law Edward Bowden) for £725, of which he paid £181 5s. in cash. In May 1852, he sailed to Melbourne with his brother-in-law John Bowden—possibly to try his luck, with many others, on the goldfields; we do not know the date of his return. He continued to reside at Bothwell; and a local valuation roll, printed in the *Hobart Town Gazette* of 20 November 1860, shows that, at this time, his property of "Grantham" was assessed at an annual value of £75; in addition, he owned ten acres of land at an annual value of £10 in Dennistoun Road nearby. He died at Bothwell on 22 May 1871, aged 64. His wife Sarah, his junior by sixteen years, died ten years later, aged 58.

Robert Blake, a 26-year-old shoemaker, was also sentenced at Salisbury to seven years' transportation. Like North, he was living at Bothwell in April 1834, having been assigned there for service two years before. In September 1835, he received permission to marry Mary Bowden, elder sister of North's future wife. Like North again, he was pardoned in February 1836, though his record may not have been quite so clean: he was charged, at least, in August 1831, with having issued a counterfeit dollar; yet there is no record of a conviction. In 1840 (so it appears from a local residents' petition), he was living at Bothwell with his wife and four children; and, soon after, was sharing a farm with his brothers-in-law, William North and John Bowden, in the same district. By January 1848, he was living in his own brick house at Bothwell; at this time, he had four sons and four daughters and is described as a farmer and Wesleyan Methodist; a fifth son was born in April 1850. He acquired further property; for, according to the local valuation rolls, besides occupying his own house and property of thirty acres (assessed in 1861 at an annual value of £30), he owned at least three other houses at Bothwell in 1858 and seven (with a gross value of £108) in 1861. Robert Blake was still living at Bothwell in 1867, when a local Directory describes him as a "landholder"; but his death was not recorded in the Bothwell district. His wife Mary had died of consumption in 1861. Two of his sons, William and Isaac, became brewers and carriers—the former at Bothwell, and the latter first at Bothwell and later at Hobart. Isaac's Hobart brewery, the Jolly Hatters in Melville Street, purchased in 1885, was bought by a mammoth rival, the Cascade Brewery Company, as recently as 1922.[14]

These two were, of course, among the few that became prosperous and successful, and that is why their records have survived. Shorter case-histories, with far more considerable gaps, might be perhaps constructed in the case of another twenty or thirty Tasmanians; the rest, once they ceased to be convicts, resumed their former obscurity. Very occasionally, however, the names of some not listed in the census returns or marriage registers or on the valuation rolls reappear after an interval of several years—such as that of John Case of the *Eliza* who died in the General Hospital, Hobart, in 1857; of John Perry, also late of the *Eliza*, who died at Port Arthur (how he got there is not recorded) in May 1866; or of William Smith who, last heard of in Campbell Town in 1834 and pardoned in 1836, was sentenced to two years' imprisonment on an unspecified charge at Launceston in 1874 at the age of 77.

By and large, as we have seen, these men stood out from their fellow-convicts both by the nature of their crime and by their general respectability and high moral character. But there is nothing in their later careers to suggest that they brought with them from England any particular ideology, or political opinions or outlook, that mark them off from other settlers, whether free or bond, in the Australian colonies. The tradition of "Captain Swing" appears to have died with their conviction and transportation; or, more accurately perhaps, with the two letters that Robert Mason sent from the hulks at Portsmouth. Yet, a few years later, we catch a faint echo of the riots in an incident in New South Wales. When James Brine, one of the six Tolpuddle Martyrs transported in 1834, returned to England, he related how he was greeted on his first arrival at his master's estate on the Hunter River with the challenge: "You are one of the Dorchester machine-breakers; but you are caught at last."[15]

Notes to Chapter 14

1. Charles Bateson, *The Convict Ships 1788–1868* (Glasgow, 1959), pp. 288–341.
2. See A. M. Colson, *op. cit.*, pp. 156–60.
3. Bateson, *op. cit.*, pp. 56–65, 198, 232–41; Coulton Smith, *Shadow over Tasmania* (Hobart, 1941), pp. 29–39.
4. Bateson, *op. cit.*, pp. 65–7; C. Smith, *op. cit.*, pp. 27–8, 43–5; L. L. Robson, *The Convict Settlers of Australia*, pp. 91–2.
5. For this and most of what follows, see G. Rudé, " 'Captain Swing' in New South Wales", *Historical Studies Australia and New Zealand*, April 1965, pp. 467–80; and " 'Captain Swing' and Van Diemen's Land", *Tas. Hist. Res. Assoc. Papers & Proceedings*, October 1964, pp. 6–24. For Australian sources, see Bibliography.
6. Tas. Arch., V.D.L. Co. Despatches of the Court of Directors to the V.D.L. Agent, 31 January 1833, NP 30/31, p. 315 (our italics).
7. *The Times*, 9 February 1831.
8. Tas. Arch., GO 1/15, pp. 455–6; GO 1/17, pp. 165–6; GO 33/17, pp. 519–20.
9. Tas. Arch., CON 31/16, p. 76; CON 31/46, p. 143; CON 40/7, p. 48; CON 40/9, p. 105.
10. Mitchell Library (Sydney), MS. 4/1123.1.
11. Tas. Arch., CON 31/43/568; CSO 8/76/1706.
12. *Hobart Town Advertiser*, 3 May 1853.
13. Census 1851; *Hobart Town Gazette*, 25 May 1858, 28 March 1865 (valuation rolls); *Mercury* (Hobart), 5 September 1896.
14. For these two case-histories we are largely indebted to Mr. Geoffrey Stilwell, Keeper of Special Collections, Hobart.
15. *A Narrative of the Sufferings of Jas. Loveless, Jas. Brine and Thomas & John Standfield . . . displaying the Horrors of Transportation* . . . (London 1838), p. 11. (Four of the Dorset machine-breakers of 1830 were assigned for service in the Hunter River Valley.)

15

AFTERMATH

The historian of the Last Labourers' Rising may be fascinated, touched and moved by his subject, but he will not be able to avoid the final question: what did it actually achieve? Like all such questions, this one is ambiguous. "Achievement" may be the attainment of ends desired by the rioters or consequences of their actions outside the range of their intentions. "Failure", which is only negative achievement, may equally be failure in the rioters' own terms, or a failure not intended by them. They may or may not have succeeded in their obvious aims of raising wages, creating more employment by the destruction of machinery, improving the conditions of employment and of poor relief: or the wider aims implicit in all these, namely the reversal of the general currents which had, for generations, swept agricultural labourers towards pauperisation, demoralisation and an even lower social status than traditional society granted them. On the other hand they may have succeeded in quite unintended and unpredictable ways in leaving their mark on history; for instance, by contributing to the acceleration of Parliamentary and Poor Law Reform. Or else, they may have failed in unintended ways, for instance, by actually accelerating, through their immediate failure, the decline of their class into that slow-moving, ox-like, passive and demoralised mass, a sort of native southern Negro community, which was all that so many of their Victorian superiors saw in the English villages.

In fact, it has been widely held that this is what the rising achieved. The draconic punishments distributed by the Special Commissions, the deportation of hapless men and boys to antipodean semi-slavery are said to have destroyed what remained of the labourers' will to resist. Not until the 1870s did it begin to revive with Joseph Arch's union.

There is some evidence for such a view. Littleport, Ely and Downham Market, suppressed in 1816, failed to rise in 1830; only some of the centres of East Anglian activity in 1822 joined in the later and greater movement. Agrarian agitations abroad have sometimes failed to revive after the failure and suppression of their major acts of revolt, though it is not absolutely clear whether this is due to the effects of official terrorism, or to the demoralisation and disillusion of defeat, or a combination of both. After all, even without the executions and deportations, the contrast between the brief exhilaration of a rising and the rapid collapse of it, is quite enough to disillusion and demoralise unorganised and ignorant men, whose belief in their capacity to mould their collective fate is in any case not very strong. Still, taking the rising as a whole the pessimistic view cannot be maintained. Eighteen-thirty was *not* the last act of revolt by the labourers.

Moreover, contemporaries were impressed less with the defeat of the labourers than with the fact that they had actually risen. What shocked farmers and landlords painfully was not the feebleness but the strength of the labourers' activities in 1830, and therefore the continued necessity to conciliate them. For them the rising was not the last kick of a dying animal, but the first demonstration that a hitherto inert mass, active at best in a few scattered areas and villages, was capable of large-scale, co-ordinated or at least uniform movement over a great part of England. It was fortunate that they had risen in isolation, but not inconceivable that they might rise again in conjunction with the much more readily mobilised movements of factory and city. The hysteria of London in the autumn of 1830 was largely a reflection of this fear.[1]

How far was the fear of the possessing classes justified? We cannot say for certain, because no scholar has ever attempted to answer, or even to pose, the question. Indeed, of all the many gaps in our knowledge of the farm-labourers' world in the 19th century none is more shocking than our total ignorance of the forms of agrarian discontent between the rising of 1830 and the emergence of agricultural trade unionism in the early 1870s.* The historians of social movements seem to have reacted towards agrarian unrest very much like the rest of the urban left—to which most of them have traditionally belonged—i.e. they tended to be unaware of it unless and until it appeared in a sufficiently dramatic form or on a sufficiently large scale for the city newspapers to take notice. They were wrong. The most cursory inspection of the evidence shows that agrarian unrest of the old type continued well into the 1850s, and social incendiarism can be traced down to about 1860.[2] That rural agitation revived at certain times

* The only exception to this is the Tolpuddle incident of 1834, which is known only because of its urban repercussions. It has never been studied in relation to contemporary rural movements.

during the 1830s and 1840s ought to be common knowledge. Nor should it be at all surprising. The condition of the farm-labourer did not significantly improve until the tightening of the labour market in the 1850s, and the fundamental causes of discontent therefore remained.[3]

The defeat of the 1830 rising itself did not, as we have seen, end the labourers' agitation. It dragged on, with a few local revivals or even extensions—as in the Romney Marshes—until the middle of 1832. What is more to the point, it revived in a number of places where the 1830 riots had been suppressed with the greatest ferocity. There was a strike in Ramsbury, Wilts., in March 1831, and the labourers, on the point of repeating the old tactic of marching to other villages to recruit support, had to be dispersed by the yeomanry.[4] The men of West Lavington struck unsuccessfully against a wage reduction in June. Similar instances can easily be found elsewhere. Still, these were merely afterglows of the greater fire of 1830, though they prove that not all the labourers had been demoralised by the terror of the Special Commissions.

More impressive was the revival of unrest in 1834–35, when the introduction of the New Poor Law provided a focus for the labourers' agitation. Their resistance to this inhuman statute deserves more study than it has hitherto received, for while it was ineffective, it was touching and impressive in its desperate intensity. The *Devizes and Wiltshire Gazette* deplored the moral deterioration of the men of Wroughton who demonstrated against a proposal to alter the work-house by collectively marching out of church and smoking their pipes in the cemetery. "On Sunday last a still greater number of the poor attended church. The notice was repeated immediately before the sermon was delivered; and again every poor man, woman and child to the number of 150, walked out." Christian Malford rioted against changes in the poor law, and especially the separation of man from wife. One hundred assembled, "took possession of the Church and refused to allow the overseers to enter", later burning a rick. Delegations of labourers from Worton, Chiverell and Poulshot attended Devizes Petty Sessions to complain against the overseers.[5] In 1835, 50 men armed with sticks came from Worth and Ardingly in Sussex to threaten the Guardians at Cuckfield, 150 rioted against the new poor law in Chertsey, Surrey, while on the always inflam-mable border between Norfolk and Suffolk there were that summer "many meetings of labourers and occasional strikes", not to mention a particularly notable strike and riot against the new poor law at Bircham and Bircham Tofts.[6] These incidents—and they could be multiplied—coincided with a distinct revival of an economic movement which came close to trade unionism, and in the case of the Tolpuddle martyrs actually became trade unionism. There may have been other cases—the formation of "labourers' unions" at Rye, Eastbourne and Winchelsea (Sussex) is reported, though it is not quite certain whether these were composed of farm-workers[7] and it is possible that local research would reveal other such organisations. At all events, wage-movements and strikes of a less organised kind were common. Men in Compton Bassett (Wilts.) were charged with intimidation for seeking to draw all parish labourers into a strike in May 1834.[8] There was a strike in Goring (Sussex) whose labourers, in the old-fashioned manner, assembled on High Down Hill overlooking Angmering, Ferring, Turring and Goring in an unsuccessful attempt to draw in the neighbouring parishes, and were overawed by a display of force, a strike in Hoo (Kent), and doubtless there were others.[9]

Neverthelesss, on the whole such organised and public activity was uncommon, and after 1834–35 insignificant. The commonest, indeed the standard form of agrarian social protest after 1830 was that terrorism which found its most universal and frightening expression in the burning corn-stack. Incendiarism was a comparatively new phenomenon in the life of the English farm-labourer. Even in a region which became so proverbially addicted to it as the eastern counties, the first legal claim for damages arising out of it is described as "entirely novel" in Norfolk in 1823.[10] Taking England as a whole the commitments for this crime between 1812 and 1825 ranged from 20 to 30 a year (except in 1822 when they rose to 47), and as we have seen they tended to decline in the later 1820s. In the two years after the 1830 rising they averaged 106, and in the rest of the 1830s never fell below 43 per year; or, before the mitigation of the law in 1837, below 64.[11] In the nature of the crime, commitments measure at best its trend and not its scale, for the authors of incendiary acts were almost impossible to discover. Thus in 1831 there were 102 commitments for the whole of England and Wales, but an incomplete survey of one county alone, Wiltshire, reveals at least 20 cases.[12]

Incendiarism thus became the characteristic form of rural unrest after 1830, and over an area if anything rather wider than that of the "Swing" rising. Thus there is evidence of its significance in Warwickshire and Northants., in Devon and Gloucester.[13] Captain Swing, wrongly cast by public opinion as an incendiary in 1830, triumphed in this role for twenty years thereafter. Henceforth the degree of labourers' discontent is most easily measured by the prevalence of burning stacks. By this index it clearly remained high in 1831 and 1832, slackened a little in 1833, rose again in 1834–35, fell thereafter reaching a low point in 1841, rising in the following year and blazing upward in the last flare of old-style unrest, 1843–45: the committal figures show this surge very clearly, especially for Berks., Hants., and Wilts. (three cases in 1842, 17 in 1843), less so for the Eastern counties in which this form of action had long become endemic (Beds., Cambs., Essex, Lincs., Norfolk, Suffolk had 18 commitments in 1842, 23 in 1843). However, these figures grossly understate the actual extent of incendiarism, as given not only in the press,[14] but in the partial survey made in connection with the 1846 Select Committee on Game Laws:

Gloucestershire:	15 fires 1844–45.
Northamptonshire:	16 fires from January 1844 to March 1845.
Hampshire:	19 fires from January 1844 to April 1845.
Bedfordshire:	100 fires in 5 years, the worst period being the winter of 1843–44.[15]

The *Act to amend the Law as to burning Farm Buildings* of 1844[16] and the sharp increase in insurance premiums on farming stock in the same year reflect the scale of the phenomenon.

The last flare of unrest probably occurred in the years after 1848. It is almost unrecorded, except in such incidental observations as those of Caird[17] and in the criminal statistics. Let us recall that in Suffolk no less than 39 per cent of the rural prisoners in Bury and Ipswich jails in 1848–52 were there for incendiarism.[18] These casual notes do not exhaust a difficult subject, which still awaits full investigation.[19] It evidently deserves it, for as late as 1853 something like 40 per cent of all fire-losses underwritten by the County Fire company (and including nearly 60 per cent of the value) were classified as "incendiary fires".[20]

What interests us here is not so much the extent of these outbursts as their character. There is little doubt that after 1830 this changes substantially. There is first, a new note of embittered despair, a dark atmosphere of hatred and vengeance, which is on the whole absent in 1830. It is true that poaching mirrors the pressure on the labourers, perhaps also their rebellion against it: the militancy of 1843–44 is reflected, or anticipated, in the striking increase of summary convictions in the two preceding years in such counties as Berks. (25·6 and 11·7 per cent), Bedford (7·6 and 78·6 per cent), Bucks. (6·5 and 32 per cent), Essex (24·3 and 42·6 per cent), Norfolk (30·7 and 20·5 per cent), Suffolk (2·3 and 39·1 per cent), Warwick (101·7 and 10·4 per cent), and Wilts. (34·6 and 28·8 per cent).[21] But do such movements entirely explain the tendency of the number of gamekeepers killed in affrays with poachers to rise in times of unrest such as 1834–35, 1843–44, 1848 and also in 1838–40?* Probably not. Hatred and truculence: it was as though the labourers had at last realised that they were not Englishmen with rights, but slaves; that their demand for the modest and subaltern life in a stable hierarchical but not in principle *unjust* society had been a mistake, because the rest of society did not accept that there was justice and that they had rights. The New Poor Law of 1834 destroyed the last and most modest of their claims on society, namely the belief that it would not let poor men starve like dogs. As the song put it:

"If life was a thing we could buy,
The rich man would live—what thousands he'd give!
While a poor man he might die."[22]

Revenge is a constant theme of this rural terrorism. "Jentelmen," wrote the labourers of North Curry and Stoke Gregory (Somerset) in a tragic little leaflet, "You has taken Away All Poor men's Pay and you must take care of your Self Corn hay and stock this Wenter you will get it ham string. North Curry. Stoke St. Gregory."[23] (Commitments for cattle-maiming and killing rose to about twice the pre-1830 peak in 1831.) "Their will be a slauter made amongst you verry soone", said an anonymous letter in Sotterley, Suffolk, in 1844. "I shood well like to hang you the same as I hanged your beastes."[24] "It was evident", as *The Times* correspondent reported from East Sussex, where incendiarism and sheep-killing was rife in 1835, "that a rankling feeling of discontent and a diabolical spirit of revenge

* Gamekeepers killed 1833–48. Source: Parl. P. XXXIX of 1844, pp. 309 ff., XLIV of 1849, pp. 448 ff. The two series vary somewhat.

1833	1	1839	4/4	1844	3/4
1834	2/4	1840	3/4	1845	1
1835	5/4	1841	1/1	1846	4
1836	3/1	1842	2/2	1847	1
1837	1/1	1843	7/6	1848	5
1838	3/3				

prevailed over a large proportion of the peasantry."[25] Nor was it confined to the secret terrorists. In Wroughton (Wilts.) most of the villagers did indeed help to put out an incendiary fire in 1834; "a few, however, assembled at a short distance smoking their pipes and amusing themselves with the utmost indifference, but manifesting their recklessness and malignity by cheers and other tokens when any part of the building fell in". Moreover, "at a recent fire some of the labourers actually lit their pipes by the burning corn stacks and deliberately smoked them in the farm-yard".[26] At the other end of England, in Bacton (Suffolk)—another centre of unrest in 1830—"a bad spirit was manifested by a great many agricultural labourers present, who would not render assistance in extinguishing the fire".[27] Finally, and most significantly, the gentry itself was now sometimes the direct object of the militants. The owner of the Manor House, Tusmore, Brackley (Northants.), first found his pheasants demonstratively killed, his dog poisoned and then his house burned down.[28] He was not the only squire or parson against whom terrorism was brought to bear.

Hatred and revenge were universally felt. W. H. Hudson's story of the curse which, as the people of Doveton (Wilts.) firmly believed, rested on the squire because of the injustice his father had committed in the 1830 riots, merely illustrates how lasting such sentiments were.[29] Yet it is also probable that those who carried their hate into practice were a special section of the village; the wild, independent, savage marginal men—poachers, shepherds and the like—and the youths (or those most likely to be inspired by their actions). Such men had no doubt been active in 1830. Indeed, in East Sussex we hear of armed smugglers and poachers who accompanied mass marches and protected the rioters. Yet the core of the movement was in the respectable, married, peaceful labourers, its leadership lay among them and among village artisans, and nothing is more impressive than the absence of violence. Even the collective revenge on overseers of the poor, whose oppressions might well have released reactions of blind fury, never seems to have exceeded the conventional limits of fights at fairs or outside inns on a Saturday night. It is true that terrorist actions—rick-burning most obviously—were fairly widely established by 1830, at least in the eastern counties. However, as we have seen even these methods were used in moderation, and at the height of the mass movement, hardly at all. More than this: the limits of violence were known and not overstepped. Property was its legitimate object, life was not. The labourers' scale of values was thus the diametrical opposite of their betters', for whom property was more precious to the law than life.* The rising was not a desperate and embittered lunge against the oppressors so much as a massive collective and peaceful assertion of the labourers' rights as men and citizens, which ended either when these rights appeared to be formally granted by their betters, or when the movement was suppressed.

The character of the endemic terrorism of the next twenty years is almost impossible to document, though it may be significant that the best sample we have shows an unusually high proportion of the young, an unusually low one of non-agricultural labourers and the fully literate. In Norfolk half out of 24 were under 18—six were actually under 15—and only five over 30; in Suffolk 22 out of 57 were under 18 (eight of them under 15), and 11 over 30; a similar proportion to Norfolk. Only one quarter of the Suffolk terrorists were literate.[30] Sixty out of a total sample of 73 were described as labourers, farm-servants, lads, drovers, shepherds, etc., two more were marginal characters—a vagrant and a broom-maker. More to the point is the description of this period of village history in *Ashby of Tysoe*, which brings out very clearly the difference between the post-1830 activists and the respectable, non-poaching, non-terrorist village cadres who were to provide the backbone of the later trade unions. The terrorism of those years of hopelessness was in one sense a political advance upon the earlier movement. It was implicitly revolutionary, stripped of the illusion that the rulers of the village would yield to anything except *force majeure*—whether of violence or economics. A just cause was not enough. On the other hand its most obvious weakness was that—like the rioters in the Negro ghettoes of the U.S.A. in the 1960s—the militants of agrarian force were probably the least educated, the least organisable, and that they lacked the stiffening and perhaps also often the support of the village cadres. Terrorism was at best a symptom; it could not be politically effective.

Terrorism was the active response to defeat. Was religion the passive? There is no doubt that in some of the areas affected religious revivalism followed hard upon the heels of riot and defeat. Possibly

* "To a certain extent the burning of ricks is a mode of revenge which has always been practised among the labourers. They make a wide distinction between burning a rick and burning a house; between destroying property and endangering life." R. C. Poor Law XXIX of 1834, p. 300. This was written in the immediate aftermath of the rising, and about it.

the two flared up together here and there; certainly if they did so, revivalism continued to grow. In the Fakenham circuit of the Primitive Methodists (North Norfolk) signs of revival were evident "at the renewing of the Christmas quarter tickets" of 1830, and soon an entirely spontaneous surge developed round the village of Kelling, perhaps because the only dissenters there were a small group of the "Ranters". The Primitive Methodist preachers in the region heard rumours about a projected "Great Meeting" or "Great Friday" at Kelling, of which they knew nothing. On the appointed day in March 1831 "people came in from the adjacent villages", as did the preachers, and an unplanned but passionate camp meeting developed. The revival soon spread throughout the circuit.[31] Similar phenomena are reported throughout these years in the rest of East Anglia, where the connexion spread with great rapidity, at all events up to 1835, when the fires of religion began once again to burn less consumingly. The Norwich district of the Primitive Methodists, founded as such in 1825, had remained fairly stable at about 2,000 members in eight circuits from 1828 to 1830. Between 1830 and 1831[32] it increased by about half, between 1830 and 1832 it doubled, between 1832 and 1833 it increased by about 50 per cent again, and after a slight hesitation, continued to rise in 1834–35 By this time there were over 8,000 Primitive Methodists in East Anglia, i.e. the sect had multiplied four times over in five years. By 1840 the district contained 18 circuits.* After 1835 this religious mania declined somewhat.

It can also be traced among the Primitive Methodists in the south.

*	1829	1830	1831	1832	1833	1834	1835	1836
Norwich	109	232	332	533	720	535	641	763
Fakenham	251	223	264	467	503	394	600	563
Lynn	327	448	536	770	1,170	1,100	1,200	800
Yarmouth	348	380	501	470	300	420	600	1,000
Upwell	317	343	352	420	442	460	593	550
N. Walsham	451	534	750	600	660	680	890	545
Brandon	168	211	270	420	660	400	477	633
Matishall (E. Dereham)				310	610	510	720	555
Wangford					233	272	540	614
Wisbech					302	320	410	414
Rockland (Attleborough)						487	710	800
Aylsham							314	290
Soham							280	250
Swaffham							220	240
	1,971	2,371	3,005	3,990	5,600	5,578	8,195	8,017

In the area, familiar to the reader, where Hampshire, Berkshire and Wiltshire meet, the sect had been far from well established before 1830. Preachers ventured into it as into missionary territory from their base at Brinkworth in the Wootton Bassett–Malmesbury region, establishing a few footholds in one or two places such as Eastgarston, Chaddleworth and perhaps Aldbourn—300 members were claimed for the entire region in December 1830[33]—but meeting with bitter resistance not only from the farmers (who "threatened to turn the people out of work and out of their houses, if they either hear us preach or take us in"), but also from the mass of the ungodly, whose drinks, sports and entertainments the apostles, it must be admitted, damned with all their habitual ferocity and lack of tact. Ramsbury (first evangelised in March 1830) was a great centre of Satan; in Shrivenham the crowd joined in with a ballad-singer whom the farmers had hired as a counter-attraction, and the young men "played at 'back-swording' " so that the saints could not preach. In Hurstbourne Tarrant "Church and King was their cry; no Ranters here".[34] Yet barely had the Swing rising subsided, when the Lord's path became distinctly less stony. In Ramsbury persecution had stopped "lately"; there were now 100 members. Between January and mid-April 1831 the zealous Thomas Russell succeeded in forming at least seven societies. In Hurstbourne Tarrant there were now good congregations. In Kintbury (like Ramsbury a great centre of militancy in 1830), where no results had been reported as recently as October 1830, there was now "a crowded congregation; tears flowed", perhaps because the inhabitants of that embattled village had good cause to weep after the Special Commission.

The expansion of Primitive Methodism in south-western England, though less explosive than in East Anglia, was therefore equally impressive. Though the numbers in the "Brinkworth District" only rose at a steady rate from about 1,800 to just over 6,000 between 1830 and 1837, when they stabilised themselves, the geographic range of the sect extended remarkably. In 1830 it had five circuits covering the "Swing" area of the South (Wilts., Oxfordshire, Berkshire, Somerset, Gloucester, Dorset, Hants.). By 1837 it had 11, by 1840 18, of which four were mainly in Berkshire, five in Wiltshire, and two in Hants.[35]

Other sects show a similar pattern. The Wesleyans opened 11 new circuits in Lincolnshire and three in Bedfordshire between 1832 and 1840, and there are distinct signs of Baptist expansion in such counties as Hampshire and Lincolnshire and indeed elsewhere.[36] In 1829 there had been only one "Suffolk and Norfolk" association of Baptist congregations; by 1841 there were six in the eastern counties, three of the new ones having been formed in 1834–35. The "Kent and Sussex" association gave birth to a separate East Kent association in 1835, the "Berkshire and West London" now found sufficient to organise in Berkshire, and so on.[37] Presumably this rush into religion took place chiefly where there were local nuclei of dissenters, of whatever persuasion and not elsewhere, though—as usual—we know too little about the progress of nonconformity in the English village to say much about it. If we did we might discover, among other things, why the local equivalent of the Primitive Methodists, the Bible Christians, made no significant progress in Kent (except for a little burst in 1834–35), though they had established footholds in a few places there by 1830.[38]

There can be no doubt that this new rural religion was passionate, dramatic, and often hysterical. "The glory appeared visible", reported a Primitive Methodist apostle from the Camp Meeting at Shefford (Berks.) in 1830. "By some it was seen as a light, by others as fire falling among the people."[39] It is equally certain that the mood was such, that the right kind of millennial preacher could easily have mobilised the people for more than prayer and convulsions. A socially conscious paranoiac, an exiled Cornishman posing as—or believing himself to be—Lord Courtenay and the Messiah—actually did so in the area between Canterbury and Faversham in 1838, though he was not followed outside his own village.[40] Yet the very uniqueness of this abortive millennial revolt demonstrates that the religious revival of the early 1830s was an escape from, rather than a mobilisation for, social agitation. And though we have no real evidence, it is quite incredible that the newly saved village Baptist or Primitive Methodist, with his hatred of liquor, pubs and sports, should have taken part in the rick-burning and cattle-maiming so patently associated with the bold, hard-drinking and hard-playing poachers and their circles. They represented the last resistance of the traditional society against its destroyers. The dissenters in their way represented the forces of internal modernisation. In 1830 the two had combined. By the time of Joseph Arch's union in the 1870s, the traditionalists were no longer a significant force in village politics and organisation. But in the years after 1830 the two diverged, and the village resistance was fatally weakened by their division.

These reflections lead us naturally to the question, or rather the complex of questions, about the links between the "Swing" movement and the subsequent farm labourers' trade unions. What were these links, if any? Alternatively, why did so long a period separate the revolt of 1830 from the first national explosion of rural unionism in the early 1870s?

The second of these questions is more helpful than the first. For, since no direct continuity between 1830 and 1872 can be traced, any investigation of what the "Revolt of the Field" owed to "Captain Swing" must be entirely speculative. It is true that some centres of early riot also turn out to be bastions of unionism much later, and in some there is a consistent record of militancy over several generations, as in parts of Norfolk. It is obviously significant that in that county the start of the later movement should have been at Old Buckenham, storm-centre of so many riots since 1816, or that the father of the union leader George Edwards is supposed to have moved a resolution in favour of higher wages at a village meeting near Aylsham in 1833.[41] But the tracing of such continuity or recurrence does not advance us very far.

On the other hand the evident gap between the archaic and modern movements of the farm-labourers requires some sort of explanation, and that explanation, even though perhaps equally speculative, cannot but illuminate our understanding of village agitation, or at the very least direct our attention to the neglected problem of how they are to be understood. The point is that up to 1830, and perhaps 1835, the labourers' agitation was essentially the sort of movement which could and ought to have been trade unionist, since it was an organised (though informally organised) demand for better wages, better conditions of life and better employment. But it was at no point *formally* a trade union movement; and though one or two local labourers' unions may be discovered in 1834–35—Tolpuddle is the only familiar example—their very rarity and eccentricity merely demonstrate how wide the distance between the archaic and modern movements still was. It cannot be that farm-labourers between 1830 and the late 1860s had no opportunity to hear about such organisations. If the remote village of Tolpuddle could discover their existence, then so could plenty of other villages in much closer contact with village Radicals, with the journeymen craftsmen of local market towns, not to mention with centres of Radicalism, Chartism and artisan agitation like Norwich and Ipswich. But nothing happened.

What is the explanation? Several reasons may be suggested. In the first place, regular unionism was evidently almost impossible for the labourers until their economic situation had improved enough to allow them some of the advantages of labour shortage, not to mention income to pay regular dues. This, as we know, did not happen until the 1850s. Until then they could—they were indeed forced to—fight defensive actions against the deterioration of their conditions, but could hardly fight offensive ones for their improvement. Unions are more necessary for aggression than for defence, for spontaneous last-ditch resistance can be more readily improvised than systematic advance; and conversely, success is what encourages the spread of unionism. Pauperised labourers, clinging grimly to the raft of insecure and intermittent employment in the sea of available surplus labour, were hardly the material for regular organised militancy. They risked job, home and perhaps even a large part of poor relief or charity every time they opened their mouths. It is no accident that the spontaneous development of strikes and local unions resumes in the 1860s.

A second reason, as we have seen, was the demoralisation of those who might have been the expected cadres of the unions, reflected in the shift of the movement's centre of gravity to the wild anti-organisation men who kept the night skies red with burning ricks. This demoralisation was reinforced by the systematic and growing degradation of the labourers by their rulers, which sought to turn them into a class of helpless and abject helots, and rural society into a racialist structure distinguished from the others so dear to the Victorian upper classes only by the fact that the lower races happened also to be white. The *Life of Joseph Ashby* illustrates this process in all its callous brutality: the transformation of the poor into forelock-pulling charity-receivers, the systematic discrimination against the unusually strong, self-reliant and energetic labourers who might be less abjectly dependent on their "betters", and therefore a potential danger to them. But the dependent man could not easily risk joining, let alone leading, a union. It is no accident that the village leaders were, more often than not, men who either by their own determination or by discrimination had ceased to be farm-labourers and were economically independent, like Arch, the migratory hedger, Ashby, the small surveyor and contractor, or George Edwards, forced out of farming into the brick-yards.

Nevertheless, there still remains much to explain. Is it not probable that the very nature of trade union organisation, an urban and industrial phenomenon developed—often in the geographically remote north—without regard to the agricultural situation, made it unusually difficult for farm-labourers to understand and to utilise it? (All the more so as its most obvious form, the purely local union, was virtually useless to them.) As we have seen, the organisation of the Swing movement was entirely traditional. It rested on the informal consensus of the lower classes in the village, or in so far as it had any formal organisation at all, on the *ad hoc* choice of leaders, spokesmen, treasurers, on the "gang" or "mob". Could the labourers conceive of regular and permanent organisation for any purpose, except perhaps the traditional ceremonial ones of the village, the waits and wakes, the annual village feast which was the main purpose of the village friendly societies? At all events, the village bounded their horizon. The men might venture beyond it, in the ancient manner, to mobilise other villages in the region by direct contact, and if things were right—as in 1830—they might do so. If they were not right, then they would fail, like the men of Goring in 1834 who stood on the hill vainly waiting for their neighbours to join, or the band behind the Messiah of Boughton in 1838, who followed him to Faversham and back to Bossenden Wood before standing and fighting alone. It was not enough for modern trade unionism.

Modern forms of organisation have to be learned, like anything else. Strikes may be the spontaneous products of the wage-labourers' predicament, but unions are not. The modes of modern, i.e. urban and non-agricultural action, took time to penetrate the remote hinterland in which most farm-labourers lived, doubly insulated by distance and by the obvious *difference* of their lives and situation from even the small-town craftsman. Can we trace the process of this modernisation of their intellectual universe?

Allowing for our habitual ignorance about the labourer's world, we can do so to some extent in the case of two types of organisation closely connected with subsequent trade unionism: the dissenting sects (mainly organisations of potential cadres) and the Friendly Societies in the form of national organisations with local branches, such as the Oddfellows, Foresters, etc. The sects, as we have seen, developed very rapidly after 1830. Though their strength fluctuated after the middle 1830s, they had in several cases reached the level of the 1860s by then. However, as we have also suggested, their expansion created potential rather than actual activists, though the process by which the hell- and eternity-obsessed village Ranters of the 1830s turned into the union militants of the 1870s remains in obscurity. The progress of the Friendly Societies is more illuminating.[42]

In 1830 the typical rural friendly society was the independent village club, though by this time the gentry-organised county society (as Essex, Wiltshire and Hampshire) was already being pressed on the labourers by their rulers with varying, but normally modest, success. It is quite certain that in 1831 the degree of organisation of any kind in the Swing counties was lower than anywhere else. In Sussex, Berks., Lincs., Kent, Hants., Norfolk and Cambridge it ranged between 2·5 and 4·5 per cent of total population (the only other comparably low counties being Hereford and Westmorland), in Oxford, Dorset, Bucks., Bedford and Suffolk and Hunts. between 5 and 6 per cent and only in Somerset, Essex, Wilts. and Gloucester (all of which contained concentrations of textile workers and other artisans and manufacturers) was it above this level—though still, with the exception of the last three, below the median.[43] There is little to show any significant increase in Friendly Society membership in these counties between 1815 and 1847.[44]

This is not the place to survey, in so far as anyone can, the fluctuating fortunes of the village clubs, which remained of all friendly societies the ones with the highest proportion of farm-labourer members. Whether they grew or diminished in number, they were increasingly overhauled by the local branches (lodges, courts) of the national fraternal orders, chiefly the Oddfellows and the Foresters, who were somewhat the larger of the two in the southern counties, except in East Anglia and the south-west. By the 1870s they had overhauled the local clubs in all "Swing" counties except Berks., Bucks., Hunts. and Oxford.[45] As for the Fraternal Orders, they—and especially the Oddfellows—appealed primarily to non-agricultural workers, though about 9 per cent of the members of the Manchester Unity in 1846–48 were described as "labourers (rural)".[46] Nevertheless, their very size and distribution were bound to make them the major form of mutual organisation among labourers.

It is evident that they spread into the "Swing" counties comparatively late, partly no doubt because their original centres lay in the remote north of Lancashire and Cheshire. This delay is all the more significant because the periods of most rapid growth of the orders as a whole was in *c.* 1835–45. Yet in our counties, with some exceptions, it fairly clearly occurred *after* 1845. Thus in Kent, Sussex and Hampshire the Manchester Unity had a total of 53 lodges in

1845, but 180 in 1875; in Norfolk and Suffolk 69 and 148 respectively.[47] The Foresters, better documented, are also even more illuminating, as the following table shows:

Membership of Ancient Order of Foresters (in 000) Source: Gosden, p. 44

Region	1848	1858	1867	1876	increase 1848–58	1858–67	1867–76
Surrey, Sussex, Kent, Hants., Berks.	2,3	8,4	34,1	50,6	6,1	25,7	16,5
Northants., Hunts., Beds., Cambs., Oxon., Herts., Bucks., Middlesex	10,2	23,3	77,4	108,6	13,1	54,1	31,2
Norfolk, Suffolk, Essex	1,3	5,6	14,3	22,6	4,3	8,7	8,3
Wilts., Dorset, Devon, Somerset, Cornwall	0,8	1,3	13,1	21,4	0,5	11,8	8,3

The modest size of this Order in 1848, the leap forward in 1858–67, are quite clear.

The period of major penetration for these national organisations into the Swing counties therefore occurred, broadly speaking, between 1850 and 1870. Why exactly this is so, we do not know. But if the capacity to organise in such societies is a measure of the capacity to form union branches, or more generally an index of the spread of urban modes of social action in the agricultural sector, then at least these figures help us fill the gap between the peak of the archaic movement in 1830 and the national emergence of a modern movement in the early 1870s.

We are left with a final question: what, if anything, did the Swing movement achieve? We have seen that it frightened the rural rulers, at all events for a time. We have seen that it had its aftermath of endemic terrorism, designed not only to revenge but also to protect the labourers. Yet these do not automatically answer our question. Was Swing a mere symptom of intolerable oppression or did it have practical and measurable effects?

It would be surprising if a movement so widespread, and which frightened the government so much—for however brief a spell—had been without influence on the reform legislation of the first half of the 1830s. Contemporaries certainly thought there was a connection between Swing and Reform;[48] Cobbett and Wakefield believed it to have done more to turn parliamentary reform into practical politics than the urban agitations, though it can hardly have had any very direct bearing on the passing of the 1832 Reform Act. Still, in so far as fear of revolution influenced the legislators, this, the most widespread rising of the oppressed, acting so often in concert with the discontented urban Radicals, must have been in the minds of those who weighed the dangers of Reform against those of social upheaval. It turned out that the danger of revolution in the countryside was negligible, partly because the labourers so obviously did not set out to make one, partly because, apart from local village and small-town Radicals, they were entirely cut off from the great centres of urban agitation. There is no evidence that the London ultra-Radicals, in spite of their enthusiasm for Swing, had the faintest idea what the Kentish labourers were at, or even where to find or how to get in touch with any of them.[49] What is more, the *local* centres of industrial agitation remained quiet. The Wiltshire textile region, a fortress of extreme physical-force Chartism nine years later, did not move in 1830; the bands of roving rural rioters in Kent did not succeed in raising the local paper-workers. Nevertheless, at a crucial moment of British politics—i.e. during the actual take-over of the new Whig administration from the Wellington government—a large part of the country was in rebellion, respectable men were refusing to serve as special constables, landowners were pressed to the wall. There is no politician born who would not ponder the implications of such a situation very carefully.

Two other major statutes of the time must also have been influenced by Swing: the Poor Law Amendment Act of 1834 and the Tithe Commutation Act of 1836. There is no significant evidence for this connection, except the obvious preoccupation of the Poor Law Commissioners with the 1830 rising, which has given us so much useful source-material for its study, and the equally obvious role which discontent with the Poor Law and the tithe system played in it. It is significant that an Act to limit the clergy's full right to claim tithe was passed as early as 1832 (one to legalise the sale of game and thus to discourage poaching had been passed even earlier in 1831), and it is equally to the point that the bulk of the Poor Law Commission's material, including the "rural questions" was collected between February 1832 and January 1833, i.e. at a time when "Swing" was still vividly in the minds of witnesses and respondents. Still, the only connection which can be legitimately claimed is one of probability, and nobody would argue that the rioting labourers were more than one factor among several.

As for direct links, these may be established for minor pieces of legislation like the Allotments Acts of 1831 and 1832, which were not of great significance—"spade husbandry", though widely canvassed as a solution for rural labour problems, did not really flourish—and the 1833 Act exempting agricultural fire insurance from payment of duties. (The argument was, that as the object of incendiarism was to intimidate farmers, and as the insurance companies were reluctant to insure farming stock, special measures to encourage such insurance would encourage farmers to resist the labourers' pressure.[50]) However, such minor effects are too petty to waste much time on.

Let us therefore concentrate on the direct effects of the movement on agriculture and the situation of the labourer. It did not, and given the general situation in the labour market, could not, improve the labourers' wages and conditions for any length of time. Nevertheless, there is much evidence that in the years immediately following 1830 the wage-concessions of that year were maintained, the Poor Law alleviated, wage-cuts postponed, thanks to the fear of another 1830 or, more concretely, of burned ricks. "I am sure that more attention has been paid since that time to the comfort of the labourers", said a witness from Wiltshire before the Select Committee on Agriculture of 1833, which took note also of several instances of wage-increases due to intimidation. The character of the labourer had deteriorated, observed a witness from Norfolk: "If we had never had any fires our wages would not have been more than 10s. a week; now they are 11s."[51] The labourers still fixed the amount of wages or relief, complained the reporter from the Rape of Hastings to the Poor Law Commission, and he was not alone.[52] "And even now", wrote the curate of Westwell, Kent, to the Poor Law Commission, "they say: Ah them there riots and burnings did the poor a terrible deal of good."[53] And "they" were evidently right at the time.

How long these after-effects of the rising lasted we do not know. Nevertheless about one aspect of the rising we can speak with considerable confidence. The threshing machines did not return on the old scale. Of all the machine-breaking movements of the 19th century that of the helpless and unorganised farm-labourers proved to be by far the most effective. The real name of King Ludd was Swing.

The evidence is scattered but impressive. There is no doubt that the machines did not immediately return in the years following the rising. The witnesses before the 1833 Committee are reasonably concurrent.[54] Their recession in Essex continued to be noted in 1836,[55] and in Berkshire in 1840.[56] The spread of such machines in the valley of the Hampshire Avon had been observed in 1819; but Wilkinson's *The Farming of Hampshire* in 1861 makes no allusion to threshing machines.[57] As we know, they provoked the outbreak in East Kent in 1830; but Buckland's *On the Farming of Kent* of 1845 records them only in Sheppey, and makes no reference to them in his discussion of Thanet.[58] As late as 1843, it was still assumed as common knowledge —admittedly by a townsman—that "at this moment, in a large part of the Agricultural Districts of the South, the thrashing Machines cannot be used, owing to the destructive vengeance with which the labourers resisted its introduction".[59]

The only part of the "Swing" area in which the destruction of machinery cannot have had any lasting effect is the eastern counties, where the evidence for the prevalence of machine-threshing in the 1840s is strong.[60] Here Luddism clearly failed, as it may also have done on or beyond the western fringes of the "Swing" area. But over a substantial part of the country it succeeded, at all events until mechanisation commenced or recommenced in the 1850s.

We do not suggest that this recession of the machines was due to the simple force of the rioters or the farmers' fear of them. It was almost certainly due to the dissatisfaction of the small and medium farmers, forced against their better judgment and interest to introduce implements whose economic advantage was doubtful in the conditions of a permanent surplus of cheap labour, and in any case tending to diminish. But would they have been abolished without the initiative of the labourers? It is most improbable. For better or worse, the rioters of 1830 were more powerful than they or most contemporaries and successors thought.

Notes to Chapter 15

1. See Chapter 13, above, pp. 258.
2. *The Times* Quarterly Index provides a very approximate guide. By the 1860s such rural incendiarism as persists is specifically contrasted with the older social type, and generally put down to vagrants, tramps and the like.
3. E. L. Jones, "The Agricultural Labour Market in England 1793–1872" (*Ec. H.R.* XVII 1964–65), pp. 329 ff.
4. *Salisbury and Winchester Journal*, 7 March, 6 June.
5. *Devizes and Wiltshire Gazette*, 27 March, 13 November, 4 December.
6. *The Times*, 26 November, 2 October 1835; R. Hindry Mason, *The History of Norfolk* (1884), p. 506; Charles Mackie, *Norfolk Annals* (Norwich 1901), p. 342.

7. *The Times*, 13 June 1835.
8. *Devizes and Wiltshire Gazette*, 8 May 1834.
9. *The Times*, 7 November 1834, 26 November 1835.
10. C. Mackie, *op. cit.*, p. 218.
11. Parl. P. XXXIX of 1844.
12. *Salisbury and Winchester Journal*, 1831, passim; "*Common Prudence: a letter addressed to the Peasantry and Labourers of the County of Wilts. on the incendiary practices of some of their numbers.*" By the author of "Common Sense", etc. (Sherborne n.d. [1831]).
13. *Ashby of Tysoe*, chapter XIX; Parl. P. XXXIX of 1844 (Tables showing the number of Criminal Offenders: Committals for Arson); *Report of the S.C. on Game Laws* IX i and ii of 1846.
14. *The Times, Annual Register, The Britannia* and the *Lincoln, Rutland and Stamford Mercury* (notes on which have been kindly made available by Mr. Rex Russell, the acknowledged expert on the history of farm-labourers in his county), have been consulted. The main reports come from Beds., Northants., Cambridge, Huntingdon, Lincoln, Norfolk, and above all, Essex and Suffolk.
15. Parl. P. IX of 1846, i, pp. 816, 820, ii Q 5712.
16. 7 & 8 Vict. c. 62. This strengthened the penalties relaxed in 1837.
17. *Op. cit.*, p. 420 (Northants.), p. 467 (Cambs. and Hunts.).
18. J. Glyde, *Suffolk in the Nineteenth Century* (1856), p. 144.
19. Among the main sources which we have not been able to utilise fully are the records of the various anti-incendiary associations, formed at times of unrest (e.g. 1834, 1844). Mr. Rex Russell has studied those deposited in the Lincoln Archives. There are also the records of the Insurance companies which may, with a lot of trouble, be made to yield some data on fire-losses. The global figures for farming-stock insurance, which are available from 1834, show—as one might expect—particularly rapid increases in 1835 and 1843 and 1847, and—as one might not expect—in 1838 and 1840. (Cf. *Insurance Cyclopedia* (1874), vol. III: Farming Stock Insurance.)
20. *Ibid.*, p. 174.
21. *Journal of the Statistical Society* X (1847), p. 57. W. Russell, Statistics of Crime in England and Wales.
22. Alfred Williams, *Folksongs of the Upper Thames* (1923), p. 105. This version of a familiar theme comes from Southrop (Glos.). The song is "The Prop of the Land".
23. *Devizes and Wiltshire Gazette*, 30 October 1834.
24. *Ann. Reg.* 1844, p. 81.
25. *The Times*, 13 June 1835.
26. *Devizes and Wiltshire Gazette*, 27 February, 17 April 1835.
27. *The Britannia*, 16 March 1844, p. 173.
28. *The Times*, 1 and 5 December 1837.
29. *A Shepherd's Life* (1910), chapter 15.
30. House of Lords 258 of 1844. Ages and Descriptions of Persons Committed for Trial for Incendiary Offences in Norfolk and Suffolk.
31. *Primitive Methodist Magazine*, 1833, pp. 8, 51.

32. The membership figures given in the Conference Minutes refer to March of the given year, which is probably the annual maximum, the harvest period, when labourers had other things to think about, representing the annual minimum. (*Prim. Meth. Mag* 1831, p. 463.) Occasionally, however, we have had to use the Connexion's July returns.
33. *Primitive Methodist Magazine* 1832, pp. 263 ff. "On the work of God in the Brinkworth circuit" surveys the area since 1828.
34. *Primitive Methodist Magazine*, 1832. Journal of Thomas Russell, pp. 291 ff.
35. Shefford, Faringdon, Wallingford, Reading, Brinkworth, Salisbury, Chippenham, Market Lavington, Marlborough, Andover, Micheldever.
36. Figures from the *Wesleyan Conference Minutes* and *Baptist Magazine*, 1836, 1841.
37. The actual figures for the number of congregations and members are too unreliable to use, since reporting was pretty unsystematic.
38. In Faversham, Elham, Margate and Tenterden. Minutes of the Bible Christian Conference. (Methodist Archives.)
39. *Primitive Methodist Magazine*, 1831, p. 265.
40. P. G. Rogers, *Battle in Bossenden Wood* (London, 1961).
41. G. Edwards, *From Crow-Scaring to Westminster* (1957 edn.), p. 17. For another example of continuity, see P. Horn, Banbury and the Riots of 1830 (*Cake and Cockhorse*, Autumn 1967, p. 179.)
42. Much of the subsequent paragraph is based on P. H. J. H. Gosden, *The Friendly Societies in England*, 1815–75 (Manchester, 1961).
43. Middlesex and Surrey, being dominated by London, have been omitted.
44. For 1815, Gosden, p. 22. For 1828–47, *Insurance Cyclopedia* (1874) art. Friendly Societies, pp. 600–1. The returns on which these statistics are based are so imperfect, that all we can say—and even this may be too much—is that the order of magnitude of membership in the counties remained much the same.
45. *Insurance Cyclopedia, loc. cit.* Data for 1873:

County	Branches	Local socs.
Beds.	56	53
Berks.	43	43
Bucks.	41	51
Cambs.	64	46
Dorset	49	36
Essex	107	68
Gloucester	142	108
Hants.	168	65
Hunts.	18	20
Kent	237	101
Lincs.	202	60
Norfolk	159	88
Oxford	26	71
Rutland	138	45
Somerset	106	67
Suffolk	317	108
Sussex	151	55
Wilts.	51	37

46. Gosden, p. 74.
47. Gosden, pp. 30–31.
48. Cf. Harriet Martineau, *A History of England During the 30 Years Peace*, II, p. 73.
49. This point has been confirmed to us by Dr. I. Prothero on the basis of his researches into the London labour and Radical movement.
50. See *Insurance Cyclopedia*, III, art.: Farming Stock.
51. Parl. P. V of 1833. Questions 11085, 982 ff., 2224, 2218.
52. Appendix C. Rural Questions 53. Parl. P. XXXVIII of 1834.
53. *Ibid.*
54. *S.C. on Agriculture*, Parl. P. V of 1833, e.g. Questions 7385–6, 1235–8.
55. *S.C. on the State of Agriculture*, 1836. Parl. P. VIII ii of 1836, Q 12432.
56. *The Journey-Book of England: Berkshire* (London 1840), p. 16. "Threshing machines were common in many parts of the county, both fixed and moveable; but during the disturbances of 1831 [*sic.*] many of them were destroyed and the corn is now chiefly threshed by hand, there being always a superabundance of agricultural labourers." For their abandonment, cf. Poor Law Com. App. A Parl. P. XXVIII of 1834, p. 303 (Barton Stacey).
57. G. A. Cooke, Topography and Statistical Description of the County of Hants. (London, 1819), p. 36: "thrashing mills of two and three horse power are getting much into use in the valley of the Avon", *Jnl. R. Agric. Soc.*, England, XXII, 1861.
58. *Jnl. R. Agric. Soc. Eng.*, VI, 1845, p. 258; however, the *Reports of the Special Assistant Poor Law Commissioners on Women and Children in Agriculture* (London, 1843), pp. 173, 193, suggest some machine-threshing in Kent, but not in Sussex.
59. E. Baines, *The Social, Educational and Religious State of the Manufacturing Districts* (London, 1843), p. 61.
60. *Report on Women and Children in Agriculture*, 1843, p. 240, for Norfolk; R. N. Bacon, *The History of the Agriculture of Norfolk* (London, 1849 edn.), pp. 355–6; B. Almack in *Jnl. R. Agric. Soc. Eng.*, V, 1845, pp. 328–30; W. and H. Raynbird, *The Agriculture of Suffolk* (London 1849), pp. 229–30; *S.C. on Agricultural Customs* (Parl. P. VI of 1847–48), Q 2015–22, on the Bedfordshire customs concerning the removal of threshing-machines by outgoing tenants.

APPENDIX I

DISTRIBUTION OF DISTURBANCES BY COUNTIES

1 JANUARY 1830—3 SEPTEMBER 1832

County	Arson	"Swing" letters	Wages riots	Tithe riots	Workhouse riots	Enclosure riots	Food riots	Strikes	Political	"Riots", Assaults	"Robbery"	Burglary	Machine Breaking: Threshing Machines	Machine Breaking: Other Agricult. Machinery	Machine Breaking: Industrial Machinery	Rent Riots	"Sedition"	Total per County
Beds.	6	1	3	4	–	–	1	–	–	1	–	–	–	–	–	–	–	16
Berks.	13	5	14	–	–	–	1	–	–	2	47	2	75	3	2	–	1	165
Bucks.	3	8	3	1	–	–	–	–	–	3	2	1	7	6	5	–	–	39
Cambs.	7	1	5	–	1	–	–	–	–	2	–	–	1	–	–	–	–	17
*Cheshire	3	1	–	–	–	–	–	–	–	–	–	–	–	–	–	–	–	4
*Cornwall	1	–	2	–	–	–	4	–	–	–	–	–	–	–	–	–	–	7
*Cumberland	3	2	–	–	–	–	–	–	3	1	–	–	–	–	–	–	–	9
*Derby	2	1	–	–	–	–	–	2	1	–	–	–	–	–	–	–	–	6
*Devon	4	7	1	1	–	–	–	1	1	–	–	–	3	–	–	–	–	18
Dorset	12	–	5	–	–	–	–	–	1	4	9	1	9	1	–	–	–	42
Essex	8	4	13	1	–	–	1	–	–	1	1	–	15	2	–	–	–	46
Glos.	5	–	–	1	–	1	–	–	1	4	–	–	19	6	–	–	–	37
Hants.	15	12	14	5	2	–	–	–	1	26	76	2	45	7	3	–	–	208
*Hereford	2	2	–	–	–	–	–	–	–	–	–	–	–	–	–	–	–	4

*Herts.	5	1	–	–	–	–	–	–	–	–	–	–	–	–	–	–	–	6
Hunts.	3	3	–	–	–	–	–	–	–	–	4	–	15	–	–	–	–	25
Kent	61	11	29	4	1	–	–	–	1	5	3	–	37	–	–	2	–	154
*Lancs.	3	–	–	–	–	–	–	1	5	–	–	–	–	–	–	–	–	9
*Leics.	2	1	1	–	1	–	–	2	–	–	–	–	–	–	–	–	–	7
Lincs.	28	–	–	–	–	–	–	–	–	2	–	–	–	–	–	–	–	30
*London	–	1	–	–	–	–	–	–	1	–	–	–	–	–	–	–	–	2
*Middx.	5	6	–	–	–	–	–	–	–	–	–	–	–	–	–	–	–	11
Norfolk	19	1	3	11	1	–	–	1	–	12	–	–	29	–	11	–	–	88
Northants.	4	2	–	–	1	–	–	–	1	4	1	–	4	1	–	–	1	19
*Notts.	1	2	1	–	–	–	–	–	1	–	–	–	–	–	–	–	–	5
Oxon.	5	1	2	–	–	2	–	–	1	4	–	–	14	–	1	–	–	30
*Salop.	3	–	–	–	–	–	–	1	–	–	–	–	–	–	–	–	–	4
Somerset	2	2	1	–	–	–	–	–	2	3	1	1	3	–	–	–	–	15
*Staffs.	3	–	–	–	–	–	–	2	–	–	–	–	–	–	–	–	–	5
Suffolk, E. }	6	–	11	10	–	–	–	–	–	–	–	–	–	–	–	1	–	} 28
Suffolk, W. }	2	2	6	1	–	–	–	–	–	–	–	–	1	–	–	–	–	} 12
Surrey	23	–	1	4	–	–	–	–	–	1	–	–	–	–	–	–	–	29
Sussex, E. }	23	4	25	19	5	–	–	–	2	3	–	–	–	–	–	–	–	} 81
Sussex, W. }	11	5	22	1	1	–	–	–	1	–	12	–	11	–	–	–	–	} 64
*Warwicks.	1	–	–	–	–	–	–	–	–	–	–	–	1	–	–	–	–	2
Wilts.	18	4	–	–	–	–	–	–	–	20	62	3	97	–	4	–	–	208
Worcs.	–	2	–	–	–	–	–	1	–	2	1	–	2	–	1	–	1	10
*Yorks.	4	7	–	–	–	–	–	–	–	–	–	–	2	–	–	–	–	13
Total	316	99	162	63	13	3	7	11	23	100	219	10	390	26	27	3	3	= 1,475

* Counties only marginally affected by the labourers' movement.

APPENDIX II

SUMMARY OF REPRESSION

COUNTIES, COURTS AND SENTENCES

County	Cases heard	No. of Courts	Acquitted	Fined	Whipped	Jailed	Sentenced to death	Executed	Transported		
									Sentenced	Arr. in N.S.W.	Arr. in V.D.L. (Tasm.)
Beds.	18	3	4	–	–	12	–	–	2	2	–
*Berks.	162	2	41	–	–	78	27	1	45	40	4
*Bucks.	160	2	81	–	–	46	44	–	32	–	30
Cambs.	49	8	23	–	–	23	–	–	3	1	–
Cheshire	1	1	1	–	–	–	–	–	–	–	–
Cornwall	4	1	2	–	–	2	–	–	–	–	–
Cumberland	2	1	2	–	–	–	–	–	–	–	–
Derbyshire	1	1	–	–	–	–	–	–	1	1	–
Devon	1	1	1	–	–	–	–	–	–	–	–
*Dorset	62	2	33	–	1	15	6	–	13	13	–
Essex	123	4	31	–	–	67	1	1	24	–	23
Glos.	94	2	41	–	–	26	1	–	27	–	25
*Hants.	298	2	108	2	–	68	101	3	117	50	57
Hereford	1	1	–	–	–	–	–	–	1	1	–

Herts.	2	1	–	–	–	–	–	–	2	–	2
Hunts.	57	1	22	–	–	30	–	–	5	–	5
Kent	102	12	25	–	–	48	5	4	25	2	23
Lancs.	2	1	–	–	–	2	–	–	–	–	–
Lincs.	12	5	8	–	–	2	2	2	–	–	–
London-Middx. ..	4	1	4	–	–	–	–	–	–	–	–
Norfolk	129	6	56	–	–	59	3	1	13	1	12
Northants.	49	3	13	–	–	33	2	1	–	–	–
Notts.	2	1	2	–	–	–	–	–	–	–	–
Oxon.	75	2	34	5	–	23	–	–	13	–	11
Salop.	4	1	2	–	–	1	–	–	1	1	–
Somerset	40	3	26	–	–	13	–	–	1	–	–
Staffs.	11	2	4	–	–	2	2	2	3	–	1
Suffolk	71	5	49	–	–	14	1	–	8	1	7
Surrey	20	3	11	–	–	8	1	1	–	–	–
Sussex	52	4	18	–	–	16	3	1	17	–	17
Warwicks.	1	1	1	–	–	–	–	–	–	–	–
*Wilts.	339	3	139	–	–	47	52	1	152	36	115
Worcs.	25	2	15	–	–	9	1	1	–	–	–
Yorks.	3	2	3	–	–	–	–	–	–	–	–
Totals	1,976	90	800	7	1	644	252	19	505	149	332

* Counties in which Special Commissions sat.

APPENDIX III

TABLE OF INCIDENTS

KEY

TO TYPES OF DISTURBANCE

1. Arson.
2. Threatening ("Swing" or other) letters.
3. Wages meetings, riots.
4. Tithe meetings, riots.
5. Poorhouse riots.
6. Enclosure riots.
7. Food riots.
8. Strikes, industrial riots.
9. Political demonstrations, riots.
10. "Riots" (assault, release of prisoners, etc.).
11. "Robbery" (i.e. acquiring money or food by menaces).
12. Burglary, larceny, theft.
13. Destruction of Threshing Machines.
14. Destruction of other Agricultural machinery.
15. Destruction of non-Agricultural machinery.
16. Rent riots.
17. Sedition ("inflammatory" speeches, seditious remarks, etc.).

1

Date 1830	Place	County	Type of Disturbance 1	2	3	4	5	6	7	8	9	10	11	12	13	14	15	16	17	Target	Value, etc.
5.ii	Mildenhall	W. Suffolk		x																	
23.iii	Brandon	W. Suffolk		x																	
6.iv	Chipping Campden	Glos.		x																Farmer	
10.iv	Orpington	W. Kent															x			Overseers	
28.iv	Rye	E. Sussex									x									Government	
1.vi	Orpington	Kent	x																	Farmer	
1–6.vi	Bromley area	Kent	x	(3)																Farmers	
2.vi	Hinckley	Leics.					x													Overseers	
3.viii	Caterham	Surrey	x																	Irish	
5.viii	Blandford	Dorset										x									
3–28.viii	Nr. Sevenoaks	Kent	x	(4)																ex-Tradesman	
24/25.viii	Kidderminster	Worcs.								x										Tailors	
27.viii	Otmoor	Oxon.						x													
28.viii	Lower Hardres	E. Kent													x					Farmers	
late viii/ early ix	Bromley/ Sevenoaks	Kent	x																		
29.viii	Newington	E. Kent													x					Farmers	
1/2.ix	Brasted	Kent	x																	Farmer	£348.9.0
	Orpington	Kent	x	(2)																Farmer, J.P.	
2–10.ix	Cowden	Kent	x																	Parson	
	Otford	Kent	x																		
	Shoreham	Kent	x																		
	Ide Hill	Kent		x																"Poor Widow"	
	Sevenoaks	Kent		x																Tradesmen	

6.ix	Oxford	Oxon.						x				x								Police	
18.ix	Upper Hardres	E. Kent													x (2)					Farmer	
20.ix	Barham	E. Kent													x					Farmer	
20–26.ix	Dover/ Canterbury	E. Kent													x (3)					Gentry Farmers	
4.x	Sandwich	E. Kent	x																	Farmer	
	Middleton	Lancs.									x									Government	
5.x	Ash	E. Kent	x																	Farmer	
	Lyminge	E. Kent	x																	Parson	
6.x	Dover	E. Kent		x																	(a "Swing" poster)
6/7.x	Margate	E. Kent													x					Gentry	
7.x	Blackburn	Lancs.									x									Government	
8.x	Boughton Hill	E. Kent	x																		
10.x	Bluntisham	Hunts.		x																Farmers, Gentry	(re Th/Ms)
11.x	Saxlingham	Norfolk										x									
	Nr. Wrotham	E. Kent	x																	"Widow"	
14.x	Maidstone	Kent									x									Government	(Cobbett)
	W. Peckham	Kent	x																	Farmer	
16.x	Battle	E. Sussex									x									Government	(Cobbett)
17.x	Hartfield	E. Sussex	x																	Overseer	
	Otford	Kent	x																	Farmer	
21/22.x	Nr. Sittingbourne	E. Kent	x																	Overseer	"Heavy loss"
22.x	Upstreet	E. Kent	x																		
	Oxted	Surrey	x (2)																	Farmers	
22–26.x	Northfleet	E. Kent		x																Gentry	
22.x	Hartlip	E. Kent													x					Farmer	("Blackened faces")

2

Date 1830	Place	County	Type of Disturbance 1	2	3	4	5	6	7	8	9	10	11	12	13	14	15	16	17	Target	Value, etc.
23.x	Bekesbourne	E. Kent													x	(2)				Farmers	
	Nr. Canterbury	E. Kent													x	(2)				Farmers	
	Rainham	E. Kent			x															Farmers	
	Shipbourne	E. Kent	x																	Farmer	
24.x	Sandwich	E. Kent													x					Farmer	
	Cobham Hall	E. Kent	x																	Landowner	
	Selling Court	E. Kent	x																	Steward	
25.x	Sheffield Park	E. Sussex		x																Earl of Sheffield	
25–26.x	Ash	E. Kent													x						(9 in all)
	Goldstone	E. Kent													x						
	Overland	E. Kent													x						
	Sandwich	E. Kent													x						
	Stourmouth	E. Kent													x						
	Lenham	E. Kent			x																
28.x	I. of Sheppey	E. Kent	x	(2)																	
	Boughton Hill	E. Kent	x																		
	Hollingbourne	E. Kent			x								x								(Tricolour flag)
29.x	E. Sutton	Kent			x								x							Landlords/	
	Langley	Kent			x								x							Farmers Parsons	
30.x	Canford Magna	Dorset												x							8/– (part of th/m.)
1.xi	Boughton Hill	E. Kent			x																
	Faversham	E. Kent			x																
	Blackburn	Lancs.									x									Government	

3.xi	E. Malling	Kent			x															
3/4.xi	Chatham	E. Kent	x																Large Farmer	
early xi	Nr. Battle	E. Sussex		x															Farmers }	(Re Th/Ms)
																			Gentry }	
3.xi	Battle	E. Sussex	x																Overseer	
4.xi	Nr. Battle	E. Sussex	x																Farmer	
	Nr. Battle	E. Sussex	x																J.P.	
	Nr. Battle	E. Sussex	x																Farmer	
	Brede	E. Sussex					x												Overseers	
	Fairlight	E. Sussex					x												Overseers	
5.xi	Rayleigh	Essex	x																Small Farmer	£100–£150
	Kettering	Northants.										x								£5.19.3 pd.
	Caterham	Surrey	x																	
8–9.xi	London	—									x								Government	
	Robertsbridge	E. Sussex	x		x														Farmers	
	Sedlescombe	E. Sussex			x														Farmers	
8–10.xi	Carlisle	Cumb'd.									x								Government	
9.xi	Hurstfield	E. Sussex			x															
	Northiam	E. Sussex			x															
	Hawkhurst	W. Kent													x					
	Preston	E. Kent													x					
	Wingham	E. Kent													x (2)					
	Birchington	E. Kent	x																Overseer	
	Goudhurst	W. Kent			x	x												x		Landlords, Parsons, etc.
9/10.xi	Rodmersham	E. Kent	x																Farmer	
10.xi	Milton Constable	Norfolk	x																J.P.	
9.xi	Bodiam	E. Sussex			x	x													Farmers, Parsons	
	Brede	E. Sussex			x	x													Farmers	

3

Date 1830	Place	County	Type of Disturbance 1	2	3	4	5	6	7	8	9	10	11	12	13	14	15	16	17	Target	Value, etc.
9.xi	Ewhurst	E. Sussex			x	x														Farmers, Parsons	
	Frant	E. Sussex			x	x														Farmers Parsons	
	Newenden	W. Kent			x	x														Farmers Parsons	
	Mayfield	E. Sussex			x	x														Farmers Parsons	
	Salehurst	E. Sussex			x	x														Farmers Parsons	
	Ticehurst	E. Sussex			x	x														Farmers Parsons	
	Wadhurst	E. Sussex			x	x															
10.xi	Goudhurst	W. Kent			x	x												x		Landlords Parsons, etc.	
	Bearsted	Kent	x																	Overseer	
	Thurnham	E. Kent	x																	Farmer	
	Holyport	Berks.		x																Farmer	
10/11.xi	Portsmouth area	Hants.		x																	
11.xi	Cranbrook	W. Kent			x															Farmers	
	Yalding	Kent			x																
	Eastry	E. Kent													x					[Destroyed by farmers]	
	Wingham	E. Kent													x						
	Rotherfield	E. Sussex				x														Parson	

	Englefield Green	Surrey	x																	Gent.	
	Brockenhurst	Hants.		x																	(re Th/Ms)
	Colnbrook	Bucks.		x																Gents.	(re Th/Ms)
	Langley	Bucks.		x																Farmers	
	High Wycombe	Bucks.		x																	
12.xi	Headcorn	Kent	Farmers' & Labourers' petition to Parliament.																	Parsons, Landlords	
	Otham	Kent	x																		
	Warbleton	E. Sussex					x													Overseers	
	Watersfield	E. Sussex	x																	Farmer	
12–16.xi	Sussex Border	Kent/ Sussex				x														Parsons	
12–15.xi	Codford St. Peter	Wilts.		x																Farmer	
12–17.xi	Hadlow	Kent			x															Farmers & Overseers	(by unemployed)
	E. Peckham	Kent			x															Farmers & Overseers	
	W. Peckham	Kent			x															Farmers & Overseers	
	Nettlestead	Kent			x															Farmers & Overseers	
	Yalding	Kent			x															Farmers & Overseers	
13.xi	Bexhill	E. Sussex	x																		
	Petworth	W. Sussex					x													Overseer	
	Benenden	W. Kent			x																
	Rolvenden	W. Kent			x																

4

Date 1830	Place	County	Type of Disturbance 1	2	3	4	5	6	7	8	9	10	11	12	13	14	15	16	17	Target	Value, etc.
13.xi	Sutton Scotney	Hants.									x									Government	(Reform Petition) (re Th/Ms)
	Bluntisham	Hunts.	x																	Farmer	
	Horsham district	W. Sussex		x																	
	Lewes district	E. Sussex		x																	
	North Cove (Beeches)	E. Suffolk	x																		£450 pd.
14.xi	Boughton Hill	E. Kent	x																		
	Nr. Hythe	E. Kent	x																		
	Albury	Surrey	x																	Farmer	
15.xi	Thatcham	Berks.			x															Gentry Farmers	
	Wavendon	Bucks.	x																	Gent.	
	Alland Court (I. of Th.)	E. Kent	x																	Large Farmer	
	Boughton Hill	E. Kent	x																		
	Nr. Minster	E. Kent	x																		
	Goudhurst	W. Kent			x							x								JPs, overseer farmers	
	Battle	E. Sussex			x	x														Parsons Farmers	
	Buxted	E. Sussex			x	x														Parsons Farmers	
	Crow-borough	E. Sussex			x	x									x					Parsons Farmers	

Herstmonceux	E. Sussex			x	x														Parsons Farmers
Rotherfield	E. Sussex			x	x														Parsons Farmers
Withyham	E. Sussex			x	x														Parsons Farmers
Ringmer	E. Sussex			x															Farmers & Gentry
Uckfield	E. Sussex										x								Police
Maresfield	E. Sussex		x																
Lewes	E. Sussex	Joint meeting farmers & labourers																	Parsons Landlords
Ashington	W. Sussex	x																	
Watersfield	W. Sussex	x																	
Bersted	W. Sussex			x								x		x					Farmers Parsons
Bognor	W. Sussex			x								x		x					Farmers Parsons
Felpham	W. Sussex			x								x		x					Farmers Parsons
Yapton	W. Sussex			x								x		x					Farmers Parsons
Goodwood	W. Sussex			x								x		x					Farmers Parsons
Pagham	W. Sussex			x								x		x					Farmers Parsons
Worthing	W. Sussex			x								x							Landlords Parsons
Exton	Hants.		x																Farmers
Strathfieldsaye	Hants.	x																	Duke of Wellington

Date 1830	Place	County	Type of Disturbance																	Target	Value, etc.
			1	2	3	4	5	6	7	8	9	10	11	12	13	14	15	16	17		
15.xi	Knook	Wilts.	x																	Farmer	
16.xi	Hurst	Berks.	x																		
	Bray	Berks.		x																Farmers	
	Windsor	Berks.		x																Manufacturers	
	Mevagissey	Cornwall							x											Farmers Dealers	
	Wallington	Hants.	x																	Farmers	
	—	Hereford		x																Large Farmers	
	Moulton	Lincoln	x																	Farmer	
	Hounslow/ Heston	Middx.		x																Farmers	
	Bedfont	Middx.	x																		
	Benenden	W. Kent													x						
	Hawkhurst	W. Kent			x										x						
	Lydd	E. Kent			x																
	Sevenoaks area	E. Kent			x																
	Fulking	E. Sussex		x																	
	Hailsham	E. Sussex	Joint meeting farmers & labourers																	Parsons Landlords	
	Angmering	W. Sussex	x																		
	Chichester	W. Sussex			x															Large Farmers J.P.s	
	Nr. Horsham	W. Sussex	x	(2)																	
	Egham/ Molsey	Surrey	x																		

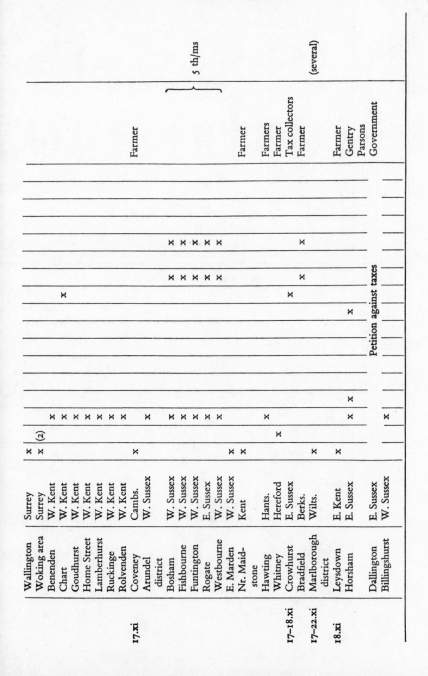

	Wallington	Surrey	x																		
	Woking area	Surrey	x	(2)																	
	Benenden	W. Kent			x																
	Chart	W. Kent			x							x									
	Goudhurst	W. Kent			x																
	Home Street	W. Kent			x																
	Lamberhurst	W. Kent			x																
	Ruckinge	W. Kent			x																
	Rolvenden	W. Kent			x																
17.xi	Coveney	Cambs.	x																	Farmer	
	Arundel district	W. Sussex			x																
	Bosham	W. Sussex			x								x		x						5 th/ms
	Fishbourne	W. Sussex			x								x		x						
	Funtington	W. Sussex			x								x		x						
	Rogate	E. Sussex			x								x		x						
	Westbourne	W. Sussex			x								x		x						
	E. Marden	W. Sussex	x																		
	Nr. Maid-stone	Kent	x																	Farmer	
	Hawting	Hants.			x															Farmers	
	Whitney	Hereford		x																Farmer	
17–18.xi	Crowhurst	E. Sussex										x								Tax collectors	
	Bradfield	Berks.											x		x					Farmer	
17–22.xi	Marlborough district	Wilts.	x																		(several)
18.xi	Leysdown	E. Kent	x																	Farmer	
	Horsham	E. Sussex			x	x					x									Gentry Parsons	
	Dallington	E. Sussex									Petition against taxes									Government	
	Billingshurst	W. Sussex			x																

6

Date 1830	Place	County	Type of Disturbance																	Target	Value, etc.
			1	2	3	4	5	6	7	8	9	10	11	12	13	14	15	16	17		
18.xi	Hellingly	E. Sussex			x															Lord Gage	
	Pulborough	W. Sussex			x																
	Wisborough Green	E. Sussex			x																
	St. Mary Bourne	Hants.	x																	Large Farmer	
	Strathfield-saye	Hants.	x																	Duke of Wellington	
	Wadswick	Wilts.	x																	Farmer	
	Havant	Hants.											x		x	(9)				Three Farmers	
	Micheldever	Hants.											x								15/–
	Overton	Hants.			x															Farmers	
	Warblington	Hants.													x	(2)				Farmers	
	W. Marden	W. Sussex			x																
	Aldermaston	Berks.											x		x						
	Beenham	Berks.											x		x						
	Bucklebury	Berks.											x		x						
	Stanford Dingley	Berks.											x		x						
	Colling-bourne	Wilts.	x																	Farmer	
	Ludgershall	Wilts.	x																	Farmer	
18–19.xi	Woolhamp-ton	Berks.												x						Labourer	(Meat)
	Southover	E. Sussex	x																	Farmer	£700–800
16–22.xi	High Wycombe	Bucks.		x																Paper-Makers	

	Marlow	Bucks.		x																Gents	
																				Farmers	
	Slough	Bucks.		x																Gents	
																				Farmers	
19.xi	Alder-	Berks.											x		x					Farmers	
	maston																			Gentry	
	Brimpton	Berks.											x		x					Farmers	(33 Th/Ms
																				Gentry	destroyed
	Shalford	Berks.											x		x					Farmers	18/19.xi)
																				Gentry	
	Wasing	Berks.										x	x		x					Farmers	
																				Gentry	
	Nr. Thatcham	Berks.															x			Manufacturers	£1,000?
	Holyport	Berks.	x												x	(2)				Farmer	
	Lambourn	Berks.	x																		
	Alresford	Hants.										x			x						
	Andover	Hants.													x					Gent.	
	Barton Stacey	Hants.	x																	Baronet	
	Basingstoke	Hants.											x								£1
	Glendesden	Hants.			x																
	Micheldever	Hants.											x	(4)	x					Parsons	£4+
																				Farmers	
	Newton	Hants.			x																
	Stacey																				
	Overton	Hants.			x								x								
	Stratton	Hants.											x								£10
	The Wallops	Hants.			x															Meeting with	
																				farmers	
	Warford	Hants.			x										x					Farmers	
	W. Meon	Hants.			x										x					Farmers	
	Winchester	Hants.		x																Farmers	
	area																				

Date 1830	Place	County	Type of Disturbance 1	2	3	4	5	6	7	8	9	10	11	12	13	14	15	16	17	Target	Value, etc.
19.xi	Stickford	Lincs.	x																	Farmer	
	N. Walsham	Norfolk		x			Riot against Threshing Machines													Farmers	
	Nr. Canterbury	E. Kent	x																	Farmer?	
	Ockley	Surrey				x														Parsons	
	Woking	Surrey				x														Parsons	
	Wotton	Surrey				x														Parsons	
	Barcombe	E. Sussex			x															Farmers	
	Cooksbridge	E. Sussex			x															Farmers	
	Rotherfield	E. Sussex			x															Farmers	
	E. Dean	W. Sussex	x																	Farmers	
	Arundel/ Worthing	W. Sussex	x																	Farmers (several)	
	Oare	Wilts.	x																	Farmers	
	Wilcot	Wilts.										x									
19/20.xi	Paston	Norfolk													x					Farmers	
20.xi	Speen	Berks.			x																
	Waltham St. Lawrence	Berks.													x						
	Andover	Hants.										x									£3,000?
	Barton Stacey	Hants.											x	(3)							5/–+
	Kimpton	Hants.	x									x	x							Farmer	
	Martyr Worthy	Hants.											x							Baronet	£20
	Nr. Ryde	Hants.	x																	Farmer	
	Up. Clatford	Hants.													x	x	x			Manufacturers	

	Herne	E. Kent										x								Farmers	(shots)
	Margate	E. Kent													x					Farmers	
	Riverhead	E. Kent	x																		
	Bacons-thorpe	Norfolk	x																	Small Farmer	
	Holt	Norfolk													x						
	Henley-on-Thames	Oxon.		x																Farmers	
	Norwood	Surrey	x																		
	Stanton St. Bernard	Wilts.	x	(2)																Large Farmer & Farmer	(re Th/Ms)
20/21.xi	Boughton	E. Kent	x																	Farmer	(using Th/Ms)
	Ampthill	Beds.		x																Gents, Parsons	(several)
20–22.xi	Canterbury area	E. Kent		x																Gentry, etc.	
21.xi	Binfield	Berks.											x							Blacksmith	(sledge-hammer)
	Enborne	Berks.										x								Farmer	
	Inkpen	Berks.													x					Farmers	
	Kintbury	Berks.													x					Farmers	
	Yattenden	Berks.			x																
	Willingham	Cambs.	x																	Farmers Overseers	£4,000–8,000
	Alverstoke	Hants.		x																Gent.	
	Crawley	Hants.										x									
	Fyfield	Hants.		x																Bishop	(verbal)
	Houghton	Hants.											x	(2)							30/–
	Kimpton	Hants.											x	(2)	x					Farmers	
	Littleton	Hants.										x	x		x					Farmers	
	Southampton	Hants.		x																Timber Merchants	
	Vernham Dean	Hants.											x	(4)							30/– +

Date 1830	Place	County	Type of Disturbance 1	2	3	4	5	6	7	8	9	10	11	12	13	14	15	16	17	Target	Value, etc.
21.xi	Blean	E. Kent	x																	Councillor	
	Hernhill	E. Kent	x																	Small Farmer	
	Riverhead	E. Kent	x																	Miller	
	Goudhurst area	W. Kent			x															Farmers	
	Somersham	Hunts.	x																		
	Benson	Oxon.													x					Farmers	
	Berrick	Oxon.													x					Farmers Gentry	
	Crowmarch	Oxon.													x					Farmers Gentry	
	Ewelme	Oxon.													x					Farmers Gentry	
	Rofford	Oxon.													x					Farmers Gentry	
	Crowhurst Park	E. Sussex	x																		
	All Cannings	Wilts.													x						
	Hippens-combe	Wilts.													x						
	Amesbury	Wilts.	x																		
	Everley	Wilts.	x																		
	Stanton St. Bernard	Wilts.	x																		
	Winterslow	Wilts.	x	(2)																	
20/21.xi	Horton	Wilts.		x																Large Farmers	(re Th/Ms)

	Salisbury district	Wilts.		x																Farmers Manufacturers	
22.xi	Ashampstead	Berks.			x															Farmers	
	Basildon	Berks.			x															Farmers	
	Chilton Foliat	Wilts.											x								
	E. Hagbourne	Berks.			x																
	Eddington	Berks.			x																
	Wallingford	Berks.																	x	Farmers, etc.	(in pub)
	W. Wood-hay	Berks.											x		x						13 Th/Ms broken on 22/11 (W. Woodhay, Kintbury, Lambourn)
	Kintbury	Berks.							x				x (7)		x (3)						
	Lambourn	Berks.													x (3)						
	Hungerford	Berks.										x			x		x				
	Fowey	Cornwall							x											Dealers	
	Bere Regis	Dorset			x															Farmers	
	Coggeshall	Essex										x								Overseer	
	Andover	Hants.											x								
	Bighton	Hants.										x									
	Basingstoke	Hants.										x									
	Broughton	Hants.												x						Shopkeeper?	(musical instruments)
	Buriton	Hants.			x																
	Corhampton	Hants.											x								£5.10.0
	Durley	Hants.													x					Farmer	
	Everley	Wilts.	x																	Farmer	
	Farringdon	Hants.											x								5/-
	Hurstbourne Tarrant	Hants.											x								£1
	Itchen Abbas	Hants.										x			x					Farmer	
	Leckford	Hants.											x								40/-

Date 1830	Place	County	Type of Disturbance 1	2	3	4	5	6	7	8	9	10	11	12	13	14	15	16	17	Target	Value, etc.
22.xi	Liphook	Hants.										x								J.P.	
	Martyr Worthy	Hants.											x								5/–
	Michelmersh	Hants.											x	(2)	x					Farmer	
	Mottisfont	Hants.											x								
	New Alresford	Hants.													x					Farmer	
	Owslebury	Hants.												x							(Iron bars) 14/–
	Penton Grafton	Hants.													x	x				Gent.	
	Quarley	Hants.													x					Gent.	
	Romsey	Hants.													x						
	Selborne	Hants.					x													Overseers	(Poor house destroyed)
	Steep	Hants.			x	Labourers' wages charter														Gentry, etc.	
	Wootton St. Lawrence	Hants.										x	x	(4)							
	Thruxton	Hants.													x					Gent.	
	Upham	Hants.											x							Parson	
	Vernham Dean	Hants.											x								
	Weyhill	Hants.											x	(2)							
	Wickham	Hants.										x									
	Alland Court	E. Kent													x	(2)				Large Farmer	(in disguise)
	Woodnesborough	E. Kent	x																	Farmer	

Melton Constable	Norfolk										x								
Walcot	Norfolk													x					
Northampton	Northants.									x									Government
Northampton	Northants.		x																Gent.
Heythrop	Oxon.			x															Farmers, etc.
Pishill	Oxon.	x																	Gent.
Battle	E. Sussex																	x	Government
Poynings	E. Sussex				x														Parsons
Cowfold	W. Sussex			x															Farmers
Hickstead	E. Sussex			x															Farmers
Hickstead	E. Sussex	x																	Farmers
Lancing	W. Sussex			x															Gent.
Steyning	W. Sussex			x															Farmers
Nr. Worthing	W. Sussex			x															Farmers
Allington	Wilts.													x					
Buttermere	Wilts.											x							
Collingbourne D.	Wilts.											x							
Collingbourne K.	Wilts.											x							
Downton	Wilts.													x					
Enford	Wilts.													x	(2)				
Figheldean	Wilts.											x							
Froxfield	Wilts.													x	(2)				
Gt. Bedwyn	Wilts.											x	(2)	x	(3)				
Hippenscombe	Wilts.													x	(2)				
Idmiston	Wilts.													x					
Mildenhall	Wilts.		x											x					
Netheravon	Wilts.													x	(2)				

10

Date 1830	Place	County	Type of Disturbance 1	2	3	4	5	6	7	8	9	10	11	12	13	14	15	16	9	Target	Value, etc.
22.xi	Newton Toney	Wilts.													x						
	Ramsbury	Wilts.										x(3)	x		x	(5)					
	Salisbury	Wilts.										x									
	Tidcombe	Wilts.													x						
	West Dean	Wilts.													x						
	Whiteparish	Wilts.													x						
	Wilcot	Wilts.													x						
22/23.xi	Edingthorpe	Norfolk				x														Parsons	
23.xi	Aston Tirrold	Berks.			x															Farmers Gents.	
	Aston Upthorpe	Berks.													x						
	Basildon	Berks.											x	(6)	x	(4)					
	Boxford	Berks.											x		x						
	Bradfield	Berks.			x																
	Buckhurst	Berks.	x																	Farmer	
	Benham Pk.	Berks.											x		x						
	Buckhurst	Berks.	x																	Farmer	
	Eastbury	Berks.											x								
	E. Garston	Berks.													x(2)	x					
	Enborne	Berks.											x	(3)	x						
	Hampstead Marshall	Berks.											x		x					Lord Craven, etc.	
	Hungerford	Berks.											x		x						
	Inkpen	Berks.											x								

Kintbury	Berks.											x (4)								
Lambourn	Berks.											x		x						
Shalbourne	Wilts.													x(2)	x					
Southridge	Berks.			x																
Streatley	Berks.													x (2)						
Welford	Berks.											x		x (2)						
W. Shefford	Berks.											x		x						
W. Woodhay	Berks.											x								
Wickham	Berks.													x						
Englefield	Berks.	x																	Gent.	
Faringdon	Berks.		x																Farmers	(re Th/Ms & Wages)
Fawley	Berks.	x																	Gent.	
Cranborne	Dorset											x								
Gosport area	Hants.		x																Parsons Press	
Breamore	Hants.											x								
Burghclere	Hants.											x (7)		x (2)					Gents. Farmers	£15.3.0
Droxford	Hants.													x					Farmer	
E. Woodhay	Hants.				x							x (7)		x (2)					Farmers Parsons	£5.17.0
Fordingbridge	Hants.														x (2)				Manufacturers	(2 Factories)
Nr. Greatham	Hants.											x								
Headley	Hants.					x													Overseers	(poor house destroyed)
Highclere	Hants.											x		x	x				Earl of Carnarvon	(Th/Ms: farmer)
Kingsley	Hants.											x								
Monk Sherbourne	Hants.										x	x (2)								£6

11

Date 1830	Place	County	Type of Disturbance 1	2	3	4	5	6	7	8	9	10	11	12	13	14	15	16	17	Target	Value, etc.
23.xi	Owslebury	Hants.										x	x	(2)							£5.5.0
	Pamber	Hants.										x	x								4/6
	Quarley	Hants.											x		x	x				Farmer	£1+
	Rockbourne	Hants.										x				x				(Iron gates)	
	Sherfield	Hants.											x								
	Sydmonton	Hants.											x		x						£2
	S. Stoneham	Hants.										x	x		x	(3)				Farmers	
																				Gents.	£1+
	Stockbridge	Hants.										x									
	N. Walsham	Norfolk													x						
	Themel-thorpe	Norfolk													x						
	Burcot	Oxon.													x					Farmers	
	Clifton Hampden	Oxon.													x					Farmers	
	Little Milton	Oxon.										x			x					Farmers	
	Bexhill	E. Sussex	x																	Farmer	
	Alton Barnes	Wilts.										x	x		x						
	Alton Priors	Wilts.													x						
	Aldbourne	Wilts.										x	x	(5)	x	(8)					
	Burbage	Wilts.											x	(4)	x	(2)					
	Chirton	Wilts.											x		x	(2)					
	Colling-bourne D.	Wilts.											x								
	Downton	Wilts.													x						
	Easton	Wilts.											x		x	(3)					

	Ham	Wilts.										x	x	(2)	x						
	Hannington	Wilts.											x		x						
	Liddington	Wilts.											x		x						
	Milton	Wilts.										x	x	(2)	x	(2)					
	Netheravon	Wilts.										x									
	Odstock	Wilts.											x								
	Ogbourne St. A.	Wilts.										x	(2)			x	(2)				
	Pewsey	Wilts.														x	(6)				
	Ramsbury	Wilts.											x								
	Shalbourne	Wilts.										x	x	(2)		x	(5)				
	S. Severnake	Wilts.											x								
	Standlynch	Wilts.											x								
	Wanborough	Wilts.											x	(8)		x	(2)				
	West Harnham	Wilts.															x			Papermaker	£18.7.0
	Whiteparish	Wilts.											x	(2)							
	Wilton	Wilts.														x					
	Wood-borough	Wilts.														x					
	Wootton Rivers	Wilts.											x	(3)							
23/24.xi	Southampton	Hants.	x																	Timber Merchants	(Bakers' saw-mills) £7,000
24.xi	Ashampstead	Berks.											x								
	Appleford	Berks.			x																
	Balking	Berks.			x										x						
	Basildon	Berks.											x								
	Beenham	Berks.											x		x						
	Boxford	Berks.											x		x						
	Inkpen	Berks.											x								

12

Date 1830	Place	County	Type of Disturbance 1	2	3	4	5	6	7	8	9	10	11	12	13	14	15	16	17	Target	Value, etc.
24.xi	Speen	Berks.											x		x						
	Stanford	Berks.			x																
	Upton	Berks.			x																
	Wantage	Berks.													x	x	x			Iron founder	(Austen's)
	W. Woodhay	Berks.														x					
	Wickham	Berks.													x						
	High Wycombe	Bucks.		x																Papermakers	(verbal)
	Boveridge	Dorset											x							Gent.	
	Handley, etc.	Dorset											x		x	x				Farmers	
	Thaxted	Essex	x																	Farmer	
	Dockenfield	Surrey			x															Farmers	
	Droxford	Hants.											x		x					Farmers	£1
	E. Wellow	Hants.													x					Farmers	
	E. Woodhay	Hants.											x								5/-
	Selborne	Hants.				x														Parson	
	Redbridge	Hants.		x									x								
	Week	Hants.														x				2 Farmers	£25
	Conington	Hunts.														x?					
	Sawtry	Hunts.														x					
	I. of Thanet	E. Kent													x	(4)					
	Wrotham	E. Kent		x	x	x														Parsons	
																				Overseers	
	Heston	Middx.		x																Powder Magazine	
	Staines	Middx.		x																Farmer	

Beeston	Norfolk	x																		
Cawston	Norfolk														x (4)					
Field Dalling	Norfolk														x (2)					
Foulsham	Norfolk														x					
Thorpe	Norfolk	x																		
Barton	Oxon.			x										x						
Wootton	Oxon.										x									
Framfield	E. Sussex			x							x								Farmers Government	(+ Taxes riot)
Alderbury	Wilts.										x	x		x						
Bishops Cannings	Wilts.											x								
Broad Chalk	Wilts.										x	x (3)		x						
Burcombe	Wilts.													x						
Barford St. Martin	Wilts.											x				x			Silk manufactured	£185.15.0
Coombe Bissett	Wilts.											x (2)		x						
Cricklade	Wilts.													x						
Draycot Foliat	Wilts.													x						
Damerham	Hants.											x (3)		x						
Dinton	Wilts.											x								
Ebbesbourne	Wilts.											x								
Fifield	Wilts.													x						
Fugglestone St. Peter	Wilts.										x				x					
Highworth	Wilts.												x (6)							
Hannington	Wilts.										x	x (2)		x						
Plaitford	Hants.										x (3)									
Westbourne Stoke	Wilts.													x						

Date 1830	Place	County	Type of Disturbance																	Target	Value, etc.
			1	2	3	4	5	6	7	8	9	10	11	12	13	14	15	16	17		
24.xi	W. Grimstead	Wilts.													x						
	Wroughton	Wilts.										x									
	Wilton	Wilts.														x					
25.xi	Hinsford	Dorset	x																	Farmer	
	Piddletown	Dorset	x																		
	Fawley	Hants.										x									
	Liss	Hants.										x									(House pulled down)
	Nr. Newport	Hants.			x															Farmers	(paupers)
	Ringwood	Hants.										x									
	Alconbury Hill	Hunts.													x						
	Northfleet	E. Kent	x																		
	Rusthall Common	W. Kent	x																	Gent.	
	Bolton	Lancs.									x									Tories	
	Caister	Norfolk	x																	Large Farmer	
	Honing	Norfolk													x						
	Kerdiston	Norfolk													x						
	Southrepps	Norfolk										x									
	Whitwell	Norfolk										x									
	Egham	Surrey	x																		
	Limpsfield	Surrey			x															Farmers	
	Boyton	Wilts.													x						
	Cricklade	Wilts.										x			x	(3)					[incitement to break]

	Fonthill Giff.	Wilts.										x									
	Fonthill Bish.	Wilts.													x						
	Latton	Wilts.													x						
	Lyneham	Wilts.													x	(2)					
	Stanton	Wilts.											x								
	Stanton Fitzwarren	Wilts.													x						
	Tisbury	Wilts.										x			x					M.P.	£353.2.5
	Tollard Royal	Wilts.											x		x	(3)					
	Bromsgrove	Worcs.		x	(2)															Parson	
	Kenchester	Hereford	x																	Large Farmer	(re Th/Ms)
	Whitney	Hereford																	x	The Rich	(a circular)
26.xi	High Wycombe	Bucks.										x								J.P.s	
	Blackgrove	Bucks.													x					Farmers	£50
	Up. Winchenden	Bucks.														x	(3)			Farmers	
	Waddesdon	Bucks.																		Farmers	£55
	Nr. Exeter	Devon		x																Farmers, etc.	
	Bere Regis	Dorset										x									
	Wolland	Dorset													x						
	Beverstone	Glos.										x		x	x						£40+£20
	Fairford	Glos.													x	x					£300 claimed
	Horsley	Glos.													x						£10
	Tetbury	Glos.										x									
	Exbury & Lepe	Hants.										x									
	Fawley	Hants.										x								J.P.s	
	Romsey	Hants.											x								
	Kimbolton	Hunts.		x																Parson	
	Alconbury	Hunts.											x		x					Farmer	

Date 1830	Place	County	Type of Disturbance 1	2	3	4	5	6	7	8	9	10	11	12	13	14	15	16	17	Target	Value, etc.
26.xi	Buckden	Hunts.													x						
	Buckworth	Hunts.											x		x	(2)					
	Hamerton	Hunts.													x						
	Old Weston	Hunts.													x					Blacksmith	
	Gt. Stukeley	Hunts.											x		x						
	Little Stukeley	Hunts.			x										x						
	Lancaster	Lancs.	= Meeting of Trades																	Government	
																				Manufacturers	
	Reepham	Norfolk										x								J.P.s	
	Warmington	Northants.											x		x						
	Heythrop	Oxon.											x		x						
	S. Brewham	Somerset										x									(threat to Th/M)
	Barcombe	E. Sussex				x														Parson	
	Nr. Battle	E. Sussex	x																	Farmer	
																				J.P.	
	Berwick	E. Sussex	x																	Lord Gage	
	Brighton	E. Sussex					x													Overseer	
	Cricklade	Wilts.										x									
	Long Newton	Wilts.													x	(2)					
	Tisbury	Wilts.													x	(2)					
27.xi	Wootton Pillinge	Beds.	x																	Large Farmer	
	Stone	Bucks.												x	x						("several" Th/Ms)

	Waddesdon	Bucks.														x				Farmer	£2
	Mappowder	Dorset											x								£1
	Pulham	Dorset			x								x							Farmers	
	Buckland Newton	Dorset											x		x					Farmers	
	Coln St. Aldwyn	Glos.													x	x					
	Eastleach Martin	Glos.													x						
	Eastleach Turville	Glos.													x						
	Quimmington	Glos.													x						
	Fawley	Hants.										x									
	Newport	Hants.	x																		
	Alwalton	Hunts.											x		x					Farmer	
	Elton	Hunts.													x					Farmer	£90
	Folksworth	Hunts.													x						
	Haddon	Hunts.													x						
	Morborne	Hunts.													x						
	S. Reston	Lincs.	x																	Farmer	£600
	Colton	Norfolk													x					Farmer	
	Lyng	Norfolk														x				Paper Manuf'rers	£700–800
	Taverham	Norfolk														x				Paper Manufacturers	£2,000
	Taunton	Somerset									x									Government	(radical poster)
	N. Staffs.	Staffs.								x										Mine-owners	(colliers)
	Broughton Gifford	Wilts.	x																	Overseer	
28.xi	Beaconsfield	Bucks.										x								Police	(to release prisoners)

Date 1830	Place	County	Type of Disturbance 1	2	3	4	5	6	7	8	9	10	11	12	13	14	15	16	17	Target	Value, etc.
28.xi	High Wycombe	Bucks.													x		x	(6)		Paper Manufacturers	£719.12.0 £10 (Th/Ms)
	Loudwater	Bucks.																			
	Long Crendon	Bucks.													x	x					£10
	Rodsley	Derbyshire		x																Overseer	
	Eastleach Turville	Glos.													x						
	Moreton-in-Marsh	Glos.	x																		
	Bishop's Waltham	Hants.		x																	(verbal?)
	Freshwater	Hants.		x																Parson	
	Rockley	Wilts.													x					Farmer	(fire)
	Bishop's Stortford	Herts.		x																	
	Burwell	Lincs.	x																		"great loss"
	Irby	Lincs.	x																		
	Monckton	Lincs.	x																		
	Swaby	Lincs.	x																		
	Banstead	Surrey	x	(2)																	
	Nr. Merton	Surrey	x																		
	E. Preston	W. Sussex	x																	Farmer	
28/29.xi	Oundle	Northants.										x								Police	(to release prisoners)
29.xi	Langford	Berks.			x																

March	Cambs.	x																		
Castle Hill	Dorset													x						
E. Stour	Dorset											x		x					Rector	
																			Farmer	
Lulworth	Dorset			x																
Stour Provost	Dorset										x			x					Farmer	
Winfrith	Dorset			x																
Wool	Dorset			x																
Preston	Dorset	x																	Farmer	
Bibury	Glos.													x						
Coln Rogers	Glos.													x						
Southrop	Glos.										x									
Freshwater	Hants.	x																	Parson	
Hemel Hamstead	Herts.	Fear of attack on Paper Mills																		
Cobham Hall	E. Kent		x																Earl of Danby	(to Th/Ms)
I. of Thanet	E. Kent		x																	
Wingham	E. Kent													x						
Easton	Lincs.	x																	Farmer	
Spalding	Lincs.	x																	Parson	£130
Preston	Middx.	x																	Farmer-Overseer	
Burnham Overy	Norfolk													x						
Burnham Thorpe	Norfolk													x						
Catton	Norfolk															x			Timber Merchants	(sawmills)
Docking	Norfolk										x									
Forncett	Norfolk				x														Parsons	
Long Stratton	Norfolk				x														Parsons	

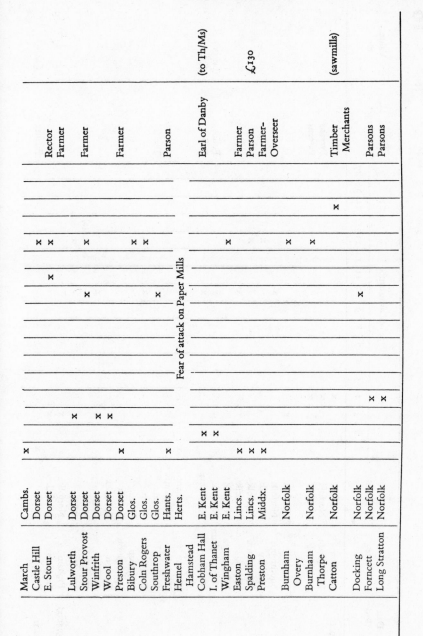

16

Date 1830	Place	County	Type of Disturbance																	Target	Value, etc.
			1	2	3	4	5	6	7	8	9	10	11	12	13	14	15	16	17		
29.xi	Moulton	Norfolk				x														Parsons	
	Saxlingham	Norfolk				x														Parsons	
	Stoke Holy Cross	Norfolk				x														Parsons	
	Roughton	Norfolk			x																
	Southrepps	Norfolk										x									
	Sparham	Norfolk													x						
	Thurgarton	Norfolk													x						
	Weston	Norfolk										x									
	Whinburgh	Norfolk													x						
	Wymondham	Norfolk										x								Police	(prison)
	Welling-borough	Northants.										x								Police	£32.10.0
	Finedon	Northants.	x																		
	Wollaston	Northants.	x																		
	Banbury	Oxon.									x									Tories	
	Broadwell	Oxon.										x			x						
	Neithrop	Oxon.													x						
	Sproughton	Suffolk	x																	Farmer	
	Denton	E. Sussex	x?																		
	Poulton	Glos.										x									
	Wingfield	Wilts.													x	(2)					
	Winsley	Wilts.													x						
29/30.xi	Binham	Norfolk			x																
	Langham	Norfolk			x																
30.xi	Ford	Bucks.	x																	Farmer	£24

Carlisle	Cumberland	x	(2)					+ "Swing" handbill posted											Merchant	£50+ £50
Cann	Dorset													x					Farmer	
Shaftesbury	Dorset										x								Police	(to release prisoners)
Brightlingsea	Essex	x																		
Lymington	Hants.			x															Farmers	
Newport	Hants.		x																Farmers	(re Th/Ms)
Bedfont	Middx.		x	(2)															Parson	
																			Farmer	
Hillingdon	Middx.																	x	Government	
Beeston Regis	Norfolk													x						
E. Tudden-ham	Norfolk													x						
Norwich	Norfolk								x							x	(2)		Silk Manufacturers	£300–400
Toft	Norfolk				x														Parson	£10.0.0
Wymondham	Norfolk										x								J.P.	
Finedon	Northants.													x					Farmer	(Damages refused)
King Sutton	Northants.														x				Farmer	
Banwell	Somerset					x						x	x						Overseers	(tobacco 2/6)
Banwell	Somerset										x								Police	(lock-up des-troyed £60)
																			J.P.s	
Bacton	E. Suffolk			x	x														Farmers	
																			Parsons	
Cotton	E. Suffolk			x	x														Farmers	
																			Parsons	
Shettle-borough	E. Suffolk			x	x														Farmers	
																			Parsons	
Thrandeston	E. Suffolk			x	x														Farmers	
																			Parsons	

17

Date 1830	Place	County	Type of Disturbance																	Target	Value, etc.
			1	2	3	4	5	6	7	8	9	10	11	12	13	14	15	16	17		
30.xi	Wickham Skeith	E. Suffolk			x	x														Farmers, Parsons	
	Wortham	E. Suffolk			x	x														Farmers, Parsons	
	Albury	Surrey	x									x								Farmer	(shooting)
	Bodiam	E. Sussex	x																		
1.xii	Stotfold	Beds.			x							x								Farmers, Parsons	
	Iver	Bucks.			x								x								
	Little Brick-hill	Bucks.													x					Farmer	
	Shredding Green	Bucks.											x								
	Wavendon	Bucks.				x														Parson	
	Carlisle	Cumberland									x									Local Tories	
	Bere Regis	Dorset	x																	J.P.	
	Lytchett	Dorset													x						
	Nr. Sher-borne	Dorset													x					Farmer	
	Stalbridge	Dorset										x									
	Tut Hill	Dorset										x									
	Ridgewell	Essex			x				x											Farmers	
	Donington	Lincs.	x																	Gent.	
	Wothorpe	Northants.	x																	Landlord	
	Draycott	Somerset		x																Parson	
	Henstridge	Somerset													x	(2)				Farmer	£10+ £10

	Ilton	Somerset			x															Farmer	
	Nr. Battle	E. Sussex	x																	Farmer	
	Hanley William	Worcs.													x					Farmer	£10
	Redmarley	Worcs.														x				Farmer	£30
	Beverley	Yorks. (E.R.)		x																Farmer	
	Crowe	Yorks. (E.R.)		x																Farmer	
	Ferrybridge	Yorks. (E.R.)		x																Farmer	
	Tadmarton	Oxon.													x						
2.xii	Stotfold	Beds.				x			x											Farmers Parsons	
	Waisendon	Bucks.										x									(unlawful assembly)
	Coton	Cambs.	x																		
	Dumbleton	Glos.	x																	Farmer	
	Hamerton	Hunts.	x																	Farmer	£200
	Banham	Norfolk				x														Parson	
	Buxton	Norfolk	x																	Parson	
	Toft Monks	Norfolk	x																	Farmer	
	Hempton	Oxon.	x																		
	Tadmarton	Oxon.	x												x						
	Redgrave	E. Suffolk				x														Parsons	
	Nr. Battle	E. Sussex	x																	Farmer	
2–5.xii	Birdbrook	Essex			x															Farmer	
	Mile End	Essex			x															Farmer	
	Polstead	W. Suffolk			x															Farmer	
	Ridgewell	Essex			x															Farmer	
	Iver	Bucks.														x					
3.xii	Olney	Bucks.	x																	Gent.	
	Stony Stratford	Bucks.			x																

18

Date 1830	Place	County	Type of Disturbance																	Target	Value, etc.
			1	2	3	4	5	6	7	8	9	10	11	12	13	14	15	16	17		
3.xii	Ickleford	Herts.	x																	Gent.	
	Bressingham	Norfolk		x											x						
	Burgh	Norfolk				x														Parson	
	Lynn	Norfolk	x																		(incitement to arson)
	Stoke	Northants.		x																	(re wages)
	Up. Boddington	Northants.													x					Farmer	
	Redgrave	E. Suffolk				x														Parsons	
	Nr. Battle	E. Sussex	x																		
	Worthing	W. Sussex		x	(3)															Parsons Landowners	
4.xii	Burghfield	Berks.	x												x					Farmer	
	Newport Pagnell	Bucks.			x																
	Long Eaton	Derbyshire	x																	Gent.?	
	Beighton	Norfolk													x						
	Lingwood	Norfolk	x												x						
	Shouldham	Norfolk	x																	Farmer?	
	Sutton	Norfolk	x																	Farmer	
	Bishops Stortford	Herts.	x																		
4/5.xii	Richmond	Yorks. (N.R.)		x																Parson	(re tithe)
	Whitby	Yorks. (N.R.)		x	(3)															Farmers	(re Th/Ms)

4/6.xii	Balsham	Cambs.			x															Farmers	
	Barnwell	Cambs.			x															Farmers	
	Bottisham	Cambs.			x															Farmers	
	Chesterton	Cambs.			x															Farmers	
	Attleborough	Norfolk				x	x								x					Parsons Overseers	
	Brighton	E. Sussex					x													Overseer	
5.xii	Cumnor	Berks.	x																	Small Farmer	£40
	Carlisle	Cumberland		x																Householders	
	Clacton	Essex													x						
	Gt. Holland	Essex													x						
	Ramsey	Essex													x						
	Nr. Standon	Herts.	x																		
	Aylesford	E. Kent	x																	Large Farmer	£700
	Etton	Yorks. (E.R.)	x												x	(2)				Farmer	
6.xii	St. Michael	Essex			x																
	Sheering	Essex											x		x					Gentry J.P.	
	Steeple Bumpston	Essex			x															Farmers	
	Tendring	Essex			x															Farmers	
	Shingay	Camberland										x									
	Flitwick	Beds.			x															Farmers	
	Lough-borough	Leics.								x										Master Weavers J.P.s	
	Deeping Fen	Lincs.	x																	Farmer	
	Long Sutton	Lincs.	x																	Farmer	
	Hanwell	Middx.		x																Parson	(re tithe)
	Rushmere Heath	E. Suffolk			x															Farmers	

19

Date 1830	Place	County	Type of Disturbance																	Target	Value, etc.
			1	2	3	4	5	6	7	8	9	10	11	12	13	14	15	16	17		
6.xii	Hadleigh	W. Suffolk			x															Overseers	(unemployed)
	Stanningfield	W. Suffolk			x	x														Parsons Landowners	
	Withersfield	W. Suffolk			x										x					Farmers	
	Oxshott	Surrey	x																	Prince Leopald	
	Redditch	Worcs.															x	(4)		Manufacturers	£26.10.0
6/8.xii	Norwich	Norfolk															x			Silk-Weavers	(date approx.)
	Surlingham	Norfolk				x														Parson	
7.xii	Chesterford	Essex	x																		
	Gt. Clacton	Essex			x										x	(6)				Farmers	£35, £40 × 4, £50
	Ramsey	Essex	x													x				Blacksmith	
	Ilfracombe	Devon		x	(4)																
	Deerhurst	Glos.	x																		
	Northfleet	E. Kent	x																		
	Nr. Leek	Staffs.	x																	Manufacturers	(silk mill)
	North Cove	E. Suffolk			x	x														Parson	
	Ixworth	W. Suffolk			x															Farmers	
	Stanningfield Green	W. Suffolk			x															Farmers	
	Whepstead	W. Suffolk			x															Farmers	
	Blockley	Worcs.										x								Farmer	£19.0.0
7/8.xii	Pershore	Worcs.										x	x								
8.xii	Shottesbrook	Berks.	x																	Gent.	£9–£1,000
	Cambridge	Cambs.		x																Univ. Dons.	
	Little Clacton	Essex													x					Farmer	£40

	Walton-Le-Soken	Essex													x					£45
	Pardon Hill	Glos.	x																	£150
	Moulton	Northants.													x				Farmer	
	Bildeston	W. Suffolk		x	(2)														Parson	
																			Farmer	
	Nr. Hadleigh	E. Suffolk			x														Farmers	
	Nr. Sudbourne	E. Suffolk	x																	
	Walpole	E. Suffolk			x	x												x		Overseers	
																			Parsons, etc.	
	Westleton	E. Suffolk	x																Gent.	
8/9.xii	Prior's Marston	Warwicks.	x																	
9.xii	Wootton	Beds.	x																Farmer	
	Keeltny Brickhill	Bucks.													x					(by fire)
	Fenny Stratford	Bucks.													x					
	Deeping Fen	Lincs.	x																Farmer	
	Dunmow	Essex														x			Farmer	
	Nr. Cottingham	Yorks. (E.R.)	x																Farmer	
10.xii	Potton	Beds.	x																	(4 Cottages)
	Arkesden	Essex }																		
	Henham	Essex }			x	(2)													Farmers	
	Peldon	Essex }																		
	Steeple B'stead	Essex }																		
	Hawkwell	Essex		x															Parson	
	Swimbridge	Devon				x													Parson	

Date 1830	Place	County	Type of Disturbance																	Target	Value, etc.
			1	2	3	4	5	6	7	8	9	10	11	12	13	14	15	16	17		
10.xii	Somersham	Hunts.		x																Farmer	
	North Frith	W. Kent	x																	Farmer	
	Cuerdley	Lancs.	x																	Farmer	
	Warrington	Lancs.	x																	Manufacturers	
	Bowen	Lincs.	x	(2)																Farmers	
	Whitechapel	London		x																Distiller	
	Watford	Northants.										x									£11.14.0 damages
	Edgehill	Warwicks.													x						
11.xii	Castle Hill	Devon			x															Farmers Parsons	
	Clavering	Essex			x																
	Polstead	W. Suffolk	x																		
	Shutlanger	Northants.	x																	Earl of Pomfret	
	Boxford	W. Suffolk	x																	Large Farmer	
12.xii	Chicksands Priory	Beds.	x																	Farmer	
	Dalston Common	Cumberland	x																		
	Buckhorn Weston	Dorset	x																	Farmer	
	Canford Magna	Dorset	x																	Farmer	
	Evesham	Worcs.																	x	New Police	(seditious posters)
	Cheam	Surrey	x																		
13.xii	Horrell	Hants.	x																		

	Bishop's Stortford	Herts.	x																	
	Pishill	Oxon.	x																	
	Hoxne	E. Suffolk				x													Parson	
13/16.xii	Hoxne	E. Suffolk			x														Farmers	
14.xii	Nr. Reading	Berks.	x																Master Carpenter	£500+
	Dedham	Essex		x															Parson	
	Finchingfield	Essex			x															
	Leyton	Essex	x																London merchant	
	Wingham	E. Kent	x																	
	Whitchurch	Salop	x																Publican	
	Bolney	E. Sussex	x																	
15.xii	Abbot's-kerswell	Devon	x												x				Farmer	
	Sandford	Devon	x																Farmer	
	Wrotham Park	Middx.	x																M.P.	
	Whitchurch	Salop.	x															x	Farmer	
16.xii	Stradishall	W. Suffolk																	Parsons Farmer	("inflammatory" papers)
17.xii	Liverpool	Lancs.	x																Sugar Refiner	
18.xii	Callington	Cornwall			x														Farmers Gentry	
	Launceston	Cornwall			x														Farmers Gentry	
	—	Essex		x															Farmers	
	Deeping Fen	Lincs.	x																	£1,500–£2,000
	Chiddingly	E. Sussex	x																Farmer	

21

Date 1830	Place	County	Type of Disturbance 1	2	3	4	5	6	7	8	9	10	11	12	13	14	15	16	17	Target	Value, etc.
18.xii	Oxted	Surrey	x																		
19.xii	Enfield	Middx.	x																	Farmer	
	Hampton	Middx.	x																	Farmer	
	Knettishall	W. Suffolk	x																	Farmer	
	Wellingham	Norfolk	x																	Farmer	
	Woldingham	Surrey	x																	Farmer	
	Cuckfield	E. Sussex	x																	Farmer	
Mid.xii	Norton	Notts.		x																Publican	
	Notts. Forest	Notts.			x	Meeting of Framework Knitters														Hosiers	
20.xii	Fowlmere	Cambs.			x															Farmers	
	Churton Hall	Cheshire	x																	Gent.	
	Nr. Chester	Cheshire		x																Gentry	
	Moreton-in-Marsh	Glos.				x														Overseer	
21.xii	Fowlmere	Cambs.			x															Farmers	
	Eaton	Notts.		x																	
	Ordsall	Notts.		x																Paper Manufacturers	
	Nr. Pulborough	W. Sussex	x																		
22.xii	Chatteris	Cambs.	x																	Maltster	
	Cockington	Devon	x																		
	Highweek	Devon	x												x					Gent. Farmer	
20/25.xii	Morval	Cornwall		x																Farmer	(re Th/Ms)
	St. Neot's	Cornwall		x																Parson	(re Tithe)

	Freiston	Lincs.	x																		
24.xii	Leicester	Leics.			x			= Wages meeting of Trades													
	Farnley	Yorks. (W.R.)	x																		
	Hawkes-worth	Yorks. (W.R.)	x																		
25.xii	Henton	Oxon.	x																		
26.xii	Preston	Lancs.									x									Tories	("Bread or Blood")
	Elsecar	Yorks. (W.R.)	x																	Earl Fitz-william	(colliery)
27.xii	Brimpton	Berks.	x																	Publican	
	Lockinge	Berks.	x																	Farmer	(re Th/Ms)
	Glossop	Derbyshire								x										Manufacturers	
	Ashton under Lyne	Lancs.								x										Manufacturers	(weavers)
28.xii	Newton Abbot	Devon													x						(by fire)
	Adbury Lodge	Hants.	x																	Gent.	
	Nr. Banbury	Oxon.		x																Large Farmer	
29.xii	Bacton	E. Suffolk	x																	Large Farmer	
	Kilmington	Wilts.										x									(incitement)
30/31.xii	Chippinghurst	Oxon.	x																		
31.xii	Stonehouse	Devon	x																	Brewers	
	Pointon	Lincs.	x																		
1831																					
1–5.i	Horbling	Lincs.	x																		
	Nr. Louth	Lincs.	x																		

22

Date 1831	Place	County	Type of Disturbance 1	2	3	4	5	6	7	8	9	10	11	12	13	14	15	16	17	Target	Value, etc.
1–5.i	Neithrop	Oxon.	x																		
	Raithby	Lincs.	x																	Farmer	
2.i	Barrowmoor	Cambs.	x																	Farmer	
	Carlisle	Cumberland									x									Government	Prop. of Pol. Union
	Basildon	Essex	x																	Large Farmer	
	Chapel Brampton	Northants.																	x	Government	
	Armthorpe	Yorks. (W.R.)	x																		
3.i	—	Derbyshire								x											
	Aston	Oxon.	x																		
4.i	Dunton	Beds.	x																	Farmer	
	Carlisle	Cumberland		x																Clerk of Peace	
6.i	Nr. Whitchurch	Salop.	x																		£40
	Albury	Surrey				x														Overseers	
7.i	Boston	Lincs.	x																		
8.i	Langton	Dorset	x																	J.P.	£500+
	Aust	Glos.	x																		£120
	Glentham	Lincs.	x																	Farmer	£400
	Swanton Abbott	Norfolk	x	(2)																J.P. Farmer	
	Huntingfield	Suffolk	x																	Parson	
8–12.i	Nr. Blandford	Dorset	x	(3–8)																	

6.1	Tilney-all-Saints	Norfolk	x																		
10.i	Upton Lovell	Wilts.	x																	Parson	£400
11.i	Bromsberrow	Glos.													x						
	Tilney A.S.	Norfolk	x																	Farmer	£300
	Potterne	Wilts.	x																	Parson	£400
	W. Lavington	Wilts.	x																	Publican	
13.i	Ockbrook	Derbyshire	x																	Maltster	
	Bedfont	Middx.	x																		
	Ilketshall St. John	E. Suffolk	x																	Farmer	
	Polstead	W. Suffolk	x																	Large Farmer	
14.i	Nr. Dover	Kent	x																	Large Farmer	£1,200
	Heydon	Norfolk	x																	Parson	
	Thorpe	Norfolk	x	(2)																Parson	
	Swindon	Staffs.	x	x																	
mid-i	Ilminster	Somerset																		Parsons Landlords	
	Langport	Somerset	x																		
16.i	White Cross	Hereford	x																	Farmer	
18.i	Stickford	Lincs.	x																		
20.i	Adbury Lodge	Hants.	x	x																Gent.	
	Gt. Hallingbury	Essex																		Parson	
	Nottingham	Notts.	x																		
22.i	Queensborough	Leics.	x																	Farmer	
	Nr. Bath	Somerset	x																		

23

Date 1831	Place	County	Type of Disturbance 1	2	3	4	5	6	7	8	9	10	11	12	13	14	15	16	17	Target	Value, etc.
22.i	Amesbury	Wilts.	x																	Farmer	
23.i	Nr. Leicester	Leics.	x																		
	Benning-holme	Yorks. (E.R.)	x																	Farmer	
24.i	Chowley	Cheshire	x																		
	Coppenhall	Cheshire	x																	Parson–	
25.i	Modinton-ham	Cornwall	x																	J.P.	
30.i	Standon	Herts.	x																	Farmer	£400
end.i	Dover	E. Kent	x																	Publican	
1.ii	Woodford	Northants.											x							Overseer	
3.ii	Burghclere	Hants.	x																	Farmer	
																				Overseer	
5.ii	Hadlow	W. Kent		x																Overseer	
	Kettering	Northants.					x													Overseer	
6.ii	Hadlow	W. Kent		x																Parson– J.P.	
15.ii	Penzance	Cornwall							x											Dealers	
22.ii	Helston	Cornwall							x											Dealers	
1.iii	Steventon	Berks.	x																	Farmer	£2,000
7.iii	Spilsby	Lincs.	x																		
12.iii	Stickford	Lincs.	x																	Farmer	
29.iv	Rye	E. Sussex									x									Tories	(election riots)
—.v	Potteries	Staffs.								x										Manufacturers	
23.v	Battle	E. Sussex	x																		
28.v	Whitehaven	Cumberland									x									Tories	(election riots)
11.vi	Coleford	Glos.					x													Landowners	

—.vi	—	Kent	x																		(several fires)
23.vii	E. Hendred	Berks.	x																	Farmer	
31.vii	Patrixbourne	E. Kent													x					Farmer	
	Boston	Lincs.										x								Irish	
early viii	Lower Halstow	E. Kent										x								Farmers?	(re wages?)
	Sitting-bourne	E. Kent										x								Farmers	(re wages?)
2–3.viii	Walton	Northants.										x								Irish	
5.viii	Ripple	E. Kent													x					Farmer	
	Boston	Lincs.										x								Irish	
14.viii	Romney Marsh	Kent													x					Farmer	
15.viii	Romney Marsh	Kent													x					Farmer	
16.viii	E. Hendred	Berks.	x																	Farmer	
24.viii	Barham	Kent													x						
27.viii	Wingham	Kent													x						
28.viii	Broad Chalke	Wilts.	x																	Farmer	(re Th/Ms)
29.viii	Oakington	Cambs.	x																	Farmer	
31.viii	Barham	Kent	x																	Farmer	
6.ix	Dilham	Norfolk													x					Farmer	£10
1–27.x	Tiverton	Devon								x										Hosiers	
8.x	Derby	Derbyshire									x									Tories	(Reform Bill)
9–10.x	Nottingham	Notts.									x									Tories	(Reform Bill)
12.x	Chatham	E. Kent									x									Tories	(Reform meeting)
22.x	Tiverton	Devon									x									Tories	(Reform meeting)
	Yeovil	Somerset									x									Tories	(Reform meeting)

24

Date 1831	Place	County	Type of Disturbance																	Target	Value, etc.
			1	2	3	4	5	6	7	8	9	10	11	12	13	14	15	16	17		
29.x	Bristol	Somerset									x									Tories	(Reform meeting)
	Rye	E. Sussex	Labourers' Joint Wages Meeting Anticipated																		
17.x	Ramsgate	E. Kent	x																		
22.x	Nr. Guildford	Surrey	x	(2)																	
1.xi	Chalgrave	Beds.	x																		
—.xi	Coalbrook Dale	Salop.							x											Mine Owners	
19.xii	Bassingbourn	Cambs.					x														Superintendent of the poor.
29.xii	Kirtling	Cambs.										x									
1832																					
3.ix	Tadlow	Cambs.													x					Farmer	£10

APPENDIX IV

THE PROBLEM OF THE THRESHING MACHINE

Why should the labourers' movement have taken the form of a general and widespread destruction of threshing machines? The obvious answer (because the machines took away winter employment) is true, but begs some rather puzzling questions. For why should labour-saving machines of this description have been common enough at this time to provoke such generalised Luddism? Was not the main characteristic of the English agricultural labour market the growth of an increasingly large surplus of the under-employed and unemployed, and consequently the availability of ultra-cheap pauperised labour at almost all times? Why then mechanise? What is more, were not the savings of labour-saving machinery offset by the corresponding rise in the poor rates, which the employers of it had also to pay? Indeed a Scots writer (virtually all literate agricultural experts seem to have belonged to that nation) wrote in 1811:

> Some objections have been offered by English farmers, as if the saving in one way would be compensated by the increased expence in another; in other words, that if the thrashing machines were brought into general use, a great many labourers would be thrown out of employment, which of course would raise the poor rates.[1]

These questions cannot be answered without an analysis of the nature of machine-threshing in the early 19th century, a subject on which, as usual, quantitative evidence is extremely scarce.

Let us first consider what is actually known about the progress of this aspect of mechanisation on the English farm. The first practical "thrashing mills" were pioneered in Scotland in the second half of the 18th century, and settled down in the form devised by Andrew Meikle of Haddington (1785), in which the grain passed between rollers, and was shaken out by beaters in a revolving drum; rakers and shakers were added a little later.[2] Fixed mills of this kind, water- or horse-driven and priced at a minimum of £100—and often considerably more—[3] spread fairly rapidly in the Scots lowlands, but not in England where the first patent (by Wigfull of Lynn in Norfolk) seems to have been taken out in 1795. For practical purposes machine-threshing in 1800 was entirely confined to the North of Britain.

It spread with considerable rapidity during the Napoleonic wars, because of the increasingly acute labour shortage.[4] The various "General Views" of the agriculture of different counties, leave no doubt about this, particularly for the years after 1805. However, such general statements as "these machines are becoming very prevalent" and the lists of a dozen or two of particularly celebrated installations, hardly tell us enough about the extent of their use. One English—and almost certainly East Anglian, perhaps more exactly Suffolk[5]—innovation throws an oblique light on it. This is the development of a much cheaper "portable" machine "to be fixed in any barn, or in the open field", and worked by as few as one or two horses,[6] and therefore more adapted to the smaller farmer, who hired them from itinerant small contractors at so much an acre or for a percentage of the harvest.[7] The farmer provided power and labour. Their cost was much more modest: £30–40 is the price most commonly quoted in the post-Napoleonic period,[8] but the compensation for machines destroyed in the riots was sometimes much less. This was the type of machine which spread most rapidly in southern and eastern England.[9]

What happened between 1815 and 1830? How common were threshing machines in the year of the rising? Our evidence is scanty, for the next systematic series of county surveys after those of the Board of Agriculture in the 1790s and the early 1810s, that organised by the Royal Agricultural Society, only began in the early 1840s, and throw most light on the 1850s. Two things can be said with different degrees of confidence: southern England remained (perhaps with the exception of the eastern counties) backward in the adoption of mechanised threshing, but nevertheless, the machines (presumably in their portable form) made some progress *even in the worst years of the farming depression.* We know the first fact from the concurrent statements of the much more machine-conscious Scots experts, of which Ritchie is typical:

> "This machine, though it came gradually into use over the agricultural districts of Scotland, made but slow progress in England. . . . At the present day (1849), although, perhaps, some of the finest threshing machines in Britain may be occasionally met with in England . . . still it cannot be said that threshing machines, except in the border districts, are at all in general use. . . . Where machines are used in many counties, perhaps for the smallness of the farms, the labour is still performed with the small portable threshing-machine, going from farm to farm, but still the greater part of the thrashing in England is done by flail."[10]

We know the second directly from the output figures of Ransomes of Ipswich, perhaps the largest firm in the business, which certainly rose until at least 1819,[11] and more doubtfully, from various statements in connection with the 1830 rising about the recent introduction of such devices in particular areas.[12]

Their actual distribution and prevalence remains uncertain. The only attempt at a systematic, though cursory and patchy, survey, is in the second (1828–31) edition of Loudon's *Encyclopedia*. This notes that the machines were rare in Middlesex, Surrey, Sussex and probably Herts., suggests they are rather more common in Beds., Cambs., Suffolk (nothing is said about Norfolk), Berks., and Dorset, and says nothing, or nothing of significance, about the other counties mainly affected by the rising. As we have seen in the text (cf. p. 203) there is evidence of widespread, if not general, use of the machines in the corn-growing zone of East Kent, in Wilts., Hants. and perhaps Berks. The distribution of agricultural machinery manufacturers enables us to supplement this impression. For what it is worth hardly any such firms in 1830 describe themselves as "agricultural implement manufacturers" (as Ransomes already did). Tasker of Andover, for instance, the leading Hampshire firm—and attacked by the rioters in that year—is still listed only as "blacksmith" (though in 1839 it is "Iron Founder and Agricultural Implement Maker").[13] The leading Wiltshire firm certainly had hardly got beyond the embryonic stage in 1830.[14] On the other hand Maggs of

Wincanton (Somerset, near the Wilts. border) was already in serious business in 1815.[15]

The more comprehensive lists and catalogues of the middle of the century confirm the general impression that the eastern counties were the main centre of machine production, and the South was much less developed. Morton's Cyclopedia lists four major manufacturers in Lincs., three in Suffolk, two in Norfolk and one each in Beds. and the East Riding, as against six in all the southern counties (two in Berks., one each in Sussex, Gloucester, Somerset and Hants.).[16] The Annual Register of Agricultural Implements for 1843–45 lists seven for the whole of the counties of Kent, Surrey, Sussex, Hants., Berks., Wilts., Dorset, Somerset and Gloucester, as against nine for the counties of Lincs., Beds., Suffolk and Essex.[17] The 1851 Exhibition which presumably attracted all the more important firms, exhibited threshing machines by 11 makers from Lincs., the East Riding, Norfolk, Suffolk and Beds., and only two from rural southern England (both from Berks.).[18] Since no doubt many small machines were knocked up by local carpenters and blacksmiths this is not conclusive, but it nevertheless suggests a rough distribution map of this type of machinery. The concentration in the eastern counties is undoubted, the persistent absence of any manufacturer in, say, Kent, must be significant. A large local demand could be expected to provide the basis (as in Suffolk with Ransomes or Garretts of Leiston) of flourishing manufacture. Conversely an area lacking a local manufacturer of substance could hardly be very machine-conscious.

The relative sluggishness of mechanisation is readily explained. As we have already seen, cheap labour and increased poor rates resulting from the rise in unemployment discouraged them. Certain local threshing-customs and the economic value of good quality straw (for thatching or for sale in the nearby metropolitan market) both made them less desirable. Scythe-cut stalks—and all grains except wheat were cut by scythe and not sickle—were not automatically bound up in sheaves, and therefore—or so it was argued—passed irregularly through the rollers, with consequent inefficiencies in machine-threshing.[19] The damage to inefficiently machine-threshed straw is mentioned time and again as an argument against the machines.[20] But above all the sheer economic saving of machine-threshing on smaller farms was marginal, all the more when we remember that even the cheaper machines were considerably more expensive than the next-most elaborate pieces of equipment,[21] and that their repair and maintenance might come high.

Certain crops—oats and barley—were definitely cheaper to thresh by hand, at least in Suffolk where "it is a very general opinion that wheat is the only grain that it is profitable to thresh with the portable".[22] But even for wheat, the actual saving due to machine-threshing—estimated at perhaps 5 per cent of the harvest—was not so much in money, as in the more effectual separation of grain from straw, in diminished pilfering, etc.[23] An interesting table (overleaf) from the 1840s shows the marginality of the saving for smaller producers.

We do not know the reliability of this estimate, but the diligent Hamm undoubtedly based it on information gathered in England.

If this estimate is realistic, the difference in cost between machine- and hand-threshing at the 675 bushel level was about 10 per cent, or £1 in cash. Assuming an average yield of 25 bushels per acre and a four-course rotation, this might

Cost of hand and machine-threshing

Number of "sheaves"	In bushels	Cost of threshing in Thaler by machine	by hand
5,000	675	54	60
10,000	1350	64	120
20,000	2,700	96	240
40,000	5,400	152	480

Source: W. Hamm, *op. cit.*, p. 695.
Bushels converted at author's rate of 1 Bushel=0·66 Scheffel.
6·25 Thaler=£1.

correspond to a farm of about 110 acres, or the English average in 1851. (More precisely, in that year 135,000 farms or over 60 per cent had 100 acres or less, not counting holdings under 5 acres.) Hence, using farm acreage as the roughest of guides, something like two-thirds of English farms would gain negligible economies from machine-threshing except in a very good harvest. The minority of 17,000 who farmed 300 acres or more would of course make substantial savings of at least £20 or so. Even allowing for a three-crop rotation, or a much higher yield, the farms which did not on average make any substantial saving from machine-threshing would still be all those below about 80 acres.[24]

All this explains why farmers were or ought to have been doubtful about machines. Why then did they continue to spread? The variations in harvests between one year and the next would certainly make it desirable to have machines available for extra-good years, and the "portable" machine solved this problem. It was available to the smaller farmer, while saving him from tying up capital in expensive plant. It could also be argued that it saved the cost of building barns for storing the harvest during the long months of hand-threshing; the argument does not seem very strong.[25] But essentially, it may be suggested, farmers continued, often against their inclination, to adopt machine-threshing because it saved precious time. Broadly speaking, grain prices began to fall immediately after the end of each year's harvest, and did not stabilise themselves again until the late autumn. The fall could be both rapid and heavy: thus in 1820–23 wheat prices in 12 maritime districts fell between 15 and 20 per cent in the three or four weeks of post-harvest decline. Speed in getting the grain onto the market evidently made a considerable difference to the price it might fetch. In a period of general recession success might mean not merely the difference between a moderate and a good profit, but between profit and no profit, especially for farmers too pressed to hold their stocks until the spring rise in prices. That this was one of the major factors of the spread of machines after 1815 is known.[26] It is hard to avoid the conclusion that it was the most important. On the other hand, the more machine-threshing spread, the less the possibility of stealing a march on competitors by mechanisation, except of course for the very large operator, who genuinely enjoyed its economies of scale while throwing the displaced labour on to the rates of which other people paid the largest share. The small farmer would therefore now gain by the destruction of *all* machines.*

* The statistics of price-movements for wheat are not inconsistent with this argument. We would expect the spread of machine-threshing to produce a more rapid post-harvest

All this should explain the most mysterious aspect of the 1830 rising, namely the widespread sympathy not only of the gentry but of many *farmers* for the men who broke their machines, not to mention the well-attested auto-Luddism of several of them. It was clearly not due mainly to fear or the desire to propitiate the labourers, though this played some part. Had it been the major cause, then the machines would have returned to the farms as soon as possible after the rising. As we have seen they did not. The reason for the general sympathy with machine-breaking was rather, we suggest, that the Luddite mobs appeared as a sort of fortunate "act of God" which alone, short of the unthinkable banning of machinery by law, could extricate all farmers from a situation into which they were forced against their better judgment. For the individual was helpless against the process of mechanisation. If he returned to hand-threshing, he would merely ensure that others got their corn to market faster. Nor was voluntary action more effective. As we have seen, it was tried on several occasions—in East Anglia in 1822, in Kent in 1830. But voluntary agreement was always at the mercy of the sharp or greedy farmer who would gain an advantage by breaking it, not to mention the minority of large operators who never gained any advantage from abiding by it. As we have seen this is precisely what happened in East Kent in the autumn of 1830 and led to the rising.

But when the labourers rose and virtually ensured that *no* machine in the village, the hundred, even the county, remained in action, many farmers must have heaved a sigh of relief. The problem was solved. No wonder that they failed to resist the Luddites, exposed their machines for destruction, and even publicly helped in breaking them. No wonder that in many regions they were in no hurry to bring them back. In their different ways the farmers were as Luddite as the labourers.

NOTES TO APPENDIX IV

1. R. Brown, *Treatise on Rural Affairs* (Edinburgh, 1811), I, pp. 337–8. The same point in *Lords Ctee on Poor Law 1831*, pp. 323–4.
2. R. Ritchie, *The Farm Engineer*, A Treatise on Barn Machinery particularly on the application of Steam and other motive powers to the *Thrashing Machine* (Glasgow, Edinburgh, London, 1849), pp. 19–23. J. Allen Ransome, *The Implements of Agriculture* (Ipswich, 1843); G. E. Fussell, *The Farmer's Tools* (London, 1952) for general surveys.
3. For prices of early machines see Rev. John M. Wilson, *The Rural Cyclopedia* (1849), vol. IV, p. 443. R. W. Dickson M.D. *Practical Agriculture* (London 1805, 2 vols.), estimates the cost (including shed) at £100 plus £5 interest on prime cost and £5 per annum for maintenance and repair.

fall, its retreat (after 1830) a slower decline. In fact, the average period from the maximum to the post-harvest stabilisation in 1827–30 was just under 6 weeks, in 1831–34 just over 9. (Figures based on *Accounts Relating to Grain and Flour*, Parl. P. XL of 1841–42, pp. 361–4, and Parl. P. XVIII of 1828, X of 1830–31) Since the movement of grain prices is determined by many other factors than the technicalities of harvesting and threshing, the only conclusion that can be drawn from such figures is that they do not automatically invalidate our argument.

4. The point is made in W. Stevenson, *Gen. V. Agric. Dorset* (1815), p. 144.
5. W. L. Rham, *The Dictionary of the Farm* (revised and re-edited by W. and H. Raynbird (London, 1853), p. 431: "The custom of hiring out drills and threshing machines probably originated in the eastern counties, at all events Suffolk men practised the custom of hiring out drills at so much per acre as early as 1804, and introduced the system into other districts of England." Raynbird evidence on Suffolk is first-hand information.
6. J. C. Loudon, *Encyclopedia of Agriculture* (3rd ed., London, 1835), p. 439.
7. Wilhelm Hamm, *Die landwirthschaftlichen Geraethe und Maschinen Englands* (Brunswick, 1845), p. 673.
8. Loudon, *op. cit.*, p. 439. An 1843 catalogue (C. W. Johnson and C. Hare, *Annual Register of Agricultural Implements*, lists two H.P. machines at £35, and one H.P. machine "ready for travelling" at £38 (p. 63); John C. Morton, *A Cyclopedia of Agriculture* (Glasgow, Edinburgh, London, n.d.), vol. VIII, at £30–40. Similar prices are quoted for 1813 in *The Farmer's Companion* (London, 1813), p. 53.
9. Morton, *loc. cit.*, p. 970; W. and H. Raynbird, *The Agriculture of Suffolk* (London 1849), p. 229; H. Stephens, *The Book of the Farm* (Edinburgh and London 1844), II, p. 327; Ransome, *op. cit.*, G. Fussell, The Suffolk Farm Machinery Industry (*Suffolk Review*, II, 1959–64) all concur on this point.
10. Ritchie, *op. cit.*, pp. 32–3. Allowance must be made at this date for the effect of the Swing rising, which reduced mechanisation. Ritchie should carry more weight than the foreigner Hamm (*op. cit.*, p. 137) who notes much more general mechanisation (but cf. his observation on p. 660). Doubtless by German standards there was, but not by Scottish ones.
11. N. Gash, *op. cit.*, pt. I, chapter 1.
12. E.g. for Lincolnshire *S.C. on State of Agriculture* 1836, evidence of F. Iles, for Monkton Farleigh, Wilts., Poor Law Comm., Rural Question; see also VCH Wilts., vol. IV, p. 85; for the recent extension of machinery into East Kent, cf. above, p. 85.
13. Pigot & Co.'s *National Commercial Directory* (South) 1830; Robson, *Commercial Directory* for 1839. These sources should not carry too much weight.
14. VCH Wilts., V, p. 84.
15. W. Stevenson, *Gen. V. Agric. Dorset* (1815), p. 27 ff., notes it as one of the three leading manufacturers (after Geikie of Scotland and with Bates of Exeter). John C. Morton, *op. cit.*, lists it among the leading national manufacturers.
16. *Op. cit.*
17. C. W. Johnson and C. Hare, *op. cit.* I have taken the maximum number listed in any of the three years for each county.
18. Catalogue, vol. I, Sec. II, Class 9. We have counted only those machines exhibited by makers described as "manufacturer" and not merely as "inventor".
19. R. Brown, *op. cit.*, pp. 337–8, criticises the English for this practice, which "is much against the use of the thrashing machines; and indeed it is against the process of thrashing in whatever way it is performed".
20. Ritchie, *op. cit.*, p. 33; Raynbird, *op. cit.*, p. 230, perhaps also *The Farmer's Companion* (1813), p. 55.

21. D. Low, *Elements of Practical Agriculture* (London and Edinburgh 1840) estimates the total capital equipment in "implements" of a farm at £470 of which a good threshing machine would come to £100, a Roller to £12, a broadcast sowing machine to £10, pp. 659 ff. For views about the marginality of the machines' advantage, see *Lords Ctee on Poor Law 1831*, pp. 96, 111, 324.
22. Rham, *op. cit.*, p. 474.
23. Society for the Diffusion of Useful Knowledge, *British Husbandry* (London 1837), vol. II, p. 201. Also *Lords Ctee on Poor Law 1831*, p. 324.
24. To turn from speculation to actuality. We happen to have details of the 1835 wheat crop for 11 Bedfordshire parishes including 147 farmers. The crop per farm averaged under 600 bushels for the whole area. The only parishes in which it averaged 750 bushels or more per farm were those containing only one farm of less than 100 acres. *Journal Stat. Soc.*, I., p. 89 ff.
25. *S.C. on Agriculture* (Parl. P. V of 1833) Q 1235; *S.C. on the State of Agriculture* (Parl. P. VIII of 1836), Q 4256.
26. W. Hamm, *op. cit.*, pp. 697, 700–1, for a discussion; *Lords Ctee on Poor Law 1831*, p. 111, Poor Law C. Rural Questions 53 Kent (Chilham).

[illegible]

[illegible] the [illegible] would [illegible]

[illegible] in saving [illegible]

[illegible] of the machine [illegible]

[illegible] Riots, [illegible]

Society for the [illegible]

[illegible] among [illegible]

[illegible] only [illegible]

[illegible] one [illegible]

[illegible] Vol. VIII [illegible]

[illegible]

SELECT BIBLIOGRAPHY

I. MANUSCRIPT SOURCES

1. *Public Record Office*

Assizes: Gaol Books, South Eastern Circuit, 1826–36, 33/11–12; Oxford Circuit, 1830–31, 5/150–51; Midland Circuit, 1830–32, 11/5; Western Circuit, 1829–31, 25/21–22; South Eastern Circuit, 1830–31, 35/270–1; North Eastern Circuit, 1830–31, 44/145–6.

Home Office Papers: Criminal Entry Books, 1830–31, H.O. 13/52.

Criminal Register England and Wales, 1830, H.O. 27/39–42; London, 1830, H.O. 26/36.

Disturbances: Correspondence, 1822, H.O. 40/17, H.O. 41/6–7, 1830, H.O. 40/25–7.

Entry Books, 1830–31, H.O. 41/8.

Law Offices' Reports and Correspondence, 1830–31, H.O. 40/28.

Military, 1830–33, H.O. 50.

Municipal and Provincial Correspondence, 1830–31, H.O. 52/6–11 (1830), 52/12–16 (1831).

General Muster of Convicts, New South Wales, 1 December 1837, H.O. 10/32–36.

Treasury Board Papers: Rioters, 1831–32, T. 1/4193–4.

Treasury Entry Books General, 1829–35, H.O. 36/22.

Treasury Solicitors' Papers: T.S. 11/849 (Berks.), 865 (Bucks.), 943 (Kent), 1031 (Oxon.), 4051 (Sussex).

2. *Guildhall Library Muniment Room*

Hand-in-Hand Fire and Life Insurance Society, General Minute Books, 1826–33, MS. 666/34; General Letter Book, 1752–1842, MS. 8670; Policy Register, 1823–31, MS. 8674/148.

Royal Exchange Assurance Co., Agents' Books, 1826–33, MSS. 7253/93–98; Head Office, 1828–34, MSS. 7254/64–66.

Sun Fire Office, Gen. Meeting, Ctee of Accounts, Management Ctee, County Ctee. Minute Books, Policy Registers, Claims (MSS. 11,931–7, 11,963.)

Globe Insurance Co., Insurance Ctee Minutes, Treasury Ctee Minutes, Ledger (MSS. 11,657–8, 11,674).

3. *County Record Offices*

Beds. QS. Minutes, 1830–33 (transcript); QS. Rolls, 1830–31.

Berks. QS. Order Book, 1828–31; Clerk of Hungerford division: papers relating to riots, 1830–31.

Bucks. Clerk of the Peace, Correspondence, 1830–31.

Cambs. QS. Order Book, 1830–33; QS. Rolls, 1831–2.

Cumberland and Westmorland Joint Archives Committee. Carlisle City Corp'n, Correspondence, 1830–31; Lord Lonsdale Correspondence, December 1830–January 1831.

Dorset. Registers of prisoners in Dorset gaol, 1830–31; Marquess of Anglesey's estate accounts, 1830; "Account of the Regiment of Dorset Yeomanry Cavalry raised in the year 1830" (n.d.).

Essex. QS. Process Books, 1824–31; QS. Rolls, 1831; Treasurer's Accounts, 1829–40; S. Hinckfield division, 1830 Constabulary Force.

Glos. QS. Minutes, 1831; County Gaol Register, 1829–31.

Hants. Treasurer's General Account Books, Vol. 28 (1831).

Hereford. QS. Minutes, 1830–33; QS. Roll, Epiphany 1831.

Hunts. QS. papers, 1830.

Ipswich & E. Suffolk. QS. Minute Book, 1829–35.

Leics. QS. papers: correspondence, 1830.

Norfolk & Norwich. Norfolk QS. Minute Book, 1827–32; QS. Proceedings Minute Book, 1830–35. Norwich City Assembly Book, 1830–35; QS. Minute Book, 1830–32. Land Tax Returns.

Northants. Kettering Petty Sessions, Draft Minute Book, 1830–32; Treasurer's Account Book (Western Division), 1830–31.

Oxon. QS. Minutes, 1830–31; QS. papers, 1830–31.

Somerset. QS. Rolls, 1831; Treasurer's Account Book, 1830–31. Earl of Egremont's correspondence relating to his Ilton estate, 1830.

Wilts. Treasurer's Account Book, 1831–32; draft Minute Book, 1830–32.

Worcs. QS. Order Books, vol. 12 (1830–33); QS. papers (miscell.), 1831.

4. *Australian Records*

Mitchell Library, *Sydney*. Convict records: 4/1123 ("Machine-Breakers"), 1116, 2196, 2443, 3676, 4016, 4099–4108 (Tickets of Leave), 4119, 4130, 4491, 4508–14 (Books of Marriages, 1825–50), 4524, 4540, 4549, 4569; C 37/979–46/487 (certificates of freedom).

Tasmanian State Archives, *Hobart*. Census returns, 1842–51; Colonial Secretary's Correspondence, CSO 5, 8; Governor's Letter Books, etc., GO 1, 25, 33, 52. Convict records: indents, conduct and marriage registers, description and assignment lists, esp. CON 14, 18, 22, 23, 31, 32, 40, 52, 54.

5. *Private Collections*

Norwich Union Fire Insurance Society, Surrey Street, Norwich. Board of Directors' Minute Book, March 1826–October 1831.

The London Assurance, 1 King William Street, London, E.C.4. Minutes of the Committee of Fire, June 1827–31 December 1831; Minutes of the Court of Directors, vol. XXV, 1829–32.

Wilts. Arch. and Nat. Hist. Society, Devizes: J. Cobb, Correspondence.

II. PERIODICALS

The Annual Register.

Baptist Magazine.

Berrow's Worcester Journal.

Brighton Gazette.

Britannia, The.

British Almanack and Companion.

Cambridge Chronicle & Journal and Huntingdon Gazette.

Cambridge and Hertford Independent Press.

Conference Minutes: Bible Christians; Primitive Methodists; Wesleyan Methodists.

Cobbett's Political Register.
Devizes and Wiltshire Gazette.
Dorset County Chronicle and Somersetshire Gazette.
East Anglian, or Norfolk, Suffolk and Cambridgeshire, Norwich, Lynn and Yarmouth Herald.
Gentleman's Magazine.
Hobart Town Advertiser.
Hobart Town Gazette.
Ipswich Journal.
Jackson's Oxford Journal.
Kent Herald.
Kentish Chronicle.
Lincoln, Rutland and Stamford Mercury.
Maidstone Gazette.
Mercury (Hobart, Tasmania).
Northampton Mercury.
Norwich Mercury.
Primitive Methodist Magazine.
Reading Mercury.
Salisbury and Winchester Journal.
Times, The.
Westmorland Advertiser and Kendal Chronicle.
Worcester Herald.

III. CONTEMPORARY WORKS OF REFERENCE

Annual Register of Agricultural Implements (ed. C. W. Johnson and C. Hare, 1843–45).
British Husbandry (Society for the Diffusion of Useful Knowledge 1837).
Clarke's New Law List (1830).
G. A. Cooke, Topography and Statistical Description of the County of Hants. (1819); Berkshire (n.d.); Norfolk (n.d.); Suffolk (n.d.); Sussex (n.d.).
Great Exhibition, Catalogue I, Sec. 2, class 9 (1851).
J. Glyde, Suffolk in the Nineteenth Century (1856).
Insurance Cyclopedia, The (1874).
Journey Book of England: Berkshire (1840).
London and Provincial Medical Directory (1847).
J. C. Loudon, Encyclopedia of Agriculture (1835).
J. C. Morton, A Cyclopedia of Agriculture (n.d.).
Names and Descriptions of all Male and Female Convicts arrived in the Colony of New South Wales during the Years 1830–42 (Sydney 1843).
Pigot's Commercial Directory (London and Home Counties) 1832–34.
Pigot's National Commercial Directory, 1830.
Pigot's National Commercial Directory, Northern Counties, 1834.
Poll Books: Norfolk 1817, 1830; Suffolk 1830.
Post Office Directory, 1845.
W. L. Rham, The Dictionary of the Farm (1853).
Robson's Commercial Directory, 1835; 1839.

H. Stephens, The Book of the Farm (1844).

S. Tymms, The Family Topographer: being a Compendium of the Ancient and Present State of the Counties of England, 7 vols. (1832–43).

W. White, Gazetteer and Directory of Hampshire and the Isle of Wight (1859); of Suffolk (1844); of Norfolk (1845).

Rev. J. M. Wilson, The Rural Cyclopedia (1849).

IV. PARLIAMENTARY PAPERS

1816 S.C. on Game Laws.
1817 S.C. on Poor Laws.
1818 S.C. on Poor Laws.
1818 Vol. XVI, Criminal Returns.
1821 Census.
1821 S.C. on State of Agriculture.
1822 S.C. on State of Agriculture.
1823 S.C. on Game Laws.
1824 S.C. on Labourers' Wages.
1824 S.C. on Poor Rate Returns.
1826 S.C. on Emigration.
1826–27 S.C. on Criminal Commitments.
1826–27 XIX Criminal Returns.
1828 S.C. on Game Laws.
1828 S.C. on Poor Laws.
1829 XVIII Criminal Returns.
1830 XXVII Hop Duty Returns.
1830–31 S.C. on Poor Laws.
1830–31 XI Returns of Poor Law expenditure.
1831 XVII Hop Duty Returns.
1831 Census.
1831–32 Criminal Returns.
1833 S.C. on Agriculture.
1833 S.C. on the Sale of Beer.
1834 Report on the Poor Laws (vols. XXVII–XXXIV).
1834 S.C. on Drunkenness.
1835 XVII Returns of Poor Law expenditure.
1835 First Report of Poor Law Commissioners.
1835 XLV Criminal Returns.
1836 Second Annual Report of Poor Law Commissioners.
1836 S.C. on the State of Agriculture.
1837 S.C. on Poor Law Amendment Act.
1837 S.C. on Transportation.
1840 Report of Registrar-General.
1841–42 Accounts relating to Grain and Flour.
1842 Report on the Sanitary Condition of the Population.
1843 Reports on the Employment of Women and Children in Agriculture.
1844 (House of Lords) Ages and Descriptions of Persons committed for Trial for Incendiary Offences in Norfolk and Suffolk.

1844 XXXIX Return of Gamekeepers killed.
1846 S.C. on Game Laws.
1847–48 S.C. on Agricultural Customs.
1847–48 LIII Poor Rate returns.
1849 XLIV Return of Gamekeepers killed.
1849 XLVII Return of Poor Rates.
1850 Report to the Poor Law Board on the Laws of Settlement.
1893–94 R.C. on Labour (XXXV Agricultural Labour).
1900 Report on the Wages and Earnings of Agricultural Labour.

V. DISSERTATIONS AND SECONDARY WORKS WITH SPECIAL REFERENCE TO THE LABOURERS' RISING

Alice M. Colson, The Revolt of the Hampshire Agricultural Labourers and its Causes, 1812–31 (unpublished M.A. Thesis, London Univ., 1937).

Monju Dutt, The Agricultural Labourers' Revolt of 1830 in Kent, Surrey and Sussex (unpublished Ph.D. Thesis, London Univ., 1966).

Norman Gash, The Rural Unrest in England in 1830 with particular reference to Berkshire (unpublished B.Litt. Thesis, Oxford Univ., 1934).

J. L. and B. Hammond, The Village Labourer (2 vols., Guild Books, 1948).

Pamela Horn, Banbury and the Riots of 1830 (*Cake and Cockhorse*, Banbury, Autumn 1967, pp. 176–79).

A. S. Humphreys, Bucklebury. A Berkshire Parish (Reading, 1932).

Barbara Kerr, Bound to the Soil. A Social History of Dorset 1750–1918 (1968), esp. cap. 5.

Barbara Kerr, The Dorset Agricultural Labourers 1750–1850 (*Proc. Dorset Nat. Hist. and Arch. Soc.*, LXXXIV (1962), pp. 158–77).

Notes and Queries: vol. 161, pp. 377, 427.

W. H. Parry Okedon, The Agricultural Riots in Dorset in 1830 (*Proc. Dorset Nat. Hist. and Arch. Soc.*, LII (1930), pp. 75–95).

A. J. Peacock, Bread or Blood. The Agrarian Riots in East Anglia 1816 (1965).

P. F. Rogers, The Battle of Bossenden Wood (1961).

George Rudé, "Captain Swing" and Van Diemens Land (*Tasmanian Hist. Res. Assoc. Papers and Proceedings*, XII (1964), pp. 6–24).

"Captain Swing" in New South Wales (*Historical Studies, Australia & New Zealand*, April 1965, pp. 467–80).

P. Singleton, Captain Swing in East Anglia (*Bull. of the Soc. for the Study of Labour History*, August 1964, pp. 13–14).

SUBJECT INDEX

INDEX OF PLACES

NAME INDEX